T0305340

Mike did a great job of defining the significant areas relating to the management of risk into clearly defined chapters that offer a contracted consultant, the security professional or other senior management an easy reference guide. It provides a complete view of the potential pitfalls complex contracts may encounter with an eye towards helping both the consultant and client mitigate risk.

Robert G. Molina, Jr., Global Security Manager, LyondellBasell Industries

Mike has created an excellent handbook which provides the reader with a clear path through the labyrinth of industry procedures and practices so necessary to deal effectively with the business of protecting people and businesses as they set about operating in evermore challenging environments.

Dick Stiles, Program Manager Parsons Iraq Joint Venture

Whether an on-site visit or simply office-bound, Michael's risk and contingency management procedures created the safest possible environment for staff to carry out their duties. Other security and risk professionals would do well to follow his lead.

Tim McNeill, Risk Analyst, Shell

Business is routinely conducted in dangerous and volatile regions of the world and companies often don't know, or don't understand, the associated risks and security management requirements. Mike Blyth's excellent work addresses just this issue and provides a valuable one stop reference guide and primer for risk and security management. His book is a must read resource for business leaders pursuing opportunities around the globe, and risk and security management professionals seeking to hone their skills.

Wayne Ashcroft, Executive Vice President, Bowhead Technical and Professional Services

This book brings together all that is necessary to enable law enforcement agencies, the military, commercial companies, government agencies and prospective clients to work together with common understanding. Protecting people and assets to ensure business continuity requires a multi-disciplined approach, with significant investment of resources. Working with Mike and his company made me realize we were talking the same subject but with different words; this led Mike to draw together widely used methods and provided the comprehensive book for international cooperation and cross agency activity in this complex area of investment.

Paul Harries, Police Inspector, London England

Michael Blyth has used his deep knowledge and wide ranging experience of security matters to produce a timely and truly perceptive book in which he addresses the fundamental need for protective measures with a pragmatic and sensible approach to risk management. Having personal experience of working with him in the most demanding security environment, I cannot commend this book too highly.

Adam Peters, Commander British Forces Diego Garcia and Commissioners Representative for the British Indian Ocean Territory 2001–2003.

Just when you think you've seen the best and the brightest of the international security set, along comes Mike Blyth with one of the most comprehensive, useful books I've seen in my 35 years of mitigating threats worldwide. In fact, Mike has taken me to school on a couple subjects. His breadth of knowledge of the threat equation is superb, but more importantly, he has mastered the art of the elusive RFP. This book is a must for anyone who is serious about conducting security ops abroad.

Ray Baysden, International Security Expert

This volume astutely illustrates the need to "speak the language" of corporate executives in order to successfully indoctrinate risk management protocols into a business program. The guidelines and specific, actionable plans presented offer just the right tools for a corporate security professional to demonstrate their immense value to corporate executives.

Greg Hoobler, Senior Global Security Analyst

Michael's breadth of experience comes out in this comprehensive look into the security and risk management world. The themes he has captured encompass the full spectrum of security consulting and management from concept to capture to execution.

Mark Cusick, Counterintelligence Agent, US Army

Mike brings a wealth of knowledge gained from both his military and corporate experience operating in many of the harshest regions of the world. He has managed to lay out this book in a clear and concise manner and offers practical advice for both the novice and most experienced security professional.

Gary Oliver, Director, BSG LLC

This book is both informative and thought provoking. It is an extremely helpful tool for all those, ranging from independent consultancy through to head of security for corporate organizations, who work in the security industry—Highly recommended!

Ian Daniel, Security Consultant

Risk and Security Management

Risk and Security Management

Protecting People and Sites Worldwide

MICHAEL BLYTH

John Wiley & Sons, Inc.

Library of Congress Cataloging-in-Publication Data

Blyth, Michael, 1972–
  Risk and security management: protecting people and sites
worldwide/Michael Blyth.
      p. cm.
Includes index.
  ISBN 978-0-470-37305-7 (cloth)
 1. Risk management. 2. Emergency management. I. Title.
  HD61.B55 2008
  658.4'73–dc22   2008006391

10 9 8 7 6 5 4 3 2 1

To my wife, Kristen, who practiced poor contingency management when she decided to marry me, and has been crisis managing ever since. And to our children, Alex and Amber, who test our crisis management skills daily.

Contents

CHAPTER 4
Threat Evaluation and Risk Management   **107**

CHAPTER 10
Evacuation Planning   295

Preface

It is estimated that the risk management and security market could be valued at over $300 billion by 2010, fueled by rapid business intelligence needs and the growth of physical security service requirements that enable government and commercial activities to occur, especially in remote, volatile, and commercially challenging environments. Despite the significant market for these services, industry expertise is often developed within government organizations and then applied to the commercial sector with very little in the way of transitional awareness or appreciation of the unique principles of commercial application. Even the largest and most well established international risk management and security services companies often lack detailed policies, procedures, and information capture structures. The same is also frequently true for commercial entities with organic risk management and security departments working under pressure to manage multiple business and project activities, with limited resources and budgets. Few organizations provide adequate instructional programs, resulting in inefficient uses of time, effort, and resources, while concurrently risking business continuity and company resources and assets through inadequate project and management controls.

When entering the risk consulting and security management sector after 14 years as an officer within the British Royal Marine Commandos, I quickly realized that often both industry standards and internal company policies and procedures were limited or, at times, absent throughout the industry. The management teams across the leading security companies (and the contracting client companies) I worked with, for, or alongside were often populated with impressive leadership that brought dynamic, pragmatic, committed, and innovative solutions to support government and commercial projects under challenging and fluid conditions. I and many others gained commercial exposure and training while on the job, situations that at times in retrospect exposed the companies to avoidable risk when managing a wide spectrum of crisis events such as mass evacuations, complex attacks, and industrial accidents within critical infrastructures. It was also evident that support structures and the sharing of well-established materials, concepts, and information occurred mainly in a disjointed manner, and often through networking and relationships rather than through organized channels, policies, or information custodians. Many reasons exist for a lack of commercial risk and security structures: these include transient consultants flowing through dynamic and uncertain contracts; the fact that policy and procedure development frequently is viewed as a cost center rather than a business enabler; and the fact that the time and resources required to establish and maintain such systems can be considerable, often exacerbated by fast-moving, underresourced, and fluctuating commercial environments.

While in the Royal Marines, I led the development of some relatively complex and unique risk management policies and security plans for the protection of strategic facilities and large geographic regions with multinational and multiethnic security groups. These exercises provided me with a solid framework for running large and complex commercial operations at the point of delivery as well as managing the corporate requirements as the client interface. Like many ex-government employees entering into the risk management and security industry, the learning curve moving straight into volatile program management functions was steep, and many lessons came about through watching experienced and competent leadership and then developing new or adapted solutions to suit fluid, business requirements. Throughout my career I have been fortunate to work with professionals with a wealth of experience and knowledge, and much of my professional development has been gained through absorbing and adapting their expertise to evolving requirements.

As such, this book is designed to support executive company leadership, chief security officers, risk and security directors, program and project managers, and contract and procurement officers in understanding how risk management and security services can be used to *enable* business to flow seamlessly and productively, even under the most challenging conditions, bringing convergence to often complex and disjointed organisations. The content of this book is also designed to illustrate how business recovery can be better achieved following a crisis event, as well as to framework what companies might expect from security providers contracted to support projects in new, remote, or dynamic operating regions. It is also designed to support commercial and government bodies in enhancing and structuring policies, procedures, and project management groups to better identify and manage the spectrum of risk, whether companies face challenges supporting United States Agency for International Development (USAID) programs in the Federally Administrated Tribal Areas of Pakistan; are seeking to conduct health projects for the Department for International Development in Nigeria or southern Sudan; are supporting reconstruction, development, or hydrocarbon initiatives in Afghanistan and Iraq; are operating commercial enterprises in crime-ridden regions such as Mexico and Kazakhstan; or are entering new and uncertain market regions such as Libya. The book is also designed to support risk consultants and security managers currently operating within the industry, as well as those seeking to enter this dynamic and diverse field with concepts, frameworks, and observations that might provide additional ideas for enhancing existing structures and approaches. In addition, it brings further clarity on some approach methodologies, systems, and tools to make for more efficient and effective risk and security management.

The book captures some main themes of risk management and security provision in 13 chapters, most of which overlap in terms of implementation and impacts. A chapter-by-chapter breakdown of the topics covered follows.

Chapter 1. Risk consulting and security management services are two distinct but often overlapping fields, forming the basis of how security services are planned, resourced, and conducted. Inserting risk advisory support at the outset of the business cycle will likely determine the extent of a project's success. Sound security management will then sustain the business enterprise, ensuring service delivery meets contractual expectations. This chapter captures how the company and its vendors should develop relationships, understandings, and quality assurance methodologies that will better support the management of risk and ensure the most productive business activities.

Chapter 2. Risk consultants and security managers play an increasingly important role in program design and business case justifications, especially as companies operate in more challenging or remote regions. By understanding the business process risk and security advisors can be better positioned to assist their companies in successfully entering new and challenging environments safely and productively. This chapter provides the premise for understanding business activities, which can then be placed into a risk management and security services context.

Chapter 3. Service delivery is the provision of agreed products or services within specified timelines and cost frames. It forms the basis for productive business activities. Both companies and security vendors must understand the specified and implied services contracted, collaboratively developing policies, systems, and regulatory mechanisms to ensure that high-quality services are performed. Problem solving, accountability, and agreed methodologies will create the framework from which productive business results will flow. This chapter supports both companies and vendors in maximizing organic resources and leveraging supporting organizations in order to punch above their weight in terms of capabilities.

Chapter 4. The areas of contingency planning and crisis management have grown in prominence during recent decades as both governments and businesses suffer significant losses through a combination of inadequate risk analysis and poor management of emergency situations. Such losses have necessitated comprehensive risk management plans and crisis management structures. This chapter provides a framework for ensuring that business continuity is achieved through the protection of people, resources, and reputation, as risk management enables forward planning through the identification and management of risk, allowing businesses to weather, and recover from, a crisis most effectively.

Chapter 5. Business activities are susceptible to a variety of risks, ranging from the more intangible threats to a company's reputation, to the harder physical risks resulting from criminal or terrorist threats or events. Understanding the spectrum of risks and how the risks might impact the company, employees, the business enterprise, and corporate reputation forms the basis for risk management and successful business continuity. This chapter provides insight into the scope of risk that many companies face, allowing managers to understand and navigate complex and changing risks to their company's activities, enabling a greater degree of business continuity assurance.

Chapter 6. Risk consulting services require the greatest blend of intellect and expertise. Often such areas create the most frustration, or achieve the worst results within the risk management and security industry. Consulting services are complex and unique, requiring the application of well-grounded management skills, task-specific knowledge and the ability to capture information and recommendations in a concise, logical, and well-structured manner. This chapter explains the unique service of risk consulting, which often bridges the gap between risk management and project success in order to support business activities, often under challenging and shifting conditions.

Chapter 7. Project management is the discipline of organizing and managing resources to ensure a business goal meets its defined scope, quality, time, risk, and cost constraints. A project can be considered a temporary and one-time endeavor, with a defined exit strategy, undertaken to create a unique product or service that brings about beneficial change or added value to an organization. Even within conventional business environments, projects are prone to failure, and project risks are exponentially increased when companies operate in remote or challenging regions. This chapter demonstrates how the alignment of business and security project management is critical for activities to succeed in any business environment, especially where unconventional or unfamiliar risks are present.

Chapter 8. Mobile security is a term used to define the movement of people, assets, and materials by land, sea, or air. It presents some of the highest risks and most dynamic management activities faced by businesses today. Mobile security ranks as one of the most complex and challenging areas for risk management and security provision due to often prolonged risk exposure. This chapter illustrates how mobile security services must be subject to robust and comprehensive planning and service delivery oversight in order to best protect the company's business interests and employees' safety.

Chapter 9. Critical infrastructure or facility security protects the company's assets, structures, personnel, and activities and should be viewed in a holistic manner, considering how the site operates within the larger context of surrounding and supporting communities and organizations, as well as how to best secure and manage the site itself, through a combination of structural, human, and technological measures. This chapter discusses how facility protection solution design should integrate organic resources, leverage external capabilities, and reflect both risk and business needs.

Chapter 10. Evacuations are singular events in that they can involve large numbers of people under stressful and difficult conditions, often without time for detailed planning or preparation. Evacuations impact both individuals and the company as a whole. This chapter discusses how evacuation planning is a significant element of any risk management plan and requires prescripted coordination, clear lines of decision making, and buy-in at all levels in order to be effective.

Chapter 11. Disasters come in many forms, from intrastate conflicts to catastrophic man-made or natural events. Companies with existing infrastructures or employees within disaster-struck regions, or those supporting disaster response requirements, are faced with unique challenges and a wide spectrum of risks. This chapter provides an understanding of the stages of a disaster and how they impact the company, requiring the development of tailored crisis management plans around postulated risk factors. Such plans enable companies to manage risks and ensure business continuity when these crisis events occur.

Chapter 12. Some companies have detailed and well-established security documents and exhibits, methodologies, and protocols, while others have limited structures in place or reinvent the process repeatedly. The unique nature of each task often demands a tailored approach to security documents. Often consultants are faced with the problem of not what to say but how to structure and deliver information in a consistent and concise manner. This chapter demonstrates how to avoid significant resource wastage and to enhance information capture through effective design, structure, and data management.

Chapter 13. Commercial and U.S. government contracting methodologies have many similarities. However, they also have fundamental differences that determine how both companies and their vendors undertake business activities within risk environments. This chapter introduces how business, contract, project, risk, and security managers must understand the nuances of each business approach in order to ensure that project activities are compliant and best support the overall business process.

For those wishing to comment or pose questions regarding this book, feel free to contact me at Michael@riskandsecuritymanagement.com.

Acknowledgments

Many people have contributed either directly or indirectly to my professional growth and the content of this book. The list is long and spans those whom I have worked for and with, as well as those who have worked for me. It is impossible to recall all those who deserve some level of thanks, and so to all those I have missed and who have helped me in some shape or fashion throughout my professional life, my thanks. In particular, however, I would like to pay tribute to a select few who have helped develop my knowledge or professional capabilities at various strategic junctures of my life.

Foremost I would like to thank my father, Alexander D. Blyth, a retired army colonel whose stories and anecdotes led me to join the Royal Marines (he didn't mention sleeping in muddy ditches during his stories!) and who has provided a continued source of much-respected and sound advice throughout my various careers. I attribute much of my success to his counsel, although I would never admit this to him, as being a Scotsman he would seek some form of monetary compensation.

My thanks also goes out to Adam Peters, whom I worked for under the auspices of both the Foreign and Commonwealth Office and the Royal Marines. Adam gave me the latitude to develop territory wide security policies and plans that were then adopted by the U.S State Department. He also provided the rare environment in which a British officer could command several hundred U.S security personnel as well as strategic assets in what was a highly effective multinational operational group. Adam proved a levelheaded and effective leader under interesting and challenging conditions, and is now a lifelong friend.

For my civilianization to the risk world, my thanks to Tom Mulhall, Director of the Security Management Programme at Loughborough University, whose patience in bringing an academic approach to my militaristic style exposed me to different ways of perceiving the commercial security industry and led to the early commercialization of my professional skills. I continue to direct those seeking to move into management levels within the risk management field toward such valuable courses as run by Tom and Loughborough University.

In addition, Tom Valentine has been both a mentor and a friend from the outset of my commercial career(s) and has provided a source of pragmatic and candid advice and guidance since I departed the Royal Marines. I had the pleasure to work with Tom as he handled the corporate business for Control Risks Group, and I managed large program operations in Iraq. In addition, I had the pleasure of briefly working alongside him in Washington, DC, as he undertook the role of business director, and I assumed the position of director of operations. Tom is well respected and highly experienced within the risk management field, and he and his wife are good family friends.

My thanks also to Glenn McLea, the corporate security director for Parsons Corporation, with whom I worked closely in both Iraq and the United States. Glenn's support as both a client and a friend within a complex and challenging operating environment did much to ensconce me into the commercial risk management and security services industry. His candor, balanced management, and pragmatic approach to ensuring both business success and safe project operations set a great tone for my commercial career. Glenn has been a good friend and an invaluable sounding board.

My personal thanks also to David Amos and Kevin Drake, whom I worked with closely during my time in Iraq as well as in the corporate world. Consummate professionals, bringing both balance and flair to some of the most challenging and complex projects, their advice and guidance was instrumental to my professional development within the commercial environment, and their friendship and comradeship made even the most trying periods both enjoyable and positive in nature.

I would also like to express my appreciation of Michael Frayne, one of the most professional senior operations managers and risk consultants it has been my pleasure to work with. Michael ensured the smooth and effective running of some of the most complex and dynamic commercial projects within Iraq, managing all tactical aspects of service delivery as well as maintaining a first-rate client relationship under challenging conditions. His professionalism, commitment, and ability to think around corners, combined with a good sense of humor and unruffled approach, especially under crisis conditions, was priceless, and made for a thoroughly enjoyable working environment in Kirkuk. Michael is a good friend and consummate professional.

Finally, I would like to thank Dick Stiles and his team at Parsons Iraq Joint Venture. Dick was the epitome of a good client, always willing to listen to advice and invariably implementing solutions that best met project and security needs. Dick maintained a levelheaded demeanor when most project managers would be seeking cover. Always calm, even when we conducted mass evacuations of remote sites. Never without a moment to discuss important issues and approachable despite a hectic work schedule and incessant project demands, he quickly became a good friend and respected client.

CHAPTER 1

Risk Consultancy and Security Management

Most organizations would not go into business without insurance coverage, yet surprisingly few have systematic and integrated programs to address the issue of business continuity, or have qualified in-house expertise to support risk management and operational delivery. The globalization of commercial risk has led to a greater appreciation of the need for corporate planning to identify and manage a wide spectrum of threats to business success through the use of risk consultancy and security management.

Although no organization can prevent all crises from occurring, everyone can lower the odds of their occurrence while also mitigating the negative effects a particular crisis might have on brand confidence, business and operational productivity, market reputation, employee morale, and corporate liability. The importance of risk consultants and business managers in the field of business continuity—as a means by which to identify, address, and manage crisis events—has grown during recent decades, primarily because both government agencies and commercial businesses have suffered significant losses through inadequate risk analysis and the ineffective management of crisis events. Business continuity (and those security professionals who assist companies in the design and implementation of associated policies and plans) forms the foundation of how any organization prepares for situations that might cause business interruption, thereby jeopardizing the core mission and long-term health and sustainability of a group or enterprise.

Risk consultants and security managers manage the relatively unaddressed and widespread needs of convergence within an organization; they bring together often disparate groups and resources to achieve a unified and holistic risk solution. Given the current global climate, every business, regardless of its nature and geographic footprint, should hire qualified and experienced security professionals to establish comprehensive risk management policies and plans. Such plans allow companies to identify, avoid, manage, and recover from a crisis, sustaining business continuity under the most challenging circumstances.

Companies should also understand that risk consultants and security managers provide more than just security-related services. They can be leveraged as business enablers, allowing businesses to make better-informed decisions before committing finite company resources to a venture, allowing corporate leadership to map risks against potential commercial gains. Security professionals can positively affect all layers of an organization's management, from supporting business managers in developing more competitive business solutions, to enabling project managers to design more efficient and productive project plans prior to investment or risk exposure.

As security professionals play increasingly important and elevated roles within companies and their corporate boardrooms, advising chief executive officers (CEOs) and executive leadership on their company's risk exposure while concurrently coordinating multi-disciplinary solutions, the importance of making risk management an integral element of a broader corporate strategy increases. Companies now better understand that they can choose to avoid, transfer, share, mitigate, or accept risk and that risk and security managers are evolving to bridge the gap between corporate leadership, strategic business units, program managers, and other company divisions.

While many of the benefits derived from risk consultants and security managers overlap, companies should understand that security consultancy and management services are entirely different in nature and scope. Each comes with unique and particular requirements and professional skill sets, both within a contracted security company, as well as among the managers or consultants the company may field. Companies should also understand the nuances of expertise connected to both categories; the selection of qualified management personnel should reflect the specific functions the company expects from them. By understanding the differences associated with each area, as well as how they might be merged to provide a combined service, companies will achieve more productive risk mitigation and security management, and therefore better business and operational results.

Often companies with limited in-house risk consultancy and security management resources seek external support on a case-by-case basis. The provision of successful security services as a whole often depends on a security provider's ability to determine what the company wants as well as what it actually needs; many times companies require professional assistance with determining their security requirements. Both parties should have a clear understanding of consulting and management service expectations, capturing these needs under a contract that sets the parameters of services, both *expected* and *funded*. Although this may seem to be obvious, often companies are unsure of the scope of what is required and will seek more support than is either envisaged or funded during the life of a contract—effectively resulting in *scope creep*. This can present both positive and negative challenges for the security provider, as the company (or clients) becomes reliant on the provider and offers opportunities to further develop the relationship and explore new market opportunities. Conversely it also presents a challenge to contracted vendors, as the company's management may make requests or create requirements for support outside of the contractual and funded agreement. Careful balancing of both factors is necessary to ensure success by both parties and also prevent the company from placing unrealistic expectations on their provider for work that does not result in revenue generation or, worse, results in financial or capability losses.

Fundamentally, consultancy and management are distinctly different services, although both may be required in unison under one contract. Risk or security consultancy is basically the provision of specialist security advice and guidance, whether it is providing security surveys, audits, policies, business recommendations, or procedures, often with an eye for concurrent business development opportunities. Risk or security management is effectively the managerial and administrative control and coordination of personnel and assets, providing advice and guidance in terms of how best to manage project operations, with a smaller degree of attention to business opportunity, as shown in Exhibit 1.1. These two services can be provided concurrently as a unified service, where the specialist supplies advice to establish the need and approach, then services or directs the resulting tasks.

The distinction between the two services, consultant[1] and manager, is, however, often unclear to a company, which may envision a combination of the two functions supporting their task when actually contracting for only one service. Both the company and the service

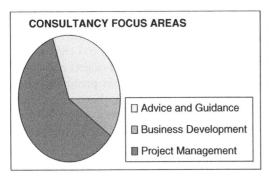 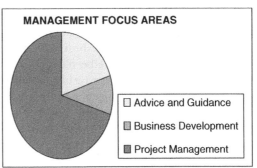

Exhibit 1.1 Risk Consultancy and Security Management Focus Areas

provider must clarify and articulate the difference. Likewise, where a combination of both elements is required, and as the project grows in needs, both company management and the security provider should seek modifications to a contract to support the provision of unforeseen services. This is important to both parties, in terms both of staying within the parameters of the contract and in avoiding problems associated with providing services that could come with legal or reputational issues, or result in the provider breaching the contract's service deliverable terms by focusing on the wrong task areas.

It is also easy for local vendor management to slip into a habit of providing more and more assistance, to the point where they are supplying a considerable amount of additional unpaid effort. This is more so the case for security managers, where they are asked to contribute to policies, plans, and strategies rather than focusing on running the security resources. For vendors and companies alike, this can be considered good business practice up until a point, but in some cases it can negatively affect both the company and the provider if a sensible balance is not struck. While clear distinctions and agreements should be made with regard to the funded services being contracted for, it is worthwhile to remember that it is often useful to provide *additional* services in the short term (until a contract modification can be made) in order to retain a healthy intercompany relationship. The service provider should seek to achieve the balance of helpfulness and pragmatism, without being taken advantage of or alienating the company's management, and the company should seek to compensate the service provider to acknowledge the additional and often unfunded efforts undertaken.

The distinct differences between consultancy services and program security management are discussed in greater detail in the chapters that follow. This chapter is designed to set the scene regarding how security services, both consulting and management, operate between company and service provider or vendor organizations.

PROJECT PLANNING

Ideally the company will engage a security provider or individual consultant at the beginning of the business activity's life cycle, prior to any actual work being started. Consultants therefore are best placed to gain a better understanding of the project requirements and dynamics before any plans are made and resources are allocated by the project team. This allows consultants to influence the strategic planning of the company from the outset, preferably in alignment and partnership with the business team targeting a specific opportunity. Consultants arriving midway in the business or project life cycle will face additional challenges; concepts and plans will have been developed independently of advice, and budgets and funding may have been set. As a result, it will be psychologically harder, and probably more costly, to modify such concepts and plans as resources may have already been contracted and mobilized, and changes may interfere with an activity or incur unaccounted-for costs. In the ideal situation, consultancy or management services will be provided before plans are made and resources mobilized, ensuring that the company's and the project's plans are developed and aligned with actual needs, saving time, money, and effort in the long run.

It is important for the consultant to understand the dynamics that affect different individuals within the company and project organization, not just in terms of the roles and responsibilities, but also regarding the organizational peculiarities, structures, human dynamics, and office politics residing in any group of professionals. By understanding the goals, objectives, and concerns of different company managers, the consultant will be better positioned to offer observations and recommendations in a manner more likely to gain traction. In addition, the security or risk management element of some companies might have an equal voice within the overall management structure, while in others they are relegated as an afterthought and might even fall under the health and safety officer or in the human resources department.

While security providers and their consultants may interface with multiple parties within a company, from the CEO to legal, contracts, and projects, typically there are three practical interfaces the consultant will deal with to complete the actual task itself:

1. *Business manager.* Business managers are responsible for targeting opportunities and gaining board approval to enter new markets or expand existing regional business opportunities. Often business managers are motivated by financial targets and have quarterly or annual targets to meet in order to grow client portfolio and business revenues. They lead capture teams in order to present business solutions that meet client quality and cost needs, and often view security as a cost element that might undermine the probability of their success. Business managers who are grounded in risk and security management seek security as a component of their solution, understanding that it will increase the value of their proposal. Those who are unfamiliar with operating in remote or challenged environments will be less inclined to consider the applicability of risk and security within their approach.

2. *Program/project manager.* Program/project managers normally seek to achieve the milestones set for the activity in terms of objectives, schedule, and cost. Their task is to ensure that the business activity achieves what is expected, when expected, and within budget. Aside from their professional responsibilities, most companies link the career and bonuses (perhaps a percentage of the actual contract value) of program or project managers to achieving these objectives, with every cost and delay to the project reducing the value of the personal incentive award. As such, poor management typically focuses on getting the job done rather than focusing appropriately on risk, while strong managers will seek advice and guidance to identify and manage risk as a proactive project approach. Both company risk managers and security vendors will need to balance the corporate and personal drivers against their own task of mitigating risk and providing

good service. Good managers will balance both project goals and risk consideration; others may view risk and security an unnecessary hindrance.

Security providers or in-house security managers who are able to offer recommendations that directly focus on objectives, schedules, and costs, while concurrently mitigating risks, will better support the company's project success and will more likely gain better traction with executive leadership. Those security providers or in-house security managers who focus on risk mitigation in isolation, and who do not consider the business objectives within every risk decision, will have a limited ability to place their role within the wider context and will not enable the most productive business results.

3. *Security manager.* A company may assign a different name to the management position responsible for managing risk and coordinating security services, or may subsume the role within a more generic corporate position, such as under health and safety, human resources, or the legal department. For those companies operating within more challenging environments, a defined position is often required to directly focus on risk mitigation. Security managers are often in the difficult position of providing observations or recommendations that might be viewed as constraining the productivity and speed of the project as well as incurring unnecessary costs. Typically security is considered a cost center rather than a means by which to conduct productive business or project activities.

The difficulty is further exacerbated as the security manager is embedded within the company, and thus the manager's career and livelihood may depend on retaining a good relationship with the business leaders as well as the program and/or project manager, rather than offering frank but unpopular recommendations. The security manager will be focused on balancing his or her own company's office and management politics, ensuring that the recommendations do not discredit him- or herself or increase activity costs. The security manager will also seek to ensure that any security vendors are best exploited on the company's behalf, while also that ensuring risk is mitigated and security is provided at an appropriate professional level. The security provider should be aware of these factors in order to best support the security manager, as well as to identify the best approach to achieve the desired risk mitigation and security measures needed to protect the company.

BALANCING SERVICE DELIVERY

While every contract and project has unique needs, the general principles of security consultancy and management remain the same. There are three interconnected areas a company and their security provider must balance when managing a contract:

1. Contract requirements and company expectations.
2. Provider's business needs and service delivery standards.
3. Project and environment risks factors.

The weight of each factor will differ, depending on the company's business goals, expectations, and the corporate risk tolerances associated with both the project and the environment in which the contract operates, shown in Exhibit 1.2. The security provider will also

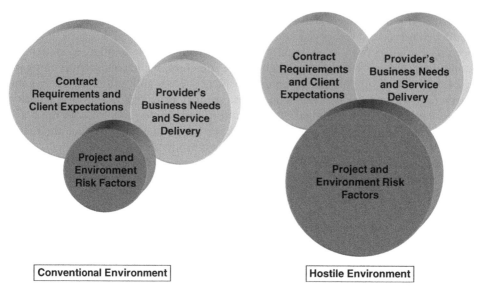

Exhibit 1.2   Balancing Service Delivery in Different Risk Environments

bring its own needs to the task, including its business objectives and corporate risk tolerances. In a conventional or nonhostile project environment, the relative importance of these three areas will vary depending on the contract's specific requirements. A consultancy or security contract in a conventional environment generally will focus more on the company's expectations and the provider company's business needs, with risk mitigation concerns being a smaller area of consideration. Conversely, in a hostile environment, the risk factors and mitigation measures play a more significant part of contract consideration, with company and provider business needs and project interests being proportionally reduced in relation to risk considerations.

Of course, all factors are interconnected and must be viewed holistically, as risk is connected to the company's ability to perform project tasks to standard, on time, and within budget, and effective risk management protects the company from physical, financial, delivery, reputational, and liability risks. It is also important for both the company and the security provider to understand that every action creates a reaction, and that the project activities themselves may increase the risk factors by raising risk profiles or providing opportunities for unwanted attention and thus in turn influencing the contract requirements and subcontracted security provider's business needs, creating a cyclic process of reevaluation and contract change.

Contracted risk consultants or security managers supporting a task will be most effective if they understand the business needs of both the company and the contracted vendor, placing these needs into the context of the varied risks faced by both, from corporate and strategic concerns to the more personal or granular levels. Balancing service delivery requires consultants to be positioned to offer the best advice and service, meeting as many individual and group interests as possible. For example, at the granular level, the consultant and the company's risk manager may wish to identify where a project manager, whose bonus relies on the timely completion of a task, may be more inclined to place him- or herself and others at risk, increasing the focus on contract requirements while reducing the value of input from the security provider as well as the attention paid to mitigating postulated risks. Often robust service delivery management is necessary to balance business needs against those of risk management.

Alternatively, a company with a low risk threshold that is unfamiliar with a new environment or activity may view the risk mitigation advice and security services provided by a vendor as a means of operating within an environment that it otherwise would avoid, thus increasing the importance of the security provider's input within a contract. Company risk managers should be cognizant of the vendor overtly or covertly imposing its own tolerance levels or risk perceptions to executive management and seek to ensure that the correct balance is achieved.

The table below offers some considerations to indicate how both the company and the security provider's focus on each area of consideration may vary.

Expectations	Impacts	Risk Focus
Company payment tied to schedule	More inclined to take risks to ensure timely project completion	Low
Company payment tied to performance	More inclined to allocate monies to mitigate risks during contract	High
Company has low risk threshold	Likely to withdraw from project if risks increase or injuries occur, or invest in risk mitigation	High
Company accepts high risk threshold	Higher likelihood that risks are accepted; possible cavalier attitude and lower investment in risk mitigation	Low
Company defers security responsibilities to vendors	Company may force definitive provider agreements to achieve project needs and may demand unrealistic or high-risk services from security vendors	Low
Company dependent on security provider/vendor for decision making	Company reliance may result in greater acceptance of advice and guidance, limiting the ability to conduct quality assurance of security vendors	High
Security vendor values its own reputation	Security vendor may refuse work, or take a strong position on accepting risk in order to protect its reputation or liability exposure	Varies
Security vendor's business development goals important	Security vendor may accept higher-than-normal risks in order to grow business quickly	Low
Security vendor has low liability tolerances	Greater focus on liability risks, especially injuries and deaths, thus driving more candid and realistic recommendations and approaches	High
Security vendor's experience in service	Experience varies the balance of company/risk/business needs	Varies

(continued)

Expectations	Impacts	Risk Focus
Risks posed direct to project	Threats posed directly to a project result in greater focus on risk through specific project-targeting threats	High
General risks high for region	General risks may result in more balance between project needs and risk levels	Medium
Project faces low risks	Low risk levels may result on a greater focus on the business needs	Low
Only provider faces risks	Providers who face all risks focus on their own business needs; companies may accept higher risk levels as they will not be affected	Varies

The company effectively has the final vote on what level of security is provided, as it controls the budget and may change security providers who do not meet its requirements or expectations. That said, sound company management will consider the advice and guidance offered by security professionals, both internal and external, in order to strike the correct balance between business needs and risk management. Good security vendors will offer candid advice in order to provide the best service. However, human dynamics play a significant role in how effectively management decisions are made. Often the balance is not achieved and risks outside of corporate tolerance levels are accepted at a local level.

COMPANY AND VENDOR RELATIONSHIPS

The development of a strong professional relationship between the contracting company and the security provider's management often underpins the levels of success of the business venture, as well as the ability to provide productive consulting and management services. Disjointed management relationships, groups operating in isolation, or the failure to understand the business needs or to acknowledge risk factors will place all personnel and companies at avoidable risk. As with any management structure and process, integration is vital, especially within hostile, remote, or new business environments.

It is also important that the company and security provider management and personnel understand that often the contracted company cannot force an issue, only advise and manage risk. Thus if project management or staff choose to ignore advice and guidance, often the risk consultant or security manager is authorized only to raise and document concerns, rather than physically force the correct measures to be implemented. In the most extreme cases, security providers can refuse to conduct a task or undertake an activity; however, they still have limited control over the activities undertaken by their clients independent of their support. Clear parameters of authority and responsibility need to be established between the company and vendor so as to address, effectively and clinically, areas where professional disagreements may present risks to personnel and activities. The sections that follow offer real examples of cases where company management has been both dismissive and receptive to their security consultant's advice.

Client Meeting

The security consultant operating within a high-risk environment advised the project manager that the meeting should be held at an alternative venue due to high physical risk levels at the proposed venue. The project manager insisted that the meeting go ahead as planned. The consultant then offered documented mitigation measures to protect the manager's plan, citing the use of armored vehicles during movement within the venue area, the conduct of discussions within hardened buildings, and the need to stay at a defined distance from the perimeter boundary. The project manager subsequently ignored most of the advice during the visit. During the manager's visit, a mortar attack resulted in an unexploded mortar round becoming lodged within the engine of the soft-skinned vehicle used for the manager's movement. (The project group was standing 80 feet from the vehicle when it was struck.) Two soldiers were also injured by snipers on the perimeter fence. The consultant had documented each assessment and recommendation for clarity and audit, thus fulfilling his and his provider company's obligations to provide risk mitigation services. It was not within his authority to prevent the visit, only advise on the risks and mitigation measures associated with each task component.

Project Planning

The security consultant provided detailed risk mitigation measures required for the development of a project site located within a remote and hostile area. The security footprint involved the use of local police and military personnel to provide an outer security layer, with a secured and hardened compound to permit construction activities to occur within a relatively protected space. The consultant advised against frequent site visits due to the high incidence of attacks along the limited routes to the project site. The project manager opted for frequent site visits, with the project remotely managed using entirely local contractors. It was recorded (prior to the manager's decision) that each day a visit was conducted, an improvised explosive devise (IED) had been placed on one of the routes used (although not directed specifically at the visit team). Several weeks after the assessment, a complex attack was mounted specifically at the project team. The project closed prior to completion, resulting in approximately $50 million of failed project costs to the funding government.

Threat Prediction

The security consultant advised the program risk manager that intelligence resources had reported a serious surface-to-air threat within the local region as well as specific targeting details. The consultant advised that air movement be delayed and countermeasure equipment be installed within the company charter aircraft. The program manager, noting the agreement reached between the company and security vendor risk managers, authorized aircraft to be grounded for 20 days until the postulated threat had diminished and invested in counter surface-to-air equipment. These actions resulted in significant costs and disrupted operations, however significantly reduced risks to the company and employees.

Misinformation

A specific project manager was known to be discussing large-scale personnel movements and project plans with a wide local audience, placing himself, his project staff, and the security team at significant risk. He provided verbal and written details on the dates and times a project location would be demobilized, offering an ideal opportunity for insurgent targeting. The provider consultant advised the company risk manager and program manager of the unnecessary and avoidable risks being created through poor information security, advising that misinformation relating to demobilizations be provided to the project manager and all project staff. The program manager agreed, and false dates and times were provided to his subordinate, which were duly passed to the same wide audience. The extraction of the project location then occurred early morning, 24 hours prior to the false extraction date, with no resulting incidences.

CONSULTANTS' OBJECTIVES

It is important that both the company and the security provider's management understand the objectives and responsibilities of their consultants. Consultants will have three main objectives during their appointment:

1. To look after the interests of the company they work for (the vendor).
2. To provide the best level of service to support a contracting company's project.
3. To ensure that they maintain their moral obligation to ensure the safety of those individuals they are responsible for. (This aspect becomes particularly important in challenging environments.)

The next lists capture some key areas consultants should consider when providing services to a contracting company on behalf of their employer.

Interests of the Provider Company

- Provide services that best reflect the standards of the provider company.
- Identify reputational, liability, and contractual risks to the provider company.
- Provide services meeting (or exceeding) contractual requirements and/or company expectations.
- Ensure further company requirements are identified and raised to the appropriate vendor management personnel, then contractually bound.
- Ensure invoicing is accurate and timely and that problems are identified and resolved.
- Ensure further business opportunities are identified and raised with the appropriate persons.
- Ensure all documentation is produced to the highest of standards.
- Ensure that internal and external auditing requirements are identified and addressed.
- Ensure quality control over all subordinate security management.
- Ensure that safety and security are central to all operations in remote, challenging, new, or hostile environments.
- Ensure a strong company relationship is maintained at all times, exploring new business opportunities.

- Report all pertinent matters to the appropriate management in a timely and detailed manner.
- Ensure all materials, assets, and equipment are accounted for.
- Keep clear documented records of significant project matters, problems, and incidents.
- Quantify and evidence all recommendations where possible.

Interests of the Contracting Company

- Understand the technical nature of the project, its schedules, incentives, terms, and conditions.
- Understand project risks, problems, and impediments.
- Understand the risk tolerance levels of the company as well as the program/project manager.
- Proactively identify possible project delay factors, with recommendations for mitigation.
- Provide succinct and accurate verbal and written materials to support project operations.
- Establish methods in which the company might succeed rather than offering negative solutions. Also offer varied options.
- Assist company management in their business goals, working as a partner where possible.
- Be able to work with limited information and evolve plans in alignment with changing needs.
- Identify provider company shortfalls and resolve them before the company becomes aware of them.
- Offer (permitted) additional support, in order to grow further business.

Interests of the Contracted Staff

- Refuse where necessary (last resort) to sanction activities that exceed risk security provider company's risk tolerance levels.
- Clearly articulate and document risks faced to personnel; address them with mitigation measures.
- Seek written direction for unwarranted risk acceptance by the company or security provider company.

CONSULTANT SKILL AREAS

A number of factors define the skill sets required of a consultant: the nature of the service being provided, the type of company being serviced, the environment in which the project is operating, the cost allowances, and so on. Each consultancy role may have particular needs that define the unique requirements of each service or task. The next list details some of the generic skills often found in successful consultants.

- The ability to identify and foster further commercial opportunities.
- The ability to balance the operational requirements with a sound commercial awareness.

- A solid foundation of knowledge and experience within the service to be provided to the company or client.
- The ability to quickly grasp new concepts and industry areas to enable the provision of more tailored solutions.
- The ability to inspire confidence and trust within a company, notably in hostile environments; an authoritative and credible manner when speaking on relevant subjects.
- The ability to communicate clearly and concisely with the company, both verbally and in writing.
- The ability to take a contract from inception, through the proposal stage, into contractual terms, and then run the contract in terms of delivery, expansion, invoicing, and standards, handing off to security managers.
- The ability to understand all forms of risk, to the company, the vendor, and contracted personnel.
- The ability to establish information and relationship networks to support both company and vendor interests.
- The capability to relate to the company on both personal and professional levels.
- A balanced and levelheaded demeanor under trying conditions.
- A clinical and focused approach with a keen eye for detail.
- The ability to view complex security issues holistically, placing them into a project context.
- Strong management skills, fostering good team spirit under challenging conditions.
- The aptitude to deal with crisis situations with confidence and professionalism.
- The ability to quickly adapt to new requirements and changes, in both risk and project terms.
- Good information technology skills, allowing for the presentation of information in an understandable and professional format.
- A proactive and imaginative manner in approaching contracts and in developing new systems and policies to enhance service delivery.
- The ability to research and analyze information quickly and effectively.
- The ability to view operational requirements from a commercial perspective.
- The ability to identify resources that may be leveraged to support the company at no or low cost, especially governmental agencies.
- The ability to establish external relationships that bring value to a project or contract.
- The ability to see cross-utilizations to best use limited or finite resources.
- The ability to think at both a strategic and tactical level, bringing innovation as well as common sense to bear.
- The ability to design policies and plans that lend themselves to efficient adaptation and adjustment.
- The ability to balance tact and diplomacy with honesty and candor.

PRINCIPAL CONSULTANT ERRORS

The field of *security services* encompasses a number of industry sectors, from the more management-oriented services such as risk consulting, investigations, due diligence, project operations, cybersecurity, intelligence, and business facilitation to the harder edge and more practical services such as close protection, cash in transit, critical infrastructure, and event protection. Although service leaders generally have a solid grounding in many of the principles of risk and security management, many have little transitional awareness between government to commercial appointments or an appreciation for the unique principles of commercial application. Government-sector risk tolerances and perceptions are also very different from those in the commercial sector, and many companies are exposed to unnecessary risks by failing to structure or define their contingency and crisis management approach. In the past, too few companies required, supported, or provided education and standards for those responsible for developing risk management policies and implementing security procedures within the corporation.

Today's well-grounded security professionals understand the principles of convergence, helping their company bring together multifaceted resources to leverage organic and external capabilities, reducing operating costs, and increasing overall organizational performance. Commercially attuned security professionals also understand the tenets of business continuity; they are able to identify and avoid risks as well as develop policies and plans that allow an operation to function during a crisis or to recover following a catastrophic event. To be successful in this evolving and maturing field, security professionals must also understand the holistic nature of risk and how both tangible and intangible risk impacts can result in ripple effects that move through an organization. Security professionals are increasingly integrated as part of business and project teams, supporting both business leaders in developing an environment in which a pursuit may occur and program design within a risk context. Increasingly security professionals are becoming facilitators for business success, important cornerstones for corporate planning and decision making.

Consultants entering into a contract may have a background within the commercial sector they operate in or may have recently left military, law enforcement, intelligence, or other specialist organizations. Those consultants new to a particular field may inadvertently place themselves, their client, and their parent company at risk. While those entering the commercial consultancy or management fields from these backgrounds may on the surface have a solid foundation of experience and capability that might support their newfound civilian careers, the transition between government and commercial operations is often surprisingly difficult, even for the most senior-level managers.

Typically the management risks posed to a company do not take the form of physical threats, as those with the relevant backgrounds within security naturally identify and mitigate against these more obvious and tangible threats. However, noninstinctive risks, such as contractual requirements, invoicing, legal issues, policies, and reputation, tend to be errors common among new consultants. Many lessons are learned the hard way with consultants assuming knowledge in areas for which they have no real expertise, or by being overly eager to help a company in a manner that later compromises the provider company's ability to compete for future contracts. These errors include:

- Jeopardizing the security vendor's contract.
- Undermining the vendor's professional standards and reputation.
- Placing the vendor and its employees/subcontractors at liability for professional or personnel misconduct.
- Preventing the vendor from billing/invoicing the client effectively.

- Preventing the vendor from demonstrating that proper operational procedures were carried out.
- Preventing the vendor from demonstrating that policies and procedures were adhered to for audit purposes.
- Undermining the safety and security of company and vendor's company personnel.

The next list illustrates some of the most common and serious errors within the consultancy and management field that can affect both the company and security vendor.

- *Providing inappropriate documentation to a client.* In an attempt to assist clients in their proposal-writing tasks, consultants have often unwittingly excluded the vendor from competing for certain contracts. This occurs principally in government contracts when a consultant provides written inputs that a client later uses within a formal statement of work, which is then included within a scope of work for a government contract for which numerous bidders offer proposals. The vendor may then be legally excluded from competing as it violates government conflict-of-interest regulations, resulting in loss of considerable potential revenue. (See Chapter 13.)
- *Treating the client as a friend.* Living in close proximity with clients for protracted periods of time, often under difficult conditions, can naturally result in the formation of strong personal relations between the consultant and company management. When the fine balance between establishing a strong relationship and being inappropriately friendly is crossed, consultants may offer inappropriate personal opinions, thoughts, or advice to company staff. Management personnel may also use consultants as tools by which to achieve personal goals, thereby jeopardizing the contract and contractor as well as damaging a vendor's reputation.
- *Using incorrect pricing for services.* Consultants may offer the company a price for a service or assets without clearing it through the appropriate contracts, finance, operations, or other appropriate managers. The product or service offered then may be found to cost more than the stated amount. The vendor may have to change the price offered, damaging the provider/company relationship; worse, it may not be able to bill for the correct amount, thus incurring considerable financial losses. This is not in the interests of either party as it creates uncertainty and impacts both business groups.
- *Discussing wage rates or actual costs with clients.* Vendor consultants may not fully understand the hidden costs of sourcing, procuring, and managing labor and equipment, thereby passing incorrect and proprietary information to client company management. This places the vendor at a competitive disadvantage if the company uses information as leverage against the vendor, assuming the vendor has lower overhead costs than it actually has. Secondarily, it may cause the company to doubt the consultant's ability to guard sensitive information that it may not wish have exposed to a third party.
- *Speaking of specialized areas without the relevant experience.* Consultants may offer information based on limited or out-of-date knowledge regarding a specialty or technical area. The project team may take this as specialist advice as truth and plan their project requirements accordingly, leading to the implementation of poor operational or contractual plans that might threaten company personnel and incur reputational or liability risks to the vendor.

- *Assuming knowledge of regulations.* Consultants might make unilateral decisions regarding contract provisions based on a faulty assumption that they possess sufficient knowledge of corporate, government, or legal regulations. This could result in significant financial losses to the vendor as a result of failing to follow these regulations; notably it may prevent accurate and timely billing for services rendered.
- *Offering services without contractually binding documents.* Often project management request services that have not been formally or contractually authorized. Only recognized authorities within the company's corporate structure have the authority to commit funds and this authority may in fact not rest with the management element requesting services. There are contractually recognized means of communicating these requests, and consultants must ensure they are used and present before rendering services. Verbal agreements, e-mails, or requests from unauthorized project management personnel may not be sufficient to justify later invoicing for services—although with well-established relationships, these may be sufficient. If proper and binding policies are not enforced, the billing for services may be denied, leading to considerable financial loss and project disruptions.
- *Auditable operational planning documents.* Consultants may not document operational activities properly. Proper documentation can later be used to demonstrate that the correct intelligence and risk mitigation was conducted and that operational planning was professionally implemented. During an audit, or after a serious incident, a lack of documented proof that appropriate planning measures were in place for a task or project may place individuals and both the company and the vendor at liability or reputational risk.
- *Not retaining detailed and well-structured databases.* The consultant's hard-drive information may be owned by the company or funding government and may be subject to audit several years after a contract has been completed. Also, when a contract closes, consultants invariably are difficult to locate or use to assist external parties in navigating their databases to identify or mine required information. If information is not kept in a well-structured format, the ability of the vendor or company to mine data and provide clear, accurate, and timely information will be considerably impaired and may be prejudicial to the company's success in future contract bids. In addition, much of the information gathered during the conduct of a program is used in new proposals and other areas. Being able to manage and source this critical information permits effective bidding on new work. It is in the interest of the company to ensure that its subcontractors' databases are well organized and can be mined for information once a contract is completed.
- *Timely reporting of serious incidents/matters.* Consultants are required to provide timely and accurate reporting of serious incidents or matters in order to permit the provider's management team to implement effective control measures, as well as to notify the appropriate company management staff. However, consultants might be so focused on dealing with the incident that they forget that other crisis measures are required and that corporate management discussions between the vendor and company corporate offices are also required. Due to poor information integration or transmission, company corporate and program managers have on occasion been embarrassed by not knowing that serious issues or incidents have occurred. Establishing an effective reporting system helps both the company and the vendor conduct more efficient business.
- *Honesty with clients.* Consultants lying or misinforming project staff on matters that should be transparent undermine the company's confidence in the vendor's personnel and threatens the vendor's reputation as well as the actual contract.

- *E-mail chains.* Consultants forgetting that their response to an e-mail will have a chain of previous e-mails attached can lead to inappropriate or embarrassing information being made available to the company or other inappropriate parties.
- *E-mail content.* Including inappropriate comments or suggestions in any e-mail related to a contract might present challenges during an audit or review for both the vendor and the company. Any offhand e-mail comments may be taken at face value, unintentionally placing the vendor at reputational risk or inaccurately suggesting inappropriate actions were taken, thus incurring fraud or other investigations or allegations against the company.
- *Understanding who holds budgetary control.* The consultant must identify who in the company's structure has budgetary authority and must accept authority to proceed with services only once confirmed by these appropriate parties or persons in a contractually valid and legally binding request. Documentation provided by an individual lacking budgetary authority will not permit the billing of services to the company, placing the vendor at risk.
- *Failing to offer options.* Consultants may fail to identify innovative solutions that might enable activities to occur. Project management staff should always feel that the consultant is attempting to solve problems, however difficult or even costly the solution might be. The company will view the consultant, and by extension the vendor, as a hindrance to operations rather than a facilitator to success if options supporting its needs are not provided.
- *Failing to explain and document task refusals.* When a task cannot be conducted due to unavoidable risk or other factors, the consultant must support the rationale behind the refusal with documented evidence. A lack of documentation calls into question the decision process used to refuse services to the project. It is imperative that the company clearly understands why the task cannot be conducted; otherwise the company may conclude that the grounds for refusal are unsubstantiated, rather than being based on an accurate and well-founded risk assessment. This situation may call into question the consultant's competency and be a liability to the vendor's reputation as well as to the intercompany relationship.
- *Contentious e-mails.* Consultant's sending contentious or heated e-mails that can never be recalled, or that may be sent to persons to whom the consultant never intended, undermines business operations on multiple levels. In addition, the recipient (or others) might use such e-mails out of context, or to support their own agendas, undermining the consultant, the vendor, or indeed the company.
- *Taking sides in an intra- or interclient dispute.* The consultant should always attempt to remain neutral in any dispute within a company's organization or between two managers. The final outcome of an argument between project staff is never certain, and the consultant might be accused of a lack of loyalty or professionalism if on the losing side. Vendors should always be impartial and only offer clinical and well-founded advice and guidance.
- *Not retaining accurate documentation of contract changes.* A contract will invariably change over time as different variables alter the nature of services provided. This is normal. However, e-mail records do not accurately capture fundamental changes adequately. These should be formalized for confirmation with the company as well as for historical reference. Failure to do this can create a breach of contract or disrupt effective

billing. Retaining accurate documentation is particularly necessary for back-to-back (job-sharing) positions where consultants must understand and explain to the company the rationale behind such changes or decisions.

■ *Applying inappropriate management approaches.* Consultants who have recently left a particular field after many years may habitually apply known management approaches, standards, and logic that do not always fit into commercial or specific project operations. Although consultants will have been selected due to their background, knowledge, and experience, it is essential that they understand that different drivers regulate the commercial sector and that applying out-of-place or inappropriate logic can undermine the contract or business activity.

Some examples of how consultant errors have negatively impacted contracts and operations follow:

■ *Speaking of specialist areas without the relevant experience.* During informal discussions, local project staff asked a close protection team leader questions regarding electronic countermeasure (ECM) equipment. The team leader used out-of-date information based on prior military knowledge (nonspecialist), which then undermined efforts of the company's security director to procure ECM equipment, impeding risk mitigation efforts and damaging the company/provider relationship.

■ *Offering services without contractually binding documents.* Armored vehicles were rented to a company for several months without contractually binding documents. When invoices were produced sometime later, the company insisted that the use of the vehicles had been a favor, not a cost service, resulting in a significant loss to the vendor.

■ *Applying inappropriate management approaches.* An operations manager making an error on leave rotations opted to consider morale before service delivery and planned to stand down a monthly contracted service for two days to permit personnel to go on vacation. This would have had direct cost impacts on the contracting company for paid-for but used services and also would disrupt project requirements. Had the manager followed through with his flawed decision, it would also have placed the vendor in contractual breach.

Risk consulting and security management services form the foundations of successful corporate business continuity and are a central management component for convergence within any organization. Risk consultants and security managers are often responsible for determining how security services are planned, resourced, and conducted. Experienced vendors will provide to companies consultants and managers who understand the different requirements of these two distinct fields as well as those who can bridge the gap and conduct both concurrently. Companies seeking to own in-house risk and security resources should leverage their security professionals in order to support risk management, business enterprises, and operational planning for projects. Selecting qualified and experienced risk and security managers, either from external vendors or as part of the in-house organizational structure will enable better corporate decision making and more productive business results.

It is also important for contracting companies and their subcontracted vendors to understand the need to include specialist support at the right point within a business cycle as well as how to develop a mutually beneficial intracompany management and operational relationship. The objectives of the consultant or manager should be clearly understood and, where necessary, documented to solidify agreements. In addition, the skill sets and competence of each post should be scoped and defined to ensure the avoidance of errors that can impact both the company and vendor. Understanding the common errors made by management, both within the company and by the subcontracted consultants, will also enable projects to mitigate both business and operational risks.

This book addresses in detail both areas of consultancy and management services and the peripheral requirements associated with both: that is, the services that they directly manage. Readers should remember that there is no one answer to the issue of how security consultancy and security management should be conducted, as each company, business activity, and environment will be different. However, the aim of this book is to provide the foundations upon which individual and unique requirements can be based.

Note

1. For simplicity, the term *consultant* will be applied to the functions of both a security manager and consultant, unless stated otherwise.

CHAPTER 2

Initiating New Contracts

It is in the interest of both the company and the security vendor personnel to understand the process by which new business is sought and won. Understanding the manner in which both the contracting authority and the supplier think and operate will enhance the efficiency of both groups as well as improve the services delivered to the company, and thus the productivity of the business activities overall. Security vendors who also understand the processes and objectives can be better positioned to support the business objectives of their clients, and thus their own corporate goals and objectives. This chapter is designed to set the scene for how security companies get to the point of delivering risk consultancy and security services, defining the drivers that lead to security service delivery, as well as what sustains these activities during the life of a contract.

A good consultant is able to provide the services agreed under the contractual terms as well as support the contracting company beyond stated contractual agreements, or in areas not anticipated, and offer strong and flexible service support while concurrently fostering intercompany relationships. If balanced appropriately, this benefits both the company and the vendor in developing a mutually beneficial relationship that supports the company's business and project goals, as well as the vendor's long term business opportunities.

It is important for both the company and the vendor, however, that consultants concurrently identifying new business opportunities do so in a manner that does not negatively impact on any principal tasks and that business development is undertaken with agreement and support from the vendor's management. Some vendor companies do not expect, nor desire, consultants to operate independently in this matter, as the consultant may not be best positioned to exploit a business opportunity to its fullest, may confuse business development plans, or may be viewed by the contracting company as distracted from the paid task when seeking out new opportunities. At worst, a consultant may be viewed as not meeting contracted services by becoming an irritant, by exploiting a contractual relationship to establish further business opportunities for their parent company.

While certainly not a black art, business development is an area of expertise in itself, with a spectrum of skill sets and approaches defined by the nature of the business a consultant may be engaged in. A consultant selling labor services (manpower) will have a different methodology for identifying and engaging in business development than a consultant selling specialist equipment. Conversely a consultant whose clientele are commercially funded will approach business development differently than a consultant whose companies are government based. This chapter provides some overarching understandings on the business process to support the planning and delivery, or receipt of risk consulting and security management services.

BUSINESS CYCLE

Business can be viewed as a cycle, a sequence of events that form a chain of activities ensuring business is established, contracted, conducted, and maintained. A break in any element of the business cycle will reduce the productivity of a commercial activity. Business cycles affect both the company and the supplier, and it is in the interests of both to align their approach and activities as closely to the other so that business can be achieved and projects can be best supported. Often in challenging environments, security and risk management will form a key component of business. It is of interest to the company's business team to ensure that they engage in-house, or external security vendors who can support their own business cycle. In effect, company and vendor business cycles become intertwined, although often they are out of sequence. As illustrated in Exhibit 2.1, the core elements of successful business cycle are comprised of:

- Selecting a market area.
- Finding business opportunities.
- Winning business.
- Contracting the activity.
- Servicing or doing the business.
- Expanding or exploiting business opportunities.

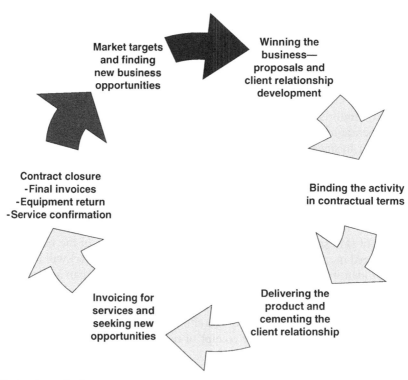

Exhibit 2.1 Business Cycle

- Invoicing for services rendered.
- Contract closure
- Finding new business opportunities.

This chapter does not aim to provide either company or vendor management or consultants with a detailed explanation of business development skills or processes, as that is a separate book in itself. This chapter seeks to illustrate the principal elements of business development to support a rounded perspective in both the major and peripheral roles and responsibilities the consultant might be tasked with, and how business processes affect risk and security services, from inception to delivery.

The following principles are pertinent to any form of business development activities:

- Clients are people and work with people they like and trust.
- Clients appreciate consultants who make their lives easier.
- Reputation is essential; lying once can destroy a long-term relationship.
- Clients are busy; if you waste their time, they will quickly stop coming back to you.
- Long-term relationships often result in repeat or follow-on business.
- Clients need innovators and problem solvers.

Repeat Business

Winning the business is, of course, the first step to successful business activities, without which no activity can occur. However, keeping the business and ensuring the contracting company returns to the security vendor is likely to provide longer-term profitability yields as well as greater operational stability for both. It is therefore essential that the vendor's focus does not rest only on winning the business, but also on successfully servicing the contract and expanding the portfolio of work, where possible and appropriate. This will benefit both the company, which gains a known and reliable service provider, as well as the vendor, which can grow and expand business. A strong combination of business and project activities enables both groups to become closely aligned, ensuring that business activities are quickly and effectively managed in a contractor/vendor partnership. In addition, established relationships enable the company to quickly move through its own business cycle more confidently, bringing in a trusted security partner who already understands the contractual, legal and service delivery processes and standards required.

Business Pipelines

Accessing business opportunities can be a time-consuming process, especially where personal relationships need to be developed or where existing incumbents or provider's personal relationships need to be countered within a competitive market place. Within some markets, opportunity release is open, and selection assessment is made on a case-by-case basis of performance and value. In other markets, human dynamics play a greater role, and company confidence first must be established, with initial smaller-yield contracts leading to larger opportunities. These variances require different business models to reflect the business pipeline subtleties.

The value to a company of establishing personal relationships with a known provider are clear, as more of a "team" approach is developed over time, and the vendor instinctively knows how best to support the company while offering cost efficiencies and operational streamlining through concurrent service delivery. The downside comes with a decreasing desire to impress and offer innovations as the relationship becomes settled, and commercially competitive drivers to sustaining the relationship might diminish.

The value of a case-by-case selection comes with new vendors seeking to impress prospective clients with unique and competitive offers, cutting margins and offering more services for a new contract. Vendors will be keen to establish a foothold to enable longer-term opportunities and growth potential. That said, the company will go through the management pains of operating with new vendors and service delivery may often not meet the required standards.

PROPOSALS

The proposal process is the medium by which a company defines the services it requires through a Statement of Work (SOW) contained within a Request For Proposal (RFP), and prospective vendors illustrate their capabilities to service the need through the responding proposal. It is of equal importance to both company and vendor that the proposal process is managed well, so that the company receives the support it requires in a logical and unambiguous manner, and that the vendor wins business by best presenting its strengths and concepts.

SAMPLE PROPOSAL TEAM

- Capture manager
- Proposal manager
- Technical writers
- Financial analyst
- Subject matter experts
- Desk topper
- Editor
- Graphic artist

The proposal element of business development is the most likely area security consultants (rather than business development consultants) will be asked to participate in. Security consultants will often be subject matter experts (SME) or technical writers for an RFP or proposal team, offering management and service delivery (operational) requirements for the company, or conversely methods by which to undertake the activity as well as innovations and ground knowledge or truths for the vendors. Within the company's management team security professionals may also validate the proposal solutions presented by vendors, assisting corporate management to select the most viable option for the task. For both the company and the vendor, security professionals may also support the development of pricing components particular to a region or field. Their input is therefore essential to this process, on both sides, in order to provide a pragmatic and realistic requirement, as well as a winning proposal, as companies may rely on a consultant's ability to offer realistic assessments as to the risks and mitigation measures if it is unfamiliar with the environment. In order to review the multiple proposal submissions and rationalize the solutions offered, either an in-house or external risk consultant should be engaged to conduct a technical review of the materials to ensure they are sound.

The art of proposal writing is one that on the surface may appear simple, but in truth requires a full understanding of how companies evaluate such offers for service and how the offer is best structured and designed to achieve the greatest win potential. The consultants selected to support the development of an RFP or the creation of proposals should be carefully considered, as the art is a fine one and requires an appreciation of operational and business needs, as well as strong writing skills. Often those field elements requested to support proposal processes are either not qualified or trained in best supporting the development of a clear and defined RFP, or a winning and sound concept.

It is also easy to simply answer the question a company has asked (i.e., directly responding to cited needs). However, it is often in the innovations that the technical section of a contract is won, and best service is offered to the company. The direct pricing of a service may also appear straightforward; however, it is in the trimming of costs that advantages may be gained and costs saved to a business budget. Additionally, if a vendor has weakness or inexperience in certain fields, the identification of suitable partner or teaming companies can augment or address areas that might have resulted in a contract loss. In order to get the most from the bidders, it is essential that the company defines how it will evaluate the submissions. The company should also seek to identify innovations and cost savings as part of its assessment criteria in order to positively exploit vendors that seek to support the business activity. Companies that do not define the structure, evaluation criteria, and expectations of the proposal will do themselves a disservice come the evaluation stage, as well as when receiving security services.

The effort involved in writing successful proposals should not be underestimated by neither the company nor vendor. A considerable amount of focus, energy, and expertise is required to ensure that a proposal is well written and reflects the stated and inferred project needs, and thus stands a good chance of winning against what is usually very stiff competition. Companies should therefore provide sufficient time and guidance to enable vendors to submit a detailed and well-planned proposal; and misleading information or insufficient time will compromise their own business activity. The company evaluation team should also seek to provide clear indications as to where a vendor may not have fared well, so that they might better present their strengths for the next opportunity.

While every proposal will be different and require unique needs, the proposal team illustrated in the table on the preceeding page forms the basic structure for creating a winning proposal. A well-established vendor company should have a strong in-house team focused on proposal production, in terms of analysis, writing, legal interpretations and compliance, contractual evaluations, financial analysis, and technical support. However, field consultants are ideally placed to gather commercial intelligence about any upcoming work a company may soon be undertaking, or to provide detailed and firsthand knowledge about a particular area or field that a proposal team will likely not have. Thus, each proposal team might require augmentation with specialists pertinent to each new opportunity. This is often where consultants are called on to lend their support as subject matter experts. Conversely, the company may also need to bring in regional or specialist expertise in order to evaluate proposal submissions in order to identify the more appropriate solution for each task.

To expedite the proposal writing process, it is useful for the vendor proposal team to provide writers and subject matter experts boilerplates, or past examples for the area they have been tasked with, thus setting the scene, style, and content expectations. Providing training, guidance, and past examples will greatly enhance the drafting of the proposal elements, saving considerable time and effort during what is a hectic and time-limited process. The company issuing the request for proposal (RFP) should consider the effort and various components contributing to the proposal effort as an indication as to the depth and capability of the organization seeking to support the project. A shortfall in any area of the proposal structure, which might be apparent within the submission, might indicate gaps in ability or capability within the vendor organization—and thus possibly indicate shortfalls in subsequent service delivery.

The RFP should also be well written and structured so that management elements can compare like against like within multiple submissions. Instructions should be clear and consistent, and the needs should be clearly articulated. The balance between providing the necessary level and granularity of information to elicit an accurate response should be weighted against the desire to see what solutions and innovations the bidding companies propose. Companies may also seek to limit the length of the proposal, but should allow additional elements to be added as appendices when necessary. A well-written RFP will support well-written proposals; the reverse is true for poorly developed RFPs.

PROPOSAL CONCEPTS

For most consultants, the involvement with a proposal will be limited to providing support to the technical and foundation price components. It is, however, useful to understand what other elements are included within a proposal to better appreciate the level of focus and effort required for the proposal effort (see Chapter 13). Before discussing the proposal process, it is useful to understand some of the basic principles associated with developing successful proposals. The proposal itself is the crystallization of various elements, from directly responding to a company's requirement in a legally binding manner with calculated costs, to innovations and strategic planning. By placing the proposal in a holistic context, the team will better understand the levels of effort, organizational and administrative needs, resource allocation, and lateral thinking required to best position a bidding vendor company for a win. Failure to provide a commercial opportunity with the correct focus and resources is like entering a race without any training. If a company understands the approach methodology, it will be better positioned to ascertain where a vendor stands out from the competition and where artistic license is in play.

Win and Do

There is a fine balance between what the proposal contains that enables a vendor to win a contract and what actually happens when the award is made. On occasion, elements of the proposal can be considered an offer rather than a contractually binding agreement; often any difference lays in the wording. This is especially relevant should the company's RFP provides vague or ambiguous information or does not clearly define the granular scope of the requirement—permitting a certain degree of ingenuity or latitude to be used within a proposal, without being dishonest or misleading. It is important that the concept of what is said to win and what is intended to be done are separated by the Capture Manager so that the proposal content is not unnecessarily constrained for the prospective vendor. Likewise, it is important for the company to be able to differentiate these differences evaluating the submissions. This is especially relevant when a vendor uses a partner vendor's strengths as an indication of the ability to service the contract. Implying that the strength is held within the prime bidder might in some cases strengthen the proposal, while the actual service might not be undertaken by the parent (or prime). Companies should consider whether the bidding agent (prime contractor) is a front for a larger company or whether they present a second layer of cost to the contract. In addition, a positive aspect of the proposal is the use of specialist resumes to indicate a company's human resource strengths; those mentioned in the proposal might not be expected actually to undertake the work, but might represent the quality of service to be supplied. Companies should define key positions where personnel cannot be changed in order to hold vendors to those managers or specialists represented in the proposal. Certain degrees of artistic license are common and to be expected—extensions or expansions of fact rather than lies are normal parts of a proposal. Companies receiving proposals from multiple vendors must be able to identifies the subtleties and differences between artistic license and hard fact, enabling companies to determine the most suitable vendor to undertake the task.

Win Themes and Innovations

Simply answering the RFP requirements may result in a bland and even playing field that prevents a bidder's unique strengths and ingenuity from being properly expressed to the procuring company. The first aim of a proposal is to answer the RFP questions. The Capture Manager must quickly identify what sets the vendor apart from its competitors or the weaknesses of current providers, allowing the bidder to strengthen their proposal significantly. The company should look for new ideas, innovations, and concepts to augment its own expectations and business needs. Such ideas also demonstrate that the vendor is imaginative in its approach, seeking new ways to enhance performance while reducing costs for the company.

Asking Questions

In open bidding processes, there are risks associated with posing questions to a company, if those questions and subsequent answers are transparent to other bidders. Questions can alert competitors to unrecognized problems or issues, or tip a vendor's hand in terms of proposal strategies or competitor uncertainties. Asking questions might also imply uncertainty or a lack of knowledge within a certain area, undermining the company's confidence in a vendor even before the proposal is submitted. Often vendors adopt a strategic approach when considering the value of asking questions to clarify issues, or decide not ask a question and make educated assumptions instead. Questions might also be spiked by the Capture Manager to ensure that the company answers them clearly rather than offering a vague response that generates a second question. The company should seek to answer questions as clearly as possible to avoid repetition of questioning or confusion. It is in the company's interests to ensure that all bidders are aware of the questions and answers to enable all offerers to present a solution that best services the company's need.

Time Frames and Goals

The time taken to provide a strong proposal is often underestimated. Often proposals are under review and being edited until the last minute. Clear timelines and goals should be established early by the Proposal Team to prevent late or weak proposal submissions. Companies should also avoid making unnecessary changes to the RFP or reducing submission time frames; as vendors will commit considerable effort, resources, and money to developing a strong proposal. It is not in the company's interests to receive poor proposals, as their source selection capability will be undervalued and they may not select the right match for their requirements as a result. Companies should answer questions in a timely manner to enable technical concepts to be addressed and also should provide sufficient warning of site visits, especially within hostile or remote environments where mobile resources may be scarce and operational planning for the safety and security of visiting vendors may take time.

Identifying Tasks

Often the proposal team underestimates the time it takes for external resources to gather and provide necessary information to support concept development. Should specialist information be required, or geographically separated technical writers or subject matter experts be expected to draft sections of the proposal, sufficient time and guidance should be provided. Breaking the proposal into manageable chunks, and issuing writing tasks or assignments with guidance and examples is pivotal to ensuring that the final product is completed in a timely and professional manner. The proposal team might also forget that external resources often have other responsibilities and that the team's request is in addition to current workloads. In addition, technical or subject matter writers may lack literacy flair and polish; the schedule should build in time for the proposal team to rework sections into the proposal. Company contracting managers and assessors should be aware of the challenges facing a proposal team and understand the effort taken to draw multiple vendor organizational units together to submit a solid proposal.

Client References

Companies may seek references to gain a degree of assurance that the vendor has performed the services before and achieved satisfactory results. Strong relationships with other companies can result in the vendor's ability to seek references or commendations to support a proposal. These references may be used to demonstrate past performance strengths and client satisfaction. Old references and recommendations should be stored for repeated use, saving the need to ask other companies for favors or assistance. Client references can provide evidence of suitability for the proposal assessment board.

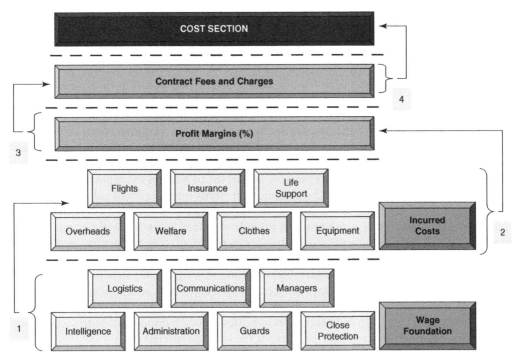

Exhibit 2.2 Proposal Pricing Foundation Elements

Pricing Foundations

Pricing is a key component of a proposal. Poor pricing data and analysis undermines the win potential, as well as exposing the bidder to financial and liability risk. If the price is wrong the proposal might be too expensive for a company, or might be noncompetitive. Alternatively, the company might accept a low priced bid, holding the provider to prices which have been miscalculated, resulting in a poor profit margin, or worse, a loss. Pricing foundations should be established early, based on direct service or equipment costs to initially ensure that the work can be done, with peripheral and profit margins then added on as the second step. Pricing calculations involve a myriad of elements, as illustrated in Exhibit 2.2, and might include labor wages, insurance, rotational costs (flights, food, accommodation), personnel handover periods, morale, recruitment, training, administration, management, movement, life support, profit, and retention levels. It is therefore important that foundation pricing is done early, in detail, and accurately to allow time for further revisions and assessments to be conducted in a timely and measured manner. Companies will need to understand the various elements associated with developing a price model, and should also be wary of companies which come in significantly cheaper than the majority of bidders. To a degree price can reflect quality, and there are certain price levels which will determine whether the vendor is realistic, or providing good quality services. Price is also tied closely to the technical solution, and companies may wish to request Cost Line Item Numbers (CLINs) which indicate the complete cost for a specific service; a guard, manager, armored vehicle, so as to compare like against like for complex projects where multiple solutions might be acceptable. Equipment and mobilization should also be broken out so that assessors might determine what material support and start-up costs are associated with each proposal.

Tailored Solutions

Often some of the company contract requirements match or are very similar to other proposals provided by vendors, enticing vendors to provide generic proposals for a service, with little modification or adjustment to the concepts being provided. Both operational and proposal boilerplates are very useful tools for saving time and effort during a laborious and time-limited proposal process. However, it is important to address the unique requirements of each project or business activity, by placing their needs into a tailored solution. It is also useful (where possible) to place the solution into the context of the business activity. This might sound obvious, but it is tempting to provide standard solutions without mentioning the technical areas of the company's activity—for example, placing engineering problems of a bridge construction project into a security environment concept; the bridge legs are a structurally weak point and are more vulnerable, resulting in a significant structural problems if damaged (i.e., by improvised explosive devices), or that communication towers in Africa are powered by individual generators, and the theft of fuel might disrupt the entire communication infrastructure. This form of observation indicates an understanding of both security and project risks, personalizing and making relevant the solution offered.

Boilerplates

Establishing a library of boilerplates will significantly shorten the time required to draft technical or price sections of a proposal. Each boilerplate will require a degree of modification or tailoring for each new proposal; however, many of the concepts will remain the same. The boilerplates will also provide consultants who are not experienced in proposal writing, but expected to be subject matter experts or technical writers, an idea of the style, format, content, and structure required. In reviewing proposals, companies should identify where vendors have inserted boilerplate without consideration for the specified requirement, as this will denote a lack of effort, understanding and focus.

Linking Elements

The company may indicate performance work statements (PWSs) as part of the RFP that defines the quality and levels of service expected within a statement of work. These PWSs are useful as they set the service standards expected from the vendor. It is often useful to annotate where a PWS is met throughout the proposal, as often a PWS may be achieved in multiple areas. This indicates clearly to the company the bidder's appreciate of the importance of the requirement, as well as drawing the company's attention to where the PSW standards are achieved. In advanced vendor proposals tables or hyperlinks can be used to connect a PWS element to a specific element of the proposal's text. The difference between a company statement of work (see Chapter 12) and PWS must be understood, with the SOW indicating the actual services required by the company, and the PSW indicating the standards and performance levels to be achieved.

Proposal Limitations

The company should set limitations on the bidders, whether it is delivery time or page count. Often companies will not accept late proposals or read pages beyond the agreed number, which undermines the value of the proposal. The company may also ask for proposals to be formatted or structured in a certain manner to achieve consistency among bidders. The bidder should seek to avoid frustrating the company by not adhering to instructions, as this will reduce the win potential or, worse, make the proposal noncompliant, and thus void. Limitations may also be placed on value, indicating a ceiling beyond which services will not be accepted. These limitations will determine the service delivery approach as well as the costing of the proposal.

Personnel Selection

Selecting the right human resources to service the contract is important for three reasons.

1. It demonstrates the strengths of the vendor in terms of expertise and experience in a field.
2. It indicates an understanding of the requirements of an activity.
3. It sets the cost levels for the contract.

The right balance between expertise and cost should be sought in order to make the proposal both technically and cost competitive. If a third-country national can undertake the duties of a more costly expatriate, then that model is likely to result in a stronger chance of a win, as well as savings to the company. If a local provider is unlikely to be able to perform a function due to a lack of expertise or poor reliability, then a Western option might be technically more acceptable (see Chapter 7). The company should identify where vendors are using the correct personnel and nationalities in order to deliver the correct standard of service, rather than where they are too focused on price.

Resumes

The company may request resumes to indicate the type and level of person expected to be used within the contract, if won. Often people whose resumes are submitted within a proposal are not actually those expected to perform the work, unless the award is expected shortly after proposal submission or key roles have been defined. Long proposal assessment periods often result in candidates seeking other employment rather than waiting several months for possible work; this use of strong resumes unlikely to undertake the work is known as bait and switch. As such, proposals often include *sample* resumes that indicate the strengths of the human resources available. On occasion the company will seek to avoid this proposal trait and will request a key post. In this situation, the resume should match the person who will undertake the role in the event of a win, with company permission required for any personnel change (which can be refused).

Use of Subcontractors and Their Strengths

More frequently vendors are merging into consortiums to provide solutions to complex business activities. A parent, or prime, will own the contract, with subcontractors providing services within specific areas as partners or subcontractors. The proposal should seek to capitalize on the strengths of the entire group in order to present a stronger image to a prospective company. This is useful when the prime is lacking in certain areas that the subcontractor might be able to cover. Vendors should sign nondisclosure agreements with subcontractors and partners to provide a degree of protection regarding sensitive information during an individual business pursuit or arrangement, as in other fields these companies may remain competitors. Combining multiple organizational strengths also benefits the company as it has better leveraged support from multiple providers.

Past Performance

Past performance lays the foundation of why a bidder is competent to undertake the work on behalf of the company. Past performance also indicates the bidder's experience and knowledge within a field and why it will be able to undertake this new contract quickly and effectively. The strengths of the bidding prime and subcontractors should be merged, where appropriate and best suited, to best illustrate the strengths of the proposal. Although this information is very important, the administrative burden of collating and processing a large company's past performance often makes gathering this information time consuming and laborious, especially when spread across multiple divisions, or encompassing statistical information within both a prime and subcontractor. Ideally the bidder will have collation and custodianship processes in place. If not, past performance requirements should be identified early to ensure that details are gathered in time for proposal evaluation, inclusion, and submission. Past performance provides a degree of assurance that the vendor is fit to undertake the task.

Use of Language

The proposal should seek to use the same language as the company requests in the RFP. Differences in terminology should be avoided, even if company/provider product names differ. If the client company is American, U.S. spelling should be used. If the procuring group is military, appropriate terminology particular to the armed forces should be adopted. This use of language indicates that the vendor understands the client and is familiar with how it operates and communicates. In addition, it reassures companies that the contractor speaks the same language as their team.

Visuals and Tables

Pictures say a thousand words, and tables several hundred. It is often useful to provide visual illustrations of data or place key elements into well-structured and easily understood tables to better demonstrate information. Illustrations also can save space if the proposal has page limitations. Mapping can demonstrate geographic experience and facilities and photography can display facilities and training.

Statistics

Statistical information is useful in providing clear and clinical information of certain facts rather than the usual fluff of verbiage contained within a proposal. For example, the sentence

"Despite managing 123 acts of crime against facilities in Southern Sudan, the company has not lost 1 day or operation" clearly shows the vendor's strength. The use of statistical information also quickly demonstrates a servicing strength; consider this statement: "The company has dealt with 7,900 days of crisis management in over 134 countries." Large companies, whether vendors or their clients, often find it difficult to gather and collate useful statistics, and mining for useful data to support the proposal can be time consuming. Vendors should substantiate and where necessary evidence such data; they should avoid guessing or providing erroneous information to the company.

Answering the Question versus Innovations

The proposal should always answer the RFP's questions or requirements first. There is a risk in openly questioning the company's assessment of what is required, as this may alienate the assessors who grade the proposal. However, innovations are useful in demonstrating the vendor's ability to provide immediate solutions, lateral thinking, and proactive support to a company. These innovations may be in the form of suggesting diplomatically (after answering the question) that alternative approaches or structures might provide a more efficient or cost-effective solution. Innovations should always be linked to performance or cost—supporting the activities' goals and efficiency—as well as the safety of personnel or materials.

Price versus Quality

There is a fine balance between quality and price during the development of the proposal and for any services delivered following a win. It is important to understand how much emphasis the company places on quality versus price: Is the company restricted in terms of budget, or is it willing to pay more for higher-quality services? Exhibit 2.3 shows possible trade-offs between quality and price, although good-quality service often can be achieved at a reasonable price through considered planning and resource leveraging. Companies must examine where they fit within a price verses quality perspective, and then align their selection criteria based on how much additional service or resource they might require, against what they can afford—as shown within Exhibit 2.3 where costs are aligned with planned budgets and all service expectations are met in full, but with little in terms of surge capacity or value added service.

Normally a company has quality and service expectations but is not willing to pay significantly more for a premium service that is significantly higher than required; in other words, for platinum versus bronze standards. This factor is also defined by the vendor: Is its reputation based on platinum levels of service, and is it therefore unwilling to lower service levels to meet client expectations and needs? The vendor's proposal team must determine whether the vendor is flexible regarding the quality of services: Will the vendor decline to bid, or will it offer a solution it knows will be too costly for the client? Balancing price and quality is a fine and fluid requirement, and both the company and vendor may wish to use versions of Exhibit 2.3 to define what level of service and cost they are willing to operate at. Vendors must carefully consider their options in order to retain their reputations, provide a realistic proposal solution, and stand a better chance of winning an opportunity.

Exhibit 2.3 Price versus Quality Considerations

	Best Solution – Meets all client needs, with surplus resources for hidden or surge requirements, or special services not originally anticipated	Effective Solution – Meets all primary client requirements, however lacks additional margins to deal with unforeseen needs, offering only basic services	Minimal Standards – Offers only specific services, a baseline for minimal professional standards and risk tolerance, below which the client/provider company will not go
High Cost – Significantly exceeds the predicted budget for the services, posing challenges to the client and their activity			
Medium Cost – Is in general alignment with expected costs of the requirement, offering a degree of movement to save cost, or engage additional services		✓	
Low Cost – Falls below the budgeted amount for the requirement, possibly offering additional scope for further services, or significant cost savings			

How to Save the Client Money

Unless the company has specifically defined what it requires, there may be opportunities for the vendor to offer solutions or innovations that can reduce the business activity's cost. While the commercial goal of a vendor is, of course, to make money, the only way of achieving this is to win the business in the first place, or keep it in the face of tough market competition. Innovations, flexibility, shared cost overheads, stretching initial cost impacts, multiple position responsibilities, and other approaches can be used to demonstrate an ability to provide the required levels of standard for the service while reducing costs to the company. Obvious methods may include reducing wage or profit levels, using collocated facilities and personnel to offset costs, sharing equipment between personnel, or reducing the numbers of rotations between staff to reduce mobilization costs. In addition, the staged modification of nationalities might offer a way to reduce costs in the second year of the contract (e.g., training local nationals to undertake the roles of more costly third-country nationals). In addition, if subsequent contracts are being opened to tender, it might be worth reducing the profitability of an existing contract to demonstrate how further engagement will reduce the company's overall budget with a savings incentive. Offering cost-saving options is a useful tool to demonstrate financial awareness and flexibility to support the procuring company's wider goals.

Disguising Costs

The comprehensiveness of the RFP will be constrained by the time available to the company management team, the level of effort they can afford to invest into the RFP, the details they have provided when describing the needs, and the company's ability to describe the entire and complex requirements of the activity as well as changing environmental factors that might affect the need throughout the project's life span. As such the vendor proposal team will seek to address some of the identified shortfalls, gaps, and ambiguities of the RFP's request through modifications *only after a contract is won.* Raising these issues during the bid phase likely will increase the cost as well as call into question the company's ability to define its needs properly. Often a sizable portion of the contract value is gained through subsequent modifications after the award of the contract. Thus, unless clearly stated, costs can often be hidden due to a lack of RFP clarity, enabling vendors to make assumptions which permit a lower cost solution. Vendors may also use careful wording which provides the legal scope for additional funds to be allocated based on any ambiguous needs indicated in the RFP, and the assumptions subsequently made in the proposal, such as: We will service surge requirements quickly and effectively, we will meet client training requirements for additional services, we will source and procure necessary equipment, we will seek to streamline management structures to save cost—thus allowing the vendor to cite additional needs and associated costs when those undefined services are required by the company.

In addition, proposal effort and costs, management overhead, training and recruitment, and other incurred expenses might be wrapped within the complete cost package rather than being defined specifically within the costing component. Some vendors provide implied free services whose costs actually might be absorbed within the management fees, in order to suggest that they are investing additional effort on the company's behalf. The balance between an implication and a lie is fine, and at no stage should the proposal include literal or clinical inaccuracies.

Packaging of Proposals

Some companies specifically define the packaging requirements of the proposal, from font size, spacing, page sizes and page numbers, to whether an electronic or hard copy is required. Vendors should pay attention to any requests in order to be compliant with the company's needs. Compliance can be especially important if the company is using multiple screens to view electronic aspects of the proposal during the evaluation phase and the font is too small to read easily, or the company has a limited time to evaluate a proposal and the bidder has offered too long a document.

Use of Graphic Artists

A picture paints a thousand words, and the professional presentation of information can best be offered through specialist support. Poorly presented visual information looks shoddy and implies poor quality of service, a lack of professionalism, and limited bidder resources. Most important, it does not present information most effectively.

Technical Experts

Rarely does an RFP or proposal team have all of the knowledge and experience to deal with each SOW or proposal that it writes. Drawing on internal or external resources is important to ensure that the proposal is accurate, contains information that strengthens the chances of the company getting a accurate and detailed response from a vendor, allows a bidding vendor to win, or adds the local flavor to what would otherwise be a stale repetition of other work. Both the RFP and proposal team need to be aware that some of the resources it will draw on may not understand the proposal process, goals, timelines, and formats, and that team members may need to invest time and effort to educate external parties regarding team needs.

Modifying the Request for Proposal

The company has the right to modify or change entirely the requirements within its RFP at any stage in the proposal process. Late changes can create enormous burdens and frustrations for vendors, as entirely new sections, significant changes, or new data are required. The company should seek to avoid changes after the RFP has been released, although the vendor proposal teams must of course remain flexible in meeting any changes in order to deliver the correct proposal to the company, within the time frames provided. Companies, for their part, should try to limit last-minute changes in order to get accurate and well-presented proposals to support their needs, as late changes will undermine their business process and result in less than optimal responses.

Bid or No Bid

The vendor typically has to decide early whether it wishes to bid on an opportunity. Deciding not to bid after dedicating time, resources, and effort to a proposal is frustrating and undermines the productivity of a business unit. Often vendors must weigh their chances of winning against the investment of effort and determine whether the financial or strategic rewards warrant a proposal effort. Companies should be aware that considerable vendor investment is placed into a proposal, and that their vendors may need to make hard business decisions leading to some opportunities being declined if it does not make sense for them to pursue a task.

PROPOSAL PROCESS

Creating a proposal is a logical but complex and dynamic process that usually is restricted only by the factors of time, effort, and resources. Some opportunities might be identified well in advance of the proposal being required, notably with government contracts, or when strong commercial relationships have been developed. Some RFPs may be released at short notice, permitting the bidders only a short window to evaluate and respond to the company's request. Even when an opportunity has been identified well in advance, the proposal process still usually is fast moving and intensive, as changes to the draft outlines and specific needs will require considerable effort and resourcing to accomplish adequately. Therefore, the process should be a combination of a regimented and a systematic approach, combined with imagination and a sprinkling of chaos, as illustrated in Exhibit 2.4. It should be noted that a sound proposal process will be organized in a very complex and detailed manner in order to ensure multiple party participation.

If the proposal team is fortunate, the company may release a pre-solicitation notice, or a warning that a solicitation for services is pending, possibly with a draft SOW. In both government and commercial terms, this is known as a pre-solicitation. The actual request for a proposal is, as mentioned, a request for proposal (RFP), which defines the final scope of work

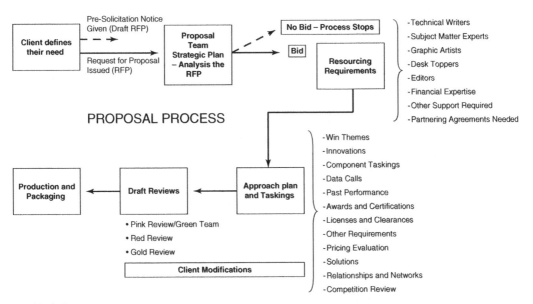

Exhibit 2.4   Simplified Proposal Process

and contractual and compliance requirements. The RFP also might outline how a proposal should be presented in terms of structure, content, and number of pages. It is important for vendors to understand what the company wants in terms of a response in order to stand the best chance of winning the award. Poorly organized and resourced proposal teams invariably fail. Focused and organized teams stand a better chance of success.

ANALYZING THE REQUEST FOR PROPOSAL

Carefully analyzing the company's needs and objectives forms the foundation for how the proposal will be approached as well as the structure, content, and pricing. Only by reading the RFP several times in detail and identifying the key areas and needs, will the final proposal product be developed that has the best chance of compliance and success. Well-structured vendor proposal teams devote the first several days to understanding and evaluating the RFP, as well as establishing the proposal strategy and structure. Teams that start writing immediately are likely to waste time and effort through a lack of planning and organization.

It is important for the proposal writing team to identify early any limitations established by the company or resulting from the provider's inability to meet certain qualifications or areas of expertise. Constraints may result in a need to establish partnering agreements, use subcontractors, or seek clearances or certifications. Constraints may be placed on both the prime and subcontractors from the company as a flow-down (where rules applied to the company are then applied to the contractor) of rules and regulations, and such constraints also should be considered in terms of proposal and delivery impacts. Certain factors might initially preclude the opportunity to bid; lateral thinking might be needed in order to overcome or navigate these problems. If problems are recognized only late in the proposal process, the vendor may fail to comply with the company's needs, thus wasting considerable time, effort, and resources, or the quality of the proposal may be degraded, resulting in failure to be competitive.

When evaluating the RFP, it is important also not to assume that the company understands or is familiar with the vendor's strengths and experiences. This is especially relevant with government contracts, where the evaluation is normally designed to be fair and balanced, and any unwritten elements will not necessarily be considered (such as the companies past exposure or experience with a bidding vendor) during the assessment of multiple proposals. During the RFP analysis, it is also useful to consider what project and financial pressures the company is facing and what internal and external dynamics may influence its thought processes, selection approach, and evaluation parameters. These could involve weaknesses of incumbents, pressures to complete a project on time, political influences, limited budgets, or an interest to use the first project as a lead-in for other opportunities. A review of the competition is also very useful, as it establishes likely win themes, strengths and weaknesses, partnering arrangements, past performances, and general strategies. This review also can help a vendor determine whether it is worth pursuing the opportunity. If the competition is expected to win, other opportunities may afford a better application of time, effort, and resources.

The RFP analysis should include a vendor bid or no-bid decision point at the outset of the process, determined by such factors as the chances of success, the ability to service the contract, the vendor's interest in the activity, the profitability of the venture, and cost constraints to the contracting organization. If an opportunity is considered worthy of pursuit, the proposal team should consider a series of options to be offered to the contracting company, based on the service delivery requirements and constraints. Win themes, unique approaches, innovations, and strategies should be at the forefront of the proposal team's mind during the analysis stage. At this time, the team also can begin drafting the proposal. The next sections form the basis of the RFP analysis.

Statement of Work

The company should provide relatively clear instructions on what services it requires, when, and where. At times, a company may provide only a basic outline of the general need and ask the bidders to define the structure and delivery of the services, placing the onus on the provider. Companies should seek to make the statement of work as logical and clear as possible, structuring it in such a manner as to enable the company to equally compare vendor services, without necessarily constraining innovation and lateral thinking.

Instructions

The company should provide instructions as to the structure, content, and delivery of the proposal. It may also indicate the certifications, qualifications, and licenses needed to bid. The vendors may need to meet certain requirements, such as established offices in the activity area or country, proof of holding sizable contracts, valid commercial licenses, or security clearances.

Evaluation Factors

The company should state how the proposal will be evaluated. It may indicate a percentage of value to certain aspects of the proposal—for example, that the solution is worth 50%, the past experiences and strengths 20%, and the price 30%. Alternatively, a company might state that the price and technical sections are equally weighted. This will provide guidance to vendors regarding how much emphasis and effort should be devoted to each area of the proposal.

Analytical Considerations

The table on the following pages, while not an exhaustive list, provides sample considerations that may help the proposal team better analyze the RFP key components in order to decide whether to pursue the opportunity, and, if so, how best to identify risks and requirements in order to be successful. If the vendors consider these factors when writing the proposal, the company is likely to get a better selection of proposals from which to choose.

Conversely, the company should seek to determine from the proposals submitted who presents the most realistic, effective and competitive offer—which places the company and their business activity at least risk.

Defining the Service

As illustrated in Exhibit 2.5, the service itself will be defined by corporate and project needs, policies, and methodologies as well as how the risk environment influences operations in a

Risks	Factors
Threat tolerances and security issues	Company risk-tolerance levels
	Provider and subcontractor risk-tolerance levels
	Company minimal security standards
	Provider and subcontractor minimal security requirements
	Values placed to company and subcontractors' equipment
	Reputational damage if equipment destroyed, lost, or stolen
	Impact factors on company operations, delay, costs, project closure, and so on
	Who will security be provided for (just the company, or also subcontractors)?
	Company's desired security level (expatriates versus local nationals)
	Reputational threats and tolerances associated with the activity
	Likelihood of specific targeting based on the nature of the activity
	Crisis response plans and measures (casualty, evacuation, etc.)
	Threat assessment for the activity, and specified projects
	Liaison with military and other security organizations
	Different areas of risk, geographic and activity based
	Can risks be mitigated, transferred, avoided?
	The cost impact for risk mitigation; is it appropriate and realistic?
	What other companies will the company manage—their performance capabilities and other areas of concern?
	Is the opportunity value worth the risk: Bid or no bid?
Intelligence gathering	Company budget parameters, expectations, and limitations
	Project scope and duration
	Project location and environmental influences
	Life support requirements
	Logistical and administrative support requirements
	Is the company intent on procuring equipment/resources; if not, who will?
	Activity timelines and phases
	Company pre-deployment training requirements (i.e., hostile environment training [HET])
	Pre-company deployment briefing and information
	Pre-contract or activity surveys, training, and preparation requirements
	Contract nature and financial, risk, liability, and legal factors
	What other companies will the provider company be managing to service the contract (i.e., convoy security, static security groups, etc.)?
	Likely non-specified interests, preferences, and desires of the company
	Company relationships with competition, strengths, problems
	How much can the vendor find out to enhance the win potential?
Competition evaluation	What are the strengths and weaknesses of the competition?
	What areas of weakness need to be addressed to make the provider more competitive, or capable to service the company's needs?

Risks	Factors
	Can weaknesses be addressed through teaming or partnering arrangements (a consortium approach)?
	Where can vendor weaknesses be turned into strengths?
Logistics, budgets, and contracts	Specialized equipment time lags (i.e., armored vehicles × 3 months)
	Weapons and specialist equipment licensing requirements
	Any registration and other licensing, tax or legal requirements
	Specialist support available (i.e., medical, military, government)
	Local procurement sources and import limitations
	Communications, evacuation, risk and logistics plan and networking
	Outsourcing options (i.e., hotels, hire vehicles, equipment, etc.)
	Formal capture of contractual company requirements
	Subcontractor authorizations and approvals if contract won for subcontractors
	Partnering agreements and formal NTP
	Defining the provider and subcontractor scopes of work
	Establishing necessary budgets to begin work (advances and escrows)
	Consolidating labor contracts and billing policies and procedures
	What pre-deployment or training requirements are there?
	What mobilization factors need to be considered?
	What recruitment influences will affect the timelines for delivery?
	What budget is required to deliver the proposal, especially if using external or direct cost resources?
	What is required to position the company to service the contract?
Win themes and innovations	What is the company asking for and how can these be best presented in terms of the vendor's experience, knowledge, and capability?
	What additional benefits can the vendor bring to the contract?
	Why is the vendor better than the competitors: *Why choose us?*
	What competition weaknesses or failures can be appropriately exploited?
	What internal and external resources or capabilities can be leveraged?
	What government or agency relationships might support the company in their endeavors?
	What is the company's core goals, objectives, and problem areas?
	How can the vendor set itself above the competition?
Compliance requirements	What compliance issues have been defined by the company?
	Can gaps or shortfalls be addressed within the company, or are external resources or agreements required?
	Can the company even bid for the work?
	Who can confirm compliance or be tasked to resolve problems?

(continued)

Risks	Factors
	What must the vendor do to be legally/contractually positioned to bid?
Supporting Needs	Who is best positioned as the regional and local expert to reflect the providers' understanding of the activity site and environment?
	Who will be tasked as subject matter experts and technical writers?
	Is there information at hand to support the content of the proposal?
	What missing data needs to be resourced? Data calls
	What information is required from any subcontractors?
	Is information required from other companies for the proposal?
	What information is available and where are there gaps? Issue tasks or requirements to parties early!

particular theater, any budgetary constraints and parameters the company must operate under, and the availability of external support that might augment the company's activities or reduce security costs. It is by considering these factors that the proposal team may be better placed to determine the scope and nature of the product the prospective client may desire.

Vendor Self-Analysis

It is important for the vendor to make a frank and honest appraisal of its own strengths and weaknesses when considering the client's requirements as well as competitors' capabilities, as illustrated in Exhibit 2.6. From the outset and throughout the proposal-writing process, the vendor should reevaluate and keep an eye on the competition in order to understand how the competition may deliver a stronger bid for the contract. In addition, by spotting gaps or weakness, the vendor may decide it needs to partner, team, or subcontract elements to present a stronger proposal as well as better delivery of service. Reevaluation also can allow a vendor to avoid areas where it may feel uncomfortable in terms of risk and reputation. The choice to subcontract or partner should be made early when evaluating service, experience, or quality gaps.

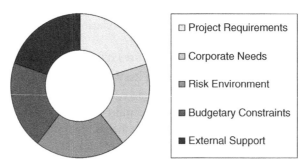

- □ Project Requirements
- ▨ Corporate Needs
- ▨ Risk Environment
- ▨ Budgetary Constraints
- ■ External Support

Exhibit 2.5 Defining the Service

Exhibit 2.6 Vendor Self-Analysis

Experience Area	Nil	Weak	Medium	Strong	Delivery
Client Industry				√	Prime
Geographic			√		Joint
Networks	√				Subcontract
Consultancy				√	Prime
Intelligence			√		Prime
Close Protection				√	Prime
Convoy		√			Subcontract
Static Guards	√				Subcontract

Lateral Thinking

The proposal team must consider the company's needs in a holistic manner, focusing not only on the requested service—such as providing a single consultant at a project site or a close protection team for a project—but also such elements as communications, intelligence, operational management, training, administration, logistics, crisis response, policies and plans, audits, evacuation, networking, and other specialist support, as illustrated in Exhibit 2.7. The vendor's complete set of services should be reviewed and best exploited to illustrate the direct, indirect, and peripheral value it can bring to the award. This not only allows the proposal team to demonstrate the structural, historical, and specialist capabilities and grounding of the vendor, but can also lead to further business opportunities for the vendor, while concurrently better supporting the company's interests. Both vendors and companies should seek to identify where a contracted organization's other strengths or capabilities might be brought to bear to supplement or enhance the initial service requirements, if needed.

Compliance Matrix

Tabulating the requirements of the proposal in terms of what is a defined requirement and what is useful to include helps the capture manager and team to structure their overall approach. Such tabulation also can be used to break down complex and sizable requirements into more manageable sections, leading to an allocation of work to groups and individuals. The list of company-defined and bidder-assessed requirements should also have annotated reference pages or sections for simplicity of management confirmation or tracking. Compliance matrixes can be complex and sizable; however, for simple proposals, they can be short key-point capture

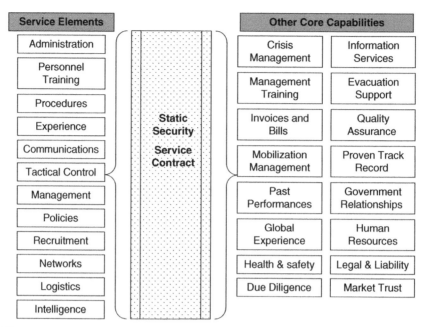

Exhibit 2.7 Complete Service Offering

documents. The key factor is to identify all aspects of the proposal and then ensure they are met in a timely and accurate manner. Discovering that the vendor company is missing a government license, has not established the correct security clearance, or has failed to gain a simple accreditation at a point too late to correct, and after significant time, effort, and resources have been expended, is frustrating and a waste of valuable time and resources. It also undermines the credibility of the bidding unit as well as the company as a whole, both internally within the vendor's organization, as well as potentially to prospective clients. Establishing tasks, problems, and solutions at the outset of the proposal process is an important part of winning the award. The proposal schedule should crystallize the key elements of the compliance matrix within a time setting, aligning the requirements against a deadline. The compliance matrix should seek to cover evaluation factors, contract requirements, and tasks, as shown next.

Evaluation Factors	Contract Requirements	Tasks
Statement of work	Licenses	Technical and management sections
Performance work statements	Experience	Past performance
Weighting factors	Past performance	Plans and documents
Innovations to enhance scores	Certifications	Certifications and licenses
Supporting data requirements	Clearances	Resumes

Evaluation Factors	Contract Requirements	Tasks
Partnering or subcontracting requirements	Defined equipment specifications	Data calls and graphic designs
	Human resources qualifications and clearances	Partnering contracts
	Financial record Delivery Packaging	Pricing Review teams

Compliance may also take into account how the proposal will be evaluated, the contractual requirements stipulated by the company and determined by the vendor, as well as the delivery of responsive answers and details for the actual tasks or services themselves. This forms a checklist to ensure that the proposal is developed with a clear understanding of the varied needs and inclusions required for successful bidding.

Proposal Schedule Plan

It is typical for proposal timelines to run over. Having no defined schedule will result in a proposal being poorly managed and often rushed in the final stages of production. Adequate time should be provided for such elements as packaging and checking the proposal's presentation. Data call deadlines (requests for key information by the proposal team to supporting elements) should be adhered to, with only vital information being accepted after the close period for new material submission as often external parties will bring new innovations late to the proposal process and fail to understand the multiple conceptual and physical changes their idea may incur. Review periods, task settings, and delivery deadlines should form the basis of a timetable for proposal development. Sufficient flexibility should be incorporated (where time permits) to address unforeseen problems, or late but critical information submission. Data call time frames, reviews (technical and financial), and external quality assurance should be factored into the process.

PROPOSAL

The perfect proposal that is incorrectly structured or the proposal that has the perfect answer to the wrong question will be rejected, wasting the vendor's time and resources and being of no use to the sourcing company. Once the RFP analysis is complete, the vendor must take as much care and pay as much attention to detail when writing the proposal. Clinical and candid reviews and assessments at critical junctions by impartial judicators will ensure that the proposal meets all requirements. Proposals can take a variety of forms, depending on what the company expects or demands. However, the five fundamental elements, or volumes, of a proposal include:

1. *An introduction or executive summary.* Here the proposal introduces the vendor their expertise and capabilities to the company.
2. *Technical volume.* This provides the answer to the company's needs, in terms of how the service will be performed and any innovative concepts or solutions that might make the activity of efficient, safer, or less expensive.

3. *Management volume.* This defines how the activity will be managed and administered. It also typically involves such aspects as company structure, responsibilities, and quality assurance.
4. *Past performance volume.* This lays out why a bidder is effective within the service required, demonstrating experience and competence. Resumes indicate the quality, strength and experiences of the human resources identified to service the activity. The certification and licenses evidence the vendor's ability to legally undertake the work.
5. *Cost or business volume.* This should encapsulate all costs, usually as a wrap rate of what the service will cost the company, as well as legal aspects.

Commercial and government proposals can differ in their complexity and structure. Companies may also dictate the manner in which information is presented, sometimes to the degree of exact areas to be covered and in what order. Usually these generic areas are included, although perhaps in a different sequence.

Structure

It is important to get the right draft structure in place from the outset of the proposal process in order to focus the proposal team on the approach strategy as well as defining individual sections to be drafted and materials to be gathered. The company may offer guidance or clear instruction on how it wishes the proposal to be structured, as illustrated in Exhibit 2.8. In U.S. government proposals, these instructions are contained within Section L of the RFP. The SOW and PWS might also offer guidance on how to lay out a proposal if Section L is limited or does not exist. Should guidance not be offered, common sense, experience, and logic need to be applied. Serious consideration should be given structuring of the document if the proposal team does not agree with the structuring offered by the company; disregarding the structure given, however faulty, and offering a cleaner solution should be balanced by how any deviation might affect the company's evaluation of the proposal.

Past performances, certifications, resumes, and other elements might be requested to substantiate the proposal content. The sections that follow provide a brief introduction to the proposal elements as a guideline to understanding how proposals are developed and structured.

Executive Summary   The executive summary sets the scene for the technical solution(s) to the company's requirements and usually includes (but is not limited to):

- *Vendor company overview* (plus partners). Includes global and regional footprint and experiences relevant to the award, specialist strengths, and any other organizational capabilities. Maps depicting global and regional offices, key statistics, and accreditations are normally included in this section.
- *Main discriminators.* This section lists why the vendor company is the best value: experience, expertise, relationships, accreditations, and footprint.
- *Risk environment.* This section offers an assessment to place the technical solution into a risk context: political, economic, hostile groups, crime, natural, and man-made risks.
- *Any key relationships.* The section lists relationships or local arrangements—government, military, other agencies—that place the vendor company ahead of its competitors.

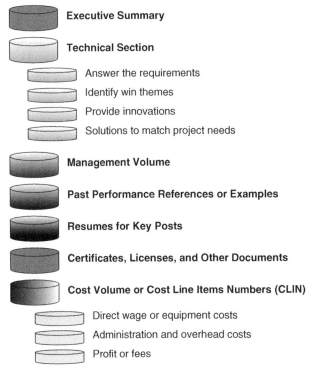

Exhibit 2.8 Proposal Structure and Elements

Technical Volume The technical solution(s) provides the methodology for and approach to delivering the services, specifying how the vendor brings benefits and innovations to the company, as well as explaining work processes and outputs, while ensuring risk mitigation. This section may include references to key relationships and networks as well as external support. Relevant experiences might be included as well as the details of how the vendor actually will conduct each task. Complex RFPs might require the technical solution be broken down into distinct components to better present the information. Each section might include these elements:

- *Threat summary and analysis.* This element relates to how the risks and the operating environment may influence and affect the program and projects, from a strategic to granular level for programs to individual tasks. Threat or risk factors can include tribal groups and influences, criminal elements and risks, hostile groups and targeting methodology (terrorists and insurgents), the political situation and any associated instabilities, sovereign security groups and their reliability and activities, foreign security groups and their support and limitations, as well as hydrographic, topographical, demographic and economic influences. A historical review of the country's problems might place the current risks into a context, and references to how adjacent country or regions influencing the situation might also be useful. The threat summary should focus on how the threats might impact the activity, allowing the technical solution to be linked to the threats reviewed in terms of solutions.

- *Concept of operations.* This section demonstrates an understanding of how the activity will be conducted, as well as how the technical elements will be aligned with the client goals, objectives, and methodology. It also demonstrates an understanding of the project timelines and milestones as well as any previous problems or concerns. In this way, the vendor demonstrates an understanding of the unique needs of the company, highlighting how the services offered serve these requirements as well as reflect the risk environment the activity will operate in.
- *Tactical approaches.* The tactical solution is the manner in which a specific activity will be conducted, rather than the peripheral factors and administrative and management elements. This may include providing an intelligence organization, communications center, operations command cell, liaison expertise, or close protection and static guards to support project activities. The use of technology and working in cooperation with external agencies might also be included. The tactical solution is the mechanical conduct of the service at the granular level and forms the foundation of how the provider intends to meet the company's needs. It should form the nucleus of a fuller answer to the RFP requirement, drawing on other factors to supplement the response.
- *Group breakdowns and mobilizations.* If appropriate, different group structures and categories for the award itself should be defined, along with mobilization goals, schedules and timelines. For sizable contracts, a separate mobilization plan should be included, defining the goals and objectives of any advance teams and contract start and continuation requirements. (This information may be included in the management volume.) The fusion of contract groups and external agencies (local and regional) and how they relate to other elements of the vendor might prove useful.
- *Communications.* A communications concept and plan is useful to define the practical requirements of information system establishment and use for a contract. This is especially relevant where communications may be poor or projects dispersed. The establishment of a communications and management center is a common theme for sizable contracts, as well as how it interacts with external agencies in terms of networking and communication connectivity systems. Communications is a key component to dealing with normal project activities as well as responding effectively to a crisis event.
- *Crisis response.* The management volume may contain the risk management aspects. However, it is useful to mention how different groups and individuals fit into crisis response. This information can explain how the communications and management center will act as the focal point for crisis management, as well as secondary roles of security personnel within that response: static guards, close protection. In theory, the whole security structure should have functions defined within a crisis response plan.
- *Incident management.* Incident management usually is defined within a set of policies and procedures, effectively a cheat sheet for management in order to make their initial response to a problem more effective. The company might value the establishment of a detailed incident management plan (see Chapter 12) tailored to the project in order to mitigate the impacts of risks occurring. Reference to creating and maintaining such a plan, in consultation with external agencies, when appropriate, will prove useful. The obvious example is the establishment of an evacuation plan (see Chapter 10), drawing on the resources of government, embassy, and military groups to safely extract personnel and resources from a crisis event or location.

- *Relationships.* The ability to draw on information, support, and experiences of external agencies is particularly useful to a company, as it is effectively gaining free services. This is notably important when working in hostile or remote environments, where serious crisis events may be dealt with only by using external agencies to supplement project resources. Relationship building will play a key role in effective project operations, both directly and indirectly, and offer a company ways of gaining access to key government or other agency officials. The proposal should exploit existing relationships to demonstrate the vendor's capacity within a region and indicate the additional assistance it might be able to offer outside of the actual service itself.
- *Services.* Services may be wide ranging, from senior consultancy services, to static guards and life support (see Chapter 9). It is important that the proposal does not focus purely on the tactical elements—how a security service will be provided in granular detail—but rather how the service fits into the project requirements, connected to the risks identified, training and recruitment referenced, and work productivity levels contracted for. For example, a holistic approach might illustrate the relationship between a static guard and the crisis management plan, community development and socioeconomic programs rather than purely on how the guard will undertake a gate sentry duty.
- *Work outputs and processes.* The company will wish to know how the various services are being delivered and what it can expect for its money. This can be explained in terms of job functions and work outputs. It can also be captured in how many hours, days, and months personnel will work—allowing the company to be assured that a Quality Assurance Plan is in place and can be audited. For example, an operations team might be expected to provide a daily report, weekly intelligence reports, movement plans for each trip, and a serious incident report for each crisis event. A table or visual illustrating the responsibilities and output of each group or individual will define their appointment processes and functions as well as work outputs. The table on the next page captures the roles to nationality, days per week worked, hours per day, and how many months they will be expected on-site.
- *Full answers.* The tactical approach should form the nucleus of a subject area answer, with organizational breakdowns, mobilization factors, communication networks, crisis response measures and plans, and other factors augmenting the answer to the tactical requirement, as illustrated in Exhibit 2.9. It is important that the proposal does not miss the opportunity to draw on other vendor (or subcontractor) strengths, which might provide a stronger case for making the award to the vendor company. A full answer brings into play every strength and experience that the proposal team can identify to sell the vendor as the best solution to the company. Integration of strengths, such as illustrated within Exhibit 2.9 which highlights the elements contributing to the tactical service approach, is important to show how the solution is layered, bringing into play a range and depth of capabilities rather than only a linear or flat service.

Management Volume   The management volume provides an understanding of the organizational structure of the vendor and its partners or subcontractors. It should demonstrate how the management elements will draw on the vendor's wider strengths and geographic footprints as well as connect to external agencies and support. The management volume also demonstrates how the client company's requirements will be managed, and by whom,

Group	Positions	Class	Days	Hours	Rotations[*]
Program management	Program and deputy manager	XP	7/7	14hrs>	2/2 months
	Security coordinator and deputy	XP	7/7	14hrs^	2/1 months
	Finance/Logistics manager	XP	7/7	14hrs>	2/2 months
	Medic	XP	7/7	14hrs^	2/1 months
	Liaison manager	XP	7/7	14hrs>	2/2 months
	Intelligence Manager	XP	7/7	12hrs^	2/1 months
Operational management	Tactical operations center (TOC)/Deputy manager	XP	7/7	13hrs^	2/1 months
	Operations supervisor	XP	7/7	13hrs^	2/1 months
	Senior shift supervisor	XP	7/7	13hrs^	2/1 months
	Dog handlers	CCN	6/7	12hrs	6/2 days
	Translators	CCN	6/7	12hrs	6/2 days
	Communication staff	CCN	6/7	13hrs	6/2 days
Operational Staff PSD	Personal security detachment (PSD) personnel	XP	7/7	14hrs^	2/1 months
	PSD personnel	CCN	6/7	14hrs	6/2 days

Key: All staff provide management overlap briefings between shifts to ensure the passage of knowledge. All personnel form part of the crisis response and quick reaction force organizations during periods of high project operations tempo or emergency response.

[*]Certain rotations come with advantages and disadvantages. For example, a two-month on, one-month off (2/1) rotation will provide fresher management and security personnel to the company, compared to a five-month on, one-month off rotation, reducing performance fatigue. However, this rotation will also come with higher cost factors due to mobilization and handover transition costs. In addition, management step-ups will require management to increase the tempo of activities as they cover for those on leave. This reduces costs to the company but implies that the position can be gapped without serious problem, which undermines the value of that appointment.

^Indicates three people undertake two positions, ensuring a smooth flow of management staff through the work leave cycle, maintaining consistency, and overlapping of knowledge.

>These posts require a back-to-back system as it is a single post with 24/7 requirements.

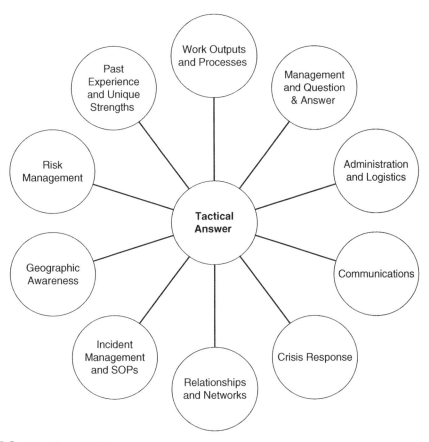

Exhibit 2.9 Providing a Full Answer

explaining how the contract will be serviced and how quality controls will be established, maintained, and recorded. It also determines what quality levels are expected as well as covering risk-mitigation measures, recruitment and training of personnel, and any administrative and logistical factors. A sample of factors for consideration follows.

- *Overall management.* It is useful to include a well-structured organizational chart, to show to the company how various levels of vendor and company management will interact and how other elements of the vendor's company will be used to support the contract. Fusion at corporate, country, and project levels is useful between different levels of provider and company management to establish effective activity controls and communications.
- *Management controls.* The contracting company will wish to be assured that the contracted services will be managed and assessed, and how expenditures will be tracked and reported. Performance measures and a quality assurance plan should be mentioned.
- *Facilities and mobilization.* The vendor's existing facilities and resources should be highlighted, if used as part of the overall contract package. In addition, the ability to mobilize specialist or sizable resources and personnel to support the company should be illustrated if relevant.

- *Risk management plan* (see Chapter 7). Demonstrating an understanding of risk as well as how mitigation measures and supporting plans will be used will indicate the vendor's ability to best protect the company's interests. This plan should be an overarching one, compared to the granular factors or approaches for individual tasks within a wider service.

- *Recruitment, training, retention of personnel.* For a labor-service-focused contract (people), the quality and ability of the human resources will be fundamentally important to the company. The provider should assure the client that it is able to source, recruit, vet, and train appropriate personnel to undertake the roles required, as well as meet unforeseen requirements at short notice. Immediate mobilization or surge requirement capabilities should be included.

- *Procurement and subcontracting management.* Some contracts may require the procurement and management of expensive equipment and resources. The company will wish to be assured that proper purchase procedures and policies are in place in addition to a well-structured and tested equipment management system and policy. The subcontracting of external parties must also meet with full contractually and legal requirements, as individual service delivery will affect performance, invoicing, and liability of the contract overall.

- *Key personnel.* It is useful to provide the resumes and perhaps a short biography of key or critical position holders to demonstrate the quality of management and specialists dedicated to support the client's activity. The company may request resumes, at which point the differences between those persons who must occupy positions in the event of a win and those who can be used to demonstrate the type of quality and experience available must be determined internally. The proposal team may seek to bait and switch personnel based on stronger resumes available at the time of proposal submission, based on the knowledge that by the time the award is actually made, those individuals may be engaged on other projects. Key positions may require the person listed in the proposal to occupy the role, preventing bait and switch. The value of the bait and switch is that the proposal is not constrained by time and resource constraints required to acquire readied specialists able to undertake a task, in order to demonstrate the vendor's strengths in terms of human resources.

- *Administration and logistics.* The company will not wish to be distracted from business goals by poor subcontractor administration or logistical matters. A sound accounting and logistical system, with experienced practitioners, should be considered a cornerstone of service delivery.

Past Performance   Companies will need to be assured that their selected subcontractor has proven competence in providing risk management or security services, especially in politically or commercially sensitive, hostile or remote environments. Past performance examples and documents demonstrate how the vendor has undertaken similar services successfully in the past. These examples can include the next contract details.

- *Key personnel.* This section should include the names of key personnel (e.g., project manager, technical leads) with a brief description of their contribution to achievements in the early delivery of product or service, significant cost savings or cost avoidance for company (must be quantifiable), a current count on quantifiable services performed, and the number of tasks undertaken, projects led and in terms of security positions, sites or people protected.

- *Quality of performance.* This section should include evidence of high levels of service delivery in similar or associated areas, including letters or certificates of commendation; performance ratings by a client, particularly in relation to challenging tasks; innovative service delivery strategies developed; potential risks averted; effective incident or crisis responses; systems and procedures that increase performance levels and accountability structures.
- *Capability statement.* The company may request the vendor's global and regional capabilities within the proposal or as an attachment or appendix.
- *Sample documents.* The company may request sample documents—for example, intelligence reports, incident management plans, and standard operating procedures.
- *Recommendations and awards.* The company might ask for other client recommendations and awards to supplement the information provided within the proposals and attachments.

The company may ask for previous or existing clients' contact details to confirm the details provided. It may also dictate the format and content of the past performance materials required.

Cost or Business Volume   Establishing the right price for the proposal is fundamental in creating a winning proposal. Cost models are useful in speeding up the process of establishing the myriad of cost elements that will make up the final price. The use of benchmarking is also a sound planning tool to establish a range of prices for particular and often-used services. The pricing of the proposal should start soon into the process rather than being left until the end. Price foundations can start the process with the definitions of labor rates, mobilizations costs, equipment quotes, and other factors. Manning numbers or the numbers of a commodity can then be quickly modified within a cost model. Effective cost models also enable the company to seek price modifications quickly and accurately from a vendor if the scope of requirement changes.

It is essential that the technical part of the proposal team liaises with the financial manager in order to lay out the scope of the contract and determine unique or unusual operating costs that might not have been included within the cost model. If the technical section is outstanding but the cost is too high, the proposal will always fail. In addition, if costs are not identified, the vendor may be at significant financial risk as it could be liable to provide a service at loss—or lose the contract and diminish its reputation, and the company may find business operations are disrupted. The next sections may be included within the cost or business volume,

- *Cover letter.* This letter is a formal verification that the drafter is offering a commitment to perform the services according to the costs and specifications included within the proposal.
- *Work breakdown structure.* This document lists the exact labor assigned for a task or group of tasks.
- *Labor categories and rates.* This section defines the specific costs to billeted positions or labor categories. It can also include cost and pricing data, if a client requests the labor

rate component to be broken into administration fees, wage and profit elements, and the like.

■ *Representations and certifications.* This section includes documents that prove that the vendor has the required certificates and licenses as well as compliance with host country, market or federal regulations.

■ *Deviations, exceptions, or assumptions.* These elements clarify risk aspects of the proposal in terms of pricing or service delivery. Examples might be future changes in project scope or country environment that could impact the company's costs or performance. Unfeasible issues should be raised in this section, as the vendor could be held liable for not meeting stated requirements. Exceptions should be carefully considered; otherwise the proposal may be declared nonresponsive.

■ *Grouping costs.* The company may provide cost line item numbers (CLINs) to allow it to more efficiently compare prices for services. CLINs, however, can create problems if the organizational structures are to be defined by the bidders, as some may aim unrealistically low in terms of manning and could win on price, but not provide a realistic operational solution. For example, the cost of the operations room in one proposal might include 10 personnel but 5 in another; however, a direct price comparison will not necessarily identify the larger number of personnel, only a higher cost, nor whether 5 personnel are sufficient to effectively undertake the task.

EVALUATING THE PROPOSAL

The team involved directly with creating a proposal can quickly become desensitized to any shortfalls or areas of weakness of their work, requiring an external panel to review a proposal prior to final changes and submission. Depending on the size and complexity of a proposal, several evaluation teams may be required. It is common for teams to be divided by color.

■ The *Pink Team* is an internal review by the proposal team once the first complete draft is ready.

■ The *Red Team* is a group of external experts who have not played any part in the proposal development. Thus they should provide an impartial review, in terms of structure, content, compliance, and likelihood of success.

■ *Green Teams* review price as an individual component.

■ A *Gold Team* might be used with a final impartial panel to review the final changes made after the Red Team, if time and resources permit, as illustrated within Exhibit 2.10.

Review teams typically consider the broader areas of:

■ Structure
■ Content
■ Compliance (legal, PWS)
■ Win potential
■ Missing elements (innovations and win themes)
■ Company reputation issues or risk concerns

Exhibit 2.10 presents a typical proposal evaluation cycle.

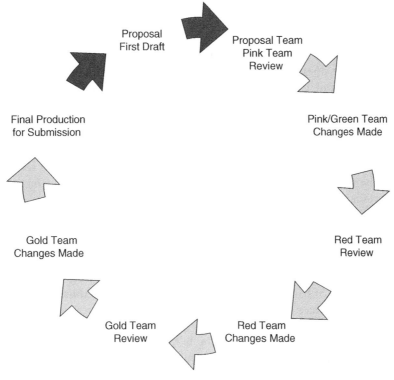

Exhibit 2.10 Proposal Evaluation Cycle

PROPOSAL PRODUCTION

The production of the final proposal can be time consuming and fraught with last-minute changes and technical problems. Computers may inextricably alter fonts; documents may become corrupted; spacing and alignment when various sections are placed together may be affected; and hyperlinking sections take considerable time and focus. Sufficient time and resources should be allocated to putting the proposal together as well as producing hard or soft copies for the company. Delivery time should also be carefully calculated, as late submissions may not be accepted.

The company may define how the proposal should be packaged (Section L for U.S. federal activities), including paper size, margins, fonts, copy numbers, attachments, and delivery instructions. A sample of factors to consider in proposal production and delivery follows.

- *Copies.* Prepare the proposal in accordance with instructions provided by the company (e.g., a three-ring binder, spiral bind, tabs, disk, e-mail, etc.). If submitting the document electronically, it should not be too large for the company mailbox or server; it is useful to send a test copy internally to ensure it can be transmitted. If it is larger than two megabytes, it may have to be broken down into small portions. The client should be approached for advice if necessary.

- *Submission.* The cover letter must be signed by authorized management within the vendor company, as this document binds company to company. For U.S. federal proposals submission should be at 1700 hours the day before the deadline to ensure that sufficient time is permitted for slow IT systems to forward mail, as well as to permit a second delivery if the first does not arrive. When delivering a proposal in another city or country, be aware of time differences and be sure to permit sufficient time to address local problems and factors. If the submission is to be delivered in person, submit it by a reputable carrier that can track the document's movement and notify you when it was received—with a receipt acknowledgment for the client to sign and return.
- *Follow-up requirements.* Vendors should be prepared to respond to company questions both verbally and in writing. Archive all proposal materials for future reference and in the event the proposal is audited by government or company management, should the vendor win the contract.

Basic Ordering Agreements

Once a vendor has been selected and the work is under way, both the company and vendor should consider the use of basic ordering agreements (BOAs) to establish a price schedule for common or frequent services. The BOA enables business and risk managers to conduct internal evaluations of how much additional security services will cost rather than request specific proposals for every contract modification. The BOA is effectively a shopping list with static costs associated with fixed services (people, equipment) and dynamic elements associated with unique factors (mobilization, special stores). BOAs should provide sufficient details to enable unambiguous procurement, using job or service descriptions to define a service expectation and associated cost.

While company risk and security managers may not have a direct interest with the granular-level details of the business and proposal process, or contract management, they should play a significant part in the business planning and proposal process if an activity or project requires any form of security services. The involvement of a company's risk and security advisory elements early within both the business and the proposal process will ensure that all risk elements are identified and that RFPs are accurate and meet all project support requirements. Company risk managers should draft the security statement of work and then assess the technical competence of bidders. These management elements may also provide guidance on associated costs to ensure that vendors are within realistic cost parameters, neither quoting too high nor too low. Integration of risk or security management within a company's business and proposal process will significantly improve its risk mitigation measures, enabling more productive business activities. Vendors also need to utilize security professionals if an aspect of the task requires risk management or security services, and should engage professional support in developing concepts and innovations which support a realistic and winning solution.

CHAPTER 3

Service Delivery and Quality Assurance

Service delivery is the provision of agreed products or services to a procuring organization, meeting defined or common standards, and within the time and cost frames agreed. Within the business cycle, service delivery plays a fundamental aspect of ensuring that the company is able to achieve its business objectives, and that the vendor security company is successful in its market—as such, service delivery directly impacts the business goals and productivity of the procuring company and the success of the provider. Poor product or service delivery will quickly result in loss of business for vendors, potentially marring a company's reputation for the existing contract and follow-up work, or within its overall market area. Because poor service delivery also undermines the confidence and activities of the procurer, vendors should consider good service delivery as fundamental as winning the actual business in the first place. Service delivery is normally centered on results, which should be measurable, sustainable, and designed in collaboration with the procuring company. Service delivery should also be flexible and responsive, meeting changing requirements proactively and dynamically to best support the company's needs.

The core components of good service delivery are the development of strong provider-to-procurer relationships and communications, professional service delivery meeting all defined needs, and sound administration as the foundation of operational delivery. The failure to meet any one of these areas will quickly reduce the reputation of the provider as well as the business activities of the procurer. It is therefore incumbent on both vendor and procurer to establish policies and systems by which service delivery can be defined, measured, and addressed. Exhibit 3.1 presents fundamental requirements of solid service delivery.

COMMON VENDOR AND COMPANY FAILINGS

Security vendors often lose company confidence through some basic failings within one or more of the three core areas shown in Exhibit 3.1. On some occasions these problems are unavoidable: a clash of personality, a disagreement over how to conduct a specific activity, or external influences or unforeseen changes that might undermine the vendor's ability to perform as expected or contracted by the company. Instead of attributing fault to vendors who may be subjected to unreasonable requirements or unforeseen circumstances, companies should be mindful that on occasion the problem may lay in-house, or may be a result of external environmental factors. However, more frequently these issues are avoidable with sound management, diplomacy, and planning by both parties. The next sections provide some frequent failings that undermine the vendor's service delivery to a company and thus the business cycle as a whole.

Exhibit 3.1   Fundamental Requirements of Solid Service Delivery

Aspect	Key Considerations
Strong Relationships	• Ensures that the vendor is considered part of the company team. • Ensures that the vendor management are included in leadership meetings, and have a voice within the management group to contribute to business goals. • Allows the company to indicate areas of concern to the vendor before they become a serious problem, allowing early resolution—with least impact. • Company management will be more inclined to listen to the advice and guidance offered by a vendor management–making them more effective in their role. • The company will be more inclined to favor the vendor with future work opportunities as inter-company confidence and familiarity is established. • Problems can be resolved more readily—avoiding contractual and legal issues.
Professional Delivery	• Ensures that contractual obligations are met—or exceeded, supporting business goals. • Forms the basis of reputation and company confidence, both for the vendor and company. • Avoids liability and legal issues. • Fosters further business opportunities, as confidence is established and the service quality becomes a known and reliant factor.
Sound Administration	• Supports the practical provision of contracted services. • Reduces distraction from the core focus, preventing project performance being undermined. • Ensures morale of employees is maintained, resulting in a positive impact on the contract performance. • Indicates professionalism and competence to the company by the vendor. • Ensures invoicing/billing can be conducted with minimal disruption to the company. • Ensures the provider will pass external audits, avoiding liability and legal issues.

Not Understanding the Client

A vendor's consultant or program manager must quickly gain a sound understanding of the company's activity as well as the problems the project or activity faces. Program and contract management will quickly become frustrated if they are forced to explain the fundamentals of the actual activity while being under business or project constraints and pressures them-selves. A good vendor will hit the ground running and will contribute to, rather than slow, the business activity. The vendor should attempt (where possible and appropriate) to con-duct sufficient research prior to an engagement in order to speak with a degree of confidence on the area being supported, thus more actively contributing to the services being provided.

Invoicing

The inability to provide timely and accurate invoicing frustrates companies immensely, yet it is generally a mechanical process through which accountants ensure that documentation is accurate and matches the contractual agreements and services delivered. Within any activity a degree of confusion will remain, notably over unique requirements or misunderstandings, or when an activity has been provided ahead of the contractual agreements or through changes midstream. A sound relationship between vendor program and finance management is required to ensure that errors and confusion are minimized prior to invoices being submitted. Poor invoicing also means the company cannot accurately assess the status of its own budget. This problem undermines the company in its ability to undertake effective financial planning and prevents it from billing its own client quickly and effectively, if the cost is passed through, creating cash flow and contractual problems. Vendors should have well-established processes and educate all staff within the service delivery chain to ensure that errors are identified early and resolved before they undermine contract performance, and subsequent invoicing.

Human Dynamics

Company project managers are unlikely to respond well to headstrong or brash external advisors. Candid advice and solidly supported recommendations are normally welcomed; however, a degree of tact and diplomacy is required, with consideration paid to company internal dynamics and office politics. Agreement through persuasion should be the goal of the vendor, not through bullying, posturing, or demands. On occasion, vendor personnel forget that the company is paying for their services and that its staff should be accorded the respect deserved, no matter what personal difficulties or professional differences might occur. That said, company management should also respect frank advice and guidance from vendors who seek to offer the best information and guidance, even if this undermines their standing within the contract. Good vendors will always attempt tactful honesty rather than place the company or its personnel at risk.

Poor Administration

Poor administration, even if unavoidable due to external factors, tends to reflect on the vendor's overall competency. In many respects administration is the simplest of the services provided, as it is usually based on systems, processes, mechanisms, and tools rather than the lateral thinking and imagination required for risk management and operational delivery. However, administration provides the foundations on which all activities operate, and companies do not wish to be distracted or have their business activities undermined by the vendor's inability to book flights, source personnel, arrange life support, or maintain equipment and records. Such failings will quickly frustrate the corporate and project management and devalue the principal services being provided.

Appropriate Levels of Support

Many companies unfamiliar with security services, or that are entering new and challenging environments, may be reliant on the vendor's consultants to specify the resources and associated finances required to undertake a service. Often a great deal of trust is required between the company and vendor to ensure that the vendor is advocating real needs at appropriate levels, reflecting a pragmatic and economic level of effort for the activity. Companies should seek to establish some benchmarking, where possible, from multiple vendor bids, if only to establish some evidence as to why services should come with the associated costs—thus effectively auditing a vendor's costs. Company risk managers should also have sufficient experience within the service and operating area to identify excess requirements or abnormally high service costs, where possible. External support should be sought where the company's officers cannot determine whether the level of service and associated costs might be out of the required scope.

Changing Service Parameters

Vendors that change the parameters of requirement (and thus the cost) during the contract through modification requests that could have been identified and raised during the initial service scoping create a range of difficulties for the company, especially if budgets have been established with no contingency factor. Project operating factors may also be affected, including life support impacts, increased travel requirements, and equipment needs. As a preemptive measure, the company should seek advice from the vendor as to how increases within the risk environment may change the level of service and costs required, and should consider these as part of a contingency planning budget. Doing this safeguards the company and enables effective responses to changing risk or operating conditions.

The company should also be cognizant that the provider may not have been tasked with estimating the impact of changing conditions, or may not have been able to predict escalations in threat. While the vendor may not be responsible for a dramatic change in condition, it should seek to indicate to the company the most accurate need at the time of requirement, while noting the impacts of certain potential events or changes on the project and budget. The company should raise the issue of cost contingency planning with the vendor if the project activity is within a dynamic environment subject to change.

Knowledge of Limitations

The vendor and its personnel must know the parameters in which their company works, in order to understand what can and cannot be achieved in support of the company. If overpromising occurs, and the vendor cannot deliver agreed services or meet significant or short-notice expectations, the situation will be embarrassing and undermine confidence and performance. Company management should seek honest answers regarding vendor capabilities and constraints, and should attempt to foster a spirit of candid dialogue, minimizing penalties for these limitations, where possible. Vendors should avoid using this trust as a tool for approaching company needs in a more sedate manner, or as an excuse to add in additional resources of budget margin, but rather as a means of ensuring that services can be delivered fully and within time frames agreed. As such, vendor management should ensure its staff understands the operating and capability parameters of the vendor company, and procurers should attempt to work with vendors to achieve a mutually agreeable understanding of service delivery.

Operating Parameters

A frequent occurrence within field vendor management is a strong desire to support the project, by providing effective and timely services, both within and outside of contract scope. This is often a result of strong professional and personal relationships, loyalty to the project goals, and a desire for individual managers to be successful. While this vested interest should be applauded, and supports the business and operational company needs as a whole, on occasion it can result in a vendor's consultant offering a service or support that is outside of his or her authority. The vendor's consultant should clearly understand the level and scope of his or her authority and what permissions need to be sought for sanctioning certain service and contractual matters. Like any organized structure, levels and areas of authority and sanction exist to support the vendor organization in its delivery of service, as well as to protect the recipient company by ensuring delivery of services promised.

Conversely this can also be true of the company management as well. In their desire to ensure that their activities are effective and successful, project staff might misrepresent their authority in order to mobilize vendor resources as they concurrently seek corporate sanction. This situation frequently occurs where vendors are forward leaning in their efforts to support a task and projects are moving forward quickly to achieve milestones and objectives. Often the corporate element is several steps behind the project, and vendors make decisions assuming the company will agree to them formally after services have started. Expending significant resources to support an activity that had been asked for, but not correctly sanctioned, or contracted, can place the vendor in a difficult position, and also embarrass company management.

While vendors may be inclined or forced to attempt to meet the unauthorized promises made by their staff, or may have mobilized resources under the assumption the documentation would follow shortly afterwards, it is more effective for both parties if field management understand the permissions and limitations of the management staff within both the vendor and the company organizations.

UNDERSTANDING THE ACTIVITY

It is important for both company and vendor management to understand the structure of the contract, whether it is a complex program involving multiple task orders and projects, or whether it is a singular business activity with a smaller organizational structure. Terms often are subjective or follow company or industry terminology; however, for simplicity, a single task is often called a *project*, while a collection of tasks is called a *program*. The manager responsible for managing the activity may be a project manager, or a program manager with several project managers below them. For large programs, a company operations manager may oversee the administration of all aspects of the program in a support role, similar to a military executive officer or second-in-command. For significant programs, a task order manager will be responsible for multiple programs or projects of the same nature—for example, 42 border forts, 12 hospitals—with a project manager responsible for each individual activity, overseen by the program manager. Some programs are simple, linear commercial enterprises; some are complex and dynamic. All have unique and diverse requirements. Exhibit 3.2 illustrates an example of a possible program structure, and what management positions might be found associated within such a complex program.

It is important that both the vendor and company consultants understand the structure of the activity, as well as the roles and responsibilities contained within, in order to best coordinate and manage his or her knowledge, activities, and support to service a contract. For example, a program may be broken into a grouping of task orders with multiple projects

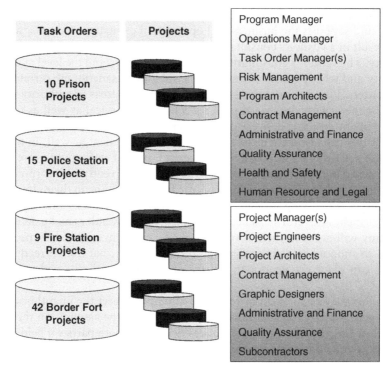

Exhibit 3.2 Program Structures

within each. The complexity of a program will define the expertise and structure of support provided to a client. Complex programs may require the consultant to have the ability to manage hundreds of personnel, handle accounting and contract requirements, focus on service delivery, and provide detailed official security documentation. Simple programs will require a reduced version of this, perhaps even a single consultant operating within the activity.

SERVICE DELIVERY SUPPORT

Vendors should always have a depth to their service, and rarely operate at a single level in terms of contract support. Additional in-country management and operational resources might be in place to support multiple contracts, and corporate infrastructures will support the vendor company's overall activities. In order to gain the best level of service delivery, it is important that both the vendor's consultants and the company's management are aware of the full spectrum of resources available to be drawn on to meet or service a project's contracted requirements, either direct or peripheral. Corporate and project management should understand additional service areas to draw on if required from both within the vendor and company structures, enabling a more effective and efficient response to new requirements, because operational integration and cost savings often result from using a single vendor to provide multiple services, or from being able to leverage other elements of a company's

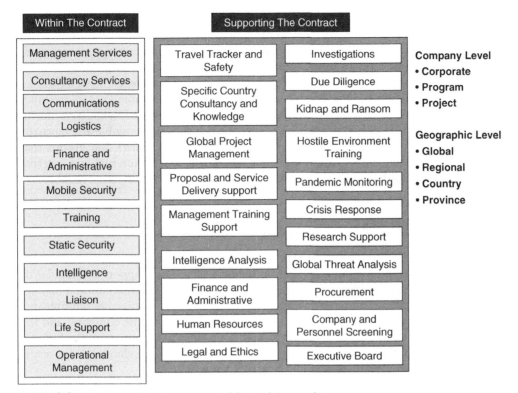

Exhibit 3.3 Contracted Services versus Additional Areas of Support

resources or expertise. Direct project support should be specified within the contract but might also include some "assumed" level of support for standard or unforeseen requirements. For example, quality assurance support is a standard requirement from vendors, while crisis management support might be an assumed additional service area for major incidents.

Ideally the vendor's consultants and staff should stand at the top of a pyramid of knowledge, expertise, capability, and experience, all of which should be readily available to supplement the contract's needs, although subject to contractual agreements. Exhibit 3.3 indicates how a vendor's contracted services may be strengthened by its complete service offerings. Some may directly support the contracted tasks, others may be called on for new service offerings. Additional services provided by the vendor, beyond contracted arrangements, can help foster a stronger vendor/company relationship and lead to an expansion of the vendor's business opportunities. However, the company should be mindful that each effort or service costs resources and money and that some form of direct or indirect compensation (additional funding or favorable consideration for further work) should be provided to reflect vendor's efforts in providing more than the contract calls for.

The company should also consider how it and the vendor might best leverage non-organic resources, such as military and government organizations, to support the business activities. This is especially relevant for government-funded tasks or for those projects that have perceived connections or political benefits to a government. Typically liaison with government or supporting groups can result in a degree of additional resource, often at no cost. This might range from an agreement to provide medical evacuation or military quick reaction support in the event of an incident, to providing dedicated air movement, intelligence, and personnel to support a task. Where appropriate, vendors should be used to develop supporting mechanisms to assist projects in challenging environments through external group relationship building and the development of agreements (memoranda of understanding). These agreements or collaborations might involve host nation or foreign government and security organizations, other commercial organizations that bring tangible and mutually beneficial resources to bear, or provincial and local community leaders and groups that might be of value to the project. At all times, the leveraging of both internal and external resources should be considered to maximize the resources directly or indirectly available.

MANAGING SERVICE DELIVERY

The requirements of service delivery management will vary from company to activity. One project may require a single vendor consultant providing advice and support for singular or limited business activities, another project might require a group of consultants and managers to coordinate specialists and large groups of security personnel involved in multiple disciplines and contract activities. As such, it is fundamental for both the company and the vendor to understand the principal elements of service delivery management as the foundation for the company's overall leadership approach. As illustrated in Exhibit 3.4, success is not a complicated process but involves three principal areas:

- Solid management and administration.
- Flexibility and innovations.
- Good communications and confidence.

A solid management and administration structure combined with mature polices and procedures will enable services to be provided, or received, in the most effective manner. Most services are in themselves simple tasks to perform, with failure occurring mainly within the management of the activity, either as a direct result of activity management or

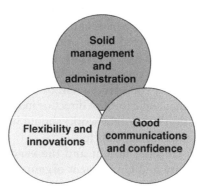

Exhibit 3.4   Pillars of Service Delivery Success

due to poor corporate oversight. Solid management and administrative breeds intercompany confidence and information sharing, creating an environment that supports success. If management structures and processes are poor, the reverse is often true, creating an environment that supports failure or hampers both parties' productivity.

Forward planning, responsiveness, lateral thinking, and innovations are often key for success within fluid risk environments, where significant changes may occur on a daily basis. While rigid processes and policies are often required to create the framework for sound contract and operational management, a degree of maneuverability is required to meet dynamic needs. Often productivity is increased, and costs reduced, by vendors that can provide innovative solutions and where companies are willing to consider them. Flexibility can also be considered in terms of vendors knowing when to provide out-of-scope services, or when to move ahead of the issuance of contractual documents to support a business activity, although this willingness to expose a company to commercial risk by moving ahead of a contractual agreement is often based on trust and good communications.

The closer the company and the vendor operate, the better the communications and overall productivity of the contract. While there are, of course, limitations on information sharing, proven vendors should be included early in the company's business cycle to enable projects to exploit their expertise and resources. By understanding the company and having a strong professional and personal relationship, the vendor can offer the best solutions during project inception and sustain solid strategic planning during the life of the contract. Sound management and insightful support engenders good communications and intercompany confidence, resulting in enhanced productivity for both parties.

Some key considerations that support successful service delivery to the company follow.

- The vendor understands the company's current needs, goals, objectives, milestones, problems, and methodology.
- The vendor actively forecasts and supports future company requirements or problems.
- Both parties develop personal relationships and intercompany confidence, at multiple levels.
- The company understands the vendor's objectives, limitations, and capacities.
- Both parties develop and consolidate external networks of support for the contract.
- Both parties present information in a clear, timely, and concise manner.
- Both parties understand the balance among operational requirements, project goals, and costs.
- The vendor presents multiple solutions to meet the company's needs.
- The vendor is regarded as an enabler, or problem solver, not a barrier or hindrance.
- The vendor presents risk in the context of project operations and business impacts.
- The vendor maintains quality assurance levels with documented evidence.
- The vendor and the company ensure invoicing and administration is accurate and timely.
- Both parties ensure logistical and resource accounting is accurate and detailed.
- Both parties keep clear records and databases of all materials and reports.
- Both parties provide reports and documents to maintain information flow between the company and the provider.
- Risk managers ensure that security, crisis, and incident plans are accurate and implemented effectively.

- Both parties understand the contractual processes and limitations, as they apply to the specific contract or activity.
- The vendor creates efficiencies and innovations to enhance service delivery performance.
- The vendor gains the trust of the company to become a core member of the project team, with an active voice (where possible).
- The vendor identifies problems ahead of occurrence in order to avoid or mitigate, with transparency of errors and mature responses by both parties.

While this list is in no way exhaustive, it outlines some fundamental principles of sound service delivery management. The next sections provide more granular aspects of service delivery, which should be considered as the underlying principle for each subject chapter.

Problem Solving

The vendor should seek to structure any solutions for the company with both security and business needs foremost in mind. The solution that focuses purely on one or the other will be of little value in protecting the company's corporate or business interests, project activities, personnel and assets, or budget. In addition, both the company and the vendor will have their own reputations, risk tolerances, and objectives in mind. Where possible, these need to be balanced to meet both parties' needs to achieve a "win–win" situation for both. The company will naturally be driven by project goals, milestones, liability issues, costs, human dynamics, and other external limitations, and the vendor should seek to offer solution options with these in mind.

Where high-risk services are needed, the vendor should be mindful of the company's tolerance levels, as well as its own, and present the risk and impact implications with each solution option. The vendor should be considered an enabler and should seek to avoid (where possible) flatly refusing to support an activity; rather it should present the approach and resources necessary to offset risks sufficiently to conduct the task. Where the risk is unavoidable, clear, focused, and clinical data should be presented as a matter of course to demonstrate to the company the rationale behind advocating not undertaking an activity, or as a last resort, declining a task. The vendor should also consider how materials might be viewed by multiple parties within the business activity, rather than purely focusing on the intended report recipient, as the vendor's client may themselves have clients or joint venture partners who might be affected by any decisions or operational changes.

Problem solving is a fundamental aspect of solid service delivery. Vendors should approach solutions in a holistic manner, considering every risk angle, each organic and external resource that could be leveraged to support a company activity, and what impacts a course of action might result in for both parties.

Threat Perceptions

Threat assessments are subjective and driven by a myriad of factors: experience, opinion, knowledge, exposure, agenda, background, maturity, and tolerance to name but a few. Managers' appreciation of the threat environment is also limited by the information they might be provided, the time they allocate to considering nonbusiness risks, and their background and knowledge. In addition, risk perception can become dulled by sustained exposure to threats.

Exhibit 3.5 Concealed Risks and Threat Perceptions

Source: Copyright © 2006, M. Blyth, Engineering Project Site IRAQ.

A company as a whole, or managers within the group, eventually may become largely blasé to risks rather than retaining a sharp perspective and appreciation of risks and associated impacts. Conversely, overexposure to risks can have the reverse effect of making managers overly sensitive to risks, undermining their ability to make sound judgement calls. Exhibit 3.5 illustrates how a peaceful scene might disguise underlying risks. Several days after this photograph was taken, a client visit was subjected to a complex ambush at this location, resulting in a combination of improvised explosive device and small arms fire. Threat perceptions are similarly subjective and often viewed from an individual standpoint.

It is also common for the field and corporate managers to have significantly differing viewpoints on risks, and the vendor can find itself in the middle of polarized client viewpoints and demands. Companies need to understand the common us versus them mentality between field and corporate offices, especially within challenging environments, where field managers regard corporate officers as a hindrance and believe they should make risk determinations and conduct impact evaluations, rather than being directed by some geographically remote and emotionally distanced executive officers. Companies should provide unambiguous and transparent guidance and directions to address the issue of *camps of opinion*, as vendors often seek to appease both field and corporate offices concurrently in order to best service the contract—often resulting in overall friction and confusion.

Companies unfamiliar with operating within challenging environments should also consider the difference between "safety" and "security." Historically, safety officers have concurrently managed security, especially for domestic business; however, the nature of many projects now requires a pure risk consulting and security management element to meet the more dynamic nature of the risks they face. While safety officers remain a key component of addressing industrial risk factors, external threats require a different skill set, as perceptions will be based on different values and understandings. Conversely, security specialists are unlikely to have the knowledge and experience required for health and safety, and so differentiating the two functions is often required.

Project Methodology

It is important that the vendor is fully conversant with the company's requirements and methods of operation, which allows the vendor to place the business goals and activities into an applicable threat context. Project methodology defines how business will be conducted, setting the scene for risk managers to identify risks and seek solutions to enable business success. Vendors that understand how a project will operate can better tailor solutions around component activities, as well as the project as a whole. If vendors cannot visualize or understand how the project will operate, they will present inefficient and ineffective solutions based on assumptions. In addition, solutions will fail to address innovations and efficiencies that might otherwise enhance business productivity as part of the overall program design. It is incumbent on both the vendor and the company project staff to ensure that methodologies are clearly understood to maximize service delivery.

Financial Tracking

It is rare that the underlying rationale for any project is not to make money. Other factors may play a part—patriotism, supporting struggling governments or democracies, assisting in the stabilization of a region, or helping impoverished people; however, any nongovernment organization needs to be paid in order to conduct business, and procuring bodies need to make timely payments for effective budget management. However, even though financial management generally is a mechanical and process-driven function, it is often a point of weakness or failure within either the vendor or the company management structures.

For programs that have a dedicated vendor finance and accounting staff, a financial tracker document is useful to establish an accountancy and expenditure overview from the source of costs: the project or program. This document may form the basis for a vendor company's cyclic review of the billing process, with the cost-raising organization being that closest to confirming the services being delivered (typically the program), and the invoicing organization (typically the corporate office) reviewing, auditing, and then submitting invoices to the company for billing. By having some financial structure at the point of service delivery many mistakes and inaccuracies that occur as invoices are raised can be avoided. It is not uncommon for a billing lag to occur within the billing cycle, during which time discrepancies and errors will grow as they move from the billing source to the invoicing agent. A financial tracker document can track each step of the process, allowing all parties to have an instant and more accurate picture of all costs incurred, invoices raised, and bills paid.

By creating an end-to-end financial management approach, the early identification and resolution of problems can be achieved, with errors or issues being quickly raised and resolved prior to the company being invoiced, as illustrated in Exhibit 3.6. It is not uncommon for vendor companies to be forced to write off millions of dollars due to *avoidable* poor,

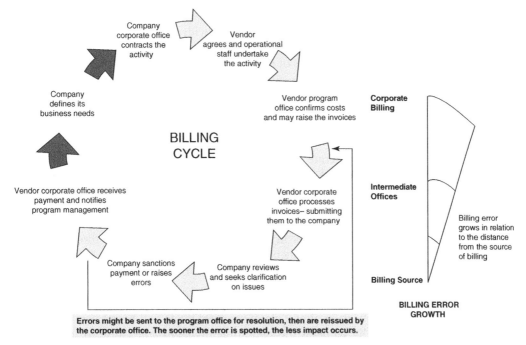

Exhibit 3.6 Typical Billing Cycle

inaccurate, or slow accounting practices. Effective financial tracking also enables vendors to notify companies when funds are running short or might be exceeded (typically at the 75% fund expended point). Should a vendor proceed beyond the contracted funding levels, it is often held accountable for proceeding *at risk*, and it might not be able to invoice additional costs to the company. This situation undermines both the vendor and the company as it creates a myriad of problems for both organizations.

Procurement

Vendors may be required to procure materials on behalf of the company, and for large contracts a significant amount of money may be set aside for a specific material or requirement. Both the company and the vendor should ensure that clear authorities and permissions are established at the outset of the contract to define where monies can be spent and how policies and records are documented and addressed. No procurement outside of defined budgets should be conducted prior to the requisition order (or purchase order) being produced by designated company officers. The vendor must be advised that it will run at risk if it expends unauthorized monies, or fails to follow set company policies. By aligning approach methodologies and working through a common understanding, both vendor and company management groups can create efficient policies and processes which avoid frustration, friction and liability issues.

Unambiguous and legally binding documentation that monies have been officially allocated are also required from authorized company managers, and vendor procurements should be conducted in accordance with any policies the company may have (i.e., providing three sources for procurement selection, using specific providers or vendors, limiting expenditure natures, etc.). The vendor should retain clear records and supporting documents for procurements for review and audit. Audits of materials procured by vendors on behalf of the company should also be conducted and documented to ensure the vendor has procured the amount and quality or materials invoiced.

Insurance

The vendor may be required to operate under its own insurance, or the company may provide insurance as part of the contract. At times, specific insurances will be required to meet corporate liability needs or government standards. Insurances are complex and may cover different areas in different ways; for example, a driver may have a different policy coverage than a radio operator within the same project, based on risk exposure. Vendor insurance shortfalls may impact the company, either in terms of secondary liability or through image or reputational issues. A clear understanding of the required insurance policies and coverages should be confirmed at the outset of the contract, usually provided by the corporate legal offices.

Insurances are designed to deal with a crisis of some sort, and vendors or companies forced to seek insurance clarification after a claim has been made will have to contend with significant challenges, typically while at the same time managing the cause for the claim. Understanding the parameters and rules of the insurance policy is also important, although many managers are unwilling to review reams of paperwork to define those risk areas that may affect their project or staff. Both vendor and company management have a responsibility to ensure those under their charge are adequately covered by insurances, as often the wrong wording within a post-incident report might invalidate a policy and could have catastrophic effects on individuals and families, as well as the company's business or project as a whole. Managers should receive formal instruction on how to structure a post-incident report and what information will be pertinent. The use of language and facts should be carefully considered to ensure that the report does not adversely affect an insurance claim through poor representation of data.

Insurances are calculated based on the business, activity, and associated risk levels. For U.S. government contracts, the Defense Base Act (DBA) is an insurance policy calculated on the daily wage rate of those operating for, or on, behalf of U.S government contracts. When calculating costs, the party responsible for providing DBA must be identified, whether it is the vendor or company, with the additional costs added into the proposal costs. The DBA also has some unique categories (i.e. such as a coxswain of a maritime vessel), so care must be taken to ensure that all employees working directly for the company or those subcontracted by the company are correctly covered.

Operating Licenses

Company's operating within new geographic regions might need to establish a locally licensed entity, or work in partnership with a local company. The same might be true of vendors, who might be brought into service within a new region under the umbrella of the procuring organization, subcontract themselves to a local company, or form a new local company themselves. Operating licenses can have significant impacts upon both the company and vendor, as it defines operating permissions, taxation issues, industry sector licenses, employment regulations, visa permissions and other legal and corporate responsibilities. Some countries might also have unique rules and regulations, restricting the number of foreign employees, requiring a certain ratio of local labor to expatriate staff, and restricting the importation or exportation of services, information or commodities. As such it is in the interest of both the company and vendor to understand the manner in which they will both operate within a foreign country, and where individual or group responsibilities lay.

Labor Service Tracking

There are many ways to account for people on task, and both electronic and manual means can be used to track the labor services provided to the company. The detail required may also change, from individual time sheets to group rosters. Some vendors use a personnel report (PersRep) as a tool in which labor services are captured for billing, at a frequency defined by the company. These reports typically are used for less refined contracts where nominals are signed off by defined managers to account for the number of actually provided persons for an activity. More advanced systems, such as Patrol Log or Deltek, can be used as a semi-automated system, sometimes with time sheets signed by the employee. It should be remembered that the number of positions contracted for and the number of personnel listed within the PersRep may differ due to handover periods, sickness, or travel restrictions. These overlaps or peculiarities are often operationally related and should be covered within the contract agreement to avoid billing disputes. Any costs incurred outside of the standard agreement should be captured within an anomaly log, so that the company has evidence as to why additional costs were incurred and so the vendor can be paid for additional appropriate services provided. Full company involvement and transparency is required so that both parties can ensure that the right number of personnel are provided to task and that out-of-scope costs are identified, explained, and processed where appropriate.

Any form of personnel tracking process should be signed off on a regular base by company officers, as the ebb and flow of personnel can be difficult to track, and questions raised several months down the billing chain are difficult to resolve. It is in the interests of both parties that frequent personnel accountability audits are conducted and documented to ensure services are delivered and invoices are processed.

Technical Directions

In dynamic environments, the company may need to frequently modify vendor services to meet changing business, operational or risk needs. The company should seek to provide technical directions to the vendor, such as the modification of personnel numbers, dispositions, mobilizations, dates, or other administrative changes. Such directions should be captured documentally rather than on e-mails, as these are easily lost and often do not clinically capture the change data for historical audit within a formal and standardized format. A mutually agreed-upon company-to-vendor technical direction form or report is useful to capture and confirm company change requirements. These directions should operate within the parameters of the defined budget and service-level agreements and should never exceed the contract parameters. This is especially important when a project is phased in with several waves of personnel and equipment rather than a unified deployment, as a single mobilization of personnel and resources is easier to manage than multiple or phased deployments. Staged mobilizations can create confusion when calculating the total numbers of personnel required or the monies allocated to the task. Clear tracking of both numbers and costs incurred should be maintained to avoid overstaffing or over expenditure. While not necessarily a legally binding document, a technical direction form will help to focus both the company and the vendor on what is being asked for, in what quantity, and when, as well as provide a paper trail of who sanctioned which requirement or change, and for what reason. Typically a technical direction form should capture such details as:

- Company name.
- Vendor name.
- Project name and number.
- Budget number (work release authorization [WRA]) or reference.
- Date, name, appointment of the company manager raising the change or modification.
- Name and appointment of the vendor's manager.
- Description of the technical change: personnel numbers, equipment, nature, dates, locations, and so on.
- Service, operational and cost impacts of the change.
- Final sanctioning authority and signatures from the company and provider management elements.
- Confirmation that the directions were implemented, and when, from both parties.

Understanding the Requirement

Understanding the company's requirement is fundamental to delivering the correct services. Typically the company will issue a scope of work that defines the services expected, and the vendor works toward this scope of work. The more complex the task, the harder it is to ensure that the scope of work matches the vendor's services, either at the beginning of the project, or throughout its lifespan. Understandings or perceptions of the company's level of need will be affected by perspective and experience, and vendors might over- or underestimate what may be required, either before or during delivery. Vendors might also misrepresent (either intentionally or unintentionally) their understanding of the requirement, overselling what they say they will undertake, while underperforming on task. This is particularly common for consulting tasks where the requirement is more conceptual rather than a hard service, which might be easier to define. It is incumbent on the company to ensure that the scope of work is as detailed and clear as possible; the vendor has the responsibility to clarify any issues or questions to ensure that its service best reflects what is actually called for. Where companies have frequent requirements, such as a security survey, evacuation plan, or simple static security services for a facility, it is often useful for the company or vendor to develop a detailed task description to form the basis of the requirement, specifying the complexity of the task, unique personal or professional qualifications needed, and any other factor of influence. These descriptions can then be modified and adapted to suit peculiarities between each project. Examples are provided in the following paragraphs.

Level I Facility Risk Assessment The Risk Consultant will review the physical security structures and general policies in place to secure a project facility. This will include the threat implications of the surrounding risk environment and how these affect the protection of company assets, materials, and personnel. The Level I Facility Risk Assessment will be delivered in a detailed written report with schematics and photographic materials, as required and appropriate. The assessment will cover the following areas in detail:

- Threat Picture
- Key Risk Elements
- Site Vulnerabilities
- Structural Vulnerabilities
- Safe Havens
- Guard Force Competence
- Access Control
- Perimeter Measures
- Recommendations

Project Evacuation Plans The Risk Consultant will support the company in developing a Project Level Evacuation Plan in order to enable company staff and high value materials to be withdrawn from a threat environment before, or during, a risk event. The consultant will leverage government and other organizational capabilities and facilities to augment the company's project evacuation options. The Project Level Evacuation Plan will include:

- Layered Threat Picture
- Key Risk Elements
- Vulnerabilities
- Management Structures
- Alert States
- Trigger Points
- Decision Matrixes
- Response Options and Plans
- Safe Havens
- Communications Plan
- Route Options
- Supporting Agencies
- Evacuation Checklists
- Destruction Plans
- Mapping and Diagrams

Contingency and Crisis Response Plans The Risk Consultant will assist the company in developing Contingency and Crisis Response Plans in order to enable the organization to identify and address risk, as well as manage any risk events should they occur. The consultant will support the company in structuring management organizations and decision making, as well as identifying and addressing risk factors. The Contingency and Crisis Response Plans will include:

- Corporate Decision Making Structure
- Roles and Responsibilities
- Decision Matrixes
- Authorities and Permissions
- Risk Types and Impact Evaluations
- Company Risk Tolerances
- Risk Evaluation Metrics
- Risk Tracking Tools and Policies
- Risk Cascade Chain Evaluation
- Risk Management Approaches
- Organic Resources
- External and Leveraged Resource Use
- Information Management Plan
- Media and External Communications
- Report Management and Tools
- Data Management

Both the vendor and/or company might also develop defined job specifications as well, aligned with typical or common required so that both the company and vendor have a clear and accurate picture of what is required.

By developing standardized service and labor definitions, basic ordering agreements (BOA) can then flow from these services specifications, and companies can establish defined service-level agreements with vendors that provide sufficient specificity to ensure swift and accurate quality assurance for services requested and delivered.

QUALITY ASSURANCE PLANS

Quality assurance is the mechanism by which service delivery is kept on track, meeting the professional standards of the vendor and the business expectations of the company. Ensuring that quality assurance is established and maintained is vital for the effective management of a project, and should cover all areas of service as well as supporting functions. A common shortfall for vendors and companies is to focus only on getting work done rather than periodically pausing to look critically at how business is being conducted. That said, quality assurance audits are difficult to conduct during high-tempo operations by in-house staff who might concurrently be managing the operations, and external audits can also distract or undermine managers from meeting immediate project requirements.

In addition, companies are unlikely to fund a period of vendor or company internal examination, where operations cease for a review and might slow or delay project goals. The involvement of external auditors can be a means by which to provide an impartial quality assurance review of activities, without directly disrupting the project, although this comes with a price and will always require a degree of project attention and support.

Where internal quality assurance is required, vendor and project managers should seek to conduct concurrent activities, such as operational assessments during training periods. Logistical audit checks and operational reviews should also be considered part of general management processes, and can be used to actively enhance performance, with little impact on the productivity of the service if sensibly scheduled. Both vendors and the company should evidence with clear and documented materials or proof all quality assurance reviews or performance-related activities for internal management confirmation that a contract is being best serviced and also for audit purposes.

Quality assurance can be subjective, unless clinical and unambiguous measuring standards are established. The methodology for measuring quality of service should be agreed between the vendor and the company to avoid differing perspectives or standards. Where possible, quality assurance should be quantifiable and transparent to both parties, as this enables vendors to discover and address shortfalls early, and the company to hold subcontractors to account where necessary.

The company should consider scheduled and random quality reviews over the life of a project to ensure best quality of service, both from vendors and the company's own staff. Post-incident reviews should also be conducted following a significant incident that incurs liability issues, such as injuries, deaths, significant business disruption, or the loss of valued or sensitive equipment. In order to establish an agreed-upon and effective quality assurance approach, the company and vendor should develop a quality assurance plan that can quantify and measure the delivery of service to the company. This plan can involve training, management performance, division of tasks and accountability, and a quality capture matrix for documenting performances, shortfalls and resolution requirements of a quality treatment plan. Performance assessment will be based on a variety of factors, with related performance indicators.

Management Responsibilities

It is important to define the different management responsibilities and accountabilities within a complex organization, as this will define who is responsible for ensuring success and quality for different activities. The vendor should initiate defining the scope and nature of authority and remits for subcontracted services, and sanctioned where appropriate by the company. Internal company quality assurance responsibilities will be more easily defined as the company has full visibility of its own organizational structure, operating methodologies and where certain responsibilities lay; however, those personnel auditing vendor services should also be identified, and clear policies and duties should be documented to ensure that both internal and external auditing can be successfully achieved.

Quality Management Systems

The vendor should implement a quality assurance system that conforms to company expectations and contractual agreements, with transparency and company input capacity. Policies, procedures, and tools can be used to administer quality management and present findings and action points, internally within the vendor management structure and, more important, to the company. Systems do not need to be overly complex. They can be simple training audits, equipment serviceability checks, and other spot checks for standard processes or activities. Indeed, where possible systems and tools should be as succinct, pragmatic and as

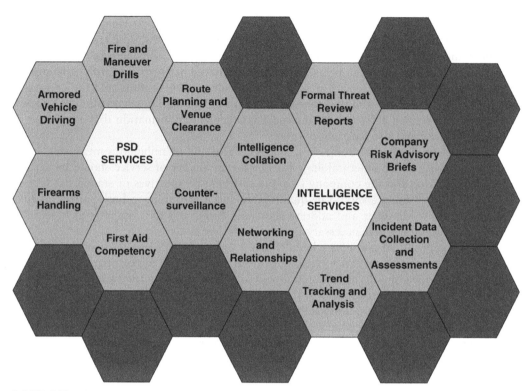

Exhibit 3.7 Identifying Quality Assurance Targets

user friendly as possible, to reduce any burdens upon the company and vendor organizations. As illustrated in Exhibit 3.7, the key service area and associated performance areas should be identified and reflect the quality assurance goals and systems. Defined quality levels can then be developed against a schedule to implement the quality management system.

Where service targets have been established, the company might outline the delivery of services expected from a vendor over a protracted period. Doing this might be especially relevant for training contracts, where a student body must be trained over several training cycles until a certain volume is achieved, or where a construction contract requires certain milestones to be reached over the course of the build phase. Where appropriate, the contract should be broken into periods of performance where targets are set and measured. The company can then establish whether the vendor is achieving, missing, or exceeding expectations, as illustrated in Exhibit 3.8.

Resource Management

In order to ensure that the vendor meets its own standards as well as those of the company, both human and asset resources need to be managed effectively. Resource scheduling and cross-utilizations should be components of the overall service delivery goals, and accounting for resource usage is a good way to ensure that best value is achieved and to prevent resources from being exhausted by over tasking. The company and the vendor should reach an

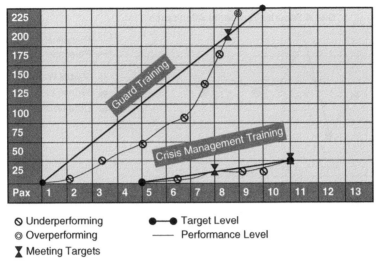

⊘ Underperforming   ●——● Target Level
◎ Overperforming   —— Performance Level
⟊ Meeting Targets

Exhibit 3.8 Setting Contract Goals

agreement as to how resource time should be allocated to different business activities, including rest, travel, training, and maintenance periods. Some form of resource application accounting should then be established to determine whether resources are meeting quality goals, underperforming, or exceeding targets, as illustrated in Exhibit 3.9.

Regular quality performance audits not only of resource use but also of resource availability should be conducted. These audits define whether the vendor is providing the resource levels agreed, rather than focusing on the delivery of actual services. In complex and large programs, it might be is especially important when attempting to ensure that large numbers of staff are on-site providing services to contracted levels, as illustrated in Exhibit 3.10. As discussed, clear measuring methodology should be established to remove ambiguity or subjective assessment, allowing clinical and transparent quality control to be established by both the vendor and the company. These systems and methodologies should, where possible and appropriate, be established with input and agreement from both parties, with a clear understanding of goals and achievements required, such as: *provide 100 men, deliver 50 tons of*

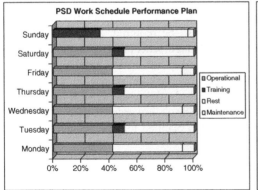

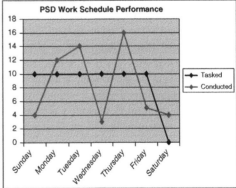

Exhibit 3.9 Personal Security Detail Work Schedule and Performance Plan

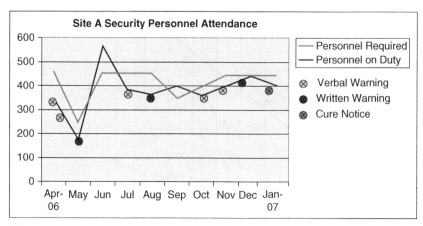

Exhibit 3.10   Resource Availability Audits

equipment, produce 3 daily reports. To prompt remedies and track overall project perform-ances influences, documented warnings and cure notices should be issued when vendors fail to meet resource delivery or performance requirements. Cure notices should be issued as the last resort and only when the vendor is about to be removed from task. External audits should also be conducted to provide impartial reviews of the contract performance levels and to ensure that project managers implement correctly and sustain the quality assurance plan. It is the interests of neither party to allow service delivery performance levels to reach the stage where a vendor must be replaced, as this will undermine both organizations, finan-cially and operationally, while also presenting additional business and operational risks dur-ing any transition phase to a new vendor.

Professional Standards

Training is fundamental not only to the quality delivered to the company's activity, but also to maintain standards in relation to good industry practices. Training might range from manage-ment tabletop exercises, to weapons and driver training. It is important that qualifications and certifications are both current and assessed throughout the life of a project, to avoid skill fade by both company and vendor personnel who might be on task for several months at a time. Theater-specific awareness training and education might also be required, and the company should account for this requirement as part of its own planned scheduling. Companies place themselves at risk if they do not include the time and resources for critical training and skill maintenance of vendor personnel, and they should avoid overtasking, which on the surface will increase productivity but may significantly affect a vendor's ability to perform the task to standard over a prolonged period. Companies should also look inwards to their staff, and ensure that skill sustainment and professional development is planned for and implemented.

Company Training

An important part of the contract may be the vendor's training or education of company staff, although this need or service is often overlooked, as other business requirements take precedence. Vendors can provide highly useful educational packages as part of their services, including management and personnel crisis response training, tactical procedures and emergency response drills, first aid, hostile environment and situational awareness training. The company should consider whether the vendor might bring other skills to supplement its own training regimes and incorporate these into any training cycles. This additional element of service can be especially relevant where certain skill sets, such as first aid in Africa or cross-decking (i.e., moving from one vehicle to another during an incident) in Iraq, might be useful for company personnel to receive instruction on. Either the vendor or the company should document training program attendance and adjust other service area expectations to account for time expended on developing and imparting vendor-to-company training packages.

Product Realization

It is important that company management understand which services have been contracted from the vendor as well as the applicable standards associated with each task. Policies and plans should then be established according to defined services so that unrealistic goals or expectations do not develop over time. Mission creep can be kept in check if defined and agreed-upon expectations are established between the vendor and the company at the outset of the contract. All additional services can then be identified as outside of the expected scope of work, either as additionally funded activities, or value added services.

Representing Quality Assurance

There are many methods, some simple and some complex, by which to illustrate the levels of service delivery being provided by a vendor, as indicated in Exhibits 3.8 and 3.9. An executive summary or representation that captures all key areas at a macro level is a useful management tool to indicate that service standards as well as contract needs are being met, as illustrated in Exhibit 3.11. The simple process of color coding performance against a task, based on defined expectations, is a useful way to track performance levels, prior to managers seeking more granular level demonstrations that services are being performed.

These tools should be used by both vendors and companies to ensure that shortfalls are identified and addressed quickly. Managers should keep a log of the shortfalls and remedial actions planned (a treatment plan) and achieved to ensure that service-level shortfalls are addressed quickly—as well as documentally recorded for future audit. Performance levels can also be presented in terms of percentages met: for example, manning numbers, reports provided, equipment delivered on schedule, and so forth.

REPORTS AND RETURNS

The flow of information both within the contract and to external parties is vital for both service delivery and overall contract management. Information flow between the vendor and the company is also important, ensuring that multiple plug-in points share relevant information to ensure a unified management approach. The company and the vendor should establish a simple and effective reporting system, with defined reports and returns that capture periodically provided information or incident-related data. A variety of reports and returns

Exhibit 3.11 Simple Quality Assurance Grading Systems

	GREEN The contractor is providing service levels defined within the contract—and is performing well	AMBER There are some minor shortfalls in service levels, however these are within acceptable levels	RED The contractor is failing to meet minimal standards—the contract is being adversely affected
Staffing. All sites/positions fully staffed at all times in accordance with the contract.	√		
Reports. Are completed in full and on time—Target 95% timely and accurate report provision.		√	
Training. Target of 90% for staff training—to contract performance standards.			√
Billing. Target of 98% accuracy of administration. A 2% inaccuracy is permissible.	√		
Deployments. Target of 85% is expected, with personnel deployments conducted within 10 days.	√		

may be required, depending on the nature and scope of the activity as well as dynamics within the company organization or the vendor group.

The distinction between a *report* and a *return* is subjective. However, fundamentally, a report can be considered a medium by which managers provide information, assessments, and recommendations, whereas a return is purely the provision of requested statistics or hard data. While both vendors and companies might initially perceive the establishment of a range of documents to meet report and return requirements to be an additional administrative burden, in retrospect most managers find that a defined reporting structure makes information management easier over the course of the contract, especially when historical data is required for project reviews, or during quality or incident audits and trend assessments. In addition, sensible report structuring systems can also remove repetitive and duplicative efforts within the organization overall.

A sound reporting structure with sensible and pragmatic information requirements will support all managers in establishing a more efficient organizational process. Consistent templates and materials flowing through company and vendor structures enable more effective decision making, as well as monitoring accountability and performance within contract leadership. Reporting chains should also have nodal points, where several sets of information flow into a report manager, who generates a consolidated report and forwards that report to a series of other recipients. This process reduces e-mail traffic and best coordinates

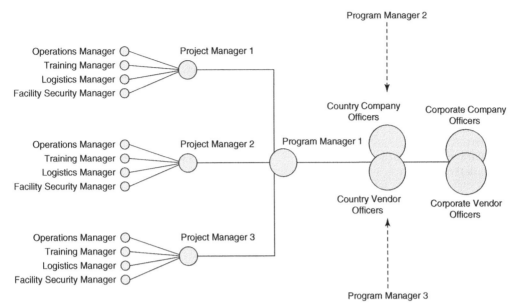

Exhibit 3.12 Information Flow Management

information management, as illustrated in Exhibit 3.12. A mature vendor will have a raft of standardized reports and returns, which the company can modify to suit its own needs, reducing the burden on the company when establishing new reporting structures or templates.

To avoid reports and returns becoming burdensome during periods of high-tempo operations, they should be focused and cleanly structured. The use of appendices for sections might also allow management to focus only on the areas of interest to them, rather than having to sift through volumes of data to get to their area of interest. Reports and returns typically reflect generic needs, risk issues, operational activities, delivery of services, manpower levels, and significant events.

Scheduling reports and returns is critical to ensuring that information flows effectively and contains the right details within a reporting system. Issuing responsibilities and accountabilities also defines who is responsible for ensuring that a process is followed, that systems are adhered to, and that quality assurance is established. A simple and clear reports and returns table often helps illustrate what is required, and can then be used as a quality assurance tool to confirm that the documents are being delivered according to specification and schedule, as illustrated in Exhibit 3.13.

Reports and returns should be standardized where possible and appropriate, as this ensures information is presented in the same manner, contains the same content, and meets the same objectives across multiple projects. The documents should seek to support, not hinder, business activities; thus, only those matching a specific need should be used. Reports and returns might need to be modified to reflect unique local or activity factors. Reports can also be generated for specific requirements outside of a scheduled system, although these might be classified as security documents and exhibits (see Chapter 12) if they are outside the norm or contain complex information.

Exhibit 3.13   Reports and Returns Scheduling Table

Report Scheduling Table	Delivered	Remarks
Contracted manning table	Sunday	All contracts provide
Serious incident report data base	Sunday	All contracts provide
Serious incident report report	As occurs	All contracts provide
Project overview	Update monthly[1]	All 1+ month contracts provide
Weekly project report	Sunday	All contracts provide
Daily report	Daily[1]	All contracts provide (only if client requires it)
Historical travel threat matrix	Sunday[2]	All projects with frequent site visits provide
Specific task threat matrix	Sunday[2]	All projects with project sites or visits provide

Report Requirement Table	Company W	Company X	Company Y	Company Z
Contracted manning table	Yes	Yes	Yes	Yes
SIR database	Yes	Yes	Yes	Yes
SIR reports (template)	Yes	Yes	Yes	Yes
Project overview	Yes	Yes	Yes	No
Weekly project report	Yes	Yes	Yes	Yes
Daily report	No	Yes	Yes	Yes
Historical travel threat matrix	Yes	No[1]	No[1]	No[1]
Specific task threat matrix	Yes[2]	Yes[2]	Yes[2]	Yes[2]

[1]The Vendor or Company may wish to add caveats, such as differences in approach from a unique to common task.
[2]Only for those contracts which provide this specific service.

Weekly Report

It is useful to establish a succinct weekly vendor report to capture programmatic activities, services delivered, and problems encountered. This report supports management awareness for both the company and vendor, and enables better decision making and issue tracking. Weekly reports also assist vendors in formally raising or capturing issues and information that can be used as a reference point for audits. The weekly report should provide an executive summary to allow management to determine key points without having to read the entire document. If the program is complex or contains a significant amount of information, a series of appendices to capture component elements, such as project performance, service delivery, and logistical and accounting issues, may be required. Tables and graphics should be used to succinctly present information to the recipients where possible. At all times managers should seek ways to capitalize on supporting reports or capture documents in a manner that reduces the effort required to produce reports and returns. Supporting documents should be aligned with the report so that elements can be taken directly and inserted easily, as illustrated in Exhibit 3.14. It should be noted that the information which feeds the reports might be considered returns. Program observations and recommendations should be clearly highlighted, with action points and responsibilities. References to previous reports can be used to illustrate ongoing problems or issues. A clear understanding of who within the

System – PSD Scheduling

PSD Task Schedule Project 1

Day	Operational	Training	Rest	Maintenance	Hours	Conducted	Delta
Monday	5	0	12	2	19	5	0
Tuesday	4	2	12	0	18	6	2
Wednesday	4	0	12	2	18	3	–1
Thursday	4	2	12	0	18	3	–1
Friday	4	0	12	2	18	2	–2
Saturday	3	2	12	0	17	5	2
Sunday	0	8	15	1	24	2	2
	24	14	15	7	60	26	2

System – PSD Task Record Keeping

SERVICE DELIVERY POWER GRID PROJECT
12–18 April 2008

Service	Project 1	Project 2	Total
PSD Tasks	26	15	41
Clients Moved	32	16	48
Patrols Conducted	56	48	104
Vehicle Searches	234	157	391
Facility Escorts	156	200	356
Risk Surveys	1	3	4

Client	Construction Ltd	Dated:	12th April 2008
Project	Power Grid Project	Dist List	Program Manager, Risk Manager, Safety Officer, Logistics Director...

WEEKLY REPORT

Program Executive Summary	
Project Executive Summary(s)	
Significant Issues or Risk Factors	
Significant Incidents (see Appendix B)	
Project Reviews	
Services Delivery	
Service Delivery Statistics	

SERVICE DELIVERY-POWER GRID PROJECT
12-18 April 2008

Service	Project 1	Project 2	Total
PSD Tasks	26	15	41
Clients Moved	32	16	48
Patrols Conducted	56	48	104
Vehicle Searches	234	157	391
Facility Escorts	156	200	356
Risk Surveys	1	3	4

Program Finance	
Logistics and Procurement	
Recruitment and Personnel	
Administration	
Recommendations or Action Points	
Outstanding Issues	
Program Forecast	

Author	
Role	
Title	

Exhibit 3.14 Efficiencies in Information Presentation

company and the vendor should receive the report should be developed in collaboration between both parties to ensure that sensitive materials are shared only within a specified group. Exhibit 3.15 illustrates an example format of a simple weekly report, although requirements will differ between companies and business activities. Daily reports might be required for complex business activities or where the activity is starting; these should be simplified or reduced versions of the weekly report.

Security Modification Reports

The security of projects is often a dynamic element, and may require continued revision to reflect the changing operational environment and project needs. Security modifications may encompass a change in approach or technique required within a project; for example, patrol patterns will be changed, access points will be closed during certain hours or personal security detail (PSD) resources will be amalgamated for certain trips due to risk levels. Thus security modification reports should be considered tactical rather than contractual changes. The company should seek to document these changes through an official report, which captures why such changes are being implemented and the resulting impacts. Security modification reports should be reviewed by both the company and the vendor program and corporate offices to ensure that transparency and accountability is maintained at all times. Serious operational or administrative concerns associated by a change should be raised to appropriate management as soon as possible. Often these changes may have implications in terms of

Client:	Construction Ltd	Dated:	12th April 2008
Project:	Power Grid Project	Dist List:	Program Manager, Risk Manager, Safety Officer, Logistics Director

WEEKLY REPORT

Program Executive Summary

Project Executive Summary(s)

Significant Issues or Risk Factors

Significant Incidents (see Appendix B)

Project Reviews

Services Delivered

Services Delivery Statistics

SERVICE DELIVERY POWER GRID PROJECT 12–18 April 2008			
Service	Project 1	Project 2	Total
PSD Tasks	26	15	41
Clients Moved	32	16	48
Patrols Conducted	56	48	104
Vehicle Searches	234	157	391
Facility Escorts	156	200	356
Risk Surveys	1	3	4

Program Finance

Logistics and Procurement

Recruitment and Personnel

Administration

Recommendations or Action Points

Outstanding Issues

Program Forecast

Author	
Role	
Title	

Appendices:

A.   Historical Risk Tracker Report
B.   Regional Intelligence Review and Threat Assessment
C.   Significant Incident Reports

Exhibit 3.15   Formatting Weekly Reports

improving or hindering business or operational activities, and these reports ensure that the rationale for any changes is logged to ensure management gaps or historical reviews have a paper trail to account for such modifications. These reports should not be confused with contract scope change reports, which highlight service-level or cost changes, compared to risk or security policy or procedure changes. At times these two reports may overlap, and an amalgamation of data from both into a single report will be required.

Contract Scope and Technical Change Reports

Project needs or the risk environment may require minor or significant changes in vendor services to reflect dynamic environmental or operational influences. Company managers may have budgeted for these changes and may have authority to scale resources up or down without a lengthy contracting process. Often a notice to proceed (NTP) is sufficient to mobilize additional vendor resources while the contracts are amended between the vendor and the company—this is made more efficient if basic ordering agreements are in place. This gives project management the flexibility to respond to immediate requirements that contracting departments might otherwise slow down. To avoid the same management gaps, and to support the historical auditing requirements mentioned within weekly reports, it is important to record all significant changes to the contract in terms of manning numbers, management movements and relocations, price modifications, and scope of work alterations in an official report. Doing this ensures that all pertinent points are captured and retained for future information and reference. Sanctions for such changes must come from the appropriate managers who have contractual and budgetary authority, with these reports being used as the foundation to provide and then record such decisions.

If agreed systems and contract change documents have been developed between the vendor and the company, a technical change form might be established, which operates within the agreed parameters of an established contract rather than meeting new needs. The standard report would be completed by appropriate parties and sanctioned by an authorized company representative, enabling immediate requirements to be addressed. Such documents meet service and contract requirements most effectively, and might encompass service levels, approach, or durations. These reports might capture a range of changes to a contract or approach, for example:

- *Technical change.* An additional 30 personnel are required for site A.
- *Security change.* Vehicles will now travel in pair configurations rather than in fours.
- *Contract change.* The contract has been extended by 6 months.

Specific Task Risk Assessment

Each activity should be subject to a risk assessment, either as a long-term review or for each individual task. The value of conducting such assessments relates not only to reducing risks to project staff, resources, and activities, but also demonstrates to the company that the vendor is applying the correct attention to risk mitigation and security management. In addition, such reports provide evidence of professional conduct in the event of an incident, and might be used for internal and external quality assurance or professional liability audits. Specific task risk assessments should be developed with clear risk measurements, and applied in a manner that reflects risk to personnel or activities, as well as the impact to the company. Exhibit 3.16 presents an example of a PSD specific task risk assessment. As with all reports, managers should seek to provide an efficient means of capturing this information without overburdening project staff. If a project site is visited frequently, much of the data in such a report will remain the same. That said, the report should be used as a tool to ensure risk managers consider the risks and modify their risk assessment based on any changes that might occur.

Historical Risk Tracker

In situations where risks may accumulate over a period of time or through repeated activities, the vendor should work with the company to indicate where risks might occur during the life span of the project. Risk and program managers should also work in partnership to define risk allowances against project needs; thus an activity might be permitted to occur only at certain frequencies, or agreed risk levels may be drawn for certain areas. Trigger points should be established and clearly indicated so that when tolerance levels are reached or exceeded, they are drawn to the attention of appropriate managers. Doing this will also enable an audit of common threat trends that occur, leading to possible changes in how a company might seek to do business. Exhibit 3.17 illustrates how PSD movements to certain sites may have visit frequency permissions attributed to them and how actual visits are registered with color coding indicating where allowances are breached. For example, if a color code of black represents extreme risk, automating an excel spreadsheet to change color when a certain point has been passed will more easily present risks to a reviewing risk or program manager. Color coding can therefore be linked to numerical data to ensure that critical information is more easily defined.

Intelligence Report

In areas of business or physical risk, a periodic intelligence report might be used to define the political, economic, ethnic, geographical, climatic and religious threats posed to a project or business activity. This report may then form the foundation or rationale for managers to change elements within both the business approach and overall risk management plan, as well as determine how project activities are conducted on a daily, weekly, or monthly basis. The intelligence report will influence operational or tactical approaches within the activity and will also be part of a post-incident review following a crisis event. Intelligence should drive the risk management and security policies and procedures of an activity allowing long range forecasting and planning. Intelligence reports should avoid merely reciting incidents or occurrences; they should also forecast risks or areas of concern and offer observations and recommendations to resolve issues.

Threat Assessment Report

Companies may wish to separate intelligence from threat analysis, although the two are inextricably linked. However, an intelligence manager may not be best placed to consider the business activities and goals into the over threat or business context, and so the company

TASK RISK ASSESSMENT

Client's Company Name	
Project Name	
Assessment By	
Date Assessment Conducted	
Task Location	
Task Date(s)	

BRIEF OVERVIEW OF PROJECT SITE

Task Location:

Description of Ground:

Description of Project:

Duration of Project:

Routes to Site:

Local Influences:

Local Security:

Security Concerns:

Importance of the Project to Client:

Reference Documents:

Risk Rating (1–5)	Scores	Mitigation Measures (only required if a scoring medium or ab Final Scores)	
Travel Risks			
Route options availability to site	5	*An additional route has been identified during recent days*	3
Distance to be travelled	3	No change	3
Physical nature of road (speed of travel)	3	No change	3
Number of incidents recorded for selected route's	4	Will be travelling outside of high incidence period	2
Intelligence available on routes	2	Will seek support from military intelligence	1
Availability of emergency alternative routes	2	Additional routes have been proven	1
Project/Task Site Risks			
Number of times visited task site	4	Since our re-insertion in October almost negligible—very few visits planned	2
Intelligence available on task site	3	Will seek additional support from military intelligence	2
Profile of the task site	2	Our prolonged stay has increased our profile.	2
Hostility within local area	2	No change	2
Threat posed by local hostile groups	2	Our security profile, procedures and stance emanate our control and alertness	1
Previous attack at task site, or adjacent areas	2	Two previous IDF attacks in recent months—June and September	2
Hostile Group Risks			
Specific activity on route to task site	4	Will travel outside of peak incident times	2
Specific activity within task area	3	Will conduct visit in hours of darkness	2
Specific focus on client's activity	3	Continual occupation for 26 weeks, with locals employed throughout.	3
Current level of hostile activity (relative to environment)	3	No change	3
Expected rise in hostile activity over task period	3	Not known	3
External Support			
Commercial QRF in 30 minutes	3	Military QRF on 15 min standby notice to move	1
Millitary QRF within 30 mins	4	Secured military support for this task	1
Trauma medical facility within 1 hour	4	We have placed am EMT on task	2
Importance of Project Task			
The profile of the Project Task/Site in relation to target	4	No change	4

PRE-MITIGATION MEASURE FINAL SCORE	65	POST-MITIGATION MEASURE FINAL SCORE	45
Grading of Pre-mitigations Threat	HIGH	Grading of Post-mitigation Threat	MEDIUM

Scoring Guide	Overall Grading (out of 100 points) Guide	
1 - Negligible Risk	0–20: Assessed as a negligible risk based on known facts and professionl assessment	
2 - Low Risk	21–40: Assessed as low risk based on known facts and professional assessment	
3 - Medium Risk	41–60: Assessed as medium risk based on known facts and professional assessment	
4 - High Risk	61–80: Assessed as **High** risk based on known facts and professional assessment	
5 - Extreme Risk	81–100: Assessed as **EXTREME RISK** based on known facts and professional assessment	

Authorization			
Task Graded	Auth Level	Authorization by	Date
EXTREME	Prog Mgr		
HIGH	Sar Ops Mgr		
MEDIUM	Ops Mgr	Authorized	12th April 2008
LOW	TL		
NEGLIGIBLE	Nil		
Will the Task be Conducted Yes or No ?			YES

Exhibit 3.16 Specific Task Risk Assessment

World Wide Construction Ltd						MARCH				Total	Delta	APRIL				Total	Delta
HISTORICAL TRAVEL THREAT ASSESSMENT MATRIX—OPERATIONAL PLANNING TOOL																	
PROJECT SITE/REGION	Gen Area Risk	Site Risk	Distance	PSD Tier	Week Frequency	1	2	3	4			1	2	3	4		
Site Northern Operations																	
1 Power Grid Station	5	4	45km	5	1	2	3	1	2	8	4	1	1	0	0	2	2
2 Water Treatment Plant	3	2	15km	3	3	1	2	2	3	8	4	4	4	3	3	14	2
3 Generator Station	4	3	18km	4	2	1	2	1	2	6	2	2	2	3	2	9	1
Site Central Operations																	
1 Generator House	2	1	56km	2	4	4	5	3	4	16	0	0	5	2	1	8	8
2 Power Line Facility	1	0	23km	1	5	4	5	6	4	19	1	5	6	3	2	16	4
Site Southern Operations																	
1 Power Transfer Station	1	0	19km	1	6	8	6	7	5	26	2	8	12	11	7	38	14
KEY INFORMATION																	
Exceeding Agreed Number																	
At Agreed Number																	
Below Agreed Number																	

Trend Analysis	Difference
Project North 1	2
Project North 2	2
Project North 3	1
Project Centre 1	8
Project Centre 2	5
Project South 1	14

Exhibit 3.17 Historical Risk Tracker Report

may desire a risk manager to review intelligence against its business and operational needs, forming a holistic view of threat against its larger company objectives and needs. Risk managers can also better recommend risk mitigation measures to overcome the threat rather than focus purely on the intelligence picture, as intelligence can be a highly specialized but restricted field, while risk and security managers might have a broader and more pragmatic view of the requirement. Periodic reports will track at a granular level the threats assessed as posing risks to the company on a daily, weekly, or monthly basis. More detailed threat assessment reports may be conducted to capture trends and forecast risks and impacts. Such reports can be used as planning tools for project management and general activities or to maintain an overview throughout a project's life. They might be subsumed within the intelligence report if necessary or as a section within the risk plan. Also, a short white paper version might be used to capture the attention of senior management on particular issues or concerns.

Program Overview Report

A good vendor will place program security management into the task whose first objective is to gain a thorough understanding of the company's structure, goals, and needs, so as to better support their overall requirements. The provision of such dynamic and decisive "start up managers" will be seen in their ability to both mobilize and track resources, as well as provide the foundations for systems, policies and procedures concurrently with more practical service delivery. This approach should be aligned with the services agreed within the contract between the company and vendor. Vendors that quickly develop a detailed document capturing the entire activity are better placed to understand complex program activities and also have a solid reference document to capture historical or contract changes – as well as to share with the other supporting elements of the organization. Typically a program overview report will demand a degree of effort to develop, as it requires focus and the ability to capture complex data within a logical document, however once done it provides an excellent foundation for multiple use and reference, and should then only be periodically modified, or when significant changes occur.

This report can be used to brief visitors, support audits, and provide a complete reference document for contract closure and historical audits. The program overview may include these core elements:

- Company overview.
- Company program overview.
- Relationships with external agencies.
- Threat review, referencing specific threat types and groups.
- Number and breakdown of company projects within the program (ongoing and completed).
- Maps or graphics to illustrate project locations and factors.
- Provider services to the company and service delivery statistics.
- Summaries on each task order grouping (i.e., 100 border forts, 20 hospitals) or individual large-scale projects (i.e., prison, power station, etc.).
- A list of significant incidents affecting the program and projects.
- Program closure section (to be completed only at the end of a program).

These reports will form the foundation of reference for a contract both during the activity and for years after the contract has been completed. If structured and detailed correctly, the reports can also function as detailed reference documents to assist in proposal writing or can be used as briefing tools with fluid sections being updated quickly.

Contract Status Report

Outside of the overarching reviews conducted within a program overview and weekly reports, there may be a requirement to maintain a log of the contract status in terms of how project activities are progressing, how much of the budget has been expended, and where significant issues lie. This reports might include statistics and graphics on project timelines (Gantt charts), financial issues (budget sheet), and serious events. These details may be covered within a variety of reports (weekly/program/serious incident report (SIR) database, etc.) or might be captured more cleanly on a detailed summary report used for documenting contract issues for audit and action, depending on the requirement of the provider and the company. Contract status reports can be historical, current, and predictive in nature, and might draw directly on other formal reporting systems with limited comments or recommendations, thus reducing resources and effort, while still capturing relevant details for review.

Management Handover Reports

It is important with vendors that provide back-to-back positions, that have management staff covering for personnel on leave, or that gap positions provide detailed handover reports to ensure consistency of service delivery to the company. These reports not only ensure that the contract is best administered, with least disruption to the activities during handover periods, but also establishes a degree of uniformity of approach. They also ensure a greater degree of accountability with vendor management to maintain professionalism of service at all stages.

Official Security Documents

All official security documents and exhibits (see Chapter 12) must be provided to the company with a degree of uniformity using consistent templates. While every activity or requirement will be different, the manner of structuring the document and presenting information should not vary significantly. These documents should be sent directly to appropriate management for sanction, with the initial and final versions being sent for archive and reference purposes, often in PDF version to prevent unauthorized tampering with information. Fixing the data within a static format such as PDF is especially important as these reports might form the basis of any post-incident audit, and may have implications both operationally and in terms of corporate liability.

Serious Incident Report

Companies should develop a standardized serious incident report (SIR) to document and manage information flow on serious events occurring within a contract. The report should be completed and released during and following each serious incident. Companies may wish to have staged reports to capture the details of a fluid event requiring initial, interim, and closure reports. All reports must be completed correctly and in sufficient detail, as they may be used for audit or investigation purposes. The company or the vendor might have preferences regarding formatting as well as the distribution list. An agreement should be reached between both parties to ensure that reports capture all necessary details and are sent only to agreed recipients. Serious incidents might include hostile incidents resulting in injury, death, or serious project problems; serious injury or death from natural causes or accidents; serious industrial accidents or evacuations; serious legal or reputational situation; and the loss of a critical or high-value asset. Exhibit 3.18 captures a rocket propelled grenade attack against a military aircraft over Baghdad, which would perhaps warrant an sir.

Crisis Response Guidelines

Crisis response documents aim to capture pertinent points to consider during a crisis situation, as well as the relevant points of contact (see Chapters 4 and 12). The vendor should update these operational documents and ensure that they are posted and adhered to. These guidelines are a granular aspect of the risk management plan.

Unlike reports, returns are engineered to provide data from which decisions or assessments are made or to support informational aspects of a report. It should be noted that returns are for some managers effectively reports, in that they are reporting information, but as that data is moved upwards through company structures these documents form the basis of initial information delivery, and thus come under the "returns" classification. The company and vendor management must clearly indicate which elements they wish to term report, or return. The next sections provide a sample of some returns that might be required within a contract.

Warden Return

Tracking the movement of project staff is problematic, and it is especially important when operating within remote or challenging countries, where heightened risks require immediate

Exhibit 3.18 Serious Incident Reports

Source: Copyright © 2004 M. Blyth, Iraq Surface to Air Risks.

staff accountability requiring systems are in place to manage personnel movements. Problems related to personnel accountability are exacerbated when staff move between projects, and the chaos resulting from a crisis event will further confuse personnel accountability unless robust and effective management systems are in place. These warden returns will be used to account for personnel during a crisis. A strict tally of who is where should be conducted on a frequent (if not daily) basis so that full personnel accountability is maintained.

Travel Return

Travel often presents the highest levels of risk exposure to the company as well as removing personnel from supporting management and operational structures. Much effort will go into secured movement planning. However, like the warden return document, it is essential that company managers can account for personnel traveling from a site. Travel returns do not need to be complex, but should include primary and secondary routes, timings, and who is traveling in which vehicle. Communications details, medical issues and venues, and other related activities should be included, and the specific risk assessment should be provided as an appendix. Exhibit 3.19 illustrates the need to account for project staff within each trip; doing so is fundamental for effective crisis management, should an incident occur.

PSD — C/S Z18   PSD — C/S Z19

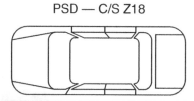

C/S Z18	Company	Name
Team Leader	Vendor	John Smith
Driver	Vendor	Greg Willis
Passenger 1	Wills Energy	Susan Vill
Passenger 2	Wills Energy	Simon Dunkle
Passenger 3	Craig Lighting	Ackmed Sills

C/S Z19	Company	Name
Team Leader	Vendor	Mike Aspect
Driver	Vendor	Fred Harris
Passenger 1	Wills Energy	John Greg
Passenger 2	Wills Energy	Lee Humprey
Passenger 3	Craig Lighting	Claire Jones

Exhibit 3.19   Travel Return Seating Plans

Contract Manning Table

At times there will be differences between the number of personnel contracted and how many persons actually are on post. External and internal influences may prevent vendor staff from leaving a site, or injuries may delay personnel arriving. Some differences will have been factored into the contract; others may require resolution on a case-by-case basis. The vendor should keep an accurate record of the number of personnel contracted to the company as well as how many personnel are on post at any given time. The contracted numbers, by labor category, should be represented on a contract manning table, while the numbers of personnel on post should be reflected in a PresRep. The differences should be captured to manage the cost and operational implications as well as for service delivery tracking and subsequent audits.

This document should be keep current and used to supplement accounting, management, and crisis response requirements. The contract manning table can have multiple applications, as it is used to determine baseline contract costs and operational capacities, as well as act as a reference document or historical data report for billing.

Serious Incident Database

Retaining a current database of serious events is useful for companies to enable them to conduct risk trend analysis, consider business viability, review project impacts, and address reputational issues through evidenced statistics and detailed documented information. This information can also feed into a company's safety statistics and might influence its insurance premiums. For companies working on government contracts, this information can also be used to demonstrate factors outside of the company's control that might result in project delays or additional costs.

Ideally a SIR database represents the range of incident areas, as illustrated in Exhibit 3.20, and will be placed on a periodically updated spreadsheet with information flows from

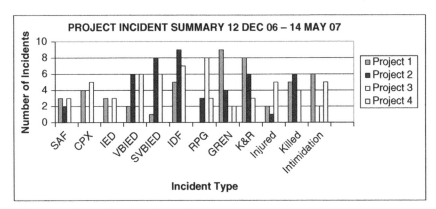

Exhibit 3.20 Presenting Serious Incident Information

each project or program to a SIR database custodian who collates all details onto a master spreadsheet. (This is preferable to all data being held solely within a single location.) This information also has applications for proposals, presentations, and corporate decision making. The database information might then be presented in a variety of ways to illustrate the historical nature of the threats facing either a single or multiple project, either as a sum total from project start to the current date, or over calendar periods.

Returns might also include a raft of administrative and logistical information, including vehicle fleet status, location and serviceability levels, ammunition expenditures and stock holdings, budgetary expenditures and reserves, group travel details and plans, service delivery statistics and incident occurrence levels.

MANAGEMENT SYSTEMS

For a company to be effective, the vendor must employ sound management systems that underpin all activities, whether operational or administrative. A management system is a tool, policy, or mechanism that, once established, will allow an activity to undertake multiple functions quickly, effectively, and, where possible, concurrently. The management system should avoid duplication of effort, maximizing the value of work already conducted, and support both existing and future requirements—at all times it should be supportive, not restrictive in nature. A management system will enhance the vendor's productivity, standard of delivery, as well as reduce the effort and stress of performing services, especially during start-up operations—allowing the company to focus more on the project needs, rather than creating new processes or planning systems. Management systems form the basis of quality assurance, service delivery, and contract management. Some of the factors discussed in the next sections may be included with a contract management system.

Standardization of Documents

Within any military or police organization are tactical aid memoirs, staff officer writing manuals, and other guidelines and protocols on how to structure and present information or plan operations in a logical, consistent, systematic, and concise manner. In the commercial

| Program Name | Project Title | Report Nature | Author's Name | Report Date |

LibyaPower – PowerHouse2 – ThreatAssessment – JSmith – 13Jan08

Exhibit 3.21   Titling Reports

sector these manuals, protocols and systems are equally important, not only to ensure that operational planning and contract management is conducted to the highest of standards, but also because the company will require proof that all appropriate and documented measures are being undertaken—and such approaches can save money and improve performance. Discrepancies in style, format, and content implies poor vendor organization, which will undermine the company's confidence in the vendor's capabilities. The company should seek to ensure that the vendor has established templates, which provide consistency of content and delivery.

Titling Documents

The clear titling of official documents permits all parties to effectively identify the nature of the document as well as other pertinent information. This ability becomes important when documents move through the company's structure and the meaning of the title might become confusing or lost. It is especially important when a contract ends and when information is reviewed several months or years later by company management, after the vendor has departed from contract. Consistency of report titling is rarely adhered to, and personal methodologies are typically adopted. The company may wish to stipulate a sensible titling system to the vendor, as demonstrated in Exhibit 3.21. Such a system enables managers to sift and mine considerable amounts of information more effectively.

Managing Information

Both companies and their vendors should seek to reduce the level of effort required to undertake repetitive tasks while increasing quality and performance. Within security documents, there are often common materials that can be reused with some modifications to suit a newer unique requirement. These materials might include the explanation and illustration of overhead protection and personnel bunkers, forward operating bases, lighting and security considerations, generic threats, the use of explosive detection dogs, access and perimeter controls, and operational approaches. They might also provide frameworks for establishing security plans, evacuation policies, or training regimes. In order for a vendor to provide a higher standard of service delivery, it should collate and retain within a reference library the most commonly used generic descriptions or approaches. The vendor should review each new piece of work and consider how it might be applied to support future tasks. Doing this will allow the vendor and company to use this initial effort to reduce subsequent time and resources expended in support of the project. While care must be taken to tailor each answer to the particular requirements of each new company activity, these generic or boilerplate materials are useful to improve performance and the quality of service. This management of information forms the foundation of data custodianship.

Forward Planning

The provision of reports, plans, or policies requires a significant amount of time and effort. Unless planned strategically, each document will often meet only a singular requirement. Vendor management should consider how the task's materials might be used for other purposes that will benefit the company or vendor, outside of the defined requirement. By considering the effort for its primary goal and secondary or peripheral benefits, the vendor and company might identify ways of concurrently achieving more than one task, for the same cost. For example:

- An intelligence report might provide the data for a security review.
- A technical section of a proposal might support elements of a risk management plan (and vice versa).
- A new component of a security plan might provide information for generic materials or boilerplates.

As such, both the vendor and company management should be proactive in organizing their approach to meet concurrent objectives, as well as future needs.

Custodian of Data and Information Flow

Within any large and complex vendor organization, there is always a risk that management works in isolation of a collating and quality assurance center, or does not draw on overall company structure or other external agencies to best service the company, or meet the vendor's needs. This also occurs within company organizations. Vendor consultants and managers often produce high-quality work from scratch, without necessarily being aware of available support from other internal groups to ensure the product does not already exist or could be produced using existing materials that might complement their new service task. Creating material from scratch reduces the effectiveness of the individual and undermines vendor service delivery levels to the company. The vendor may have a custodian manager to organize and provide document templates and useful information to contract management; however, this function is likely to be limited in large companies, as size can often be inversely proportional to efficiency. Frequently months after a product has been produced, vendor's management uncover a preexisting example that could have improved their product and reduced their level of effort. As illustrated in Exhibit 3.22, ideally some form of information flow through a central point channels useful materials and increases the effectiveness of the vendor and as a result overall service delivery.

Structuring of a Database

The structure of the vendor's project database should be clear and logical in order to permit the company to navigate through significant materials with relative ease, either during or after contract completion. A poorly organized database makes the retrieval of important information difficult, if not impossible. Mining for useful information, after a task is complete or after a project has closed, can be difficult and frustrating, and poor data management can undermine the company accessing valuable information while also indicating poor vendor

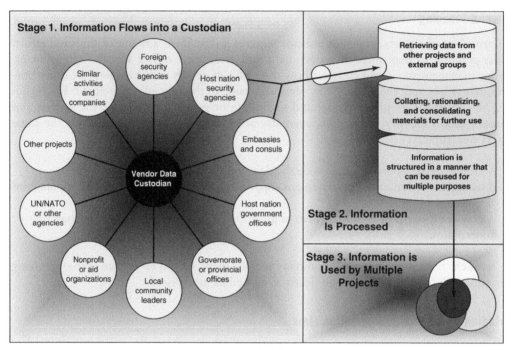

Exhibit 3.22   Information Flow and Management

administration. This is a common failing within large contracts. In the rush to establish a new and complex project, different management elements often create their own logical approach to storing information. Any external party auditing information, or those company managers inheriting the database, will find it difficult to navigate the system to find relevant materials, and this can prove especially frustrating when the contract closes and information is sought several years later. Companies should consider setting some guidelines and policies for vendors prior to the start of a project, in order to ensure information storage and structuring is consistent and logical and meets the company's needs. Exhibit 3.23 illustrates a possible database structure.

Archiving

The effective archiving of data enables companies and their clients to review materials after a contract has closed. This is especially important for government contracts, where audits can occur several years after a task has been completed. Companies should provide appropriate guidance to vendors at the start of the contract to ensure that materials are organized and retained (preferably by electronic means, as discussed above). Restrictions on material deletion or destruction should be issued, as materials created or held by the vendor may be the property of their client, and deletion or destruction might be unauthorized, or even illegal. Vendors should also be advised that for government contracts, all project-related activities and materials may be viewed by independent authorities, including e-mail traffic, Web sites accessed, reports and documents, and any other hard or soft information that may have

Exhibit 3.23 Structure of Vendor Databases

Finance and Administration	Operational Information	Personnel Policies and Reports
• Costings and rough orders of magnitude	• Security documents: surveys, plans, audits	• Sickness, welfare, and discipline issues
• Work release authorizations (WRAs)	• Manning calculations and requirements	• Job descriptions
• Notices to proceed (NTPs)	• Risk assessments	• Personnel contracts
• Technical directions and scope changes	• Incident management plans	• Injuries and deaths
• Company and subcontractor contracts	• Daily and weekly reports	• Promotions and demotions
• Invoices, receipts, and cash books	• Warden reports	• References
• Finance tracking reports and documents	• Communications plans	• Family emergency points of contact
• Procurement matters	• SOPs and evacuation plans	• Personnel appraisals
• Labor and travel costs	• Policies and procedures	• Course placements
• Anomaly and problem register	• Orders and instructions	• Qualifications and resumes

Logistics Policies and Procedures	Training Policies and Plans	Risk Assessments and Incidents
• Procurements and tracking; star items accounts	• Training criteria, standards, and objectives	• Serious incident master register
• Weapon and ammunition registers	• Training programs and resources	• Serious incident report archive
• Vehicle registers and maintenance log	• Training records and accounts	• Specific task risk assessment
• Clothing and IPE	• Lesson plans and resource plans	• Historical risk tracker
• Logistical reports and returns	• Training audits and reviews	• Threat reviews
• Destruction and write-off registers	• Training safety plans	• Intelligence reports

Management Documents	Other Information	Project Information
• Company data and project materials	• Important meeting notes and data	• Operations orders
• Handover notes	• Visual database	• Site surveys
• Company directives	• Other presentations or information	• Site plans and graphics
• Company and VIP briefing materials	• Maps and images	• Specific site management documents
• Program reviews	• Company telephone directory	• External agreements and plans

accumulated over the course of the contract. All such documents or communications must be written in such a manner as to be clear and accurate for any audit by the company or a government auditor. Any offhand comments that might be misconstrued or that are misleading should be avoided, as these might place individuals, the vendor, or indeed the company at liability risk during an audit or follow-up investigation.

Actions on Complaints

It is important that complaints are dealt with to safeguard the reputation of a company and a vendor as well as their operations. Complaints should be addressed in a professional and documented manner, and information collected should include such elements as:

- The nature and scope of the complaint.
- A written statement of the complaint.
- Details of the person making the complaint.
- Managers establishing whether the complaint has merit.
- Managers establishing the impacts of the complaint, in terms of operations, cost, and reputation.
- Managers establishing whether policies or procedures have been adhered to.
- Managers establishing if any action is required to address shortfalls.
- Managers liaising with legal representation if required.
- Managers mobilizing the incident management team to deal with the complaint, if it is serious.
- Companies making good the complaint, if appropriate, with documented evidence of actions taken and compensations made.

Securing Data

The securing of sensitive materials is an important aspect of the vendor's role, whether it is through lock-and-key security of the office, the selection of who receives certain materials within its and the company organization, or locking electronic documents with password protections. Vendors often have information that will impact the company directly. Thus, they must be held accountable for information security. Frequently in their haste to meet short timelines in high-tempo work environments, vendors do not properly manage or store sensitive documents, presenting a risk to the company.

MANAGEMENT CONSIDERATIONS

Vendor managers come from a range of backgrounds and they should be selected for their technical expertise within a specific field or industry area, as well as their past performance indicating where they have proven their capability within a corresponding environment. Outside of their professional areas of competence, some basic information technology (IT) skills are usually required to ensure that materials are delivered in a manner that best reflects the information required by the company. The next sections indicate some core areas of competence. Surprisingly enough, often these competencies are limited within the consultancy and management professions.

Technical Expertise

Consultants should be familiar with a variety of electronic tools and skills in order to enhance their productivity and improve information delivery. Many managers have a rudimentary understanding of the various computer programs on the market, and prior to entering into the risk and security management field it is useful for manager to develop some basic competency with IT tools and programs—especially relating to Word, Excel, PowerPoint, and Access, in order to deliver a higher-quality of product to the company.

Calculations

The Excel program (and subsequent versions) is an excellent tool by which to manage personnel databases, cost calculations, and logistics accounting procedures. Numerous sheets can be linked to provide collective totals. Fields can also be linked (separate boxes) to calculate key data changes automatically. The vendor's consultants should seek to become proficient in the use of Excel or similar software in order to manage personnel manning tables, risk calculation tools, accounting and logistic registers, and other management requirements.

Presentations and Visuals

Software such as PowerPoint allows those without specialist IT knowledge to provide diagrams and schematics for security documents and exhibits. Visual representations are important for all security documents in order to best distill and present security concepts and requirements to the company. Screen printing images allows vendor management to insert tables and other materials into Word documents without distorting the formatting of the document. Converting documents into a PDF format reduces the document size and reduces the ease of unauthorized tampering. PowerPoint also allows consultants to prepare presentations, inserting video clips when required. Vendor management should be advised as to preferred methods of data delivery, including style and format, where required. Vendors typically should avoid flashy graphic animations or noises, as these often distract from the delivery of information.

Compressing Files

Vendor management sometimes attempt to send lengthy files through e-mails, often clogging the system. Vendors should understand how to compress photos and other large elements of a document and how to create zip files of information.

COORDINATION WITH EXTERNAL AGENCIES

Within any project environment, but especially in challenging countries, it is useful for the company or its vendors to establish a network of external contacts who might be positioned to support the company in its business activities, whether directly for specific support or in the event of an emergency. The company should evaluate the vendor's ability to draw on the strengths and capabilities of external agencies to support activities. It is important that the vendor understands the parameters in which it is permitted to operate when engaging external resources to support the company, so that no vendor nor company policies or operational problems result. An integrated management structure will also reduce the chances of duplication of effort between the vendor and the company, as well as limit any other conflictions of interest when considering which agencies to approach. A policy should be developed and issued to the vendor to articulate how external agencies might be used to augment the business activity. These sample issues might be included:

- Confirm that liaison has been sanctioned by the company (and parent company).
- Identify where security plans can be integrated to further enhance project security.
- Confirm the extent of communications networking and emergency communications plans.
- Confirm methods of initiating external quick reaction forces and medical support.
- Confirm the location of military locations on routes and near project sites.
- Discuss the level of support available or desired.
- Confirm the availability of intelligence information or risk analysis materials.
- Discuss close cooperation between security provider and military agencies.
- Discuss repatriation procedures and support desired and available.
- Confirm evacuation plan support and integration.
- Confirm serious incident reporting procedures and policies.
- Discuss accessing warnings of military operations that might affect project operations.
- Discuss the establishment of memoranda of understanding and reciprocal agreements.

Expatriate Government and Diplomatic Support

Whether a company is operating in Africa or Afghanistan, it is always useful to establish liaison with embassies and foreign forces in order to seek additional support for a business activity. This might be direct relationship development between the company with an embassy, or through working groups organized or supported by governments. At times these external groups will offer little or no support; on other occasions their support may be critical to the success and safety of the project. Any level of international cooperation outside of organic company-contracted resources brings additional knowledge, expertise, and capabilities that would otherwise be absent. An appreciation of the external group's strengths and weaknesses is required in order to ensure the business activity does not become reliant on inconsistent levels of support. Where possible, memoranda of understanding (MOUs) between the company and government or military forces should be established to define what will, might, and will not be provided to the company.

Also, if the company's activities brings a benefit to a country—whether providing economic development, agricultural programs, or education and employment—embassies may consider a commercial project to be an indirect element of their own programs and goals and may be persuaded to offer support that otherwise might not be expected. Both the company and the vendor should seek synergies with foreign government interests in order to identify and leverage any value their business may bring to that government.

Local Government Coordination

In both passive and hostile environments, it is useful to liaise with host nation government offices and agencies, both in terms of coordinating security plans and in securing emergency support in case of a hostile incident or medical evacuation. In addition, liaison with local law enforcement and military agencies might be useful in the event of an arrest or detention. Local government and security forces can also offer information and physical support to the company that might reduce risk and perhaps provide insights into how to work more effectively within a local community. In many countries, both national and local government officials may be corrupt. In such cases, ways to avoid supporting corrupt or illegal activities, while still supporting and engaging leadership, communities and local nationals through employment should be considered as part of an overall business and security approach.

Both the risk management plan and incident management plan should address the risks faced by possible local detentions. Management discussions should be held, where possible, with local governments to establish policies and agreements on how to deal with such incidents quickly and effectively. These factors should be considered when undertaking such discussions:

- Alert the corporate legal advisor and establish an incident response team.
- Establish risks to the detained person; arrange bail, if appropriate or possible.
- Liaise with appropriate external agencies to safeguard the detained person's welfare.
- Notify the appropriate embassy or consulate.
- Determine any medical conditions suffered by the detained employee.
- Continue investigations with lawyer and embassy/consulate to confirm:
  - Facts of arrest.
  - Alleged crime (individual or corporate).
  - Time/date of court hearing.
  - Possibility of visiting or release on bail.
  - Name, rank, and service branch of most senior law enforcement officer involved in the case.
- If determined to be advisable and possible, arrange a visit to the employee with the lawyer and a representative of the embassy/consulate, taking cash, cigarettes, food, and any other items that might be useful for barter or sustenance in prison, plus any required medication.
- If an alleged crime has taken place involving injury or death of persons (or animals) or damage to property, ascertain the identity and contact details of the aggrieved party.
- Determine the level at which contact with local law enforcement should be established.

Considerations might also include such matters as imminent arrest, exit denial, investigations directed at the project, land disputes, labor issues, and any other direct and peripheral risks or support relating to the project and staff from local government offices, including risks being presented to similar or adjacent organizations which might present future threats to the company.

Local Community Liaison Plan

The success of projects often depends on local community support, and companies should leverage their vendor's local experience, relationships, and knowledge to establish a community liaison and development plan to support their business goals. This is especially relevant in challenging environments, where a local community can actively oppose operations or reduce the threat through resistance or the reporting of hostile activities. Community support or opposition is frequently found in third world or post war environments, such as some African states, where major oil companies encounter significant issues due to poor local relationships despite considerable local development efforts and social programes. Dealing with the local community requires an understanding of the culture, power brokers, and local influences. A great deal of sensitivity often is required to avoid misunderstanding or offense, both by the company and the vendor. Successful relations and communication with the local community can be the critical aspect of successful project operations in a given area, and corporate and program managers must establish the level of interaction that might be required to support their business needs.

Where possible, local communities should be included in both the planning and the implementation of all appropriate activities. During the assessment phase of project planning, various community representatives—ministries, governors, local police forces, elders, religious leaders, and representatives of various associations at provincial, district, and village level—might be included in planning conferences. It might be useful to interview these stakeholders to identify their thoughts regarding security and project impacts as well as their own community needs. These same individuals and groups should be consulted during the implementation phase of the activity, and regular meetings should be held to sustain strong local relationships.

By involving the local community from the outset of a project, a level of acceptance can be gained. Humanitarian and development organizations have a particular need to interact with community stakeholders in order to be productive, and traditional approaches to security may not adequately take these factors into account. A number of organizations prefer to approach security management based on the principles of acceptance, deterrence, and prevention. The company needs to understand that it might wish to proactively manage broad-based relationships with multiple authorities and local communities, identifying program impacts, image, and perceptions in order to operate most effectively. Engagement with the community strengthens the sustainability of the business activity by making it part of the community's socioeconomic plan and thus in the locals' interest. These guidelines might be useful in creating a successful relationship with a local community:

- Confirm the company's policy and intention of engagement with the local community.
- Establish an understanding of the local culture, especially sensitivities.
- Identify the *real* power brokers/leaders.
- Establish the best way in which to engage and communicate with local leaders.
- Conduct an intelligence review on local community involvement in possible hostile activities.
- Review possible methods by which to gain trust and support from the local community: investment in schools, medical support, and so forth.
- Consider local leadership meetings to discuss the impact of operations on the local community.

- Discuss methods by which hostile activities can be reported.
- Consider methods by which to employ the local community, where appropriate.
- Engage local businesses and ventures in partnering or subcontractor arrangements.

Other Ventures

Companies should consider establishing reciprocal agreements with other commercial organizations to leverage a consortium of support. Such organizations as the Overseas Security Advisory Council (OSAC) set up forums to centralize issues and solutions for U.S businesses and organizations abroad, and the company may wish to exploit this concept by drawing strength from other commercial groups. It might be possible and appropriate (with permissions from the company and the vendor) for the company to develop reciprocal arrangements with other commercial organizations to augment security policies and procedures. Mindful of commercial and liability risks, threats can be mitigated with measured integration of specified fields and areas with external organizations, through either loose or formal agreements.

MEDIA MANAGEMENT

The company might wish to impose strict guidelines and policies on media management, both in-house and for subcontracted vendors. Interaction with media in terms of verbal and written briefs should be closely managed to ensure that clear and accurate representation of facts is assured, through authorized and appointed representatives. Dealing with the media is an art, and inaccurate representation can undermine both the company and the vendor. A clear set of policies should be established so that all employees understand the protocols of dealing with media inquiries, whether face to face or via the Internet or phone calls. Part of the risk management plan should include the appointment of a media spokesperson at both corporate and activity levels. In the event of an incident, media queries should be directed by the crisis response teams and the embedded public relations representative to the appointed spokesperson. The public relations department should develop prewritten scripts for likely incidents to ensure that detailed and factual presentation of information is available; this will reduce management strain during a crisis and will assist with the focus and delivery of information. A clear record of any area of interests from the media, or any comments made should be recorded in order to advise the company and the vendor corporate offices as to media interests or possible intentions and story angles.

PERSONNEL AND TRAINING

Quality assurance by the vendor is important to confirm that selected staff, especially managers and specialists, meet company expectations. Poor leadership and management undermines vendor performance, directly impacting the company's business activities and overall productivity. Vendor staff who join contracts must have a proven competence within their chosen field, in terms of both knowledge and experience foundations as well as task-specific training, qualifications, and assessments. The vendor's recruiter or human resources department should conduct due diligence by confirming past experience and qualifications of individuals joining an activity by. At times, pre-selection assessments may be required to confirm the professional standards of individuals.

Typically managers and consultants have a proven background in terms of leadership and administration, as well as relevant experience within a professional area in order to permit them to deal with program and operational planning or contract administration and crisis response. Those undertaking operational tasks must have the prerequisite experience in the operational field plus additional training to prepare them for operating within the commercial sector.

Vendor managers should demonstrate to the company that they plan, implement, and document regular training and assessment packages in order to ensure that the personnel under their supervision meet the required professional standard criteria. These criteria will vary according to the nature of the individual's function. However, typically the criteria might include (in hostile regions) weapons training, weapon safety tests, first aid, communications awareness, driver training, crisis management, incident control, company training packages, hostile environment training, specialist industrial safety equipment, threat assessment systems, reporting procedures, and operational planning measures and implementation. Different scales of quality assurance may apply to various nationalities, from expatriates to third-country nationals and local nationals. Each group will come with unique challenges, needs, and selection criteria. Training and assessment should take into account different background and ethnicity factors.

Typically vendor managers will oversee the continued assessment of individuals conducting their primary and secondary responsibilities throughout the life of the activity, rather than just at the outset. This oversight will be in terms of technical competence, professional delivery of the service, and an overall awareness of the operational situation and project requirements. Those failing to meet the required standards should be formally counseled as to their shortcomings and receive remedial training, before moving on to a formal warning for dismissal on grounds of poor performance, should performance level shortfalls not be addressed. The company should be informed of any shortfalls in performance to ensure transparency at all times. Assessments of personnel undertaking tasks will also be supplemented by accurate training or performance records, which will be retained to reflect these training and assessment packages.

Training and Performance Record Database

The company may wish to conduct training or quality assurance itself, or may stipulate this requirement from the vendor. Vendor personnel who manage training activities for both security and company personnel must keep and maintain accurate and detailed training records, which, like other documentation, supports the contract and are auditable. Critical training subjects include, but are not limited to: equal opportunities, company policies, work practices, first aid, health and hygiene, industrial safety, communications and reporting procedures, hostile environment training, weapons training and weapons training tests, rules of engagement, vehicle driving, cross decking, tactics, range work, and other role-related skills sets.

Training Budgets

The company might allocate training funds (ammunition, fuel, or facilities) to ensure all vendor personnel are trained properly to support the business activity. This budget may be defined within the contract to reflect the training materials and time required to sustain professional skills. The vendor management is responsible for administering all training expenditures carefully, as there is a natural tendency in a training environment to be overzealous in using resources and to overlook budgetary constraints. If the annual training budget is spent too swiftly, the company may not make available further resources, and this may undermine vendor performance later within the project cycle. There is a tendency for those not familiar with running budgets or operating in a commercial environment not to associate materials or resources with cost. Careful control of training resources is required, especially ammunition and other expendables. A company may budget for training resources, but once an amount is committed, further budgeting may prove problematic. The vendor is placed at liability risk for exceeding material expenditure rates and being accountable for non-supported professional training if resources run out. If regulatory training is not conducted due to poor resource management by the vendor, it will also have repercussions for the company. As for other quality assurance systems, charting expenditure usage against forecast budget allowances is useful to track resource use.

Resource Expenditures

Expenditures for resources should be planned in the context of requirements, budget, and time scales. Vendors should seek authority from the company for expending resources in order to share accountability for resource use. Vendors requesting further resources should be required to justify and evidence the additional needs. Poor initial forecasting by the vendor can create frustration or prevent the correct resources from being provided. Resource expenditures should be tracked and form part of a periodic report to the senior manager for planning and adjustments. A percentage of expendable resources may be expected to be returned to the company at the end of the contract (e.g., operational ammunition reserves). Those vendors providing training resources should still be managed by the company to ensure that resources have been allocated, and that training is conducted, as some vendors may elect to avoid resource-driven training to reduce costs.

Train the Trainer

Vendors should seek to capitalize on staff expertise to strengthen all professional categories within a contract. Training regimes should be in place not only to meet stipulated needs, but also to expand or strengthen professional competence into supporting areas, where appropriate. Companies should seek areas in which vendors can, over time, further enhance service delivery through an expansion of staff skills sets, whether this is management capabilities or more practical skills. Training can also play a part in a socioeconomic plan whereby local employees receive sustainable employment training to better their economic situation as well as their community.

CONTRACT MANAGEMENT

It is difficult for a company to identify all needs prior to contract award, as often planning continues into contract start and throughout its life. As a result, the vendor may be faced with periodic or frequent adjustments and modifications to the contract. Typically the modifications can result in the greatest amount of total project revenue for larger awards, as the modification values often exceed the initial contract award amounts, and as such getting the change right is important. The lead time for identifying, scoping, planning, and implementing modifications may be short, especially within high-tempo business or operational environments. Efficient management systems are required to change or expand contractual agreements in place before any resources are committed.

Contract Modifications

Due to the dynamic nature of contracts, especially in challenging or fast moving business environments, a series of modifications may be required during the conduct of each task. Should additional manpower, a modification to equipment, or an extension to the contract time period be required, the company must issue a scope change notice. If this modification falls within agreed allowances and does not require a contractual change, it may be documented within a technical direction form or similar document. For vendor-generated requirements, vendors must provide a documented explanation of the new requirement, as well as the associated cost. These documents form an official request to add additional (defined) personnel, to extend the life of the original work release authorization (WRA), or to allocate new equipment to a budget or WRA. Only when the scope change notice is provided is the company legally requesting the subcontractor to provide these additional services. Note that verbal agreements, e-mails, or other unofficial means of communication are *not* necessarily legally binding. Only a notice to exceed, notice to proceed, or WRA may be acceptable proof that awards have been given to the vendor, although some providers will mobilize resources on relationship trust, and some organizations may use different terminology for contractual documents. The vendor must be mindful that expending any monies or committing any resources or effort prior to official and binding authority has been provided will place it at risk. Company officers who themselves may be constrained by their own company policies should understand vendor reservations about proceeding without the correct documentation.

Basic Ordering Agreements

A basic ordering agreement (BOA) defines to the company what a product or service will cost for repeat or common services. No new service can be offered by a vendor's field management without a defined BOA price from appropriate corporate or field-appointed officers. Should a new or future service requirement be identified, the vendor manager typically raises this with appropriate persons for review and inclusion as a new or modified BOA category.

Rough Order of Magnitude

The rough order of magnitude (ROM) is a ballpark price used to provide a foundational understanding of the expected costs and requirements for either the company's or the vendor's use. A cost model (Excel) calculator is a highly effective tool to estimate accurate manning and equipment prices within a short frame of time for new or existing service requirements. The ROM should be considered a highly restricted document, containing commercially sensitive information. Only authorized management staff should see the pricing aspects of the ROM, although the document may be sanitized and then used as the basis of a mobilization plan if engineered correctly.

It should be noted that the ROM is only a cost estimation for services, and thus should be considered a planning tool, not a legally binding document. However, it is the document on which a company will invariably base estimated costs and requirements for its expected business cost outline for budget planning. The vendor should seek to make the ROM as accurate as possible, as inaccuracies in ROMs may force company planners to request additional funds for their project, creating frustration and administrative problems.

ROM costs are based largely on labor and equipment costs, although separate and more dynamic elements may include mobilization costs, specialized equipment, and additional management fees. The pricing elements should include the entire costs for the service, including sharing travel costs over periods of time, management overheads, and training and recruitment costs. The ROM may also be used to spread equipment costs over the life of a contract (depending on how the costs are presented) as well as a myriad of other factors. Costs can then be calculated on a daily, weekly, monthly, and annual basis for cost estimates and budget management.

Notice to Proceed

As stated, without a notice to proceed (NTP) or equivalent, no other correspondence may be contractually legally binding. Should a vendor provide a service to the company without an NTP, the company is not necessarily legally obliged to make payment. In theory, no company should ask for services to be provided without a contract or binding document; however, circumstances may delay the issue of a binding agreement between parties, and it is up to the provider company to determine whether to proceed or not, albeit at risk.

Work Release Authority

The WRA (or equivalent) is the final and legally binding document that defines the services required and the monies allocated. The services outlined in the WRA often are defined by either the company project staff or the vendor operational management, as project and operational managers have a greater understanding of the needs. In theory, each task or task grouping should have a defined WRA allocated. In large programs, a grouping of costs may be provided under one WRA, covering multiple projects or procurements. An allocated budget might also be provided for weapons procurement, travel, equipment, and so forth. Additional company permission to expend these funds is not required so long as expenditures remain within the defined and authorized budget for these categories. If additional expenditures beyond the original budget are needed, the vendor must submit a requisition order or equivalent to gain further funds from the company for unplanned activities or resources. Budget management should be undertaken only by appropriate and trained management personnel, on both the company and the vendor side.

Service delivery and quality assurance is a fundamental requirement for the company to be productive during its business activity. The vendor must provide sustained levels of professionalism throughout a contract life through good vendor-to-company relationships, professional services, and sound administration. The vendor must understand the company and its activity, ensuring that vendor project staff stand on the shoulders of the wider group's structure and capabilities, meeting changing needs with flexibility and innovations, while also seeking to support the company in strategic and forward planning. Administration must be streamlined and efficient in order to enable project staff to focus on the task rather than be sidetracked by mechanical or process-driven issues. The vendor's employees must quickly grasp the goals and milestones of the activity, understanding the capabilities and limitations of their role, as well as those of their own company.

Managing service delivery is based on solid communications, flexibility, and strong management. The vendor should seek to be an enabler, providing a problem-solving component of the company's structure and aligning service methodologies with that of the company. The vendor must support the company in threat perceptions and present risks in a business context that can be documented and used to support audit requirements. Procurement and financial tracking will be important for large-scale or complex programs, and quality assurance plans should be established in collaboration with the vendor to ensure quality is established and measured against predetermined standards. Management must be accountable for service delivery and have the tools and systems needed to present services rendered through a series of reports and returns. Information management flow should be channeled and effective, and management systems should seek to provide structure and consistency of approach.

Vendors should seek to support the company in leveraging the capabilities and expertise of both foreign and host nation governments and organizations, allowing the company to punch above its weight in terms of organic resources against actual capability, as well as engaging local communities in outreach programs to provide a sustainable environment in which business activities can occur. Public relations through media management will be an important element of high-profile tasks. Both vendor and company management must also understand the differences between commercial and government policies and procedures, with unambiguous contractual processes and policies that best support dynamic business needs.

CHAPTER 4

Threat Evaluation and Risk Management

The debris of Hurricane Andrew, the devastation of Chernobyl, and the Tylenol poisonings vividly highlight the toll, both emotional and monetary, that a crisis, whether natural or man-made, wreaks on companies and business. The areas of contingency planning and crisis management form the foundations of Business Continuity and have grown in prominence and importance during recent decades as governments and businesses suffer serious losses through inadequate risk analysis and the poor management of emergency situations, necessitating comprehensive risk management plans and associated crisis management structures. The ability to establish a risk management plan, incorporating the areas of contingency planning and crisis management, enables a company to recognize the risks its business interests, project activities, and personnel face, as well as methods by which to avoid or reduce these risks. It also ensures that some predetermined measures are in place to allow a company to most effectively respond to a crisis situation, ensuring effective recovery and business continuity following an incident.

Executive management, or those tasked with developing management plans, might view a risk management plan as a hindrance, a set of policies and procedures that are rarely used and left on a shelf gathering dust, or that might hamper the effective conduct of their daily activities. The effort taken to develop an effective risk management plan can also be considerable, involving every facet of an organization. Risk management plans can at times be viewed as a poor use of time and resources, as frequently they bring no visible benefit to a business unit but do eat resources.

Whether developed internally or subcontracted to a risk management vendor, a risk management plan should be used as a vehicle that enables businesses to perform their project activities more successfully, safely, and cost effectively, enabling better business practices, as well as protecting the company's strategic interests. A plan should seek to engender organizational and leadership convergence, bringing together multi-faceted elements of a group in order to align company needs and understandings within a holistic set of policies and procedures. Risk management has a fundamental role within business planning; in terms of identifying business risks as well as designing the programmatic approach. It should be used as a planning tool for project operations and should be engaged at the outset to ensure that activities are planned in a context of risk mitigation, ensuring optimal project success. Typically commercial activities succeed with least loss to project effectiveness only in cases where a risk management plan has been part of the project planning, and sound contingency planning prevents every crisis from becoming a catastrophe.

Simplistically, risk management is the process of identifying the spectrum of risks facing an activity, quantifying the varied impacts, and establishing strategies to avoid or manage the risk, as illustrated in Exhibit 4.1. Company risk managers should consider risk as an indicator of threat that can be assessed qualitatively or quantitatively. Qualitatively, risk is

Exhibit 4.1   Risk Management Elements

considered proportional to the expected losses that can be caused by an event and to the probability of this event. The harsher the loss and the more likely the event, the greater the overall risk. Measuring risk is often difficult; the probability is assessed by the frequency of past or similar events, but future occurrences are based on predictions or judgments, and thus are harder to estimate. Quantitatively risk impacts may be difficult to assess. A piece or machinery or loss of production capacity can be measured in fiscal terms, but the loss of human life is generally considered beyond estimation. Risk management can be considered in terms of the equation of:

$$\text{Risk} = (\text{probability of an event}) \times (\text{loss impact per event})$$

For the management of risk within non-specialized industry fields, such as construction, development, power and water, fuels, maritime and air, consulting and training, the company or security vendor's risk managers typically come from a military or law enforcement background, where the concept of risk management has been an integrated aspect of their careers. Where risk elements are more market sector focused, such as business, financial, investigative and liability driven areas—more market sector focused risk managers may be required. Companies are increasingly drawing on this pool of generalized expertise because government groups historically have been forced to conduct contingency planning as part of their core business—from tactical orders and battle plans to responding in support of natural or man-made disasters. The unpredictability of war or criminal activities also prepares risk managers from such backgrounds to deal with crisis management as part of their daily activities, providing companies and vendors a pool of technically trained and experienced management. Both companies and security vendors, however, should understand that business contingency planning and crisis management requires a different management slant and that the skill sets brought from such backgrounds do not always translate seamlessly into a commercial setting.

Companies should seek to leverage the capabilities, knowledge, and resources of their security vendors to provide, supplement, or augment their own in-house risk management policies and plans. When operating within more challenging environments where the probability of risk is higher, companies should consider transferring both the risks and the resources required for planning to the security vendor to offset both exposure and effort. The scope of work for any contract should include clear requirements for the vendor to provide contingency plans and crisis management protocols as part of the service-level agreement. While the company can never fully defer crisis management to a subcontractor, corporate and field risk management can establish policies and procedures by which much of the burden of dealing with a crisis event is transferred onto a vendor while strategic decision making is retained by the company. These agreements should be understood, and the plans and responses clearly articulated and practiced, to ensure the most effective risk management approach is in place.

RISK AREAS

The concept of risk has different dimensions and is often subjective, as a threat is perceived differently by individuals, organizations, and groups. Company and individual tolerance levels also play a part in the assessment of risk; some companies have low tolerance levels while others are more robust in their acceptance. Risk is effectively a phenomenon that either directly or indirectly affects business and employees in terms of productivity and safety. Risks can effectively be categorized into the areas shown in the following table.

Area	Explanation
Personnel Risk	It is important that companies apply due diligence to the screening and selection of their employees through reliable background investigations. This is especially important for management roles or those positions with access to sensitive information.
Competitive Risk	Business activities are at risk if they are not cognizant of how competition is strategizing commercial activities; lack of knowledge places them at a commercial disadvantage. Investigative services and analysis can provide companies advice and guidance on how to compete in their market.
Due Diligence Risk	A company must be confident that its client, partner, or subcontractor is appropriate in terms of closing deals involving legal, liability, or capital investments. Investigative services can ensure that companies are reputable and appropriate to engage with.
Reputation Risk	Brands and reputations underpin the status and reliability image of a business; damage to either brands or a company's reputation can undermine the company's commercial productivity.
Information Risk	Information technology (IT) enhances commercial productivity; however, it also leaves companies vulnerable to data theft or loss. Industrial, criminal, government, or terrorist espionage has serious implications for businesses. IT must be physically and technologically protected.
Intellectual Property Risk	Commercial espionage or organized crime poses a serious threat to established products as well as emerging markets. Intellectual property is subject to theft or replication, which undermines the value of the producer's performance.
Physical Risk	Crime, insurgency, terrorism, civil unrest, and natural disasters are unpredictable and have significant impacts on companies and individuals. Risk mitigation, contingency planning, and crisis planning can be used to offset the spectrum of risks facing a company.
Political Risk	Political instabilities have considerable impact on global companies as well as those operating within a home country. The analysis and assessment of opaque and uncertain political environments will aid clients in complex political environments.
Productivity Risk	The productivity of the company or a specific activity will affect all aspects of the company's success, and will be tied to the other risks indicated above. Business disruptions and continuity devalue the reputation, productivity and financial status of an organization.

For many companies operating in remote or challenging environments, the more physical or base risk elements are ones that typically present the most dynamic requirements. Corporate liability, reputational risks, and other corporate concerns are ones that typically can be addressed over a more measured period and established policies and plans can be created to offset each in a timely manner, defined by the pace of business or operations. The need to address more practical threats associated with a particular region or activity will place more demands on company risk managers as each policy or plan will need to be adapted to suit shifting influences. Such risks might include:

- A facility evacuation resulting from an industrial incident.
- Injuries resulting from industrial, task-oriented activity, or hostile events.
- A natural disaster resulting in risks to the project, personnel, and assets—as well as disrupting business continuity.
- Civil disorder that present risks to personnel, facilities, or local employees.
- Disease or sickness that presents risks to personnel and impedes business activities.
- Poor service delivery performance, which undermines project activities as well as company performance and reputation.
- A facility evacuation resulting from criminal, insurgent, or terrorist groups—disrupting business and undermining corporate confidence
- A death resulting from industrial, task-oriented activity, or hostile events.
- Threats to personnel, attack, extortion, coercion, or kidnapping.
- Political instability that undermines project effectiveness and the rule of law.
- Thefts of high-value or sensitive materials that places the company at liability and operational risk.
- Supply chain assurance, reducing the delivery of critical materials and resources to support business or operational needs.

Companies should consider risk as a layered consideration; a risk to the project or business operations also presents an associated risk to the corporate managers, with some concerns and impacts being the same at each level, and others resulting in new risks or different focuses and concerns. Companies should consider how each risk element will present an impact within different elements or different levels of the company, requiring an integrated but varying management process—through organizational convergence, as illustrated in Exhibit 4.2.

RISK MANAGEMENT PLANS

A risk management plan is a logically structured policy and procedural document designed to assess and address the broad spectrum of risks in a systematic and pragmatic manner, dealing with both theoretical and tangible requirements across the company's area of interest or exposure. The company risk manager should be expected to provide a risk management plan to ensure that the business activity is planned within the context of risk, can operate most effectively, and exposes the company to the least threat level possible. A risk management plan is designed to work in a logical and often chronological sequence, identifying dangers through risk assessments, deciding whether to countermand the risks with personnel or

Exhibit 4.2 Layering Risk Considerations

resource allocation (or whether to adopt a risk avoidance policy), before implementing the delivery of risk management or security measures, in all their forms, to ensure that the probability of the risk occurring is reduced to acceptable levels or dealt with effectively. As Mitroff and Pearson say, "No organization can prevent all crises, but every organization can lower the odds of their occurrence, lower their costs, and lower potential crisis-related condemnation."[1]

The risk management plan should be aligned with three basic areas of consideration, as illustrated in Exhibit 4.3. The company or vendor risk manager should consider what range of risks the company faces and how it wishes to manage those risks. Risk managers then write polices and plans aligned to those two considerations, in collaboration with other elements of the group. The risk management plan forms the preparedness or contingency planning aspect of risk management, where a company can reduce risks before they occur and plan to best manage risks prior to an event. The risk management plan effectively forms the

Exhibit 4.3 Risk Management Plan Considerations

basis of business continuity planning, and should also consider how to address the immediate crisis requirements that typically affect the people, resources, and business goals of an affected activity as well as how the risks pose an impact ripple effect on other aspects of the company's operations and business interests, allowing companies to identify, avoid, manage and recover from a crisis event most effectively. The crisis management component of the risk management plan provides well-planned policies and procedures to reduce the impacts of the risk event through well-defined response methodologies and training. The risk management plan continues until all aspects of the risk event have been completed. Both project and corporate management review which areas of the plan were effective following an event, and which need to be improved, modified, or augmented. Risk management plans should be considered live and evolving documents. They should be continually adjusted to suit changing influences and improved as new concepts and efficiencies are identified.

In terms of providing a framework for the risk management process, risk managers should consider these three principal areas when developing the four elements that comprise the risk management plan: the risk assessment, the contingency planning, crisis management, and the post-incident review, as outlined in Exhibit 4.4.

The risk management plan may involve the development of new corporate policies, project planning procedures and tools, and employee education. It may also require specialist support for concept development and plan structuring. Plans will also include executive officers, project teams, security or risk elements, monitoring groups, and administrative resources. In many cases external agencies may also be involved, requiring security clearance, the formalization of contractual agreements, and the monitoring of the contract's standards.

When the company has contracted other groups to support its business activities, whether within the project activity or as a security component, it should consider providing, and receiving agreement on, policies and plans to enable all groups to act in unison to best

Exhibit 4.4   Risk Management Process

Area	Explanation
Risk Assessment	**Warning signs and analysis prior to a crisis event.** The value of a risk assessment as a diagnostic tool is measured in terms of accurate intelligence, specialist knowledge, and an achievable and pragmatic set of procedures to reduce the probability of a risk occurring.
Contingency Planning	**Preparation and prevention phase.** "Contingency planning" refers to measures implemented to prevent recognized or speculated serious events or emergencies. These possible activities should be identified during the risk assessment.
Crisis Management	**Incident response, damage containment, and recovery period.** Crisis management is the response to a problem while it is occurring, or after an incident, utilizing the contingency planning measures, as well as the organization able to respond quickly and effectively to unique requirements.
Post-Incident Review	**Review and modification of the risk management plan.** The documentation of all incident information should be conducted to support adjustments to existing policies and plans, as well as to identify shortfalls within crisis management policies and management teams—mitigating future crisis impact levels.

respond to risk events. Without a degree of uniformity, the response will be disjointed and confusing.

IMPLEMENTING THE RISK MANAGEMENT PLAN

The risk management plan must be supported at every level in order to be successful. At the corporate level, a risk policy strategy needs to be agreed on and distributed to appropriate individuals and groups, providing a framework for systematically developing risk assessments that corporate and program management can use to guide activities and focuses. At the program level, the plans must be usable and reflective of realistic conditions and responses. Synergies and interfaces between corporate and program-level plans should also be identified and integrated to ensure that corporate and project teams do not work independently of, or in isolation from, each other, but undertake concurrent and complementary activities. Some of these elements should be considered when developing the risk management plan:

- Establish which elements of the organization need to be brought together: both stakeholders and contributors, prior to any resources being applied, or activities being conducted.
- Provide a convenient framework for developing a quantitative risk assessment that prioritizes both goals and objectives of the company, in the context of the associated risks or threats.
- Provide a systematic and repeatable method for evaluating an organization's risks using the best available threat information. Seek efficiencies by drawing on existing templates and formats.
- Permit program, project, and other key managers the opportunity to identify their departmental and organizational risks.
- Identify information gaps in order to establish a better risk picture.
- Allow risk and security managers to express their expectations about the consequences of successful incidents. Elicit their observations and recommendations on how to mitigate these risks.
- Allow business leaders and project managers to review the risks and comment on how risk management policies, approaches, and plans might affect program design, objectives, and goals.
- Provide insights into how the uncertainty of their expectations affects the prioritization of risk or security requirements. Allow risk models to be easily updated with new input data.

Risk management should be cyclic in nature, with continuity between the users (operations and business) and managers (corporate). In addition, the process is cyclic in terms that the business need prompts the requirement for a risk assessment—used to establish which risks the new activity may elicit. These factors then feed business decision making and associated policies and plans, with new or changing events driving modifications to the policies and plans—in turn influencing business needs and decision making, as illustrated in Exhibit 4.5.

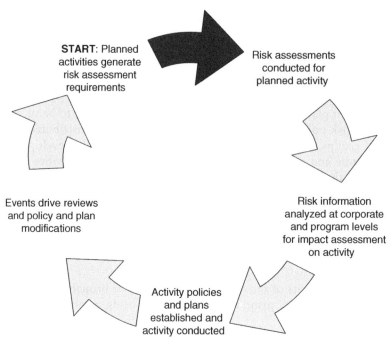

Exhibit 4.5   Risk Management Cycle

Risk information needs to be shared with appropriate groups and individuals in order to ensure that a rounded understanding of the risks is gained and that mitigation measures are most effective. Information sharing can be through training, white papers, boardroom briefings, warning posters, leaflets, or daily intelligence briefings that highlight specific risks or risk environments. The policies and procedures used to mitigate risk are a reflection of the requirements identified within the risk management plan. Depending on the size, nature, and diversity of the organization, the procedures can vary from simple and pragmatic brochures, to volumes of complicated manuals and training exercises covering a multitude of subjects, at varying organizational levels. Some of the generic procedures that should be included within any organization are the establishment of a company mission statement, general policy documents, personnel training requirements, and monitoring and validation techniques (internal and external). The identification of resource requirements (supported by appropriate budgets) is also essential to ensure that a risk management plan can be established and effectively implemented and sustained. The next sections describe the elements of the risk management plan.

Mission Statement

The company mission statement should be an unequivocal reflection of the aim of the organization. It will define in the broadest sense the nature and goals of the company. The risk management plan may also have a mission statement, which draws upon the organizational mission statement, but is specific to the intent and objectives of the plan itself.

Policy Documents

All policies should be updated to reflect the current intelligence-driven threats. All personnel should be informed of the current sources of risk, with appropriate details pertaining to how the risk might impact the organization as well as the measures taken to address them. In order to ensure that all implemented measures are effective, an established set of standard operating procedures or an incident management plan is required to educate employees on how to minimize the threat against them and bring an emergency situation under control. These policy documents can be engineered at both the corporate and field levels. They should provide general guidelines on:

- How to activate the crisis management or incident response team.
- How individuals are expected to respond to an incident.
- Whom they should inform.
- What other assets are available to support them.

It is often useful if policy documents are accompanied by relevant training and exercises to ensure that the policies are clearly understood and thoroughly rehearsed. These can be leadership or tabletop exercise–oriented, or more practical and instructional in nature.

Training Requirements

Corporate and project management education and training sessions are useful tools to run the crisis response plan through its paces. This is usually done through short seminars and training sessions, as well as tabletop exercises (theoretical and interactive management sessions focused on how to manage risk scenarios), which require little resource support and focus on key decision makers and how they undertake their individual roles as well as how they fit within the wider organizational structure. Technical and practical training may also be required in order to enable employees to be competent in using the wide variety of equipment and personal skills necessary to meet the measures identified in the risk assessment, sanctioned in the risk management plan, and implemented in the risk management procedures or incident management plan. Training agencies should be selected according to their expertise and experience, with continued training requirements identified to prevent skill fade. Training should also include relevant outside agencies and independent monitoring assessors to ensure that the measures used are current and effective. The use of tabletop exercises and practical training can help focus management teams at different levels, at relatively low cost to the company.

Human Resources

The effectiveness of any organization, whatever its purpose, is based largely on its human resources. Technical systems neither exist nor operate in a vacuum. In most cases, the causes of a major crisis cannot be traced to the isolated breakdown of a technical system. Rather, crises occur because of the simultaneous breakdown of technical, organizational, and human systems.[2] The management tools used to effectively conduct business are complex and unique, geared to the specific aims and goals of each organization. Whatever the differences within the organization, or related to a crisis, an effective command or management structure, with clear decision-making authorities and information channels, is required to best plan against as well as manage a crisis. The success of any organization is also based on selecting the right people to undertake specific roles. This is especially relevant for those deploying to remote or high-risk environments, where the use of resume validation, interviews, psychometric and aptitude tests, and more recently psychological profiling provide a means by which to ensure that the right person is appointed to the right position. Subsequent personnel appraisals, promotion schemes, personnel development policies, and competitive employment benefits, incentives, and healthy income opportunities ensure that employees remain with the organization on a long-term basis and are loyal, ensuring constancy of approach and retention of corporate knowledge.

Resource Planning

Risk management plans are closely linked to site security plans in terms of resource planning, especially where technological and physical security structures and materials might be required to mitigate risks. Additional elements, such as global communications technology linking corporate to field sites, might also be required within a resource plan, which links a site or activity to the wider corporate structure and requirements. As outlined in Chapter 9, a range of *hard* physical resources might be employed to reduce risks and protect business activities, personnel, and resources. Resources should also be considered within the context of *soft* requirements, such as training, policies, and education. Typically many organizations fail to train management personnel adequately in policies, protocols, and procedures and fail to train technical staff in the use of high-cost systems; such failures reduce operational effectiveness or make the systems redundant. While justifying the allocation of monies for the purchase of consulting services or materials procurement, installation, and maintenance, corporate officers and risk managers should consider how to sustain both policies and plans as well as systems and their utilizations over the immediate, near-, and long-term periods.

Cost Justification

It is often difficult to gain support for the allocation of budgets to risk management, as costs may be spread across multiple business units with no clear delineation of value. Often companies will seek to place risk management and security within a commercial context, aiming to minimize cost while increasing service delivery. Risk management and security are also frequently viewed as a cost center, with no identifiable tangible benefits to the business unit, but a clear cost to the project's bottom-line profits. Justifying cost can be a difficult part of the risk manager's function, especially when risk is based largely on professional judgment rather than evidenced fact. A historical cost analysis from known crisis events can illustrate risk impacts to business or project management, as well as provide a basis for cost analysis. Corporate risk tolerances and the experiences and expertise of corporate leaders will also define the approach and cost acceptance for effective risk management. Where possible a cost saving should be demonstrated, whether through reductions in insurance premiums or through the safe guarding of project operations and business productivity. Clearly indicating a potential or actual cost saving against cost factors will enable risk managers to gain traction for risk management investment.

RISK ASSESSMENT

It is questionable that every business should, or does, conduct risk assessments to ensure that its corporate needs are safeguarded from a range of risks, whether business, operational, financial, or physical. The risk assessment is especially important for companies operating within higher-risk environments, for companies that have projects which are geographically isolated, or where companies are entering new regions or business fields. The volatility of the current global climate underpins the need for companies to conduct a comprehensive risk assessment to identify potential threats, whether from industrial or commercial espionage, organized or opportunistic crime, insurgency and political instabilities, domestic or international terrorism, foreign hostile military agencies, or natural threats posed to their assets and personnel.

When considering undertaking risk assessments, companies must understand that perception plays a large part in how risk is viewed. Risk perception involves people's beliefs, attitudes, judgments, and feelings as well as social or cultural values and dispositions that people adopt toward different hazards and threats. The company must be cognizant of these facts and define how it wishes to assess risk and against what tolerance criteria risk is measured. It is often useful to provide any internal risk manager or external vendor with a generalized concept on how risks should be measured to ensure that risk evaluation is consistent with the company's approach. Exhibit 4.6 provides a simplistic evaluation of how risk might be presented to enable assessors to measure risks based on a company's risk perception rather than their own.

Once instructed, company or vendor risk consultants should seek to demonstrate the nature and validity of the information from which their evaluation is based, as risk assessments can be formed from a complex range and wide scope of information, invariably filtered and evaluated through professional judgment. Risk evaluation can be based on:

- *Hard evaluation factors.* These factors typically comprise statistics, numerical data, or trend analysis. They may also include solid evidence or human intelligence on specific risk elements, where intelligence sources have defined a specific target or activity at a

Exhibit 4.6   Establishing Measurable Risk Evaluation Criteria

Measurement Criteria	Risk Level
Unlikely to occur within the next 12 months. No intelligence or historical evidence to suggest the risk event will occur. Deemed as highly unlikely to occur.	1
May occur within the next 12 months but will be isolated events and generally low in impact. Some historical evidence of the risk occurring; none in the past two years.	2
Will probably occur in isolated areas, around specific events, but will have limited impact and will not directly affect the activity. Deemed likely, but with a limited impact.	3
Is assessed as likely to occur and will be frequent and widespread. May focus on the company and will have a noticeable impact. Has occurred recently.	4
Will definitely occur and will be focused against the activity. Events will be high impact and will present significant risks to the company. Is occurring now.	5

specific point in time. Hard evaluations typically are supported by some form of clinical evidence.

■ *Soft evaluation factors.* These factors typically are based on specialist or professional judgment, risk forecasting, and human intelligence sources. These soft factors bring multiple subjective evaluations together to form a professional opinion. Soft evaluation factors typically are predicted evaluations, based on sound judgment and experience estimating likely risks occurring.

Companies should also seek to identify the wide spectrum of risks that they face rather than focusing on the most obvious threats. Any business activity faces a wide range of risk types. These risks reflect the nature of the company's activity as well as what can be a fluid threat environment, shaped by geographic, political, and socioeconomic factors. The next table captures some of the principal areas of risk a company might face.

Performance	Reputation	Tangible Risks	Intangible Risks
• Cost	• Political	• Personnel	• Welfare
• Delivery	• Financial	• Assets	• Morale
• Scope	• Industry or Market	• Facilities	• Credibility

The risk management plan should be process and environment driven, allowing company activities to be sustained in the most effective and secure manner possible. This deliberate focus on risk mitigation at all levels, in terms of strategy, operations, and tactics, should be delivered in both managerial and operational terms—through policies and procedures, as well as the practical actions taken to reduce risk. Risks may also be specifically focused on the company's activity or may be posed in a more general manner. Both specific and general risks should be assessed in order to determine the scope and nature of threats facing any business activity.

Generic Risks

Generic categories of risk range from technical and economic crises, such as extortion and copyright infringement, to human and social crises, such as terrorism, on-site tampering, and natural disasters. Alternatively, crisis situations can fall into a number of subcategories: static and dynamic risks. Static risks are those whose impact or cost remains constant, such as the loss of industrial productivity or material damages. Dynamic risks are unstable and more difficult to evaluate; they include the impact of a fatality or the factors affecting a company's reputation. Both static and dynamic risks can be a result of man-made or natural disasters, and each may influence the other, as their effects are often interwoven.

Risks might also be considered variable in nature, as the impact within a common risk area may be altered by a change of circumstance or by other external factors heightening the impact of an otherwise isolated risk element. In addition, risk managers should consider the impact of incremental risk growth, as the cumulative effect of successive small risks may change the company's tolerance and thus the risk impact, as illustrated in Exhibit 4.7. Project

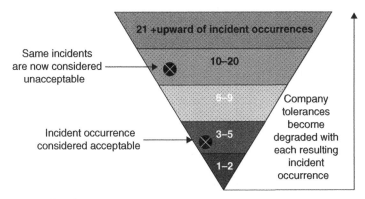

Exhibit 4.7 Incremental Risk Impact

management and field security elements may become inured to how cumulative risks change the nature of the evaluation and event tracking. Evaluation more cleanly captures event growth and frequencies to enable a more impartial evaluation of risk factors.

All aspects of a potential crisis situation should be considered while establishing the risk management plan, and risks should be considered primarily according to the potential cost to the organization as well as the probability of the risk occurring. From these considerations, the executive officers and project managers will be able to determine whether the cost of providing risk mitigation outweighs the cost impact of the risk occurring; there will always be a point of diminishing returns in terms of security provision and risk mitigation. Company management will also be better placed to identify whether resources could be concurrently tasked, or if a risk can be shared with, or transferred to, external agencies as a cost-saving measure. Risk is calculated in terms of probability, impact, scope, and nature that the company and the business activity face.

Assessment

The value of a risk assessment as a diagnostic tool is measured in terms of accurate intelligence, specialist knowledge, an achievable and pragmatic set of procedures to reduce the probability of a risk occurring (contingency planning), and measures by which to deal with any risks should they occur (crisis management). In addition, the sensible and timely allocation of resources and the identification of both company and external stakeholders (those parties that may affect or be affected by the company's crisis management) and a well-trained, resourced, and motivated crisis management team are required to allow the recommendations and action points derived from the risk assessment to be implemented effectively. Critical assumptions must be made during the risk assessment, as no crisis situation can be analyzed completely prior to its occurrence. The risk assessment should consider not only the physical threats but also security of information from theft or sabotage as well as the corporate image and morale of the company's employees. The most effective risk assessment is achieved when the risk manager has a thorough understanding of the project goals and operational approaches, the specific and general risk elements, and the operating environment in which both occur. Only by understanding all three elements can the evaluation take into account how the business needs and risk factors conjoin and interact, as illustrated in

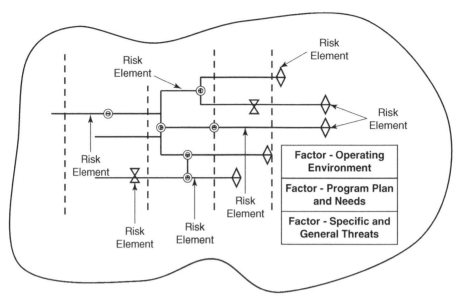

Exhibit 4.8 Credible Risk Evaluation Criteria

Exhibit 4.8, which indicates that risk elements might affect different stages of a project, different milestones and objectives, as well as different activities with the project overall.

The nature and allocation of time and resources for any risk assessment should reflect the potential threats and associated costs, should that risk become apparent. These losses can be measured in terms of fiscal or information loss, damage to assets (whether human or material), loss of business time, and diminished corporate confidence and reputation. Threats should be categorized according to some of these considerations:

- What is the organization's scope for crisis management? Are structures and plans in place?
- What is the probability of the risk occurring? Are risks unlikely or expected to occur?
- How effective are the prevention measures? Are they weak or robust? Have they been tested?
- What are the costs to intervene proactively or reactively? Where is the point of diminishing returns?
- Can the risks be avoided, reduced, shared, or transferred?
- Does the company or activity in itself draw risk? Is it a high-profile enterprise?
- How will the risk impact on the company's, short-, medium-, and long-term needs?
- What range of effects will the risk have? Will they be isolated, or will they have wider company implications?
- What are the possible cost and reputational implications if the risk is accepted?
- What budget is available to address the risk? Does it make sense to pursue the opportunity if risk mitigation costs are high?
- What is the duration of each risk? Is risk exposure short or over a protracted period?
- Does the company's approach or response elicit risks? Is the company an attractive target, is the company vulnerable?

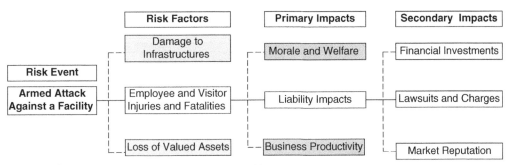

Exhibit 4.9 Mapping Risk Ripples and Impact Effects

All aspects of a potential crisis situation should be considered while establishing the risk management plan. Risks should be considered primarily in human and business terms. The human element includes the risks personnel face, both physical and psychological. The business element includes cost, productivity, liability, resource and reputational risks. From these considerations, the company's executive officers will be able determine whether the cost of providing risk mitigation outweighs the cost of the risk occurring. They will also be able to identify whether resources could be concurrently tasked, or whether a risk can be shared with or transferred to external agencies as a cost-saving measure, and as a way to reduce corporate risk exposure.

Companies should go through a formal risk estimate process in order to determine how risks might create a cascade effect and what impacts result as the effects of a single risk ripples through the company's operations. By mapping the risk, in terms of both the primary event and the secondary risk elements, each impact can be identified and addressed. Both risk and business managers should ask "what if" this happens and "what does it mean" to us. By following this chain of thought, companies can track the cause and effect of each risk, so they can discover and manage all possible eventualities. Exhibit 4.9 illustrates a simple risk impact process.

Establishing the Risk Picture

Establishing the basis of risk can be problematic, as information may be restricted or difficult to filter and process. Mature vendor companies draw on their organic resources to feed deployed consultants supporting a project with concise intelligence from which they might form a risk picture. Companies should also support deployed management to ensure that in-house knowledge and resources are best utilized. The company or an embedded vendor's risk or security manager should also seek to leverage local relationships and organizations to gain a local perspective and information sources. Any intelligence should be placed into the context of project plans and methodologies, which should be provided by the company, as these will shape how risks are graded and viewed and how they might impact on the company's activities. Exhibit 4.10 depicts project needs within risk level bandings (extreme, high, medium, low, and negligible).

The company should work closely with any security vendors to identify the risks or threats both the company and vendor considers significant to the company's operations, whether in business terms or other risk tolerances, as this will enable vendors to seek mitigations and solutions to support the overall company goals and needs. The risk manager should

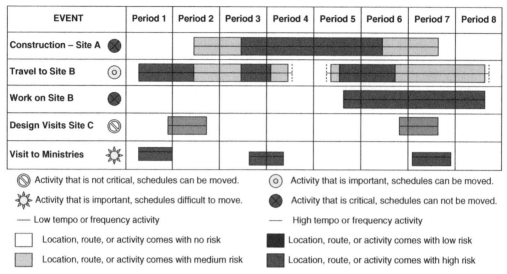

Exhibit 4.10 Establishing the Risk Picture

consider gathering information to be the foundation of the risk assessment, as well as the ability to quickly identify the core business and operational needs of the company's project or activity. Coupling gathered threat information with project vulnerabilities will permit the risk manager to establish how different risks present challenges to the company in a manner that best captures the company's interests and areas of focus. It will also enable the risk manager to offer more appropriate risk management solutions, matching each solution to a business need or tolerance level. These open sources of information can be used to support the establishment of a risk picture:

■ Information direct from the company executive officers and project team.
■ Existing information held within the vendor's company.
■ Web-based information sources: the U.S. Central Intelligence Agency, media, the British Foreign and Commonwealth Office, educational, and so forth.
■ Interviews with specialists or local leaders, as well as human intelligence.
■ Previous security-related risk assessments conducted on the region or activity.
■ Open source or confidential industry-focused reports and assessments.
■ Open and closed military, police, or government reports or interviews.
■ Physical inspections of project activities and sites.

Determining Risk Probability

Assessing the probability of a risk occurring is a challenging exercise and usually is determined by available intelligence on specific threats and the risk environment in general, placed within the context of the project activities, needs, and methodologies. Coupled with knowledge of the region, industry, and risk elements, this information allows intelligence to be used as the basis of tactical evaluations. Trend data can also provide a historical perspective or identify patterns, and might be used to indicate whether the risk is isolated or unique in nature. Risk determination can either be supported (a hard assessment) or predicated (a soft assessment), as shown in the next table.

Area	Explanation
Supported or Hard Assessment	• Specific intelligence data support the risk assessment (e.g., military reports, intelligence agency data, or direct warnings from hostile groups). • Historical or statistical data of risks occurring demonstrate or indicate a pattern or trend. • Known activities which indicate a risk is highly likely to occur. • Repeated targeting of specific activities that match the company's activity. • A collective of specialist consultants whose opinion consistently matches the risk assessment. • A known change to the political, social, or economic environment supporting the risk evaluations.
Predicted or Soft Assessment	• Targeting of activities outside of the project or company, but that are assessed as indicating a peripheral or associated risk to the activity or company. • A professional judgment that the risk environment will change (political, social, or economic), and that these changes will increase the risk. • A single risk incidence occurring that indicates possible repeat activities threatening the project or company. • Key events (political, cultural, religious, or social) that may have associated risk factors attached.

The supported risk assessment is a skilled and often labor-intensive requirement, as it necessitates gathering statistical or hard information to support a risk analysis (see Exhibit 4.11). While gathering facts is important to provide accurate foundations for the assessment, it is important to remember that statistical evidence still provides only a general picture. It can be manipulated by personal perspective, or undermined by human and environmental dynamics. If there is a shortage of reliable and quantitative data, the results may also be difficult to interpret and may not necessarily be any more objective than a qualitative description of the risk. Even supported risk assessments are usually based largely on professional judgment, unless very detailed information is available to indicate that a specific event will occur.

The availability of strong supporting evidence will allow risks to be more easily determined and presented to executive managers, who often require evidenced assessments to support corporate decision making, especially as trend or pattern setting can be used to substantiate any subsequent reviews or audits. Predicted risks, based on intelligence assumptions, experience, and a professional assessment, can be harder to demonstrate and justify. Written reports capturing the range of risks, political instability, poor rule of law, criminal activities, insurgency, terrorism, and inadequate social infrastructures are often the foundations of more pragmatic assessments; they also illustrate a risk manager's depth of

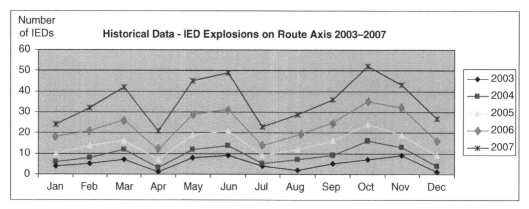

Exhibit 4.11   Trend Analysis Representation

understanding of the project region and task area. A frequent failing of many managers is regurgitating facts, without drawing conclusions and making recommendations. Managers should present potential impacts of these risks, placing the risks into context with recommendations to support subsequent decision making and planning. A combination of supported and predicted approaches is likely to provide a more complete risk assessment for the company than either approach alone.

Risk Calculations

Risk assessments are based most often on subjective analysis, or a professional calculation of a risk occurring against a general or specific activity. Even if clinical evidence is not available to support such an assessment, it can be useful for risk managers to provide a systematic assessment through a simple calculation tool whereby risks are identified and calculated in a more clinical manner, in order to focus the assessor's attention on each risk area and threat level, as well as providing a tool to indicate to project or corporate managers how a risk calculation or assessment was conducted, as illustrated in Exhibit 4.12. An assessment also

Exhibit 4.12   Risk Management Calculation Models

Project/Task Site Risks		Mitigation Measures	
Number of times visited task site	5	Since our reinsertion in October almost negligible—very few visits planned.	3
Intelligence available on task site	4	We are liaising with the local military who are providing solid intelligence.	2
Profile of the task site	4	Our prolonged stay has increased our profile. Few visits by personal security detail has lowered it.	3
Hostility within local area	3	Our security profile, procedures, and stance reduce profile and risks.	2
Threat posed by local hostile groups	3	Our security profile, procedures, and stance emanate our control and alertness.	2
Previous attack at task site or adjacent areas	2	Two previous indirect fire attacks in recent months June and September.	2

Exhibit 4.13   Historical Risk Tracking Tables

Risk Area	Freq	Apr 1	Apr 2	Apr 3	Apr 4
Route A	5 max	4	6	6	8
Site C	3 max	1	2	3	2
Site K	4 max	3	4	4	5

provides useful documentary evidence should a crisis event or incident occur for any follow-on audits or reviews, provides a tool to ensure consistency of approach, and supports quality assurance reviews both for the company and vendor management. Both complex and simple risk calculation processes should seek to address initial risk levels, offer mitigation measures, and then recalculate risks to determine whether an activity can be undertaken.

Historical Risk Tracking

Risk managers should seek to establish processes by which to track risks against project activities or incident occurrences. Tracking risks will assist in the identification of threat trends or high-risk probability activities. Within high-tempo operations, it is easy for companies to overlook activities that might escalate risks or miss trend patterns that might present real concerns to their business interests. Project managers will quickly forget that they visit a site too frequently, or that a route is used too often. High tempo activities, or complex operations can often disguise risks to company management or, worse, present opportunities for hostile activities to be planned against the company.

It is also useful, although often it is difficult, to determine what other commercial or government groups are doing outside of the business activity, as the company may be exposed to risk by association, or may be caught within peripheral risks resulting from activities undertaken by other organizations. Should other groups set patterns or increase generic, rather than targeted, risk levels it may lead to the company being exposed to unnecessary risk by association, rather than by intent. Companies presenting a robust security posture may deter hostile attention, which might be channeled to softer targets. Visualizing the risk levels is the most effective method of indicating exposure, either through a color-coded Excel spreadsheet or graphically (see Exhibit 4.13).

Risk factors should be represented as clearly and unambiguously as possible in order to highlight strategic and tactical issues. Risk tracking can show how risk impacts might be spread across a spectrum of areas or how risk levels fluctuate from recorded incidents, as illustrated in Exhibit 4.14.

IMPACT ASSESSMENTS

Traditional risk assessments that include asset valuation do not necessarily capture the essence and uncertainty of the underlying or peripheral risks. For example, it is often difficult for an organization to quantify the damage that a risk poses to corporate image, employee morale, or company stock share values. The damage to corporate image may be far more important to the organization than the actual loss of revenue caused by the risk event or the

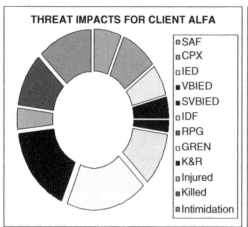

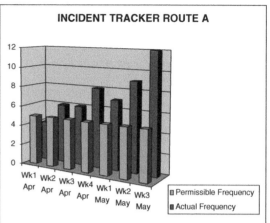

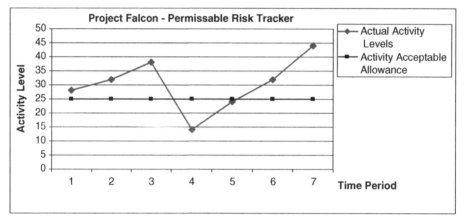

Exhibit 4.14 Tracking and Accounting for Risk

time taken to restart the business activity. In addition, the risk event may be minor, such as the theft of fuel from a generator; however the impact may be significant, such as the resulting loss of business or capacity the power source was enabling. This evaluation is further complicated when the likelihood and severity of the risk (on lives, revenue, and image) are uncertain. The costs of mitigating risks compared to the costs of being subjected to the risk impacts are therefore difficult to establish, although qualitative information might indicate the typical impact an event has on business productivity, share values, or response costs.

Risk Estimations

For some direct cost services, an estimate of impact might be possible in order to establish some cost versus reward understanding, similar to an insurance policy. For example, the direct costs associated with buying a mitigation service might be compared to known costs associated with the risk occurring. Management unable to travel might cost the company $50,000, whereas travel security might cost $250,000, thus negating the value of the

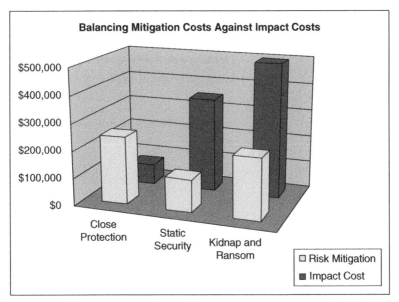

Exhibit 4.15   Evaluating Mitigation Against Risk Impact Costs

mitigation measures or requiring a different risk management approach. Providing static security for a site might cost $120,000 for three months, whereas the impact of the site being inoperable for that period may cost $350,000, making the mitigation costs a potential cost saving. Some impacts may be relatively predictable, whereas the impact of other risks may be harder to define, as illustrated in Exhibit 4.15.

Risk managers must therefore define which risks can be evaluated accurately in terms of impact and which impacts will be varied or inconsistent, as shown in the following table.

Area	Explanation
Predictable Impacts	Some risk events might have relatively predictable impacts should they occur, such as loss of life or impact of the theft of a vital piece of project equipment. This allows the risk manager to framework the risk and associated likely impacts clearly to a company, making the determination of management decision making and action easier to make for companies—i.e. if you do not provide X risk mitigation Y impact may result.
Unpredictable Impacts	Some risks can have such wide-ranging and unpredictable impacts that while identifying the risk event itself is simple, assessing how a single risk begets multiple additional risks and impacts can be problematic. For example, the risk event launched in 2001 against the World Trade Center was a terrorist attack, but the resulting risks included business continuity, public confidence, travel limitations, and others, creating a raft of impacts rippling out from that singular risk event, the effects of which are difficult to predict, evaluate, or track.

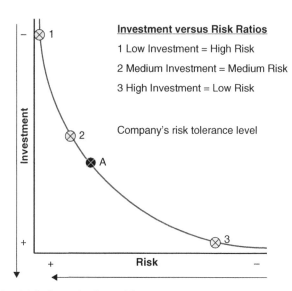

Exhibit 4.16   Balancing Risk Costs Against Risk Impacts

Risk Management Funding

Security is frequently a costly commodity for companies, often with no tangible benefits in terms of profit to a business activity. As such, seeking funding for security services to address risks is dependent on an assessor's ability to accurately present the risk and the cost impacts the company's executive management, justifying required budgets as part of a business or operational case. This can be problematic, as assessing the full impact of any risk is difficult, and it is almost impossible to gain a holistic view of every dimension of effect. However, some risk impacts have certain parameters or forms of threat and damage that can be adequately defined: For example, the loss of pumping equipment will delay project operations for 10 days, which is acceptable within the project schedule, but will cost the project $1.3 million per week in profit cost. Some risk impacts can be defined only in the broadest of senses: A hurricane of force A hitting town B will have significant social and economic consequences as well as significant infrastructure reconstruction costs. As discussed, some risk impacts or costs might be considered relatively predictable, while others are unpredictable in nature.

The project's risk tolerance levels also need to be fully understood, as the company will determine what it considers is an acceptable risk. This determination will shape what mitigation measures and what funds will be required and allocated, as illustrated in Exhibit 4.16. Those assessing threats should also identify areas of risk that the company is willing to accept, as mitigation is not required for these areas. Any monies allocated will be attributed only to defined risk areas the company wishes to address.

RISK LEVELS

Risks come in varied levels, ranging from low or negligible, where the probability of a risk occurring is highly unlikely, to extreme, where the company should expect a risk to occur at some stage. By clearly defining category levels, the company will quickly come to understand the evaluated probability of risks occurring to its business activity. Some examples are provided as a basic guide.

■ *Low risk*. The occurrence of a risk is unlikely, and no special or costly measures should be implemented other than standard company policies and procedures—unless the impact has a significant impact on the company. A detailed risk management plan may not be necessary, and risk awareness training may be useful on a scheduled or annual basis.

■ *Medium risk*. It is possible that a risk will occur, and risk mitigation measures should reflect the costs and impacts on the company and the business activities, captured within a basic risk management plan. Annual low-level management training and the establishment of crisis management project groups will be beneficial to the company as part of contingency planning measures.

■ *High risk*. A risk is likely to occur. The company is advised to establish an appropriate budget to develop policies and procedures to counteract the probability of the risk and the subsequent impacts within a detailed risk management plan. Thorough, biannual management training will support the organization in responding to any crisis event more effectively.

■ *Extreme risk*. The risk is certain to occur at some stage of the project activity's life span. The company should consider whether to continue with the activity or acknowledge the impacts and responses within a detailed risk management plan, with frequent and detailed tabletop and practical exercises for varied levels of the management structure.

Changing Tolerances

Often company risk tolerances are fluid, and levels of acceptance adjust to changing business needs or leadership perspectives. Companies can also become desensitized to a risk over time, and what might have been considered a significant issue might gradually become the norm. Conversely, a catastrophic event outside of a specific project location might sensitize a company to risks faced in other activities, regardless of proximity or project similarity. Corporate and local risk appreciation and tolerances also frequently differ. Those project managers living the risk might disagree with their corporate counterparts on how serious a risk might be and how best to mitigate these threats. Often this leads to conflicts into which a vendor or company middle managers might be drawn. Those responsible for risk and security management must be aware of these dynamics and should seek to represent risks using factual and clinical information, with an appreciation of the dynamic tolerance and perception influences at play. Formal risk management plans reduce inconsistences in perception and sustain a more balanced management approach.

PRESENTING RISK

It is often difficult for those outside of the risk field to quickly grasp the multidimensional nature of risk and the varied threats it might pose to a commercial operation. For project managers focused on accomplishing an engineering task, trying to understand both tangible and intangible factors shaping how they must plan their program or undertake their

P		IMPACT				Risk Area
R		Low	Medium	High	Extreme	A. Wellhead
O						
B	Low	A		D	C / E	B. Pipeline
A						C. Pumping Station
B	Medium			B		D. Gas & Oil Separation Plant
I						E. Refinery
L	High					F. Tank Farm
I						
T						G. Terminal
y	Extreme		G		F	

Exhibit 4.17 Representing Risks

operations will be challenging, especially if their efforts are more focused on the practical delivery of services. Providing evidence or supporting information to substantiate an assessment is useful for risk managers, as often project managers will seek to push back on constraints imposed on their activities, because every delay or resource allocation results in a cost. It is incumbent on assessors to seek to work closely with their business or project counterparts to demonstrate how risk might affect their success while offering solutions, rather than obstacles, in order to facilitate business. Risk management should be used as a tool for enablement, rather than a hindrance.

Visual Representations

The adage that a picture paints a thousand words is accurate when attempting to demonstrate risks, especially trends or patterns. Visual representations are also useful in quickly focusing the manager's attention, whether through graphs to demonstrate trends and statistical data, or risk charts to illustrate how certain activities might fall under different risk areas, as illustrated in Exhibit 4.17. This simple risk chart illustrates the impact to probability; thus a risk might be likely to happen but have a low impact upon a specific project within a wider program (i.e., theft of materials from a building site). Or a risk might be unlikely to happen but have a high impact (i.e., robbery or attack). Such charts can be used to represent granular level risk elements, or as illustrated, wider and more strategic implications. The company can then assess the impact and cost of the risk against the impact and cost of dealing with the risk. Simple risk charts are useful ways in which to quickly focus a company's attention on specific or strategic level issues.

Security Documents

While a risk or security manager may write a report for a specific individual or business group, often this report will be shared among multiple parties. The structure, format, and content of the report will be determined by the target client's preference as well as the company or vendor's standards and templates. However, the risk manager should bear in mind that the executive members of a busy commercial organization likely will not review a comprehensive report in full; thus the manager should establish the core elements and assessments within an executive summary at the front of the document to capture the pertinent points and recommendations. Supporting materials should also be captured in appendices or attachments to enable executive officers or the management users to choose which components they read, according to their areas of interest. Protecting the document from alteration is also useful, should elements within the company be inclined to modify or edit sections to meet other requirements. PDFs or WORD-protecting documents ensure that the original version is more easily defined.

CONTINGENCY PLANNING

Risk assessments are a live process and should be reviewed periodically, or immediately after an incident has occurred. The completion of the assessment enables two planning measures to be initiated. The first uses the materials gathered from the assessment as well as associated recommendations to avoid or manage risk. The second planning measure is engineered to mitigate and manage any risks that do occur. These planning measures are termed *contingency planning* and *crisis management*—both are elements of an overall Business Continuity or Risk Management Plan. Throughout the process of developing contingency and crisis management plans, the risk manager should be seeking to understand the risks and place them into the context of how to relate to a business activity. Tolerance levels, the point of diminishing returns on investment, and fluid risk environments should be central to the conceptual process of creating realistic and usable policies and procedures. Risk managers should not focus only on the physical risks when developing contingency and crisis management plans, but should view risks and their impacts in a holistic manner, in terms of tangible and intangible impacts and effects. Doing this will form the foundation for what can and cannot be achieved within the plans, and what contingency planning and crisis management measures will be acceptable to both the company and any subcontracted security vendors.

Contingency Plan

A contingency plan captures measures that, if implemented, reduce or prevent recognized or speculative events or emergencies from occurring. The contingency plan prepares organizations in advance of a crisis and is the element of the risk management plan that seeks to identify how the risks are offset by actions taken by the company and its subcontractors ahead of an event. The requirements of crisis management are also addressed within the contingency plan, as crisis management is effectively the mechanism of using elements of the contingency plan. Typically the contingency plan is structured into five main sections, although detailed components of the risk assessment and supporting policies and procedures may be held within appendices to enable ease of application. The five sections are:

1. *Executive summary.* Overarching policies, issues, and response needs.
2. *Risk assessment.* The postulated risks against which the plan is based.
3. *Contingency planning measures.* Methods to deal with each form of risk in detail.
4. *Crisis management measures.* Methods by which occurring risks are dealt with (including incident management plans).
5. *Post-incident review.* Policies for review and action following an incident.

Consideration should be given in the contingency plan to security polices and permissions, in order to determine how companies will operate as well as how management structures will function in addition to the utilization of surveys and plans as tools, to formalize security approaches and information. Crisis management measures and the post-incident review are covered within the Crisis Management section, which itself should be considered a constituent element of the Contingency Plan.

Executive Summary and Courses of Action   Within the contingency element of the risk mitigation plan, the author(s) may wish to provide a short executive summary to place the risks identified within the assessment portion against actions or decisions made by the company's leadership to manage these risks. The company may choose to modify these policy and planning decisions in collaboration with different business units or external vendors once risks are graded and countermeasures are identified, in order to facilitate organizational convergence. A number of courses of action will be available to a company within the contingency plan, and these should be determined as the foundation for any policies or procedures developed. Corporate officers should determine how they wish to approach the risks identified within the assessment phase:

- *Risk avoidance.* Not undertaking an activity as the risk is considered too high.
- *Risk transferal.* Having another group undertake a high-risk task or activity.
- *Risk sharing.* Having other groups (i.e., insurance/partners/vendors) share a risk.
- *Risk mitigation.* Implementing plans or policies to reduce a risk to an acceptable level.
- *Risk acceptance.* Understanding the risk and proceeding without changes to an activity.

Once the risk assessment is completed, the company board can assess what levels of risks are associated with a business activity and whether these risks are acceptable. Prior to engaging in or withdrawing from an opportunity, a measured assessment of contingency options should be undertaken, as illustrated in Exhibit 4.18.

The company may wish to demonstrate its awareness of the risks presented within the risk assessment and chart overarching courses of action to set the scene for the supra level policies and procedures (see Exhibit 4.19).

Risk Assessment   Elements of the risk assessment may be captured within an introductory section of the contingency plan in order to define the nature of the risks facing a company or business activity. This can be useful for those participants or readers who may not have a firsthand understanding of the nature, scope, and impact of some risks. Short definitions set the scene for understanding why certain measures and policies have been put in place, thus bringing greater buy-in to the contingency plan. Exhibit 4.20 provides a short description that might be useful to introduce the nature, scope, and effects of a risk factor, linking it to a specific mitigation measures within the risk management plan.

Those responsible for developing the risk assessment should do so in a manner that enables succinct components to be efficiently transcribed into the contingency plan, which ensures consistency of material and reduces the level of effort required to produce a detailed plan.

Exhibit 4.18 Risk Management Options for Corporate Leadership

Course of Action	Sample Example
Risk Avoidance	A company is seeking to distribute medical supplies in southern Sudan, supporting provincial and regional government offices as part of an international health care program. The risk assessment has indicated that the threat from crime has increased, and specific targeting is probable against the projects. A number of risk mitigation measures have been offered, including armed security and government support; however, both the remaining threat exposure and associated costs are unacceptable to the company, resulting in its withdrawal from the health care program.
Risk Transferral	A company is seeking to build health care facilities in Afghanistan, mainly in regions remote from Western military force support, in areas known to harbor Taliban dissidents. The risk assessment has indicated that Western engineers will likely draw the attention of hostile parties. The company has a low risk tolerance in relation to kidnappings and casualties of its own staff; however, it is willing to subcontract the task to local construction firms, transferring the risk to an Afghan company while still accepting the contract as the prime contractor.
Risk Sharing	A company has been contracted to build roadways and communication systems in Lebanon. However, the risk assessment has indicated that the political and social instabilities could result in targeting of Western engineers and project staff. The company chooses to subcontract elements of the project to other Western companies, retaining the key engineering project management and quality assurance appointments. As such, its own footprint is diminished, while Western standards are maintained, sharing the risk among several companies.
Risk Mitigation	A company wishes to develop trade opportunities in Mexico. However, it has been advised that both organized and opportunist criminals are likely to target business development staff through kidnap and ransom. The company is keen to exploit new markets and is unwilling to share business opportunities with partners. The company opts to contract a security company to provide security advice and guidance as well as close protection officers to reduce the probability of the risk occurring, while accepting that a reduced probability of occurrence remains. The resulting risk exposure is deemed acceptable, given the business opportunities.
Risk Acceptance	A company wishes to enter into the Chinese textile market and has been advised that a high degree of commercial espionage and counterfeiting occurs. It has been provided several mitigation and sharing options. However, it feels that its higher-quality merchandise will make it difficult for criminals to pose an immediate threat and considers the short-term commercial gains viable against long-term losses, as the commodity only has a 12-week lifespan. The company considers mitigation measures to outweigh the risk costs and chooses to accept the risks as they stand.

Contingency Planning Measures The contingency planning measures should reflect the threats presented within the risk assessment, matching each risk against an avoidance or mitigation approach. Contingency planning measures may be engineered to meet requirements

Exhibit 4.19 Establishing a Risk Approach Matrix

Risks	Graded	Mitigation	Graded	Approach
Commercial espionage	High	Technology and training	Medium	Mitigate
Kidnap and ransom	Low	Education and awareness	Low	Accept
Armed attacks	Medium	Security personnel and assets	Low	Mitigate
Loss of high-value assets	Medium	Subcontract services	Low	Transfer
Injuries or deaths	Low	Subcontract some high-risk tasks	Low	Share
Road travel risks	Extreme	Travel by air	Low	Avoid

at different levels, such as corporate, country, program, and project needs. The plan should be structured in a manner that ensures that tiered policies and responses are met and that any interaction between different levels is understood. Contingency measures must reflect dynamic risk environments and should be modified to suit shifting circumstances and needs. The activities of the business activity will also influence contingency measures, and documents should be written in such a manner as to permit efficient changes without undue effort. The use of tables and stand-alone guidance and policies sections for each risk area will facilitate this, although integration points should be identified so that the final policies and procedures demonstrate an integrated approach. This may also include decision matrixes illustrating which manager has authority to make decisions for certain elements of a policy or plan, as well as outlining wider remits and permissions.

Where considerable amounts of risk management and response material is required, risk managers may seek to create an incident management plan as a supplement to the overall contingency planning document, forming the granular-level requirements or response that will direct crisis management, as illustrated in Exhibit 4.21. The incident management plan should not be confused with the corporate or program-level contingency plans, as it is designed to assist with organizing immediate response protocols to practically support the response to a crisis. The incident management plan might be a set of one-page response sheets, enabling management to fall back on established protocols and procedures during the initial stages of a crisis event. This method allows more time to focus on the unique requirements of a situation rather than those that can be predicted ahead of an event. The contingency planning measures of the risk management plan are more corporate policy documents, providing overarching rather than granular-level details.

Exhibit 4.20 Providing Simplistic Descriptions to Capture Risk Natures

Risk Area	Description
Risk: Unexploded Ordinance (UXO)	Residual explosive ordnance (mines, mortars, munitions) that might remain from previous conflicts or may have not detonated through recent use. May be complete or partial components and might be exposed or covered. May be in marked or unmarked areas, typically found along disputed borders. Materials may shift over time, be washed downstream, or move through land slippage. May be activated by proximity, handling, or vibrations. May have a ranging danger zone up to 400 feet. Estimated 145,000 mines remain on Kazakhstan border regions.
Graded: Medium	
Reference: Section 1.4	

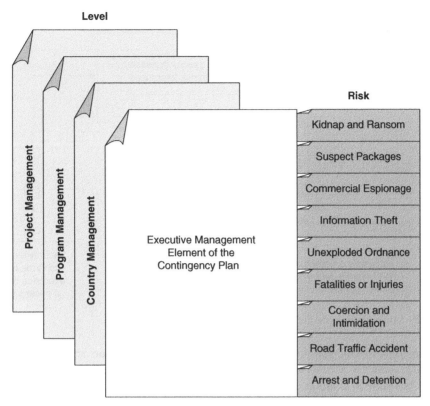

Exhibit 4.21 Contingency Plan Structuring

Contingency planning measures should be reviewed and appropriately modified throughout the life span of the activity, seeking to deter, detect, delay, and respond to a range of threats. The next sections provide sample contingency planning measures that might be used to mitigate the risk faced to a company's business activities.

Security Policies and Permissions Establishing sound management practices will invariably reduce risk to the company by a significant degree. The contingency measures will provide the foundation from which policies and procedures are developed, and will shape who is authorized to sanction risk acceptance or coordinate crisis management. Companies should work with security vendors to integrate management structures and policies to augment their internal resources, as often many of the front-end efforts can be transferred to outsourced support. Security policies may define a series of requirements or steps before a task is permitted to commence or define final sign-off authorities for high-risk activities as illustrated in Exhibit 4.22 where the Business Development Manager requests permission to conduct a business trip, which must be reviewed and sanctioned before the manager receives authority to travel.

Security Surveys and Plans Companies seeking to operate in remote or challenging areas may require a threat analysis and security survey to determine the risks presented to a facility or along a supply chain. Security surveys might be physical or conceptual, and will act as risk

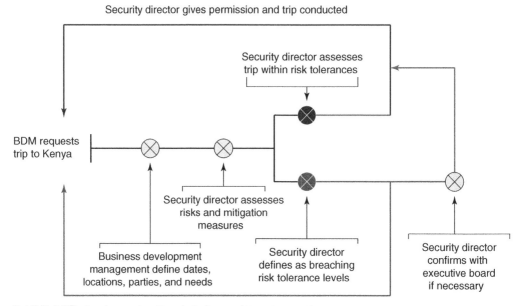

Exhibit 4.22   Implementing Simple Policy and Permission Flows

assessments for a specific activity. Security plans define how a unique activity or task will be conducted, placing the activity within a layered system of mitigation to offset risks. Further details can be found in Chapter 12.

Information Security

Informational risk presents a wide spectrum of challenges for companies seeking to retain material ownership, protect business data, and/or prevent hostile commercial, criminal, or political groups from targeting their activities. Mitigation measures might include employment screening of employees, restricting access to sensitive areas, or using IT security measures such as firewalls, restricted site accessing policies, and virus checks. The next items are some risk mitigations companies may wish to implement as part of their contingency planning measures, and include within any associated plan:

- *Security screening*. Individuals may have their backgrounds checked for affiliation with known activist or dissident groups. Their criminal history may also be investigated through government and law enforcement agencies. In addition, there may be a requirement for interviews to be conducted with family, friends, and work colleagues in order to identify any possible concerns. In some cases, a more covert method of security clearance may be employed if posts are considered critical or vulnerable within the company structure.
- *Restricted areas and identification*. Restricting areas acts as a deterrent and increases the likelihood of identifying unauthorized individuals. A series of identification methods from photographic identification cards, bar codes, voice analysis, and retinal scans are available to enhance entry restrictions.

- *Technology security measures.* Some technological security measures currently available on the commercial market include systems that prevent individuals from accessing communication or data storage media from external sources. In addition, the restriction of electronic devices that could eavesdrop on, record or access sensitive information can be prohibited from certain areas (i.e., mobile phones, computers, etc.). The threat of high-tech surveillance devices listening to verbal conversations; tapping land lines and mobile telephone calls, remote accessing computer terminals, or screens; or damaging IT equipment through computer viruses requires countermeasure strategies. Magnetic shielding, encrypted communications, virus checks, stand-alone computers, and magnetic interference equipment as well as secondary communication backups, alternative data storage systems, and power generators should also be in place as part of a redundancy policy.
- *Due diligence.* Checks should be made against key personnel and subcontractors supporting an activity to protect the company from fraud, misrepresentation, legal issues, and project failure. Investigations can be conducted remotely by database searches and public information sources, or through physical surveillance, background checks, and interviews.

Physical Security Measures

Companies may elect to use physical security as part of their contingency planning measures. Physical security measures might include perimeter boundaries, surveillance devices, secure entry points and identification checks, as well as secure access for internal sensitive areas. Specialist response teams might also be required to counter a variety of threats, whether industrial, medical, or more security related. Regular security checks on locations and materials should be conducted to deter or identify breaches of security, and strong links with external agencies are useful to augment a company's resources, as well as share risk. Some considerations related to physical security risk management measures follow.

- *Physical perimeter boundaries.* A clear delineation between public property and restricted locations is often required to isolate project areas. The use of fences, wire entanglements, concrete bollards, beams, signs and cleared land (for observation purposes) ensures that private property is clearly identified and access by all but the most determined intruder is prevented or deterred. This method also avoids accidental intrusion and provides a psychological barrier against intrusion.
- *Surveillance devices.* There are a wide selection of surveillance devices and intruder detection systems on the market, from the "trembler" devices that register movement on a fence, to ground sensors that detect low-level seismic activity (the movement of people or vehicles). Radar surveillance, laser, thermal, magnetic, volumetric, and movement intrusion alarms are useful detection systems. The use of cameras, operating with infrared, thermal, and night vision and triggered by movement can enhance security systems, alerting security personnel as well as providing accurate information on the nature of the intruder(s). Towers and aerial surveillance can also provide good intelligence from their elevated vantage points.
- *Entry points.* The physical requirements to secure entry to particular sites can encompass car and person search areas, explosive and drug detection equipment, entry-prevention

assets such as stingers and caltrops, and more permanent measures such as chicanes and bollards. Personnel manning these entry points should also have the relevant equipment and training to deal with any threat, whether mundane or unique.

- *Restricted areas.* The establishment of restricted areas involves both psychological and the physical boundary measures. A psychological impact includes creating an assumption that a certain event will occur after intrusion, from arrest to the use of firearms.

- *Material protection.* Material protection encompasses the loss of data from fire or other natural threats. Fire-retardant containers, adequate alarms, and sprinkler systems are but a few of the ways to protect against the loss of irreplaceable or high-value materials.

- *Static guards.* The use of a guard force will provide both physical and psychological deterrence as well as a response capability for a project site. Static guards can be used to provide perimeter and entry control security as well as surveillance functions. Their use provides a physical deterrence, detection, and delay factor as well as the ability to respond immediately to an incident. Local guards also can provide a socioeconomic aspect to a project, engendering local support and community investment.

- *Specialist response teams.* In the event of a potentially armed intruder, armed response teams should be available to intercept individuals at the earliest opportunity. The role of the response team will determine the equipment and vehicles required by individuals in that group. For example, a reaction force's principal task will be to intercept and apprehend individuals, so members will require the means by which to find intruders, equipment to protect themselves and any high-value assets, protection from injury, and arrest equipment to detain individuals. Bomb disposal personnel will require far different assets, from explosive detection equipment or dogs, remote-controlled detonation machinery, and comprehensive body armor.

Regular Security Checks

A regular check on secure areas is required to ensure that the integral security of a location is maintained, as well as to identify any breaches of security. Surveillance devices and intruder-detection systems should be tested frequently to ensure that no unregistered faults develop.

Vulnerable Materials

Vulnerable materials might include water supplies, food sources, and ventilation systems that could significantly impact the company if sabotaged; The deaths of eight persons in the Chicago area due to the placing of cyanide into Tylenol capsules caused Johnson & Johnson to pull more than 100,000 bottles from shelves nationwide, at a cost of hundreds of millions of dollars.[3] Vulnerable materials might also include fuel storage areas, communications equipment, and high- or critical value storage containers. Vulnerable materials and their location should be sighted in a security plan.

Supporting Relationships

Within foreign, remote, or challenging environments, it is rare that any business operates within complete isolation, whether it is a gold mining operation in Kazakhstan, an oil refinery in Indonesia, or a textiles plant in India. Establishing a good rapport with external agencies can provide some degree of sharing or transfer of risk responsibility. External agencies can provide invaluable support in identifying threats through the use of good intelligence as well as provide risk reduction measures. They may also be useful in assisting with incidents and contributing to their positive resolution and closure. A good example is the link between the civilian police and the military for the security of sensitive locations, with the provision of accurate intelligence, interception of known individuals, area cordoning support, handling of individuals, and any crime scene investigations that may result. Comprehensive joint exercises with agencies that provide assistance must be included in the risk management program. If necessary, external support representatives should be included on the crisis management team.

Crisis Management Element

The structure of the company's organization as well supporting security vendors or external agencies will govern the structure and membership of a crisis management team. The team will be responsible for coordinating all activities during a crisis event, both internally and with external groups, individuals, and agencies. The contingency plan should define the requirements expected of and from this team, their level of authority, what they are permitted to do, as well as seeking to identify the key personnel and redundancies prior to an event occurring (see the Crisis Management section).

Corporate Image and Public Confidence

Establishing a well-trained public relations department to deal with media and general public inquiries is necessary to ensure that an organization reduces potentially harmful press coverage during normal operations, but especially in the event of an emergency situation. The establishment of effective communication plan, media, and accurate reporting measures, or a "crisis communications system," ensures that the collation of information is swift and accurate, with an efficient means of delivery to the relevant elements of a crisis management team, employees, their families, often antagonistic news media, and other relevant agencies, in a timely and accurate manner. Some corporate and public image aspects to contingency planning include:

- *Public relations department.* Companies should establish an effective intermediate body between the management executive and external agencies (media, families, government) to ensure that the corporate image is promoted and maintained, while avoiding unnecessary speculation and inaccurate allocation of blame by the media or general public. Erroneous speculation often leads to a loss of confidence within an organization and undermines the aims and value of the group. A company may wish to provide training as well as pre-prepared public announcements to respond to likely threats, thus ensuring that staff are readied, with supporting materials, to deal with an incident quickly and effectively.
- *Effective communication mediums.* With the rapid technological advancements in communication systems, the swift and accurate passage of information on a global scale is now possible. This is critical for the maintenance of morale and corporate confidence

through the provision of accurate information and timely reassurance. The contingency plan aspect of the risk management plan should highlight communication shortfalls and mitigation measures to ensure that multiple communication mediums are available to support a crisis event. A detailed communications plan should be established to deal with both normal and crisis events.

- *Accurate reporting measures.* It is vital that management personnel have a clear and unambiguous understanding of how to pass on information, in what format, and to whom. Communication methodologies should form a cascade chain of reporting, from employees who might be the source of the firsthand information and incident management, to the crisis team that then takes over the management of the situation. The swift and accurate passage of information from the initial incident source to the crisis management team is critical for the successful activation of appropriate personnel and the employment of the necessary countermeasures, to minimize the potential damage a crisis event can cause. A set of clearly established protocols and information dissemination points will enhance the timely delivery of information, as well as ensure that the initial source is identified for future verification. Accuracy of reporting also reduces the potential for erroneous wasting of valuable time and resources.

Understanding Different Focus Levels

It is important both within the company but especially within supporting vendors and agencies that the different levels of focus and need are understood. Corporate officers will require support in terms of strategic planning and business continuity requirements, while project managers will be dealing with more front-end related issues, such as resolving immediate and granular-level requirements. Many focuses and needs will overlap, where both groups will be striving to reach the same overall goals. However, the focus areas associated with each will determine what information or participation is required within different groups. It is especially important that vendors understand the different needs and expectations of their clients in order to better support them: The field security management deals with the immediate requirements of the crisis while the corporate management assists with business continuity planning and strategic issues.

Contingency planning presents an opportunity for the company to reduce the level of risk to its business activity, as well as establish a plan to deal with problems while not under the pressure of the crisis event. Many organizations pay only lip service to the creation of a pragmatic and current risk management plan, which results in serious mismanagement during an incident. Those organizations that plan ahead often avoid significant problems and respond in a manner that considerably reduces the impacts of a crisis and supports overall business continuity.

CRISIS MANAGEMENT

Crisis management is the response to a problem while it is occurring, or following an incident. Should the risk mitigation measures not be successful and the security or risk management measures be breached, methods by which to reduce potential business impacts, disruption, or losses should be readied for the crisis management team to implement. According to the Reputation Institute (www.prsa.org), which conducted a survey of affected companies following the September 11 terrorist attacks, those companies identified as having a disaster policy dealt with the aftermath far better than those that did not have any contingency planning or crisis management procedures. In addition, impact studies following incidents ranging from Hurricane Andrew to the Oklahoma City bombing have shown significantly increased morale and lower distress in companies that responded with appropriate support for its employees,[4] which suggests that effective crisis management has a real and positive impact on a company's effectiveness, and that the absence of crisis management can compromise a company's reputation, operations, and productivity. There are effectively three forms of crisis that might face a company:

1. *Strategic crisis.* Changes in the business environment that call the viability of the company or activity into question (e.g., the loss of productivity, hindrances to operations, serious equipment losses, or injuries or deaths that undermine commercial ventures).
2. *Public relations crisis.* This crisis is more commonly called *crisis communications* (e.g., negative publicity that could adversely affect the success of the company, media coverage of liability claims, reputational damages, employee morale issues, and publicized government and legal investigations that can affect stock shares and company confidence).
3. *Financial crisis.* These are typically short-term liquidity or cash flow problems and long-term bankruptcy problems. Financial crisis can often result from strategic and public relations crises.

Crisis Management Flows

Crisis events may be short-lived or may occur over a protracted period of time, although even with short-term crisis events the effects may linger for significant periods and have far-reaching consequences. For short-lived crisis incidents, the event itself might occur over a very brief time frame—such as a shooting, an explosion, and road traffic accident—with the crisis management phase being completed quickly. For an extended crisis, the event may occur over weeks, months, or even years—an evacuation, an oil spill, or a kidnap and ransom case—and the crisis management phase may develop into an entirely separate entity in itself, with its own unique contingency plan. The company response and management tempo will reflect the life span of the crisis event and the implications of the post-incident management requirements. Vendors should also seek to match the pace and requirements of the company, being agile and proactive for a short-duration crisis, and being measured and responsive for more extended crisis events. Typically a crisis is defined in terms of immediate, interim, and long-term needs, with the activities within each stage of the crisis flow being compressed or extended by the immediacy of the event requirements or driven by business needs, as illustrated in Exhibit 4.23. Establishing immediate actions that bring the greatest level of control over a situation, such as stopping all personnel movement or locking down a facility, will also support the initial stages of the crisis management flow. Such actions should be part of the incident management plan. Convergence is also imperative during crisis events, as a multi-divisional approach is often required to ensure effective management and recovery.

Exhibit 4.23   Crisis Management Flow Example

Trigger Points and Decision Matrixes

Defining when a problem becomes a crisis is important as perspective may play a part in specifying when a crisis is actually occurring. The need to evacuate a nuclear reactor facility may occur when several risk levels have been breached: Insufficient electricity is being provided to power a water pump, the reactor water cooling system fails, the redundancy systems fail, and a reaction reaches a critical temperature. Contingency plans should define trigger points that identify when a problem has become a crisis; Is it at the point when electricity supplies run low, or is it when the temperate of the reaction reaches a certain point? Trigger points can also be used to avoid a crisis by identifying an approaching problem and implementing measures by which to avoid the effects. Consider these examples: Elections are imminent in a volatile region—*evacuation plans are reviewed*; public disturbances start occurring—*nonessential staff withdraw*; government forces use unnecessary force on civil gatherings—*remaining personnel move to a safe location*; mass riots occur—*the company withdraws completely from the risk area.*

Decision matrixes also enable effective decision making by those best placed to determine the required courses of action responsible for deciding what should occur, and when, as company management should not be debating which employee has decision-making authority while an emergency is under way, as this impedes clear and effective management. As a crisis escalates, the decision-making authorities may ascend upward to the executive board, and the point where the impacts breach certain authorities should be clearly defined—forming a clearly defined command structure, with each level containing certain authorities and permissions.

Information Flow

Within large organizations, information flow under the best of circumstances is often poor. Under crisis situations, the flow of information becomes even more disjointed and

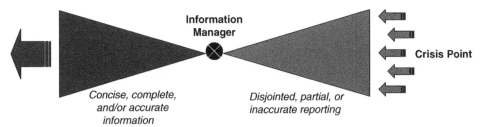

Exhibit 4.24 Information Management Flows

inaccurate, as the event will inherently create confusion, and management is often absorbed in dealing with the issues and so may fail to channel accurate information to supporting or corporate or field offices. Information managers are typically those managing the incident at the field level, or risk or security directors within the company corporate offices. Where multiple management elements are involved, it might be useful to designate key information managers (or focal points) who collate multiple sources of information to streamline information flow and assist in ensuring that information is accurate and channeled to appropriate parties. Where possible, multiple parties should funnel information into these capture points, which then feed condensed and accurate data on to decision makers, as illustrated in Exhibit 4.24.

Incident Response versus Crisis Management

The effective management of a crisis situation will be conducted by a number of response groups, each undertaking unique tasks, but with many overlapping functions. For the purposes of simplicity, two groups are often required:

1. *Incident response team.* Its responsibilities are to deal solely with the specific event in hand, the micro-crisis, focusing mainly on the security and safety aspects of the event itself. The team will have tactical decision-making authority to manage the actual event, feeding information upwards to enable strategic decision making by corporate officers.
2. *Crisis management team.* The responsibility of this team is to coordinate the activities of the incident response team in alignment with external agencies and groups, as well as manage the macro-level impacts and effects beyond the actual incident itself. This group will be looking at the holistic impacts and requirements, making strategic, rather than purely tactical level decisions.

The combined activities of both groups are designed to ensure that a company is in a position to respond to postulated threats in a timely, coordinated, and effective manner. Top-level management commitment is critical for the success of the crisis response policies and procedures. Where vendor companies play a role within both levels of a company's crisis management structure, clear understandings or responsibilities and permissions should have been established within the contingency planning section, as well as a coordinated, as far as possible, and seamless fusion of different organizational and management elements.

Crisis Event Management Tiers

It is arguable whether some groups should be considered a crisis management or incident response team. The defining point is whether the group is focused purely on the incident in isolation, or whether it is responsible for dealing with matters outside of the event: effectively micro- or macro-level decisions and responsibilities. Typically the crisis event will be dealt with at various levels, from the event source to the corporate executive level. In order to better coordinate activities and information, it is important that there occurs a management fusion at each level within the company as well as with corresponding vendors or team members. The company should expect appropriate offices and management staff to be part of any key vendor response and information chains during a crisis, rather than feeling unadvised or ignorant of the situation. A solid company-to-vendor relationship will ensure that more accurate and timely information flows between the groups, improving decision making and overall event awareness.

The company should define with any security vendor their preferences and requirements for communication traffic during a crisis event, as often the company Project or Program Managers feel that their corporate offices are too involved in the event, or that they themselves have not been provided sufficient time to understand the scope and impacts of the problems before their executive management are asking questions and demanding action. A conflict within the company's own organization is therefore common during crisis events, requiring clear guidelines and policies, as well as diplomacy and a balanced approach to multilevel involvement. Tiering the crisis management structure helps companies understand the different focus areas, as well as the spectrum of levels involved within a crisis event, as illustrated in Exhibit 4.25.

The company and security vendors should collaborate to determine the structure of the crisis response levels, functions, and responsibilities to align structures, policies, and procedures to best match crisis requirements. The event itself will also influence significantly the manner in which such response and management teams are established and how they operate. An example of a typical event chain of management functions follows.

- *Source incident response team (IRT).* A close protection team leader deals with an improvised explosive device (IED) that has damaged a vehicle and injured two passengers—this group acts as the local or event IRT.

- *Project IRT.* The project security manager coordinates organic assets to support the extraction of the team, liaising with the program security manager—this groups acts as the immediate event management or local coordination IRT.

- *Program crisis response team (CRT).* The program security manager coordinates military support and provides advice to the project IRT as well as information and recommendations to the country CRT—this group acts as the area crisis response team.

- *Country CRT.* The country CRT advises the program CRT and coordinates macro-level decisions with the corporate CRT and the executive management of the client and its own company. It may inform the embassy—this group acts as the regional or country crisis response team.

- *Corporate CRT.* The corporate CRT advises the country CRT and deals with the family and press, determining reputational, legal, and holistic company impacts—this group acts as the corporate crisis response team.

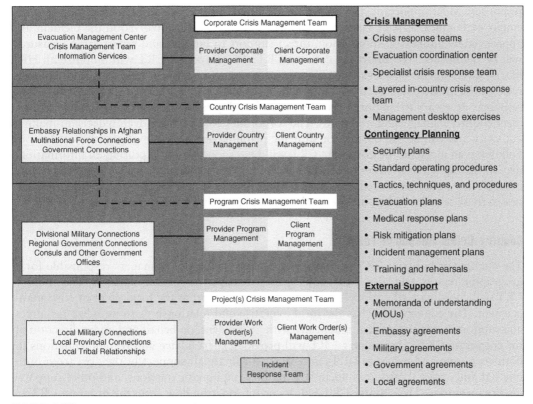

Exhibit 4.25   Crisis Coordination Planning

CRISIS MANAGEMENT TEAM LEVELS AND STRUCTURES

Companies will organize their crisis response teams based on a range of factors, including corporate structures, risk policies and management approaches, risk tolerance levels, geographic and industry influences, and partner or vendor participation. Each business activity may also bring unique requirements to the composition of a crisis team, either internally or from outsourced support. The next sections provide generic group compositions that typically are found in companies with well-established crisis management teams.

Corporate Crisis Response Team

The corporate crisis response team (CRT) will liaise directly with any vendors or teammates in order to ensure that all appropriate measures are being taken, in terms of operational support as well as business continuity, legal, liability, reputational, and media liaison. The vendor's corporate CRT should also ensure that close support is offered at corporate levels throughout the incident, providing all information and documentation requirements. In addition, the corporate CRT will ensure that human resources (HR), media, and legal groups are linked between vendor and teaming companies to coordinate any information releases or responses. Most important, the corporate CRT will ensure that information sharing with employee families, as well as support and care for any persons involved in the incident are appropriately addressed. In addition, direct support to families and repatriation measures will be established to support the country CRT. The corporate CRT will mobilize all HR, media, government, and legal specialists in order to offer support, guidance, and management of the incident and personnel in practical resource terms. This team, will also mobilize resources necessary to support a crisis event and deploy specialists and support staff to augment country management initiatives. The corporate CRT will have overall decision-making authority and will be responsible for strategic planning and senior-level government liaison. Following an incident, the corporate CRT will be responsible for capturing all information, decisions, and details in order to conduct an audit of the incident, as well as provide instructions on any policy or procedural changes. This team will also determine whether the business activity remains viable, or whether business approaches require change.

Country Crisis Response Team

The country or national CRT is comprised of the most senior managers responsible for a geographic region, typically led by the country manager or general manager. The country CRT will coordinate all national-level activities and support as the focal point of crisis management. The country CRT has the local expertise and relationships to mobilize resources and support in-country to deal practically with an incident, on behalf and under direction of the corporate CRT. The country CRT will provide expert advice and recommendations to both corporate and program CRTs and also coordinate all support in the area from both internal and external resources, including military, diplomatic missions, and other supporting organizations. The country CRT will focus information flow from the program CRT to the in-country security vendors and teammates, as well as act as the coordination point for tactical and strategic level advice, requirements, decision making, and actions.

Program Crisis Response Team

The activity or program CRT is principally led by the most senior security consultant or company program manager within the program. If a company or vendor security manager leads this team, they typically do so in close partnership with the senior company program manager. The point at which management decision making transfers from the program manager to the security manager must be defined in order to streamline decision making—as often the program manager will initially lead decision making during the initial stages of a crisis, up until the crisis has reached a certain stage and operational decision making becomes more important. The program CRT manager and their staff must ensure that all security staff and supporting military, medical, and other external service support are directed to assist the local incident response team commander in order to effectively extract personnel and assets from the risk area, as well as ensure that any medical support is readied to receive casualties. In addition, the program CRT will often integrate any vendor's or teaming partner's staff into the existing client program CRT, to ensure they complement each other's efforts, and avoid duplication or unnecessary confusion or friction. The program CRT's secondary function is to notify all company management chains of the incident, in order to initiate the country CRTs. At appropriate junctures, the program CRT manager will provide agreed-upon documented accounts of the status and details of the incident as well as formal serious incident reports. The vendor program CRT should be expected to conduct similar reports and documentation concurrently, liaising with its own country CRTs. The program CRT will typically report directly to the country CRT.

CRISIS MANAGEMENT TEAM STRUCTURE

The composition of the CRTs should reflect the personnel required to analyze and deal with any events, from the management or command elements to specialist advisors. Hierarchy and politics should not be an aspect of management selection; rather responsibilities should be attributed based on competence and experience. The role of the crisis management team is to be in a position to respond effectively to postulated threats or actual events in a timely manner. Top management commitment is critical for the success of this team; the outcome of a crisis affects not only business success and corporate interests, but perhaps more importantly can impact the lives and the jobs of employees—people who are dependent on the skills of management to see them, and at times their families, through the crisis. The various levels of CRTs will flow information and recommendations up to the corporate management or executive board while having autonomy of decision making within certain agreed and defined parameters. The level of decision making, responsibility, and authority will vary from corporate down to project CRT, as well as down to the event IRT. When considering a generic CRT, however, these appointments might be used:

- Crisis management team commander
- Administration manager
- Intelligence or information officer
- Physical/risk security manager
- Technical security manager
- Liaison officer
- Crisis communications manager
- Public relations officer
- Legal counsel
- Stress trauma advisor
- Reception team manager
- Finance officer

Crisis Management Team Commander

The crisis management team commander (CMTC) makes the executive decisions, based on the advice and information provided from relevant subject matter experts. This individual should be able to make calm and analytical decisions based on the organization's set mission statement and policies, balancing these with a clear understanding of the wider issues. The CMTC should be able to conduct concurrent activities and absorb and respond to information in a dynamic, logical, and pragmatic manner. Following an incident, the CMTC should oversee the conduct of a comprehensive review of all policies and measures in order to update the risk management program. The CMTC should be supported by a second-in-command who takes over in the CMTC's absence and provides support and advice during intensive incidents. This post may be held by, or report directly to, the CEO of a company.

Administration Manager

All events require the accurate collation and documentation of information as well as the practical mobilization of resources and support to deal with a crisis event. The administration manager may be tasked with providing documental control, gathering facts and details of those involved in the event, booking flights, allocating and making available monies to procure resources, identifying internal and external resource providers, plus a myriad of other mundane but essential tasks.

Intelligence or Information Officer

The intelligence or information officer acts as the central point for all intelligence data, compiling information into an easily usable medium. This person should provide advice and guidance in order to ensure that decisions are based on accurate and up-to-date information. He or she should liaise with other intelligence or information agencies to provide mutual support, including with government, military or commercial agencies. The intelligence or information officer should be supported with an intelligence department (where appropriate) providing all necessary task and administrative assistance.

Physical and Risk Security Manager

The physical and risk security manager is responsible for risk management advice as well as physical security measures and the management of security personnel. This manager should provide tactical advice and knowledge as a subject matter expert, allowing security countermeasures to be implemented effectively. This manager should entrust the practical command of response teams to well-trained and experienced sub-commanders, who deal firsthand with any incidents from the incident control point. This post looks at both strategic and tactical impacts and ramifications, and advises the CMTC directly to ensure best courses of action and decision making is possible.

Technical Security Manager

The technical security manager is responsible for the technical aspects of security, through the provision of specialist advice and guidance on technology systems used as part of the contingency plan and crisis management procedures in order to most effectively utilize any technical assets available in the provision of information to the CMTC as well as to prevent intruder access. The technical security manager should be supported by specialist personnel who conduct the daily maintenance and installation of equipment. Typically this post will report directly to the physical and risk security manager.

Liaison Officer

The liaison officer (LO) is responsible for interfacing with any external agencies in order to arrange support for the immediate response to an incident. This officer should identify any external assistance required, provide an initial warning to these groups, and report their readiness to the CMTC. The liaison officer will act as the intermediary between these agencies and the CMTC during and after the incident, depending on its severity and nature. The LO should also work closely with the physical and risk security manager to ensure coordination of measures and advice is achieved. For some organizations this function will be undertaken by the physical and risk security manager.

Crisis Communications Manager

The crisis communications manager is responsible for ensuring the accurate and timely delivery of information to relevant personnel. This manager acts as the focal point for all incoming and outgoing information, assisted by a communications department that will manage communications equipment. It is the communications manager's function to ensure that multiple levels of communication are available to support the crisis response measures and that a full and accurate list of points of contact are available, both internally and externally.

Public Relations Officer

While not necessarily an integral part of the crisis management team, the public relations officer is a well-trained intermediary or spokesperson between the organization and the media or civic leaders. The public relations officer can provide useful assistance in the positive delivery of information, enhancing the image of the organization externally as well as contributing indirectly to employee morale. Personnel from within the public relations department may also be involved in dealing with sensitive personal issues (related to employees or their families) requiring discretion and compassion when dealing with families and the local community. This post reports directly to the CMTC.

Legal Counsel

Serious incidents might have significant legal ramifications that will be an aspect of the crisis impact evaluation, guiding certain response measures. The legal counsel will be responsible for reviewing public announcements as well as advising executive management on the possible ramifications of the event and actions subsequently taken. This post reports directly to the CMCT.

Stress Trauma Advisor

It may be advisable for larger organizations to consider including a stress trauma advisor as part of the crisis management team, whether from internal resources or through external vendors, to provide advice and guidance on how to prevent emotional contagion, provide critical stress debriefings or crisis intervention group sessions, and minimize court settlements for emotional damage claims. This post should work closely with the Legal Counsel and Public Relations Officer, and report directly to the CMTC. Although many stress trauma measures are well intentioned, research into the Lockerbie bombing (terrorist aircraft attack resulting in the deaths of several hundred passengers) and the Herald of Free Enterprise disaster (British Ferry disaster resulting in the drowning of several hundred passengers) has failed empirically to determine whether these measures caused more harm than good.

Reception Team Manager

On mobilization of an evacuation, a crisis team may need to create a subgroup: the corporate advance and reception team (CART). This element should be prepared and equipped ready for dispatch to a reception country or point to lay the ground for a potential evacuation and relocation of company personnel. It should consist of a senior company representative and support and administrative staff. Its function will be to manage the reception of evacuees at a regional safe haven. The team's tasks will include: the booking of hotels, transportation, and follow-up flights; providing a focal point for liaison with external organizations; dealing with medical care and emergencies; procuring and preparing offices for the continuation of business; media management; accounting for all personnel and their status and reporting to corporate-level management on the general situation.

Finance Officer

The financial officer must maintain oversight over and authorize funds expended in the course of any crisis events, ensuring that procurements can be authorized quickly to support incident response requirements. The financial officer should also be available to provide expense history related to the affected operations and the forecasted implication in expenditure and incurred costs associated with a response.

INCIDENT RESPONSE TEAMS

The crisis incident will be tactically managed by several layers of incident response teams. The event IRT manager may be a working group engineer, a local manager or a security specialist—typically working within a remote or small project site. The project IRT manager will typically be a more experienced, and where possible a more trained and qualified, IRT manager, typically the operations manager or security manager within a project task. Their focus will be to maintain the safety of personnel and high-value resources as well as deal with injured persons or damaged equipment. While their primary focus will be the security and safety of personnel and critical assets, this can be best achieved only by informing relevant crisis agencies of the situation in order to leverage additional support, both in operational terms as well as for management, administration, and logistic support. The IRT will have tactical decision-making authority but will be directly managed and supported by the program or country crisis response team, as illustrated within Exhibit 4.26.

CRISIS MANAGEMENT TOOLS

Contingency planning should include developing tools and mechanisms that enable the flow of accurate information as well as authorized decision making and resource allocation to support the management of a crisis event. Communication plans, decision matrixes, procurement plans, and other tools and policies will support a crisis team to manage an event quickly and effectively.

Companies should also consider messaging plans, where appropriate personnel receive group messages to alert them to a crisis occurring. Such plans also feed information along

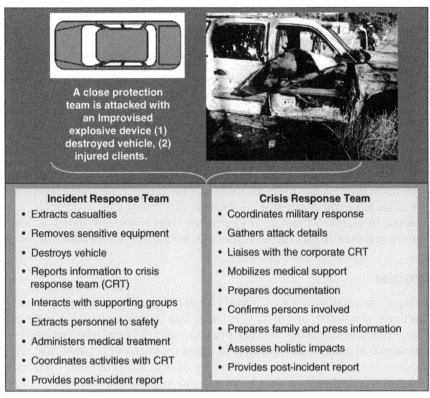

Exhibit 4.26 Relationship between the IRT and CRT

predefined channels through information managers. Messaging plans, however, should have clear parameters and methods of management to avoid erroneous or inappropriate information being released.

Information Cascade Systems

It is essential that a documented reporting cascade system is established at the outset of an activity, so that during a crisis situation, the correct people are informed as soon as possible. Cascade systems or phone trees provide an effective medium where information flows to focal or nodal points, who then have defined persons to contact. This way a clean and accurate delivery of information is achieved quickly. In addition, all contact details should be listed within an easy-to-use document, to avoid confusion and make the reporting system as efficient as possible. This document should also provide some basic guidelines, so that simple but fundamental errors are not made by the IRT/CRT during times of high stress. Such communication plans should be reviewed by all managers so that they are familiar with the requirements. These documents should be placed in operations centers and other appropriate locations, as a matter of protocol. Contact details should be double-checked and updated where necessary, as when needed the most they are often found to be inaccurate. Senior management staff should confirm that all submanagers are aware of the requirements and

Exhibit 4.27 Pragmatic Personnel Contact Sheets

Name	Appointment	Location	Phone	Email
J Smith	Program Manager	Site 1 (UK)	+ 2562235689 Off +256224789 Mb	J.Smith@client.com *The alternative point of contact is . . .*
S Jones	Security Manager	Site HQ	+2562112689 Off +256890789 Mb	S.Jones@client.com *The alternative point of contact is . . .*

guidelines and that they display these documents in the required locations. The simple chart in Exhibit 4.27 assists in the transfer of information.

It might also be useful to annotate any particular roles or responsibilities associated with each appointment if the risk management plan calls for ambiguous measures or procedures.

Report Templates

The reporting of information is also a critical element of crisis management. Often information is inaccurate, disjointed, or poorly presented. The company should develop pragmatic and user-friendly report templates in order to ensure that the right information is captured, that it is presented in a consistent manner, and that the correct people receive the reports. Serious incident reports might capture immediate data in terms of what occurred and the immediate impacts, enabling managers to receive succinct and accurate information and allow incident managers to request resources or assistance. Such templates also remove some level of burden from those reporting information, as predefined formats remove the requirement to identify information needs or presentation formats. Exhibit 4.28 provides a sample template listing some information that might be captured in such report templates. Note that each company, region, and activity may have unique reporting elements.

Exhibit 4.28 Information Management: Incident Reporting

Executive Summary:
Incident Facts:

• Project Name	• Report Date	• Report Time
• Country	• Region	• Site
• Incident Date	• Incident Time	• Incident Time Zone
• Killed	• Name(s)	• How
• Injured	• Name(s)	• Status/Condition
• Damages	• Nature	• Extent
• Losses	• Nature	• Extent
• Supporting Groups	• Agencies	• Activities
• Supported Needed	• What	• When
• Management Actions	• Current	• Planned
Reported by	Title	Phone/E-mail

Exhibit 4.29   Information Management: Strategic Planning

Executive Summary:		
Incident Facts:		

- Immediate Threat Picture
- Immediate Threats to Personnel/Business
- Immediate Response Requirements
- Sustained Response Requirements
- Highest-Risk Activities
- Low-Risk Activities
- Risk Review Requirements
- Recommendations

- Interim Threat Picture
- Interim Threats to Personnel/Business
- Interim Response Requirements
- Long-Term Needs
- Medium-Risk Activities

- Post-Incident Review Requirements
- Supporting Groups and Activities

Appendices:

* Serious Incident Reports	* Intelligence Reviews	* Causality Reports
* Communications Log	* Crisis Team Assessments	* External Agency Reports
* Actions Taken	* Policies Invoked	* Resources Engaged
Reported by	Title	Phone/E-mail

Corporate leaders may need another layer of information in order to determine strategic or macro-level operational requirements that will influence corporate decision making following an event. Vendors should seek to proactively identify business continuity considerations as well as how the company may wish to proceed in terms of risk assessment validations and post-incident audits. The template in Exhibit 4.29 indicates some areas the company's field and security vendors should be considering immediately after a crisis event.

It is essential that information provided is as accurate and detailed as possible throughout and following the crisis event. Assumptions should be avoided and educated assessments quantified so as to avoid inaccurate details being reported.

Dealing with External Groups

Each crisis event will be unique and will involve changing interactions with external groups, whether they are government support organizations or other commercial enterprises. Where a company has high-profile activities, or where a crisis event is significant, the media may seek information from both the incident site and the corporate offices. Typically program management should seek to avoid contact with the press, deferring to a nominated public relations representative. In addition, care should be taken in communicating directly with families; such activities are best conducted at a personal level rather than by indirect means, and they usually are undertaken by a corporately appointed spokesperson trained in managing sensitive situations. Companies may also seek local law enforcement support when imparting bad news to families, or when seeking to prevent press access to affected families.

Reporting and Record Keeping

Detailed documentation of the incident is essential to ensure that accurate facts are recorded and maintained, and to provide information for any subsequent internal review as well as possible government or civil audits or insurance and liability claims. Any documentation provided to external persons or groups should also be reviewed at the country CRT level (at a minimum) prior to being released, as poorly worded reporting can cause a variety of problems. Accurate and correctly worded reporting is also critical to ensuring that insurance for any injured person is awarded. Some suggested recommendations that might be part of the incident management plan information and communications section follow.

- Always gather accurate facts—never pass on assumptions or speculation as fact.
- Provide a contact report/situation report at the earliest opportunity. This will allow other management elements to provide external military and medical support to the incident management team.
- Do not liaise with press. Direct them to the program security manager, who will take instruction from the country CRT.
- Do not pass casualty details outside of IRT(s) until approval has been given by the appropriate CRT.
- Close e-mail and phone lines, if necessary, to mitigate inaccurate gossip being transmitted outside of the event country while dealing with initial stages of an incident.
- If a person is taken hostage/missing, it is critical that only those appointed to deal with the incident liaise with external agencies. Do not elevate the value of the hostage.
- In the event of an injury/death, the program administration manager will gather all personal details/medical documents to support the crisis management team. All such information should be relayed only through the program security manager.
- Injury and causality facts must be accurate—names, details, extent, location, and so forth.
- Warn military agencies for possible support requirements. This should be done at the local and regional levels concurrently where possible. Where possible, memoranda of understanding should have been established to support requests.
- Confirm facts again. Do this on a regular basis so that information is current and accurate.
- All external country liaison will be through the country CRT who will act as the initial focal point for major incidents, where possible.
- Conduct a local group brief at the first appropriate opportunity in order to pass on accurate information to the appropriate contractors. Conduct regular updates.
- When the situation is urgent, local security/operations managers must take immediate action using local military support, confirming actions as soon as possible with the appropriate CRT.
- Write all documents and reports in a manner usable for internal and external audits. Collate and deliver all materials to corporate offices for review and archiving.

TYPES OF CRISIS MANAGEMENT RESPONSES

While the aim of the contingency plan is to identify risks ahead of occurrence through the risk assessment, provide methods by which to avoid or reduce risks, and formulate response protocols and guidelines to manage crisis situations, there will always be unique elements to any event that require lateral thinking and a degree of problem solving. The company or

Exhibit 4.30 Risk Management Considerations for a Contingency Plan

Sample 1: Information Security

- **Contingency Planning**

A series of countermeasures are required to ensure that any information that may have been accessed by inappropriate individuals or groups is identified swiftly, in order to reduce further risk impacts. For example, encrypted graphic materials should be replaced if a threat of compromise is established. Security routines and policies should be amended to prevent known protocols from being used to breach security measures. Forms of identification and entry codes should be changed to reduce unauthorized access and IT assets should be checked to ensure that no interference of security measures or dormant viruses have been illegally installed.

- **Crisis Management**

If sensitive data storage materials are lost/stolen, the IRT or CRT may decide to immediately close ingress or egress to the site. The IRT may also implement searches of equipment and personnel to prevent materials leaving a restricted space.

Sample 2: Physical Security

- **Contingency Planning**

The type of physical security response will be entirely dependent on the nature of the physical threat. Access gained by passive civilians seeking publicity will be dealt with in a manner entirely different from a group of armed hostiles threatening life and property. A company facing some form of physically hostile threat should have the means by which to counter that threat as well as secure and clear key areas of unauthorized persons. Other physical security measures should be in place to support the human resources used, whether they are from the contingency planning assets (cameras, sensors, etc.) or equipment used solely as a crisis management tool (i.e., solidifying foam used to secure vital areas from intrusion or escape, tear gas, attack dogs, etc.).

- **Crisis Management**

Facility guards may be used to detain or arrest unarmed intruders. If an armed attack has been launched against a site and perpetrators have been sighted leaving the area and heading in a certain direction the CRT may call for the police to cordon the area as well as recommend roadblock locations based on known directions of travel.

Sample 3: Public Relations

- **Contingency Planning**

While not an integral part of the crisis management team, the public relations department can provide a useful link between the management and the media or general public. When an incident occurs, the focus of the executive element of the crisis management team is normally on finding and implementing a solution to the crisis event. However, the problem may have legal, ethical, and organizational ramifications, requiring the professional handling of information delivery and the positive maintenance of the "face" of the company. Clear and concise direction should be given to the PR department to ensure that the information disseminated reflects the corporate policy and any unique requirements.

- **Crisis Management**

An incident might be so dramatic that the appointed PR department is not structured or prepared to deal with the problems resulting from it. The corporate CRT might call for external specialist support to assist its own expertise in this area to better represent the company.

vendor security management provides value in its ability to use established polices and procedures and adapt them, where necessary, to reflect unique and dynamic requirements. Exhibit 4.30 provides some elements that might be included in a contingency plan—information security, physical security, and public relations—as well as possible crisis management responses during an actual event.

POST-INCIDENT REVIEW

Following any crisis, the company's management elements should conduct a detailed debriefing at all levels to ensure that mitigating measures were fully implemented and that any follow-up requirements are actioned. The post-incident review should define what went right and what went wrong in terms of the contingency plan, crisis response protocols, and management structures and decision makers. The aim of the post-incident review is to address gaps in order that future crisis situations may be avoided or better managed. Any supporting security studies, reviews, surveys, threat assessments, or other materials should be clearly stored for internal review as well as external audit. Management should be aware that audits can occur several months or years after the incident. Typically these auditing activities will occur following an incident:

- *Review the risk assessment.* Did it identify the risks and grade them appropriately?
- *Review mitigation measures.* Did they adequately offset the risks?
- *Review policies and procedures.* Were they detailed enough? Did they meet the need?
- *Review management.* Were managers properly prepared? Did they apply the contingency plans?
- *Review the vendor.* Did it provide the correct services? Did it support crisis management?
- *Review intelligence and risk data.* Are the risks still present? Is the crisis over?
- *Strategic planning.* What needs to be done in the immediate, interim, and long term?
- *Deescalating posture.* Can security postures be reduced? If so, when and where?
- *Reviews and audits.* What further reviews and audits are required? When, and from whom?
- *Adjustment.* What approaches, training, policies, and plans need to be adjusted?

The post-incident review for significant incidents should be conducted by those not directly involved in the event in order to establish an impartial review, although input and participation from the various groups that managed the crisis is, of course, required. Often, utilizing external auditing groups enables corporations to demonstrate, both internally and externally, that they reviewed the incident in a non-subjective manner.

MONITORING THE RISK MANAGEMENT PROGRAM

A risk management plan should be considered a living entity, subject to growth and change. An intelligence-driven policy will govern how the procedures are amended, adapted, or revised. The changing and evolving external socioeconomic and geopolitical influences should be used in concert with internal and external monitoring evaluations and validations, ensuring that security arrangements reflect the current threats and that the potential for complacency is minimized. An internal monitoring or assessment team can be used to test, evaluate, and exercise personnel in their responsibilities, ensuring that corporate policy is being effectively implemented as well identifying any areas for change or improvement. Such a team also is useful in the formal assessment of personnel, contributing to the evaluation of a crisis management structure as well as key individuals within it. External monitoring teams allow a fresh and impartial validation on how well formulated and relevant the current security policies and plans are. They can also contribute in a consultancy role, offering suggestions to the executive management on policy amendments and alternative methods of implementing security arrangements. External monitoring can be through unannounced spot checks, exercises, or allocated assessment periods.

External consultants may also be required to offer guidance on how to amend or adapt the risk management plan following a crisis incident. Many organizations, having successfully managed a crisis, slip into a state of euphoria, believing that they now have the expertise to overcome any future crises.[5]

In summary, it is important for any organization, whether commercial or government, to accurately determine the risks facing their corporate interests, business continuity, project activities, personnel, or facilities and establish plans and policies to address these wide ranging and often complex threats. The principal goal of a risk management plan is to protect people, resources, and the business interests of a group. Effective risk management allows companies to plan ahead, identifying and avoiding risks, or addressing them prior to occurrence. Companies with mature risk management plans and structures in place will be better positioned to weather a crisis and ensure business continuity, regardless of the nature of the crisis event. Effective risk management starts with an evaluation of risks, based on company perceptions and tolerances, and gleaned from qualitative information as well as professional judgments.

Companies then develop detailed risk management plans. These plans leverage internal, contracted, and external capabilities within a logically structured format, which identifies and meets each risk area through the logical process of assessing risk, establishing contingency plans, ensuring crisis response measures are prepared, and then reviewing and improving policies and procedures following an event. Risk management plans must be realistic, pragmatic, usable, and have group participation and buy-in to adequately reflect different levels of need. The correct focus and resources must be allocated to sustaining a risk management plan, and risk managers should propose the cost versus reward of mitigation investment as a business case.

Companies should unambiguously establish their risk tolerances to all management elements, whether internally to board members, risk managers and project leaders, or externally to security vendors who might need to align their approach and methodologies to suit their client's tolerance levels. All management elements should be aware that tolerances may change over the course of a business activity. The risk picture should be clearly defined, and risk probabilities and impacts should be clinically evaluated through quantifiable measurement mechanisms and tools. Contingency plans must reflect these risks and impacts, and should define whether a company chooses to avoid, transfer, share, mitigate, or accept each risk. Clear policies and authorities must be established to streamline management approaches, and both hard and soft risk management initiatives should be designed to meet physical and intangible threats.

Crisis management should be the last recourse of a company, as a well-designed risk management plan will avoid or mitigate most risks. However, well-structured management teams, the utilization of all available resources, accurate and funneled information channels, and prepared templates and response measures will enable the company's management to respond quickly to any incident in a well-rehearsed and coordinated manner, allowing for safer and more effective recovery.

Companies must define what a crisis is and where the tipping point between a problem and crisis lays. The flow of a crisis, from immediate to interim and sustained stages will have varying requirements, and these should be planned for. Efficiencies can be gained from prepared report templates, public release notices, and notification measures. Companies should seek to learn from each crisis event and review how well or badly their structures, managers, policies, and procedures fared following an incident, modifying and adjusting their plans accordingly, to enable them to better respond to future crises. A company that invests in risk management will transition through the crisis with less damage and confusion than a company that is forced to plan and manage a crisis concurrently.

Notes

1. Ian Mitroff and Christine Pearson, *Diagnostic Guide for Improving Your Organization's Crisis Preparedness* (San Francisco: Jossey-Bass, Inc., 1993), 23.
2. Ibid.
3. Ibid.
4. Bruce Blyth, "The Human Side of Crisis Management," www.cmiatl.com.
5. Ian Mitroff and Christine Pearson, *Diagnostic Guide for Improving Your Organization's Crisis Preparedness* (San Francisco: Jossey-Bass, Inc., 1993), 23.

CHAPTER 5

Scope of Risk

Companies operating both within their conventional business settings and in more unique operating environments will be presented with a wide scope of tangible and intangible risks. Executive leaders and risk managers must understand the nature, scope, probability, and impact of a varied spectrum of risks challenging their corporate interests and business activities, so that threats can be avoided or mitigated through sound contingency planning. Understanding the scope of risk also enables companies better to manage crisis events, as the direct and associated effects of a risk will be more fully understood and planned against before they occur. Security vendors must also be able to place risks into a company-specific and commercial context, as risks will be perceived differently and result in unique impacts for each client company. In addition, companies should also be mindful of how risks impact their teammates and subcontractors, as a direct risk presented to their activity or personnel may have significant impacts on peripheral groups, which will in turn affect their operations. Company tolerance levels vary, and risks create ripple effects where the initial cause creates new risk types and impacts. Mapping the outward effects of a risk event and how the event affects both the company and associated groups will enable more productive business continuity.

This chapter is not intended to provide a specialist understanding of any particular risk type, as each element will be unique and may require significant training or experience within a particular industry field. Rather the chapter is designed to illustrate some general risk forms, from those with tangible or physical effects that can be measured more easily in terms of impact, to those that are more nebulous in their cause or effects—many risks bridge the gap between hard and soft effects. By seeing the holistic risk picture, companies can operate within corporate tolerance levels, achieving desired business goals. Exhibit 5.1 demonstrates how a risk can move from the physical to nonphysical impact categories, as each risk impact creates new risk elements.

For readers who may not have had significant exposure to placing risk within a project or business context, it might be useful to consider how each risk type might affect a fictional business activity, at both the field level and the corporate level. The next scenario is designed to create a project picture against which risks might be placed.

This scenario provides a basic framework in which to place the scope of physical and nonphysical risks against a business activity. Readers might find greater value using their own company's activities and areas of geographic operations as the context for each risk type, considering how their company's tolerance levels, project approach, and contingency planning and crisis response policies and procedures would be applied to each threat type.

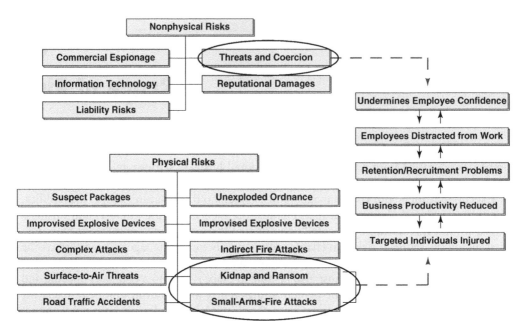

Exhibit 5.1   Varied Impacts of Risk Factors

The company has won a major health care development program in Sudan, funded by the United States Agency for International Development (USAID) with the contract award lasting up to four years. The main offices will be located in Juba and Khartoum, with 11 surrounding greenfield hospital build projects. In addition, field offices will be located within Janub Darfur and Junqali, with 32 widely dispersed community clinic projects. Four expatriate and 15 Sudanese office staff will be located in each main office, with 2 expatriate and 7 Sudanese staff in each field office. The award is valued at $210 million, and USAID has agreed to allocate up to 4% of the budget to fund security to ensure the safety of offices and the movement of company personnel, and to protect construction activities at the greenfield sites. It is anticipated that local contractors will undertake the majority of the construction tasks, with expatriate and Sudanese managers conducting quality assurance and management oversight, typically visiting each site weekly. The Sudanese government is very restrictive on Western security companies operating within the country, and only local Sudanese security companies may be armed or provide direct security services. Expatriate security managers may oversee local security personnel. Health care services are limited, and the region is politically volatile. Crime is rife and corruption common.

Some sites are large and complex, with valuable machinery and materials centralized in lay-down yards. Some sites have a high profile and sit within 100 feet of urban areas on well-traveled routes. Considerable logistical support is required, with large numbers of local project engineers and subcontractor construction workers on site, requiring varied levels of protection. The company has a charter flight to move people and small items from Khartoum to Juba, and this may be used for emergency support services as well. The company offices are open plan and used 24/7, with project information being openly accessible. Labor force payment is typically by cash, and the movement of large sums of money may be required. The company is still at the project design phase and has yet to determine what resources and approach methodologies are required. It has outsourced support to a risk management and security provider company experienced in the region.

NONPHYSICAL THREATS

There is a natural inclination for companies to focus more on physical threat forms when assessing the scope of risk, as these are simpler to envisage, and their effects often have hard and visual impacts on the company. Physical risk forms are also often more personal in nature and the psychological implications are more easily understood. However, it is important for the company to consider the more intangible risks the company or business activity may face in order to provide a holistic risk mitigation and security solution to support any business enterprise, as these more nebulous risks often cause more significant and long-term damage to a company and its employees than the more obvious physical risks faced. Nonphysical threat impacts may include:

- Loss of business competitive advantages
- Personnel or activities at psychological risk
- Recruitment, retention and employment issues
- Significant liability risks
- Loss of sensitive information
- An environment of suspicion
- An atmosphere of fear and uncertainty
- Impeded business activities and productivity
- Undermined reputation and image
- Loss of effective communications

Some nonphysical threats a company may face are discussed in the next sections.

Commercial Espionage

Commercial or industrial espionage includes the acquisition of sensitive commercial or government information through both legal and illegal means in order to steal, use, or acquire data that will give competitive advantages, technological or brand capacity, or undermine another group's business activities or reputation. Espionage can be unethical but legal, if information is gathered from discarded materials that come into the public domain. This may include riffling through the trash in order to find sensitive documents. Industrial espionage may also use both unethical and illegal means to gain information by theft of trade secrets, the use of bribery or blackmail, seduction and pretense, human and technological surveillance, and violence and intimidation. Industrial espionage may be undertaken by criminal groups, businesses or governments, or insurgent and terrorist organizations and often occurs during a tendering or product development period. Companies should identify which activities and individuals are most at risk from espionage and review the policies, procedures, and training in place to safeguard information and materials.

Threats and Coercion

Threats or coercion of company staff or subcontractors can be detrimental to the safety and welfare of individuals as well as to the productivity of the business activity as a whole. Critical personnel or entire workforces may not attend work if perceived at risk, and employees may feel forced to undermine the company by actively participating in illegal activities if they or their family are threatened. Isolated threat or coercion events, even when perpetrated by individuals or based on a hoax, can have widespread and dramatic effects on the morale of entire workforces and the success of macro level business activities, even when driven by individual and group perceptions, rather than a clinical assessment of risk.

It is important for companies to make a determination of the nature, extent, and likelihood of the risk, taking into account the welfare and safety of employees, corporate reputation, and the business continuity requirements. The company risk manager must make a pragmatic threat assessment, balancing the likelihood of the threat being implemented against the impacts the threat will have on the individual or group as well as the company operations. While the safety of employees is paramount, companies must also consider the legal liabilities in event of a threat being carried out.

The company must also evaluate whether coerced individuals are assisting (albeit unwillingly) criminal groups to protect family members, are seeking financial compensation for false claims, or are indeed at any real risk. Threats may be made to specific individuals or as a blanket statement to communities or particular groups. Threats and coercion may also be used as a business vehicle by unscrupulous companies seeking to deter competition. In some countries, criminal threats often are masked under the auspices of insurgency and terrorism. Companies should seek to determine the motive behind threats and coercion. Understanding the nature, likelihood and scope of any postulated threat can be developed, in part, by establishing the gender race, age, education level, voice characteristics, and mental or emotional state of the person making the threat, whether in person or by telephone. Any mention of a demand for money or other concessions will also assist in determining the nature and extent of the risk, confirming the motive, credibility, capability, and likely intention of the perpetrator(s).

The company should review security arrangements of employees, consider withdrawal or relocation of those most at risk, and determine mitigation measures to enable business to continue. Options may include ignoring any demands, attempting to deflect the perpetrator(s) by entering a dialog in order to cause a delay without actually dismissing the demand,

and negotiating for local government or community support. Companies may also consider threatening to withdraw from operations in the area, thereby laying off the local workforce; this move might generate external resolutions as a wider community is detrimentally affected. Law enforcement agency assistance may be sought, with the intention to plan an operation to arrest the perpetrator(s) during negotiations or a pretense of payment. Alternatively, modifications to operating procedures can be implemented to avoid or mitigate the risks. Companies should seek to quickly distinguish real from perceived risks posed by these threats, educate affected employees, and take remedial actions to protect staff and the business activity at risk.

Information Technology

The rapid advancement of computer technology has been matched with an equally swift development of computer-related crimes. In the 1980s, computer viruses were generally passed between users via floppy disks. Computer-related crimes could therefore be easily reduced through the purchase of software from reputable sources or by not copying programs onto floppy disks. Three developments in the 1990s drastically increased the variety and amount of potential damage a computer criminal could cause to a company or individual, making antivirus software essential for all computer users. The technological advancements of the 1990s also created large monopolies that naturally resulted in the development of a technological "monoculture," where the majority of information technology (IT) users run the same operating systems and applications. While this uniformity increases IT effectiveness, it also makes large groups vulnerable to the same worms or viruses, allowing malicious programs to propagate rapidly, while also exacerbating security vulnerabilities in software.

While the increase in IT efficiency and productivity has many benefits to companies, it also increases the dangers from computer-related crimes. The significant advances in IT, however, have not necessarily been matched by a realization of risk, and business operations are placed at significant danger by individuals and groups often operating from homes or from other regions and who can impact entire business lines and activities with a single contaminated e-mail. The effects of computer crime have increased dramatically since the 1980s and early 1990s, where computers communicated using normal telephone voice lines through an analog modem. By 1998, individuals wanting to use the Internet had their computer modem dial the local Internet Service Provider (ISP), which would assign a one-time numeric Internet Protocol (IP) address for that session, a dynamic or changing IP address that would automatically switch off if not used for a specific amount of time, allowing between 56,000 and 120,000 bits of information to be downloaded per second. Newer systems connect computers via cable television lines, allow for the transfer of much larger amounts of data, and are connected permanently to the ISP, which got rid of the usual connection wait time. Although this technological advancement increased the efficiency of the system, it has a negative side. It is more vulnerable to hackers downloading far more malicious data onto systems or gaining access to the computer at any stage once the IP address security measures are breached, as they are static and remain constant.

The complexity of computer systems also creates some unique problems for companies. As a typical operating system contains 200,000 to 25 million instructions, the number of logic states possible during execution in a multiprogramming or multiprocessing environment approaches infinity, making a full understanding of the program almost impossible.

It is not surprising that if the designers do not fully understand such systems, prospective infiltrators can easily take advantage of uncertainties created by such system complexity, hiding malicious programs within vast and complex programs. Many types of computer crime can be considered similar in nature to traditional crimes: theft of information, fraud, deceit, and so on. The huge scope of these offenses, coupled with a lack of physical criminal presence, sets computer crimes apart from those crimes for which a nation's laws were historically designed. Unlike a traditional theft or act of malicious damage, computer crimes can be conducted from an individual's home against a target in a distant city or country, with the amount of damage inflicted exceeding the physical limitations of traditional crime. It is estimated that the average cost of removing a computer worm or virus from each home or business is between $200 to $53,000. It is estimated that in the United States, the cost for removing each released malicious program ranges from $100,000 to $1 billion. Ironically, while the nature and scope of malicious programs has been known for decades, governments and commercial organizations are still grappling to comprehend the enormity of the situation and to provide effective countermeasures to combat computer crime. Widely available programs exist that are designed to exploit known computer vulnerabilities and contain mechanisms for self-propagation; an example is the *Ramen Toolkit* that was released for public use.

When considering computer crime, companies should define the nature of the criminal intent, as well as the activities the criminal engages in. There are fundamentally three forms of computer crime:

1. *Unauthorized use of a computer.* Stealing passwords, accessing a computer, and so on.
2. *Creating or releasing malicious programs.* Damaging systems and data.
3. *Harassment and stalking in cyberspace.* Causing fear or alarm to individuals.

Additional classifications of computer-related crimes could include the use of computers for commercial or criminal gain, the damage inflicted by voyeurs, and the harmful use of IT by hostile governments, criminal organizations or terrorist groups.

Computer crime for criminal or commercial gain prompted the 2002 United Nations Congress on the Prevention of Crime and the Treatment of Offenders to invite governments to carefully consider plans offered to formulate legislation policies to deal with computer-related criminal activities. The United Nations voiced serious concerns about the rapid increase in computer-related criminal activities, especially those connected to organized crime, notably for the sale and distribution of narcotics. In addition, the American Bar Association conducted a survey of 300 corporations and government agencies in 1987, of which 72 claimed to be victims of computer crime over a 12-month period, with damages ranging from $145 to $730 million. In 1991, another survey of 3,000 businesses indicated a noticeable increase, with 43% suffering from computer related crimes.[1]

Companies can find themselves limited in terms of legal responses when dealing with computer-related crimes. Often government agencies are also constrained by existing laws as well as the transnational nature of the criminal activity. It is interesting to note that the classic definition of burglary under Section 9 (1) (b) of the Theft Act 1968 (British law) is when a person "enters a building (or part of a building) as a trespasser with the intention to steal, inflict grievous bodily harm, rape or cause damage." The Criminal Damage Act 1971 states it is an offense to "recklessly or intentionally damage property." Computer criminals, whether working as individuals or as part of an organized criminal group, can effectively burgle a premises, whether real or in cyberspace, in order to manipulate data systems for fraudulent purposes, inflict damage, or steal intellectual property, often with the intention of damaging the organization they have illegally gained access to. The punitive actions taken against cybercriminals, however, do not reflect the level of response against physical crimes of the same nature.

Individuals who take on an assumed identity in order to convince victims to provide information for fraudulent activities are called "phishers." Criminals may set up bogus Web sites to secure credit card details or other useful information, extracting information through false pretenses. Often information is gathered by illegal intrusion of a victim's computer or by copying existing Web sites. Citibank has been a popular target for phishers, and the Federal Trade Commission has established a consumer alert on this subject. Illegal intrusions into computer systems have often been used as a source of commercial gain. In 2004, Russian hackers illegally accessed Citibank and stole $10 million from its accounts.

Malicious computer crimes are usually instigated to disrupt or destroy IT systems, whether they are specific computers, service providers, or targeted Web sites. The most common malicious computer crimes are carried out through the introduction of viruses or worms into an operator's system. These can be introduced as part of a sabotaged commercial program, as an e-mail attachment, or via disk data. A more aggressive method of introducing malicious programs can be through the active intrusion of a victim's computer. If a company applies the rationale of a geometric series of propagation to the spreading infection of a malicious computer virus, it could be assumed that if it takes one hour for the virus to locate four addresses and infect them, then within ten hours, 1,048,576 computers could (theoretically) be infected. A few examples of malicious programs introduced to cause damage to government and businesses since 1988 follow. They indicate the impact these viruses or worms have had on a global business scale and illustrate the inadequate international policing countermeasures used to deal with this problem.

- One of the earliest examples of a malicious virus was the *Brain Virus* used as a form of advertising for a shop in Lahore, Pakistan, in 1986. Relatively harmless, it was quickly followed by programs such as the *Christmas Worm*, written by a German university student in 1987, which displayed the image of a tree before deleting itself. In 1988, the more harmful *Morris Worm* (by Robert Morris) infected around 3,000 personal computers (and approximately 5% of the Internet), effectively shutting these down, as well as some university and military computers. Morris was arrested, convicted, and sentenced to three years probation and 400 hours of community service, and was fined $10,050.

- In 1999, the first serious cases of rapid infection programs appeared. The *Melissa Virus* infected Microsoft Word 97 and Word 2000 programs, propagating by attaching itself to the first 50 addresses in the Microsoft Outlook e-mail program address book. It could also be transmitted via floppy disk and disguised itself, assuming the title of a trusted person's name. The *Melissa Virus* tampered with victims' hard drives and document files, greatly undermining consumer confidence and productivity. David Lee Smith was arrested after causing an estimated $1.1 million in damage and infecting approximately half of the U.S. business computers. In addition, his program caused the U.S Senate and Britain's House of Commons Internet communications to shut down. Despite the magnitude of damage caused, Smith spent only 10 months in prison and was fined a mere

$5,100. In a study conducted over three weeks in February 2001, more than 4,000 denial of service attacks were conducted every week in the United States. This figure has drastically increased, with denial of service attacks coming in the form of a flood of continuous bogus requests that overwhelm a computer or system, causing it to stall or crash. Such attacks aimed at CNN in 1995 were considered so serious they were brought to the attention of the U.S. president. Ironically, a 15-year-old hacker instigated the attacks. Despite numerous court appearances, he subsequently launched attacks against Amazon.com, eBay, Yahoo, and many other sites, causing untold commercial damage and lost revenues.

- More recent viruses have been designed to cause the computer to stall or crash by filling the hard drive with useless data. The *Siram Virus* in 2001 filled all available space on the victim's C drive and deleted all files and directories, forwarding copies of itself in such large numbers as to overwhelm the Internet. The nature and impact of malicious programs has grown since the first relatively harmless programs released in the 1980s. Malicious programs today render computers inoperable, alter or delete information, directly prevent businesses from operating, or are used to steal valuable or sensitive information.

Additional common dangers to businesses are malicious or criminal activities of former employees who leave a company with access codes, passwords, or having installed malicious viruses within a server. Companies should instigate policies to prevent former employees from retaining access to systems or having opportunities to damage the IT infrastructure before being terminated. In recent years, individuals have also attacked businesses and government agencies, including the White House and the Department of Justice Web sites. However, according to a May 2004 report from the Department of Justice, not all hackers seek to actively cause damage when entering restricted sites. Some consider intrusion a technical challenge and enter military, commercial, bank, and telecommunication sites for the thrill of overcoming difficult security barriers. While these voyeurs may not leave behind malicious programs, they can cause damage accidentally. In 1983, a group of young hackers broke into the Sloan Kettering Cancer Institute's computer in New York, which deals with the treatment of cancer patients. Although not entering with malicious intention, damage or alteration of files within this system could have resulted in the fatalities of patients. Conversely there are also small groups who call themselves the "hacker ethic," who believe they have the expertise to move through systems and networks without causing damage and indeed identify and cure malicious viruses on occasion.

The United Nations Tenth United Nations Congress on the Prevention of Crime and the Treatment of Offenders identified the Internet as a tool used by terrorist groups for business, communications, and intelligence-gathering activities, and urged member states to implement measures to shield communications and protect data storage. Terrorist groups or individuals have been known to access sites that provide information on the construction of weapons of mass destruction or the manner by which to acquire the materials necessary to build nuclear, biological, or chemical weapons. Terrorist organizations might also seek information on, or to damage, companies associated with high-profile government activities.

Computer-related crime is diverse in nature, intent, and impact. Whether offenders are seeking to use computers for financial gain, to cause damage for the sake of anarchy, to disrupt activities against specific sites as a personal vendetta, to enter restricted areas for the technical thrill, or are members of a hostile government or terrorist group, the outcome of computer crime has significant implications for business activities. Damage occurs through the theft, interruption, deletion, or alteration of information. The resulting economic cost and security implications make computer crime one of the greatest threats faced by developed countries and their businesses.

Effective countermeasures to deal with computer crime face a multitude of hurdles, made all the more difficult by the global aspect of these unique crimes. Hackers are resourceful and determined, especially if motivated by financial or personal incentives. The majority of computer users are easy victims, having only a basic understanding of the dangers that face them and the countermeasures required to avoid becoming a victim of computer crime. The difficulty in quantifying the damage inflicted and establishing the source and primary target makes investigations problematic. The national nature of laws, which are created with the interest of sovereignty as a central principle, coupled with limited police expertise, inadequate resourcing, and a poor understanding of computer crime, reduces the effectiveness of law enforcement agencies in combating computer crime and thus protecting the company's business activities.

While computer criminals are often ingenious and determined enough to overcome any obstacle placed in their way, there are a number of ways in which both governments and companies can reduce the likelihood or impact of the computer related crimes mentioned. The Organization for Economic Co-operation and Development (OECD) in 1983 undertook a study of the international application and harmonization of criminal laws to address the problems of computer crime, aimed at establishing conformity within the legal framework across member states while also enhancing mutual assistance in combating computer crime. Despite international efforts, much remains to be accomplished, including the fact that the emphasis of the OECD focuses on Western European countries, whereas the problem is a global one. The United Nations continues to address the problem of computer crime, introducing measures for the modernization of national criminal laws and procedures. While efforts are being made, it is clear that international measures, practices, procedures, and institutions are unable to deal adequately with the threat of computer crime. The modernization of laws to reflect these new types of crime requires cooperation between nations for crimes committed across borders, violating the sovereignty of numerous nations. Companies must contend with the problems associated with weak transnational policing, which still struggles in countering the significant economic and serious security threats posed to businesses by computer crime.

Policing agencies, often overstretched and under-resourced, also struggle to deal with hackers due to the difficulty in locating and convicting them, especially considering the transnational aspect of computer crime involving multinational jurisdictional issues. In addition, the difficulty in locating specific criminals often leads to innocent users being searched accidentally, either through misdirection by the criminals themselves or as a result of their information being held on a criminal's hard drive. The U.S. Secret Service has been criticized by such organizations as the Computer Professionals for Social Responsibility for searches and seizures of suspected hacker premises. The problem concerning searches that move between the real world and cyberspace is that the interconnectedness of systems in cyberspace can lead law enforcement quickly from a simple search of one party to a multiparty, multicomputer search that could ensnare the innocent as well as the guilty.

Talented computer criminals also have ingenious methods of foiling police agencies once caught. Some plant malicious viruses in their own machines that will erase data when opened. Incorrectly closing down the computer may also activate these viruses. Some criminals plant explosive ordinance in their hardware to physically destroy the system as well as injure or kill those handling it. Magnetic fields may be employed, with a degaussing loop or ring placed around a doorway to erase magnetic data when the machine is taken from the room. A global policing approach has yet to be designed and implemented to counter the vast array of measures used by computer criminals. Companies remain vulnerable the scope of IT risks and are limited in terms of prosecuting perpetrators. Companies should consider measures by which to transfer risk mitigation responsibilities and to ensure organic protection of their communication infrastructures and data management through a range of risk management means, including:

- *Service provider accountability*. ISPs have the capability, although at some cost to themselves, to scan all e-mails for viruses with antivirus software. Although this method has confidentiality implications, ISPs could reduce or deter criminal activities to some large extent. In addition, service providers can prevent the release of harmful information used in the creation of malicious viruses. Larger companies may contract ISPs for protective measures for their systems.
- *Contingency planning, crisis management*. Contingency planning and crisis management are fundamental measures by which to prevent a computer crime from occurring or at the very least to reduce any resulting impacts. Computers serve as repositories of information as well as instruments for action within nearly every aspect of our lives. Their importance within business continuity overall, and the impacts that poor use or management can result in requires a full and proper understanding of how to manage and control evolving technology. A prime contingency planning measure is training company employees to reduce the risk of security compromise. There are no foolproof measures by which to protect the company against the ever-evolving threat from computer criminals; however, a regular update of antivirus software will prevent most malicious programs from entering a computer system. This updating can be done weekly, monthly, or whenever a new virus is identified, depending on a company's particular needs. Erecting a firewall between parts of the computer system that are accessible to external users (modem or Internet) can prevent criminals from probing a computer or gaining access to important data areas. Should security be breached and a malicious virus or worm threaten a computer system, the easiest way to resolve the problem is to reformat the hard drive and recopy saved files. Should a computer system be destroyed or corrupted, the possession of redundancy data storage facilities is essential as a crisis management tool. Where possible redundant storage facilities should be located away from main sites to protect storage facilities from malicious or accidental damage.
- *Personal security*. The use of passwords can prevent computer criminals from gaining access to data storage areas. Obvious passwords should be avoided, as should the use of actual words. If companies use randomly generated passwords, hackers are prevented from using a word list from a spell checker. Instead they would be required to generate permutations of characters and numbers, which is far more difficult and time consuming. Of course, most computer users write their passwords down or direct their computers to remember them to save them logging back on should they leave their computer for a short period of time. This defeats the purpose of using passwords. Sensible company measures should be employed to make passwords as effective as possible.

■ *E-mails.* Many viruses or worms can be transmitted via an attachment to an e-mail. Three rules can be used to counter this:

1. Never open an executable attachment (i.e., an attachment with a file name ending in *.exe* or *.vbs)* without first knowing its contents and the source of the file. This may require you to contact the person who sent you the e-mail as the computer criminal may have disguised the message under a known person from your address book.

2. Never open an attachment from an unknown source. Reply to the sender and request that they send the attachment as plain ASCII text in the body of the e-mail.

3. Use caution with any attachments that have a double file extension (i.e., a three-letter code at the end of a filename, such as *.jpg.vbs).* These are executable programs that may be disguised as a picture or web-page.

■ *Stand-alone machines and wireless connections.* The probing of systems by hackers is a serious problem with computers connected to the Internet. Many hackers randomly run programs that probe computers connected to the Internet. If the port is open, hackers can tamper with the computer and may even use it to launch malicious programs against other computers. The amount of probing by hackers has increased dramatically since 2002. One personalized statistic found that in 2002, one computer suffered an average of 1.5 probes per hour; in 2004, that number had increased to 57 attempts per hour. Using a stand-alone computer that holds all storage data or sensitive materials removes the danger of probing. While technological advancements make the transmission and storage of data far more efficient, the ease of moving significant amounts of data across cyberspace also presents serious security issues. Wireless networks have an obvious security problem in that transmissions can be intercepted easily, violating privacy as well as being used for industrial espionage or other serious criminal activities. To reduce the potential for security breaches, information should be encrypted and transmitters should be located as far away as possible from exterior walls, especially windows, to prevent unauthorized remote accessing.

■ *Computer and identity disposal.* When a computer is being disposed of, all data and document files should be erased as a deterrent, and a WIPEINFO program should be used to overwrite all free space on the hard disk, making it difficult to recover data and document files. Disabling the hard disk by removing the integrated circuits or destroying it also prevents computer criminals from gaining useful information from a redundant or discarded computer.

■ *Insurance and deterrence.* Some companies attempt to deter hackers from targeting their sites by using a logo that states unauthorized use is prohibited by law. This, however, can be a double-edged sword; it may entice a hacker by increasing the thrill of the perceived challenge. Insuring information and hardware may be the only sure way to minimize the inevitable financial loss that occurs in the aftermath of a determined malicious attack.

Despite having some of the widest company risk implications, computer crime and IT security remains, for many, a black art. It cannot be held, felt, or seen, so establishing the nature and scope of the threat, especially within a quickly evolving environment, presents a challenge to many companies.

Reputational Damage

A business reputation is an intangible commodity whose value has serious, and at times devastating, consequences to a company if undermined. Reputation is the social or commercial evaluation toward a person, group, or organization. It is especially important to businesses whose stock values and market productivity are directly connected to their status within a commercial sector, or dependent on investor and client confidence. Reputation acts on different levels of agency, individual and supra-individual. At the highest individual level, reputation concerns groups, communities, collectives, and social entities, such as firms, corporations, organizations, countries, and cultures. It affects phenomena of different scale, from everyday life to relationships between nations. The impact of reputation within companies is often ignored, with no clear or tangible connection toward associated real impacts on business success and operations.

Reputation includes image, a global or averaged evaluation of a company, its activities, productivity, and capabilities, or executive management competence. Reputation often aligns with the perceived image or branding of a business. Image is a dynamic element and subject to immediate change, through either actual events or speculation and rumor. Misinformation or erroneous reporting can severely damage a company's image and thus reputation. Contingency planning and crisis management are fundamental aspects of reputation protection as recovery is often difficult, slow, and costly and can significantly undermine the company's business activities.

Liability Risks

Most legal systems operate on the premise of fairness and justice, penalizing organizations or individuals who cause harm to a company or its employees. Liability can also be inward looking, where employees seek compensation and redress from failures resulting within their own organization, which is responsible for overseeing their general welfare, equitable treatment, and safety. Causation is required to establish liability, both in terms of *factual* causation—did the defendant's act cause the plaintiff's loss—and *legal* causation—are there policies or laws in place that hold the plaintiff responsible? Companies are subject to a range of laws and requirements that are engineered to bring about the safe management and treatment of employees within normal business environments. However, when companies operate in new and challenging environments, these policies may not accurately reflect new risk factors, and companies may place themselves at significant risk if they do not identify and address liability issues, or implement policies and procedures that show a pragmatic and real effort to avoid or mitigate risks.

PHYSICAL RISKS

Physical risks often present a hard and visual impact on a company. They also create the intangible secondary risks and impacts associated with reputation, liability, and the individual's perception of being threatened. The examples of physical risk provide a sample of some of the tangible threats commercial operations might face, whether operating in Mexico and being subjected to kidnap and ransom risks, or conducting business in a post conflict region such as Afghanistan or Somalia, where harsher risk natures occur. Physical risks may be relatively linear in nature, but are multifaceted in terms of risk mitigation and security management implementation methodologies. Physical threat impacts may include:

- Injuries and fatalities to personnel
- Damages to high-value materials
- Prevention of business operation
- Significant liability issues
- Restricted movements and activities
- Catastrophic damage to critical infrastructures
- Logistical problems for projects
- Threats posed to supply chain assurance
- Undermined employee confidence
- Secondary risks and damages

All of the risk elements mentioned above can also directly result in the non-physical risk natures already covered, as risks often span both the tangible and intangible categories. The next sections provide a sample of physical threats a company may face.

Improvised Explosive Devices

Improvised explosive devices (IEDs) have become increasingly popular with criminal, insurgent, and terrorist groups in hostile locations, especially where law enforcement and social controls are poor and where munitions are readily available. IEDs can have significant impacts on a company and its business interests by directly presenting risk to personnel and facilities as well as creating an atmosphere of fear that undermines business productivity and continuity. IEDs are a relatively simple way to cause significant casualty results to vehicles and/or personnel. Often they are placed in or carried to areas of high population density, such as marketplaces, job centers and lines, or other public gatherings. IEDs can also be used to damage critical infrastructures, with hazards formed from both the blast and fragmentation threats. IED initiation can be delivered through command wire, radio control, or mechanical activation, human delivery, and directional initiation or timer devices can be used to initiate the devices. IEDs take many forms, as illustrated in Exhibit 5.2. When assessing the risks posed by an IED, the meaning of an explosion and its effects must be considered.

- *What is an explosion?* An explosion is a sudden release of energy caused by a rapid chemical reaction, which turns what is usually a solid into heat and gas. The rapidly expanding hot gases created by the reaction pushes the surrounding air out in front of it, thus creating a pressure wave, known as the blast wave.
- *Effects.* There are six basic effects created by an explosion that cause damage and injury. These will depend on the power, quality, and quantity of the explosive material used.
  1. *Fireball.* The ball of fire is created as part of the explosive process very local to the seat of the explosion and is short-lived. However, it can cause damage to people and structures and ignite secondary fires.
  2. *Shattering.* This is the shattering and shearing effect of surrounding materials and structures (windows/doors). It is local to the seat of the explosion and is normally associated with high explosives and may cause fragmentation hazards.

Exhibit 5.2   Improvised Explosive Devices Examples
Source: Copyright © IEDS: US Military 2006.

3. *Primary fragments.* These are the fragments of the device and the packaging that are in close contact with the explosive charge. They are propelled at high velocity over a great distance. Primary fragmentation causes casualties and damage at a greater distance than secondary fragmentations.

4. *Blast wave.* This is the very fast-moving high-pressure wave created by the rapidly expanding gas of the explosion. It can bounce off hard surfaces and be channeled down corridors and elevator shafts.

5. *Ground shock.* Ground shock is produced by the effect of the explosion impacting the ground local to the seat of the explosion, sometimes creating a crater. The shock wave can cause damage to pipes, cables, and the like. Damage to gas pipes in particular may result in secondary threats.

6. *Secondary fragments.* These are the fragments that have been created by the blast wave imparting pressure on material unable to withstand the excess pressure. The materials that form secondary fragments are glass, roof slates, infill, timber, metal frames, and the like.

The U.S Embassy bombing in Nairobi resulted in significant secondary injuries to surrounding offices and buildings, which led to hundreds of serious injuries resulting from the blast wave and secondary fragment hazards. Blast-filming windows is a common method by which to mitigate the secondary effects of these threats. The hazard area associated with IEDs is defined by the quantity of the explosive materials used as well as the nature of the device. The use of chemical container vehicles may create secondary hazards, subject to wind and weather conditions. Delivery methods include being placed at the point of detonation, often either hidden or disguised, or being placed in vehicles or made to look like harmless objects. Suicide bombers, either pedestrian or vehicle-borne, or in rarer instances waterborne, might be used. Typical threat areas include the undersides of bridges, road embankments, road junctions and corners, underpasses, curbs, potholes, standing water, and culverts.

IEDs are simple to manufacture, can be created in large numbers and can be linked together to create a *daisy chain* effect. While not notably effective against armored vehicles (although the use of ball bearings as a fragmentation hazard do penetrate B6 armor), the blast and fragmentation hazard against soft skinned vehicles and people can be dramatic. IEDs can also be placed at project sites, waiting for a site visit, and can be left in place for long durations pending detonation. IEDs can also cause significant damage to critical infrastructures. Exhibit 5.3 illustrates the catastrophic effects of an incident which caused in hundreds of millions of dollars worth of damage at the Kirkuk Refinery (2006), resulting from a

Exhibit 5.3 IEDs Causing Critical Infrastructure Damages
Source: Copyright © Kirkuk Refinery 2006, M. Blyth.

small explosive device placed on a key structural feature. Intelligence-driven planning, choke point avoidance, situational awareness, route selection, and critical infrastructure protection play a key role in reducing this threat.

Unexploded Ordinance

Unexploded ordinance (UXO) presents a threat to personnel, materials, and facilities due to explosive hazard risks. There are hundreds of millions of unaccounted-for mines worldwide, typically along disputed borders or areas of historical hostility. These mines continue to present serious risks to the local populace as well as to companies operating abroad. Threat areas are rarely, if at all, properly marked. Clearance of movement corridors and work sites is often a challenge to projects seeking to operate safely within a region. Ordinance also is subject to drift, often being moved by rivers or shifting with land shifts or slides. The scattering of explosive ordinance can also make locating materials difficult to impossible, and shifting sand and dirt can also mask or uncover minefields. In some instances buildings and other structures may also be booby-trapped, with explosives inadvertently detonated by unintended victims. Companies should advise their staff on UXO awareness, including how to recognize explosive ordnance and minefields, whether marked with Western symbols or tin cans or sticks by the local communities. Companies should also invest time and resources in training staff how to avoid risks presented by UXOs as well as what to do if inadvertently caught in a minefield.

Suspect Packages

Packages left unattended by owners cause concern as potential explosive hazard threats, regardless of whether they contain harmful materials or not. Harmless or innocently left packages often significantly disrupt project operations as facilities are cleared of staff, work is impeded, and explosive ordnance teams respond to deal with any prospective hazards. In hostile regions, suspect packages can be used to waste the time of security forces or to elicit attention from security groups in order to enable hostile groups to conduct a staged ambush, effectively baiting the security forces to a location of choice. Exhibit 5.4 indicates some safety planning distances that risk and security managers may need to determine safe ranges

Exhibit 5.4   Safety Table for Unexploded Ordnance and Suspect Packages

Threat Description	Explosive Capacity (TNT Equivalent)	Threat Distances	Outdoor Evacuation Distances
Pipe Bomb	5 lb or 2.3 kg	70 ft or 21 m	850 ft or 259 m
Briefcase/suitcase bomb	50 lb or 2 kg	150 ft or 26 m	1,850 ft or 564 m
Small car bomb	500 lb or 227 kg	320 ft or 98 m	1,500 ft or 475 m
Large car bomb	1,000 lb or 454 kg	400 ft or 122 m	1,750 ft or 534 m
Passenger van bomb	4,000 lb or 1,814 kg	600 ft or 195 m	1,750 ft or 838 m
Small moving van bomb	10,000 lb or 4,536 kg	860 ft or 263 m	3,750 ft or 1,143 m
Moving truck bomb	30,000 lb or 13,608 kg	1,240 ft or 375 m	6,500 ft or 1,982 m
Semi-trailer bomb	60,000 lb or 27,216 kg	1,500 ft or 457 m	7,000 ft or 2,134 m

to place between personnel from a suspect package, as well as the implications to business continuity suspect packages or identified explosives will have upon a facility. Note that hard structures between an explosive device and personnel can reduce these distances.

Explosively Formed Projectiles and Penetrators

The explosively formed penetrator (EFP, or shaped charge) has become a form of IED that poses a serious threat to armored military and commercial vehicles used to move personnel in hostile environments, such as Iraq and Afghanistan. Capable of penetrating armor plating, the EFP is a relatively high-tech device that has been deployed using passive infrared radar (PIR) devices, much like garage door openers, to increase targeting accuracy, as historically EFPs and IEDs were detonated through physical observation of a vehicle passing the hidden device and were therefore inherently inaccurate. Hostile groups typically observe frequently used routes or road junctions to determine any patterns in order to specifically target of companies; alternatively, devices can simply be placed along commonly used routes and employed against targets of opportunity. Devices are generally used in areas where natural slowdown points exist, such as interchanges, steep curves, and traffic circles.

EFPs and platter charges may be similar in appearance, but platter charges have a flat, platter liner rather than the concave or cone-shape liner found in EFPs. An EFP's range and potential for armor penetration depends on its size. Typically explosives are packed or cast against the convex side of the cone or liner, and the projectile is formed through detonation into a liquid fingerlike object that can more easily penetrate armor. A platter charge, however, has a more blunt trauma effect, as illustrated in Exhibit 5.5. EFPs can be produced easily, often in small machine shops, using small sections of large pipe (8–10 inches long, 6-inch diameter) used for common industry purposes, as illustrated in Exhibit 5.6.

The main EFP charge may be placed on the curb alongside the road and angled upward or on top of guardrails. Charges can be covered in dirt, hidden in bags or old tires, placed into the carcass of a dead animal, or disguised using paper-mâché to look like rocks, and may be placed on the left side of the road in order to target the vehicle's driver. EFPs are

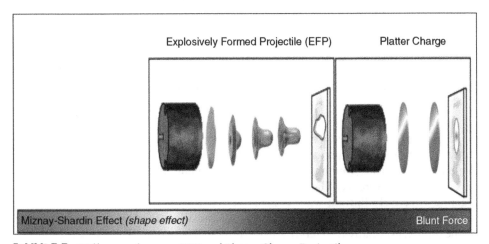

Exhibit 5.5 Differences between EFP and Platter Charge Projectiles

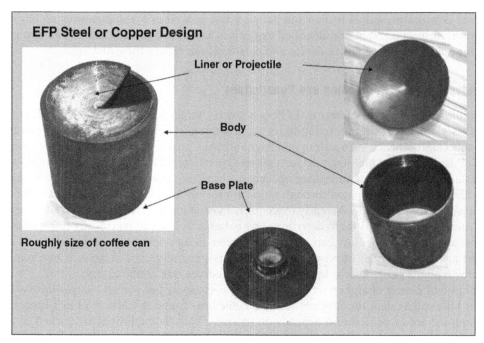

Exhibit 5.6   Small Workshop Machine Production of EFPs

effective weapons and present both physical and psychological hazards to a company. Platter charges are usually created with uniformly packed explosives set behind a metal platter (preferably round, but it may be square) in which the platter (metal plate) is pushed into the target. Penetration is rougher than with EFPs, with holes having a broken, punched-through appearance. Platter charges do not pose as serious a threat to heavily armored vehicles as EFPs do, due to the greater penetration factor the EFP poses, but they are more traumatic in nature.

Indirect Fire Threats

Indirect fire attacks (IDFs) provide easy targeting opportunities for hostile groups and have been used by terrorists and insurgents for several decades. In Northern Ireland, terrorist organizations used mortars and rockets to attack military bases with great effect and little risk to the instigator. The ability to target areas or specific structures from a distance and remotely from the weapon system reduces the risk to the user while concurrently making threat reduction measures difficult to implement by security forces, especially in urban areas, where the risk of a retaliatory strike (counterbattery) incurring collateral damage reduces response effectiveness as well as deterrence. The risks faced by IDF vary, depending on the operator's skill in targeting effectively (hitting what is being aimed at or getting a general area strike pattern), the size of the target area, the equipment used, and any secondary threats that could result from the attack, especially for facilities with combustible materials (notably oil and gas refineries and storage areas). The risks associated with IDF include:

- IDF damages to structures or buildings
- Resulting industrial hazards
- UXO clearance
- Follow-up small arms fire
- IDF fragmentation hazards
- Casualty management
- Evacuation procedures
- Follow-up complex attack
- Fires and explosions
- Mustering procedures
- Interagency support
- Civil population support

Companies can provide adequate risk mitigation and countermeasures to reduce the effects of IDF risks, including:

- Bunker requirements
- Overhead protection
- Safe havens
- Compartmentalization measures
- Retro-blast mitigation measures
- Detailed incident control plan
- Evacuation options
- Muster procedures
- Casualty management plan

Typical IDF weapons include:

- *107mm type 63 rocket*. The type 63 Rocket is a 41.5-pound rocket containing a main charge of dynamite weighing 2.86 pounds. The rocket is normally launched from an adapted launcher or from areas like dry riverbeds, pointed in the general direction of the intended target. The maximum effective range of the rocket if launched from a manufactured launcher is 16,400 feet. The blast area of lethality is 69 feet with a hazardous area of 1224 feet, which is greatly compounded if the round bursts in the air.
- *60mm Mortar*. The 60mm Mortar contains 0.5lb of dynamite. The mortar is usually fired from a single tube launcher, either hand held or bipod mounted, with or without a base-plate. It may also be fired from expedient launchers, either singly or in a series. The maximum effective range of the mortar is 8,200 feet. The blast area of lethality is 20 feet with a hazardous area due to fragmentation of 246 feet. Launchers can be wired to washing machine timers to enable the users to move away from the firing area before firing.
- *82mm Mortar*. The 82mm mortar contains 10lbs of dynamite. The 82mm mortar like the 60mm is fired from a singe launch tube or single to multiple expedient tubes. The effective range of the mortar is 16,072 feet. Like the 60mm mortar, multiple launchers can be wired to washing machine timers. The Blast Fragmentation area of lethality is 50 feet with a hazardous area of 1033 feet.

The effective use of an IDF is often hindered by a lack of effective command, control, and communications necessary for coordinated attacks. As a result, IDF attacks are rarely coordinated with the accuracy and timeliness necessary to cause maximum impact. Many groups tend to favor "shoot-and-scoot" tactics, necessitating quick and therefore inherently inaccurate setup, with a minimum number of rounds fired before moving away from the firing area quickly to avoid being apprehended. IDFs present an area risk to companies and can also undermine business activities as personnel may spend many hours in shelters while the risk is present, which can be both fatiguing and demoralizing.

Surface-to-Air Threats

While far less common than most typical threat types, in recent years air threats against commercial and military targets from insurgent and terrorist groups has become more prevalent in volatile regions. Man-Portable Air Defense System missiles (MANPADS), also known as surface-to-air missiles (SAMs), are highly effective weapons proliferated worldwide on the black market. Such devices typically contain an infrared seeker and offer little opportunity warning before impact, which is often lethal. They are designed specifically to facilitate the targeting of aircraft and do not discriminate between civilian and military targets. It has been estimated that least 500,000 MANPADS are available on the black market, making them particularly accessible to nonstate actors. Because they are extremely portable, weighing approximately 30 to 40 pounds and about 5 feet long, they can be easily disguised. Insurgent groups seek them because they are effective against the type of aircraft typically used in counterinsurgent operations, and they can be relatively cheap to purchase.

There are two principal ways in which to mitigate the threat posed by MANPADS: reduce susceptibility and reduce vulnerability. Susceptibility reduction measures are undertaken to avoid a hit or strike on an aircraft. Hit avoidance includes improved airport perimeter security measures and special aircraft ascent and descent behavior and countermeasures that divert the missile from the aircraft. Steep ascents and spiraling descents can reduce the amount of time that an aircraft flies in range of a MANPADS. Infrared decoy flares or infrared energy directed at a MANPADS can confuse the missile, leading it to follow the energy pattern of the decoy. Direct infrared energy can lead the missile off course. The use of flare systems may, however, pose a problem in heavily populated areas, due to their incendiary nature.

Vulnerability reduction attempts to increase the chances of survival if the aircraft is hit. This is particularly important for commercial aircraft, for which susceptibility reduction measures (i.e., flares and rapid maneuvers) may not be viable options. Vulnerability reduction alters or modifies the design of the aircraft and may include the hardening of vital areas that are vulnerable to MANPADS threats and the installation of fuel shut-off valves or self-sealing fuel lines and fire and explosion suppression systems. Redundancy and separation of flight controls and hydraulic systems are also design options to improve survivability of damaged aircraft.

MANPADS are highly effective and can be very lethal weapon systems. Evidence from Desert Storm (Iraq) indicates that such missiles produced 56% of allied aircraft deaths and 79 percent of allied aircraft damage. It is estimated that civilian aircraft face a 70% probability of casualties in the event of a MANPADS contact. During the Soviet occupation of Afghanistan, Stinger missiles supplied to the Mujahideen significantly degraded the threat of

Exhibit 5.7   MANPAD Capability Table

	Strela-2: SA-7 and 9K32M	
Maximum Range: 18,040 feet	Minimum Range: 1,640 feet	Maximum Altitude: 14,760 feet
	Strela-3: SA-14 and 9K34	
Maximum Range: 19,680 feet	Minimum Range: 1,968 feet	Maximum Altitude: 19,680 feet
	Igla: SA-16 and SA-18	
Maximum Range: 16,400 feet	Minimum Range: 1,640 feet	Maximum Altitude: 11,480 feet
	Stinger	
Maximum Range: 13,120 – 15,744 feet	Minimum Range: 656 feet	Maximum Altitude: 12,464 feet

Soviet airpower. Reportedly, 269 Soviet aircraft were destroyed with 340 such missiles. Among the best-known and most widely used MANPADS are the Russian-manufactured Strela and Igla and the U.S.-manufactured Stinger missile systems. Exhibit 5.7 indicates the general characteristics of different surface-to-air threats.

Small Arms Fire

Small arms fire (SAF) is the use of rifles or handguns against a target, whether person, vehicle, or structure, presenting a personal and psychological risk to employees as well as secondary hazards if fired within areas with highly combustible materials. The caliber and velocity of the round as well as its composition and nature will determine the level of damage this form of threat may pose to personnel or facilities. Typically smaller-caliber rounds will not penetrate commercial vehicle armoring, although explosive or armor-piercing rounds will. In addition, munitions can pose an indirect threat if fired indiscriminately or can create secondary hazards if igniting explosive or flammable materials. SAF can also present a risk in countries when the firing of weapons is associated with demonstrations or festivals, as rounds may land with sufficient force to injure or kill individuals or damage materials and structures.

Complex Attacks

A complex attack is when a hostile person or group uses several forms of attack against a target concurrently. For example, the perpetrator may detonate IEDs to slow or damage vehicles, then engage immobilized vehicles with rocket-propelled grenades and small arms fire once vehicles are stationary. The complex attack typically aims to kill or injure as many people as possible, significantly damage critical infrastructures, or enable instigators to effect a kidnap. Such attacks usually are more thoroughly planned than other forms of risk and are typically aimed at a specific target rather than opportunistic in one nature, due to the complexity involved and resources required. Complex attacks typically are planned well in advance of the event and may result from companies setting trends which enable hostile groups to plan specific operations, or be associated with a notable event of visit. Effective risk mitigation and security planning will form the basis for avoiding complex attacks. Training and other contingency planning factors will largely determine how a company weathers a complex attack.

Kidnap and Ransom

Kidnapping, detention, and extortion are now some of the fastest-growing crimes against companies in the developing world, with around 15,000 reported incidents worldwide each year. Kidnap and ransom are highly specialized areas. The discussion here is provided only to demonstrate some factors and considerations connected to these unique risk areas. Kidnap and ransom can be a short-term risk event or may last many years as captives are held for considerable amounts of time. There are two main forms of kidnap situation, the commercial and the ideological. The commercial kidnap is conducted purely for monetary gain; the ideological kidnap, for political or religious reasons. In some instances commercial and ideological rationales may overlap, with a commercial or criminal kidnap being conducted as a means to sell captives onwards to a religious or political group for financial gain, or where such groups kidnap persons to acquire funding for their cause.

Commercial kidnapping is most common and comes in various forms, from criminal opportunists who kidnap an individual from the street and make the person withdraw money from a cash machine, to fake kidnappings where families are informed that a member has been kidnapped and money is demanded for their alleged release. More organized kidnappings target wealthy persons; individuals or groups plan the kidnap in detail, which often results in much larger release costs. It is in the interest of commercial kidnappers to release their captives after ransoms are paid in order to perpetuate the business opportunity within this criminal industry sector. Commercial kidnappings are usually shorter in duration than ideological kidnappings and more frequently result in the release of the victims.

Political or religious groups might engage in kidnappings in order to make a public statement, to deter government or commercial activities, to effect the release of persons from detention, or achieve other political or religious demands. In the worst cases captives are killed publicly, with media releases to achieve a group's goal. Often demands are made of governments rather than corporations or families. Ideological kidnappings tend to have a longer duration, unless the planned intention is to kill the captive from the outset.

The speed and quality of decision making and the immediate actions taken in the initial stages of a kidnapping incident are likely to have a significant influence on the outcome for both the individual and the associated company. If operating within a hostile location, immediate notification of supporting Western or local military authorities might assist with the immediate recovery of kidnapped persons through roadblocks and quick response intercession, before the victim can be removed from the area. Key initial actions after a kidnapping include:

- Ensure hostage safety.
- Use external governmental or military agencies (if appropriate).
- Establish the company's negotiation policy.
- Understand the ransom policy and parameters.
- Carry out agreed policies and procedures with local authorities.
- Ensure family support policies and measures are in place.

Companies should use only a trained specialist to undertake any negotiations with kidnappers. It is important to determine a negotiation strategy in terms of whether to negotiate, make payment, or seek alternative solutions. The involvement of external parties is also a factor that requires consideration, in terms of providing time for law enforcement investigation or requesting government or military support. The extent of control permitted by external parties is also an important consideration: Some government agencies may impose restrictions on the involvement of other groups in the situation, and such restrictions, or indeed the participation of governments could undermine the victim's chances of safe release. In addition, often the kidnappers' initial ransom demand is too high. It is invaluable to have experienced and trained professionals determine whether to negotiate in order to provide the company, and or family, a measure of future protection by reducing the kidnappers' expectations and demonstrating that no further funds will be available if the hostage is not released. For commercial kidnappings, the contingency planning policy should set a target settlement figure and the level of an initial offer.

It is important for companies to understand that it is not only the captive individual and family who are affected by a kidnap and ransom situation; the future safety and welfare of other company employees, the reputation of the company, its ability to continue business within the kidnap environment, and the company's market and employees' image of the organization are also at risk. In addition, the manner in which a kidnap and ransom situation is managed may have adverse effects on the company's relationship with the host nation authorities. These requirements and considerations provide an introduction to some elements that the company's leaders should consider during a kidnap and ransom event:

- *Verify the kidnap*. Company management should explore all alternative explanations, including confirming that the individual is not late or lost, or has not been in an accident.
- *Brief personnel*. The company should brief all likely recipients of a call from the kidnappers, ensuring that the communicator is ready to ask "proof of life" question on receipt of initial call. The company should choose a dedicated telephone to use for communications with the kidnappers.
- *Gather information*. Companies should consider attaching a recording device to telephones to ensure that all instructions and information are received and evidence is gathered. If no recording equipment is available, the company should ensure that the person receiving or conducting any calls from the kidnappers makes full written notes as soon as possible afterward. Original tapes and letters sent by kidnappers may also be important evidence. Letters and envelopes should be touched only at the extreme corners. They should be placed in plastic envelopes for photocopying and then transferred to normal envelopes and secured for eventual handover to police. Tapes should be copied immediately and originals secured. Transcripts and translations should be made as soon as possible.
- *Control information*. The number of copies made of any information should be kept to a minimum and strict security control applied by delegated company management. Permission should be given by appropriate persons before any material is handed over to local police or other authorities.
- *Initial negotiations*. The initial response to the kidnappers should not include any commitment to, or comment on, monetary or other demands. The person who is in contact with the kidnappers should indicate that other management elements en route have decision-making authority. At all times should this person be conciliatory with the perpetrators, as this allows the company time to establish an approach plan and also allows experts time to be deployed to the management location in order to best manage the incident.

- *Media handling.* If the incident is known to the media, the company must monitor media reporting. Press inquiries should be referred to corporate headquarters for the public relations manager (spokesperson) to handle. If questioned, local managers might be authorized to admit there is a kidnap, stating that, because life is at risk, it would be wrong to make any additional comment. Companies should seek the media's understanding and sympathy in the matter, and request that they act responsibly in the best interests of the hostage and family. No details should be provided on the company's intentions or negotiation activities, contacts, and liaison with law enforcement agencies or the hostage, other than identity and any demands made by the kidnappers.
- *Family liaison.* The family of any victim will be shocked and in need of advice, information, support, and administrative assistance from the company. Immediate support must be provided wherever they are located. A responsible party from the company must ensure that this information is obtained: the captive's information, health, and other medical details that may not already be known, as well as recent photographs. In exceptional circumstances, families may need to be relocated to friends or relatives, although the preferred solution is to move a friend or member of the company to stay with the family. The company should ensure regular liaison and briefings are carried out by a manager trusted by the family. The representative should brief on full facts and the likely sequence of events while not being overly optimistic. The representative should avoid discussing rumors or speculation, or indicating that the incident is likely to be over in a short time. The company or external kidnap and ransom consultants should also warn family members of possible pressure tactics by kidnapers (e.g., threats or upsetting letters or videotapes from hostage).

Road Traffic Accidents

The highest risk in terms of injury within any business environment, even high-threat regions, often is from road traffic accidents (RTAs). An RTA may result from poor driving, difficult road conditions, or as a secondary risk following an attack. It is important that policies and procedures reflect the risk of road travel relevant to a particular country, region, or threat environment. Some considerations that might be useful when considering the risk impacts of an RTA follow.

- What are the risks associated with the local road conditions?
- What is the level of competence of local national drivers?
- What threats are faced from hostile groups?
- What threats are faced from security measures required (in terms of driving) to avoid hostile persons or group threats?
- What are the local laws governing actions following an RTA?
- How do local laws conflict with security risks from hostile persons or groups?
- What is the impact of a RTA, especially if a local national is injured or killed?
- What is the action following a RTA within a "safe," "medium-risk," and "high-risk" location?
- What special training is required to mitigate driver risks?
- Are the vehicles suitable for the road conditions and other threats?

DOMESTIC TERRORISM

This chapter has covered some generic forms of threats from criminal individuals or groups, insurgents, or terrorists that companies might face operating within foreign environments. It also is useful to consider domestic challenges that can have significant impacts on commercial and government activities at home.

Domestic terrorist groups represent interests that span a broad spectrum of political, environmental, economic, and social issues. Domestic terrorism is typically defined as the unlawful use, or threatened use, of violence by a group or individual that is based and operating entirely within a defined country or its territories without foreign direction and which is committed against persons or property with the intent of intimidating or coercing a government or its population in alignment with political or social objectives. Domestic terrorism might be classified in terms of special interest extremists or right-wing and left-wing extremist groups. Such groups have caused hundreds of millions of dollars of direct and indirect cost to government and commercial organizations worldwide. They also contribute to social discord, which undermines business goals and market confidence.

Special interest terrorism differs from traditional right- and left-wing terrorism in that extremist special interest groups seek to resolve specific issues rather than achieve a wider political change. Such groups focus on environmental, antiwar, animal rights, and antinuclear issues, attempting to bring about change through public focus or by creating economic risks that undermine a targeted business or project activity. Right-wing terrorist groups often adhere to the principles of racial supremacy and embrace antigovernment, antiregulatory beliefs. Often these groups operate under a nation's laws of free speech while creating social tensions based around race and religion. Right-wing extremism is of significant concern to governments and businesses as issues can quickly become volatile and encompass broad sections of a populace or workforce. Left-wing groups focus on revolutionary socialist doctrine and concern themselves with capitalism and imperialism issues. Their goals are typically to bring about change through revolutionary rather than political measures, focusing on major institutions or government programs.

Many domestic terror or activist groups are comprised of dedicated but often transient members who float between various activist organizations and who use a combination of crude and sophisticated methods to undermine commercial or government activities by targeting public images and reputations as well as facilities, materials, and personnel. Such groups often seek to elicit public support through symbolic and high-impact activities, some of which are illegal and on occasion result in significant damage and financial loss. On rarer occasions, members might engage in violence, psychological or physical, against individuals or groups.

It is important for companies to understand the methods employed by domestic terror groups in order to best protect personnel, facilities, resources, and activities. By determining the typical and atypical methods used by such groups, companies are better placed to develop risk management policies, procedures, and internal training programs and to leverage external government and commercial organizations and their capacities in order to best protect the business needs.

Domestic terror groups often adapt their methods to suit each new campaign or event. Some groups are well organized and conduct detailed planning in order to gain the most effective results from their activities; some run training and education classes in order to maximize the impact of individual activists. Groups can also be flexible and therefore unpredictable in nature, taking advantage of changing circumstances or exploiting opportunistic gaps or weaknesses. Although many events are designed to have a broad impact, some groups are very selective and focused in their targeting and may pursue a singular course of action with a distinct focus in order to achieve their desired results. Many domestic terrorist groups also seek to avoid obvious management structures and have a degree of decentralized control, although all groups have a permanent or semipermanent leadership core. During events, ringleaders may be designated to incite or channel the larger protest group, and spokespeople may be preselected to ensure that the "message" is imparted in accordance with the campaign's strategic objectives. Typically groups are guarded and suspicious and seek to retain operational secrecy to protect against government or commercial investigations. Small groups with well-established and proven members typically retain control of key information, a fact that hinders the ability of law enforcement and companies to map all threat aspects as part of a strategic countermeasure plan.

Known approach methods used by domestic terrorist groups targeting commercial and government activities are listed next.

- *Intelligence gathering.* Domestic terrorist groups might engage in distinct intelligence-gathering activities of project offices, project sites, and individual employees. Subversion of employees or subtle intelligence-gathering techniques within social contexts may be employed to gather company or project information. Activists may join work crews or office staff in order to embed themselves within an organization and gain access to restricted information, allow them to support campaign planning, or better place them to undertake acts of sabotage. Subterfuge may also be used to gather information, through misrepresentation and deceit, with activists placing fact-finding calls or posing as postal workers or sister office staff to seek addresses and other sensitive information. Subversion of employees may occur with the leveraging of disgruntled former or current employees to gather strategic information for their activities, facilitate smear campaigns, or facilitate sabotage.
- *Media attention.* Some groups may seek to leverage local, national, and international media attention in order to undermine the principles and values of the target business activity as well as tarnish its reputation and image. In addition, media attention enables activist groups to garner additional support from those supporting their specific causes. Media attention can be gained through articles, publications, radio, television, demonstrations, and more aggressive singular events. Media attention, through staged or contrived incidents, can also be used to create a situation where the target company or its employees respond in a manner that undermines their reputation, credibility, and objectives. Media attention provides an exponential multiplier to the group's activities.
- *Demonstrations.* Many extremist groups use public demonstrations through high-profile or project areas in order to gain exposure as well as impede business activities. Demonstrations may be singular events, lasting hours, or may be protracted, lasting days to months and evolving into site occupancy (e.g., tree sitting). Demonstrations are typically nonviolent and involve chanting, banners, and costumes. Organizers alert media organizations to the event, and situations may be contrived to embarrass or elicit reactive responses from the target group. Demonstrations may also involve the symbolic burning of

items or the activists leaving obstructive or unpleasant items, such as manure and tree stumps, at the target site.

■ *Facility targeting.* Individuals or groups may target project facilities or offices in order to harass employees, gain media attention, or impede business. Activists may attempt to seek covert or overt entry into facilities through deception or force, and may attempt to remove sensitive information or items from facilities. In addition, activists may deposit obstructive items or resort to unpleasant pranks, such as placing manure into air vents to create unpleasant odors. Fire alarms may be activated and hoax bomb threats placed to create tension, fear, and undermine business activities. Air vents may be blocked and air-conditioning units disabled to undermine working conditions. Convention centers may be targeted with helium balloons being released with activist slogans. Intruders may also seek to enter executive offices in order to deliver a psychological message. Facilities may be damaged create fear and tension with employees as well as impede business and incur costs to the targeted group.

■ *Intimidation.* Extremist groups may target individuals, their families, or residences in order to harass or intimidate employees. Activists may be highly focused and channel resources into a single target rather than attempting to target multiple persons. The status of targeted individuals may not be relevant, ranging from executive board members to janitors, as the effects of intimidation will cascade through an entire organization. Employees may be followed overtly or covertly, and may be heckled, challenged, and subject to physical and verbal abuse. Residences may be subject to demonstrations, harassment, and damage. Family members may be subjected to intimidating attention, to the point of children being approached at school with inflammatory remarks being made regarding their parents' employment.

■ *General harassment.* Activists may undertake a regime of pranks or general harassment in order to create tension, fear, embarrassment, and frustration. Mail may be redirected from homes to other addresses, black sheets of paper may be faxed to disrupt business communications, pornographic or homosexual materials or subscriptions may be forwarded to business addresses, and prank calls may be placed to disrupt communications. Paint may be smeared onto vehicles, oil placed onto the windshields of cars, and fuel tampered with.

■ *Event capture.* Activist groups seek to gather information through video, photography, and voice recordings to used as part of their media campaign or to enable them to seek legal proceedings against their target or police authorities. Event capture also enables activists to defend themselves against prosecution.

■ *Networking.* Extremist groups may seek to leverage other groups that have similar ideals or goals in order to increase the impact of an organized event or campaign. The mapping of relationships against the interests of the activity will assist in identifying other organizations that might become involved within a campaign or event.

■ *Resource or asset targeting.* Some activists use sabotage or property destruction (monkey-wrenching) to damage or destroy high-value materials or resources in order to slow or stop business and to undermine the profitability of a business venture. Psychologically, such activities also create fear and tension within a workforce and may result in inadvertent injuries. Sabotage is typically aimed at strategic or high-value items, seeking longer-term damages or impediments to the project goals. Psychological damage, even through inference, may also be used to undermine a project's achievements.

- *Obstructive activities*. Extremist groups may seek to impede business goals by obstructing either company project or administrative activities. Individuals or groups may place themselves in the way of machinery or access points in order to create physical blockades, on occasion chaining themselves to fences, cattle grids, bollards, or each other (blockades). Individuals may also climb trees to prevent felling within construction areas (tree sitting) and erect simple to complex structures that might enable a long-term presence that poses a difficult and dangerous challenge to police authorities seeking to evict protesters. Vehicles, barrels, concrete blocks, and tree stumps may be used to restrict movement and access to areas or facilities in order to impede business. Activists may also seek to enter facilities, resulting in sit-ins within public areas, or the occupancy of boardrooms or other sensitive and symbolic areas.

Companies should consider whether their business goals and activities, individuals, or sections of their workforce might elicit the attention of such domestic terrorist groups and how the approach methodologies of such groups might affect the company and its employees. While many of the approaches used by domestic terrorist or activist groups are relatively passive, some nonphysical activities can result in tension and fear. On occasion, aggressive attention focused on resources or people can result in substantial structural, resource, and reputational damages. Worse, injuries or fatalities to staff may result from the activities of extremist groups using more direct and robust techniques to further their sociopolitical objectives.

In conclusion, companies face a wide range of tangible and intangible risks that can significantly undermine business activities, even within normal operating environments. When companies embark on enterprises in new, remote, and challenging settings, these threats can be significantly exacerbated and can create unfamiliar and unpredictable risk factors. By understanding the scope of risk, companies can determine the interconnectedness of the physical and nonphysical risks as well as gain an appreciation how wide ranging risks might threaten their organization and activities. Contingency planning and crisis response can then be developed through an understanding of how these risks operate and how they will, directly and indirectly, affect the company, its personnel, and its operations.

Companies must be cognizant of risks that are nebulous—which cannot be held, felt, or seen. These risks often have some of the most catastrophic effects on the organization. Espionage undermines competitive advantage, weakens brand image and reputation, and filters sensitive data away from the company. Threats and coercion impact both individuals and entire workforces, to the detriment of productive operations and employees' morale and welfare. IT security risks can crash global information and communication infrastructures, resulting in irreplaceable data loss or corruption, or facilitate espionage, significantly impeding business continuity and resulting in untold revenue loss. Company reputations are also closely guarded and form the foundation of business success through individual and brand image, yet they can be easily lost and are difficult to recover. Liability issues present risks to individuals and groups as companies are held legally accountable for damages.

Companies might also face a range of conventional risks, either in the form of typical crimes against facilities and personnel or common, risks such as road traffic accidents. These risks can be exacerbated with the introduction of more unique risk factors, such as explosive device targeting in more volatile regions. Such additional risks create an atmosphere of fear and tension that undermines business activities and presents real and personal risks to personnel and facilities. Unexploded ordnance also presents significant challenges; millions of unmarked land mines remain unrecovered in many areas companies wish to operate in. Suspect packages, whether hoax devices, real explosives, or innocent items, can shut down entire facilities for long periods of time, impeding business continuity. More advanced physical risks such as explosively formed projectiles and platter charges present an evolving threat to companies, which are hindered in their ability to move freely around a business environment. Indirect fire attacks present area risks for entire construction or operating sites, presenting an invisible, general fear of attack. The use of widely available surface-to-air missiles can prevent companies entering regions or from moving to remote locations safely. Well-coordinated and opportunistic attacks, whether through indiscriminate gunfire or well organized and complex, can present difficult-to-counter risks, resulting in high cost security measures to protect individuals or critical infrastructures. Companies might also be presented within longer-term challenges that require more specialist support in order to counter criminal and ideological kidnap and ransom risks, or from special interest groups at home. Such risks can present physical risks to the victim as well as a range of reputational and liability risks to the company.

Only by understanding the scope of risk within each business and operating environment can a company determine where the risk sits within organizational tolerance levels and what contingency planning and crisis response measures are required to avoid, mitigate, or accept the risk. An understanding of the nature, scope, and impact of risk also forms the foundation for determining whether a business enterprise should be initiated or whether the risks outweighs the commercial incentives.

Note

1. M.J. O'Brian, "Computer Crime," (2004) http://www.mobrian.com/computer_crime.shtml.

CHAPTER 6

Consultancy Services

Many companies and individuals claim to offer consultancy services. However, this service is one that requires the greatest blend of intellect and expertise and is often the area that creates the most frustration or achieves the worst results. Good consultants are difficult to find as consultancy services differ from security or project management in that they supply advice and guidance through consultation and products, rather than merely controlling a process or resources to support a project's activity. A consultant is generally a subject matter expert who provides advice in a particular area, such as investigations, political assessments, risk management, due diligence, governance, forensics, or facility protection, or a particular industry field, such as communications, maritime logistics, or oil and gas. A good consultant provides a project with access to a granular and deeper level of expertise and experience within an area that may not be retained in-house, or when the company does not have the resources to apply to a requirement. This is a common business need if the service a consultant provides is required by the company infrequently, and so does not justify a full time position to support the requirement within the company.

Each area of consultancy is relatively specialized and usually requires a degree of experience within that particular field. Investigations and forensics are normally the remit of retired law enforcement or government specialists, cyber security attracts those with information technology (IT) backgrounds, and facility security often is conducted by ex-military personnel. This chapter introduces the types of consultancy services within the risk and security industry sector in order to provide a foundation of knowledge in the myriad of areas this term covers and introduces some principal elements that span most sectors of consultancy. It is not intended to be a definitive guide, nor suggest specifically the background of those engaged within a defined consulting area.

DUE DILIGENCE

Due diligence is a significant service requirement within the security sector, as confirmation of the suitability of other parties for engagement is essential to protect company reputations and transactions, such as acquisitions, joint ventures, mergers, and key hires. Due diligence services may include research and investigation of the reputation, associations, activities, and ethics of potential partners, investors, or key hires. It may also be important to confirm or refute allegations of criminal or questionable business practices prior to business activities being initiated, contracts agreed, or associations established.

Due diligence may also identify, prior to commitments being made, any undisclosed liabilities or questionable financial reporting, unusual offshore structures, and unexplained issues associated with a potential merger, acquisition, or joint venture target. Identifying relationships between target companies and various individuals, including government officials. It also allows executive management to better understand the new business landscape they wish to operate in. It is also important to understand who the real power brokers are, where alliances lay, and where they may shift to, in order to reduce business risks.

INVESTIGATIONS

Investigations may include the research and evidencing of fraud, theft of intellectual property, counterfeiting, and piracy. Investigations typically include asset tracing and recovery, the identification of fraud and personnel criminal or policy issues, allegations of embezzlement, antitrust activities, conflicts of interest, bribes and kickbacks, insider trading, security and policy violations, accounting and information irregularities, espionage, and false representations.

It is important that investigations provide not only facts from which a company can determine legal action or business response measures, but also evidence as thoroughly as possible information gathered in alignment with the laws prevalent in the area, to enable subsequent prosecutions. At a subsequent trial, inadmissible information will not assist a company in prosecuting a case.

FORENSICS

Forensic technology and investigator consultants are engaged to interpret data produced through electronic, audio, or visual means, whether recovering or searching for specific information within IT databases, or whether analyzing every byte, pixel, and sound wave that these technologies can record and hide. Forensics is a highly technical field and includes computer, audio, and video forensics as well as the ability to analyze land and mobile phones and call-location tracking. Forensics may also include voice identification, handwriting analysis, signature comparisons, document tampering assessments, reassembling damaged data, fingerprint analysis, polygraphs, crime scene investigations and evidence recovery, ballistics, DNA analysis, medical reports, and fiber and hair analysis. Information should be gathered and presented in a manner that can later be used within legal proceedings.

INFORMATION SECURITY

Information security has become increasingly vulnerable to hackers, viruses, and a myriad of other direct and malicious risks (see Chapter 5). Businesses are reliant on technology for their daily operations and thus will seek to protect both their systems as well as their data. Information security consultants may be engaged to conduct security audits, information leak investigations, unauthorized access, security engineering, information entry point, and system chain risk management.

Consultants will come from an IT background and be familiar with the various threats associated from commercial espionage, criminal elements, and hackers as well as the technological and procedural requirements to countermand these threats. Investigative skills, such as data mining and evidencing, may be required.

SCREENING

There are significant risks associated with enrolling new employees or vendors. Risk consultants mitigate these threats through background investigations in order to prevent fraudulent employees or vendors from damaging a business or activity. Employment screening is a highly effective way of combating employee fraud and providing an integrity check, as employing the wrong people can present serious financial, operational, and reputational damages to a company. There is also an increasing regulatory requirement to screen staff and confirm credentials. This can be accomplished by credit referencing and bankruptcy checks, verification of academic and professional qualifications, employment reference checking, international media searches, and criminal records checks for certain posts. Screening agencies can then provide guidance and evidence to the company with regard to risks posed by a prospective employee or vendor as well as the impact of regulatory and legal issues.

SECURITY MANAGEMENT DESIGN

Many companies have limited or no internal security or risk infrastructure or may be expanding quickly into new areas or regions and so require outsourced support for security policy design and development as well as a start-up security management element. Security management design is especially important for companies entering new geographic regions, where an awareness of local influences and existing established networks of relationships will prove beneficial. Services may include intelligence and threat analysis, surveys, audits, policies, procedures, white papers, program security design concepts, training and personnel development, supply chain and transportation risks, facility and management protective services, incident response, and evacuation planning.

SECURITY STRUCTURAL DESIGN

Companies may enlist specialist technological or architectural design support for the establishment of new facilities. The integration of closed circuit television, intruder detection systems (IDSs), and other alarm and monitoring systems may be enhanced by strengthening physical structures such as walls, windows, doors, and ceilings to mitigate physical attack. The external structures may also be designed around security requirements. Tamper- and monitor-proofing facilities, especially against physical and electronic surveillance, may be incorporated into the building's structural design.

CRISIS MANAGEMENT

Companies may engage specialist consultants to provide advisory services and practical management of crisis events, especially if the company has no in-house regional or specialist capability in the crisis area. Consultants might include kidnap and ransom negotiators, crisis management trainers, regional liaison and facilitation, medical support, political detention mediators, extortion advisors, and hostile environment project managers. Crisis response training also allows management to become experienced in crisis scenarios in order to establish how best to respond if an event occurs and to identify any changes required of the company's own management structures and approaches.

GOVERNANCE AND DEVELOPMENT

The links among security, stability, and development are increasingly apparent as globalization increases the degree at which localized instability influences international problems. The need to establish and maintain stability is paramount for countries emerging from conflict and transitional states. International donors recognize the need for quick and effective responses to instability. Consultants who have held posts in government and nongovernmental organizations (NGOs) can support governments, donors, NGOs, and the private sector with a range of services tailored to their specific requirements, including stabilization design programs, investment advisement and facilitation, compliance and ethic consultancy, networking and liaison, and community capacity building.

POLITICAL ANALYSIS

Companies seeking to invest or operate in new countries must be assured that an acceptable degree of political and social stability is in place, both at the time of engagement and during the business activity's life span. Political assessments and forecasts as well as analysis of politically driven risks will allow the company to determine whether to engage in an opportunity, or whether uncertainties within a region's social or the political future make business ventures to high a risk investment.

Consultancy services can be provided as a short-term service or may be engaged during a prolonged activity's life span. Consultants who are embedded within a company's organization as part of a project team often quickly find themselves engaging in management functions rather than the pure consultancy role. Often their advice carries a significant amount of weight, regardless of the expertise and experience of the contracting agent's in-house management.

SECURITY CONSULTING SERVICES

In order for risk or program managers to get the most from a contracted consultant (whatever his or her field), it is useful to understand some techniques and principles by which to best manage this resource. As security consultants may be hired to provide specific advice or assessments for any form of business activity, whether to support conceptual program planning or a site survey, a degree of product flexibility is required as the parameters of each task will be very different. Within challenging environments, site assessments, whether fielded in-house or by a supporting security vendor, are a common requirement. (See "Security Surveys" in Chapter 12) Without going into the granular level elements of such assessments, it is useful to understand some useful tools and approach methodologies that will enhance the services expected from such consultancy support.

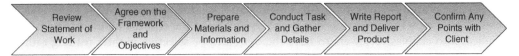

Exhibit 6.1 Consultancy Work Flow

Consultancy Work Flow

Consultants will need to follow a logical process in order to be effective, although this process may be compressed, conducted concurrently, or where necessary done in a different order. Exhibit 6.1 illustrates some major elements within the process, however, where possible the following steps should be taken.

Task Objectives

At the outset of any task, the contracting body and the supplying vendor should clearly establish the objectives and deliverables. These are commonly captured in a statement of work, which defines what is expected for the consultancy task, how materials should be presented, and which areas should be addressed. The lack of clearly defined objectives often results in a failure to meet the client's needs, no matter how professional and relevant the resulting report or product may be.

Frameworking

For complex tasks, it is useful to framework the layout of the product at the beginning. Frameworking defines the structure and presentation of the product (often a report) as well as the content. The framework will be based on the statement of work, but will also include implied and stated requirements. Some consultants will write their report freehand, not establishing a structure or framework to which they write, but presenting information as it comes to mind; and so may lose the thread of the original objectives. Frameworking should not be restrictive, and innovations or new points should be permitted; however frameworking should form the basis of the approach in order to bring a predetermined structure to the consultant's product. Some general areas that might be included in a report are:

- Executive summary
- Project objectives
- Historical background
- Geopolitical review
- Socioeconomic review
- External organizations
- Risk and threat review
- Site survey
- Recommendations
- Appendices

Often reviewers are interested only in certain sections of a report, especially if the report is a complex and sizable document. An executive summary that captures the central elements of the document and the overarching recommendations is therefore a useful feature, which enables all reviewers to gain a macrolevel understanding of the report's findings. The use of appendices also enables reviewers to have the option to be selective in their reading rather than have to scroll through the entire document. A table of contents should also be included if the report is large or complex.

Consistency

While each task will be unique and require a fresh approach, often the principal elements of tasks remain the same. When using the same consultant or consulting company again and again, companies may experience a lack of consistency within the final product, demonstrating a lack of a formalized approach. Often consultants are contracted by a security company to support a client rather than be a full-time employee; as such, they will bring their own approach to the task. While consultants and companies may grow and seek to continually improve their products, a degree of consistency in style, structure, and delivery should be sought. This will make information digestion more palatable and also ensure that quality and consistency is maintained.

Innovations

Although some consistency is necessary, all reports should bring innovations or new themes to the product. Consultants delivering a report that contains no new elements often demonstrate an inability to fully grasp the requirements and bring value to the product. Innovations illustrate how good consultants apply their intellect to each new problem and provide value to the contracting company.

Boilerplate

All companies and consultants will develop a library of boilerplate information that is generic in nature and can be reused again and again to bring quality to a report, but also expedite the speed of delivery of the product. The sensible and appropriate use of boilerplate will add depth to a report. However, often companies and consultants inadvertently add boilerplate information in order to pad out a report rather than adding the material purely through need or value. A well-written report will blend the boilerplate seamlessly into the new elements; poorly written reports will be disjointed or fractured. Some consultants may also forget to take out references to previous reports, an indication that the product has been rushed and no editorial review has been conducted—this devalues any important elements the report may contain.

Meeting the Need

Many consultants become enamored with their own work and may find it difficult to avoid including some previous materials they have developed that might not be applicable for the task at hand. This might also apply to their style and approach; after years of development in a field, a consultant may be somewhat inflexible regarding change. At all times consultants should seek to meet the client's specified requirements in a fashion that best represents those needs. While consultants should seek to augment and improve, where appropriate and agreed-upon, they should also be mindful that the client is paying for a service and that the company should receive what it requests, and in the format and manner desired.

Benchmarking

Benchmarking is the comparison of factors to quantify a recommendation or illustrate a point. Benchmarking is a useful tool both for the consultant seeking to make a referenced point, and for the client who might need to qualify a decision based on the report. Often other organizational approaches might be used to indicate why a certain decision should be made: For example, three other businesses always travel in armored vehicles, or no government employees are allowed to travel at night.

Statistics

Many professionals from an intelligence background will argue that statistics offer a false representation of facts and that they are too removed from the granular-level influences and variables, which can only be explained by verbiage. Often this might be the case. However, statistics provide a trackable analysis of information and can be useful to indicate trends or draw out specific features. Statistics should be used with care and be directly relevant to any point being sought. They should also be explained in terms of what they might represent and any limitations they may come with.

External Organizations

It is useful for consultants to draw on external bodies to augment their own expertise during a task. Thus consultants may meet with embassy officials, local government, or law enforcement or any other institutions or bodies that might offer further insight and information regarding the elements surrounding the task. These sources should be referenced in order to attribute details to the source. In some cases, sources may not want to be quoted. Common sense should be applied to how the information might be presented.

Representations

Representing information is an important feature of the final report and can often do more to explain complex facts than through a written medium. Representations may be graphs, matrixes, photographs, maps, or schematics. They should be professionally developed but often they are created through simple software media, rather than by graphic artists, as illustrated with Exhibit 6.2. While many consultants will not have access to graphic artists or complex software, sound representations can be developed easily and relatively professionally to capture the key points. Representations will illustrate both the information required by the client and also the competence and experience of the consultant. Representations will likely reduce the size of the report, while adding significantly more information.

Recommendations

There are very few instances where a task will not require some form of observation or recommendations. Recommendations should be summarized within the executive summary and

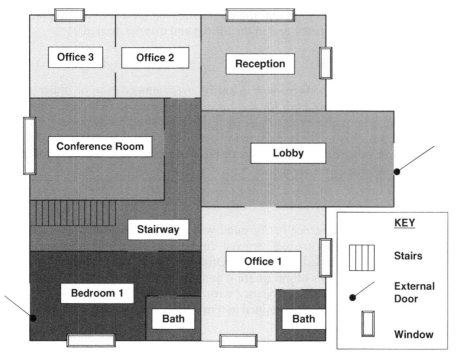

Exhibit 6.2   Simple Graphic Representations

explained, if necessary, in greater depth at an appropriate point within the report. Recommendations should always be aligned with the nature of the project as well as the statement of work. Where possible, options should be provided, rather than a straight yes-or-no answer. Options can be presented either in ascending scale or preference or as methods by which an activity might be conducted. In some instances, recommendations will be reviewed by a project manager first, to ensure that the best represent the goals of the project. On other occasions, corporate leadership will wish for consultants to be unhindered in their observations, reporting only to executive management. The approach should be defined at the outset in order to avoid confusion by the security provider as well as friction within the company itself.

Rapid Assessment

In some instances consultants will have very little time on task. This may be due to risk factors, which prevent a protracted visit, or due to other task or time restrictions. Consultants should be able to quickly and accurately record the pertinent details of the task in a manner that enables them to develop the theme of the task at a more leisurely pace, when time or circumstance permits. Consultants should therefore be adept at developing schematics, mapping, and other shorthand representations to which they can later write to. Digital cameras, global positioning devices, and video recordings as well as dictaphones allow consultants to

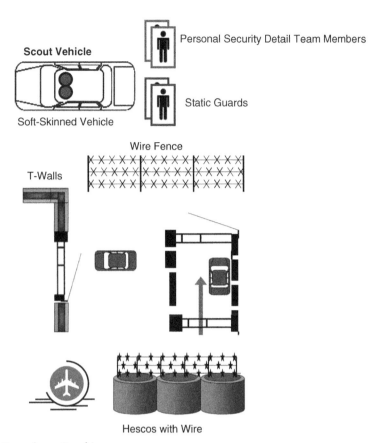

Exhibit 6.3 Consultant Graphics

record considerable amounts of information that can then be transcribed and expanded into their report away from the area of review. A well-established consultant will also have a library of graphics and other materials, developed prior to the task commencing, in order to expedite the process. Exhibit 6.3 presents some simple examples of these consultant graphics. Prior to being deployed, consultants should develop a range of materials that will form the basis of the overarching report, including:

- Intelligence information
- Mapping and imagery
- An understanding of the project goals
- Relevant and local groups and organizations
- Information restrictions or concerns
- Graphics and visuals
- Communications details
- Statistics and graphs
- Initial framework of the report
- Risk tolerances of the client

- Location of key features or supporting agencies
- Points of contact and communications details

Style

The style of the report is an important factor, one that often indicates the consultant's competence and level of written skill. Language (generally) should be clinical and factual rather than opinionated or inflammatory. Reports should be written impartially and mindful that the final audience might be varied and as yet undetermined. Language should be carefully crafted to represent the stated and assumed needs of the client. For example, the consultant may substitute "challenging" or "high risk" for "dangerous." Opinions, such as the police are *unprofessional*, might be better stated by saying that the police have significant *shortcomings* or *limitations*. While style is often based on semantics, sloppy or inappropriate language can undermine the value of the product, mislead management, or create internal and external frictions.

Service Expectations

Consultancy services often require more time and resources than initially envisaged. Reports should be edited and reviewed by an independent element within the security provider's organization to conduct independent quality assurance. Often external parties will need to contribute to the service to ensure all aspects are fully met, as the consultant may raise points which require further clarification by the company, or may lead to the investment of further information which may not have been shared with the consultant at the start of the task. Both the contracting company and security provider should be aware that while a good consultant will bring the product to a 95% acceptability level, often less experienced consultants will need additional support or time to finalize the product. A period of post-report finalization should therefore be included within the service time frame and cost estimate to ensure than the final product meets all expectations.

The contracting company should also establish the depth and amount of information that it is seeking: Is it looking for a concise ten-page report or a more lengthy document? Many providers consider quantity as an indication that their client has received a solid product; many contracting companies, however, might desire a succinct and concise report rather than volumes of information. Where possible, the client and the consultancy provider should come to a clear understanding regarding the size of the product. If a provider feels that size limitations detract from the quality of the service, either it should attempt to reach an agreement to increase the scope of the work or it might add additional materials as appendices or attachments for further referencing.

AUDITING CONSULTANCY

Consultants may also be called on to audit other commercial companies in the conduct of their service delivery or may be requested to carry out an audit of the company management or operations themselves in order to establish an impartial internal review or investigation.

Auditing services present different challenges from most other consulting services; often they create a degree of friction and hostility within the group being subjected to the audit, by virtue of the nature of the task. Auditors often have the power to indicate areas or weakness within a management structure or process and many times report directly to executive leaders with their findings. (See "Security Audit" in Chapter 12)

Auditing can come in the form of a standard process, whereby at certain intervals or junctures an audit is conducted. This standardized process might reduce any concerns of those being subject to the audit. Audits might also be conducted if a project or activity is struggling to achieve its objectives; such audits might create a greater degree of concern. On rare occasions, audits may be conducted on a competing company, where information restrictions and competitive issues will create significant challenges. At all times audits should seek to adhere to these principles:

- *Goals.* Audits should have clearly defined goals and objectives, which should be central to any activity being conducted. The auditors should not exceed the limitations of the stated task.
- *Nature of the company or task.* The auditors should understand the nature of the company and task in order to place the audit within a context and to understand and explain their findings.
- *Parameters.* The audit team should have clearly defined parameters and authorities so as to control and support their activity. All parties should understand their parameters and authorities to ensure that the right level of support is provided.
- *Measurables.* The audit team will need to have a set of standards or measurables by which to evaluate the task. These should be clinically assessable where possible to avoid subjectivity. Benchmarking might also be used to illustrate any key points or differences.
- *Confidentiality.* Audits should be treated with confidentiality. Information should be protected and imparted only to those authorized to receive it. In some cases numbered copies will be required to track restricted documents.
- *Clinical.* Audits should seek to impart their findings in a clinical and impartial manner rather than express personal opinions or sentiments.
- *Fair.* Audits should be fair and based on findings, not perspective or emotive elements. This will be especially important if those being audited are not receptive to the audit team.
- *Documented.* All findings should be clearly documented to enable review, both on immediate completion of the audit and at periodic junctures thereafter. Reports should be written in a manner that all likely reviewers can understand.
- *Friction.* Auditors will require a degree of tact and diplomacy and must be able to manage difficult or challenging audiences without adding to frictions or concerns. Audit teams must have top-level support and must be able to draw on executive leadership if needed.
- *Balance.* Audits should seek to balance, where possible and appropriate, positive findings against negative, without distorting the content of the report or its aims.
- *Reporting.* Information restrictions are likely to apply. A clear understanding of who is permitted to review what elements of an audit should be established. An agreed distribution list should be established at the outset of the task.

Auditing is likely one of the most challenging consultancy tasks as it often receives the least support from those involved directly. Typically audits are viewed as presenting challenges or criticisms to those being audited, rather than offering them support or solutions. A good audit will identify both positive and negative elements and offer (where required) recommendations to mitigate shortfalls or remedy issues, as well as commendations for those activities which are being performed well.

In summary, consulting services should be considered one of the most complex and demanding services a security provider will offer to the company. Each task is unique and requires the application of well-grounded expertise, management skills, task-specific experience, and the ability to capture information, observations, and recommendations in a clear, logical, and well-structured manner. Consultants should be innovative and be able to draw on multiple external resources as well as identify internal issues and requirements in order to best respond to the statement of work. Consultants will need to bridge the risk management and business requirements in order to offer valid and realistic recommendations to the company.

CHAPTER 7

Project Management

Project management is the discipline of organizing and managing resources in such a way that an activity or goal is completed within defined scope, quality, time, risk, and cost constraints. Every business or operational activity should be considered a project, whether it is a textile company establishing a new factory within Indonesia, or a security company protecting a major oil refinery in Saudi Arabia. Regardless of the nature of the activity, a project can be considered a temporary and one-time endeavor undertaken to create a unique product or service that brings about beneficial change or added value to an organization. Projects have a definitive start and end, and are thus different from repetitive actions or processes, which are permanent or semi-permanent activities to create the same product or service on a prolonged or continued basis. Projects may last for days or years but have an exit strategy, which distinguishes them from the permanent process. The management of these two systems is often very different and requires varying technical skills, methodologies, and innovations. Project management often requires a dynamic management approach within the risk and security field. Challenges are new and unique and conditions may change quickly to alter the original expectations and plans for the project. A process, however, is rarely required to deal with new problems but is governed more by repeated processes and static risk management concepts, although the risk environment in which a process occurs may change or fluctuate.

Companies seeking to enter into or operate in a new or challenging environment often require the integration of two project management lines into the overall corporate planning processes. The first management line is the driving force behind the project activity: the business needs and the operational delivery methodology. The second management line is the enabler that supports the business activity and delivery methodology: the risk management and security services that ensure that the project can be conducted safely and that the activity is planned to achieve the most productive results. Only when companies integrate both management planning lines from the outset can projects be planned, mobilized, sustained, and closed productively and safely.

Process mapping is a system by which a company identifies the participants and influencers of the project, whether different elements of the organization itself, external commercial suppliers and vendors, or involved or supporting government agencies. Process mapping enables diverse group relationships and responsibilities to be identified and mapped, showing interdependencies as well as management and communication flow processes. In the risk and security field, bringing multiple risk and security components together to establish a unified and coordinated security methodology is known as enterprise security. Process mapping should also be conducted for the business activity, bringing the business team, technical and administrative support, suppliers, and project managers together to identify resource needs, schedules, milestones, and objectives. Exhibit 7.1 illustrates how risk and business project

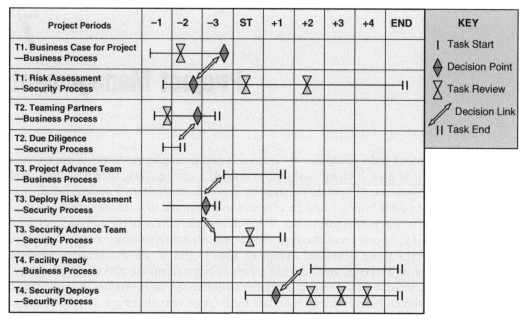

Exhibit 7.1   Aligning Business and Security Project Management

management planning must work hand in glove to ensure that business goals can operate within a risk management context.

By aligning both the activity and the enterprise security plans, rather than considering risk management a supplemental aspect to the business process, key vulnerabilities can be predetermined prior to project plans being finalized, allowing companies to identify and address risks prior to as well as during the project. Project teams who draw on the expertise and resources of risk management and security advisors, invariably finding that their approach is enhanced and the project results are improved.

Risk managers should develop a process map based on the business goals, operational and management processes, schedule and workflow needs, budget allocations and profit expectations, milestones and performance expectations, and responsibilities and relationship natures between multiple parties. Understanding who has ownership of each element of the process, where decision making and responsibilities lay, and who the passive participants are will enable risk managers to chart the management processes and decision-making authorities. By charting out responsibilities and decision making, and how these may affect other project groups, both connected to the activity or affected by decisions resulting from a specific group, risk managers can understand how a decision might create a ripple effect that might undermine or endanger a parallel processes or impinge on other business needs. Companies should avoid thinking purely along linear lines of decision making, as a decision made by one corporate executive to address an isolated project risk may have implications for multiple removed business or operational activities. The secondary and peripheral affects of a single point decision should be understood so that the ramifications are placed within a wider context. Exhibit 7.2 illustrates how mapping decision making to manage an isolated risk will create a ripple effect on other operations.

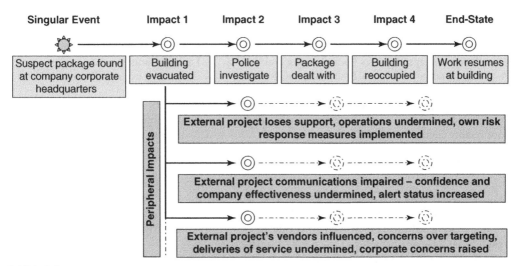

Exhibit 7.2 Mapping Process Impacts

Understanding the implications of single-point events will enable project management to engineer policies and plans that will support business continuity within their project, cognizant of, but not unduly affected by, external events.

PROJECT FAILURE

The first challenge for project managers within challenging or new business environments is to ensure that a project is delivered within defined business, contractual, and risk tolerance parameters. The second and more difficult aspect is to establish methods by which to gather and consolidate multiple areas of expertise in order to establish the most effective project plan and then to ensure that the plan is sustained and adjusted throughout its life to meet changing circumstances and needs. A project is a carefully defined set of activities that uses as resources money, people, materials, energy, space, provisions, communications, quality, and risk to meet the predefined business and delivery objectives. Frequently in unstable project environments the carefully defined resource requirements will shift. Project managers must predict how much variance from the project path might be expected, and build these into the project resource and schedule plans as contingency factors.

A project should be defined in terms of *time*, *product*, and *resources*. Projects are designed to produce measurable business products through change, or service delivery. Projects may be motivated by cost to profit, strategic objectives, or organizational necessity. Risk and security management will help support project planning to navigate risks and offset impacts that might otherwise undermine or derail a project's objectives. Risk managers should be considered an active voice on a project planning team and be brought into the business cycle early, typically at the project design phase. Risk managers who understand the project team's language, approaches, and techniques, as well as the activities inherent weaknesses or areas of vulnerability, will be better placed to offer sound counsel and practical support to project management teams as well as to represent the wider group's interests as an auditor of the

Exhibit 7.3 Typical Project Failure Points

• Lack of definitive start date	• Poor requirement definition	• Insufficient configuration management
• Poor change management	• Poor planning and control	• Lack of planning time
• Poor alignment with strategic goals	• Poor management	• Unforeseen external factors
• Insufficient budget	• Lack of commitment	• Business changes
• Fragmented project	• Insufficient resources	• Unrealistic time scales
• Poor quality control	• Inappropriate resources	• Poor business case
• Poor communications	• Failure to close	• Poor structuring
• Poor risk management	• Requirement loss	• Poor security service performance

company's overall risk management approach. The risk manager should be positioned as an enabler, seeking solutions to solve project design and implementation dilemmas, rather than throwing barriers or obstacles in the path of business success.

To be determined a success, the project must meet the defined expectations of cost, time, and quality established within the design phase. Statistically, the majority of government and commercial projects fall outside of the defined project scope, and the resources allocated to deliver a specific business product are exceeded, resulting in the majority of projects being clinically defined as a failure, at varying levels. Project failure commonly results from poor planning and management, rather than from external unique or unforeseen circumstances. Even in remote and challenging environments where the risk climate is fluid and difficult to predict, many points of failure can be identified and mitigated against with integrated project and contingency planning and sensible resource allocation. Exhibit 7.3 highlights the typical vulnerabilities that lead to project failure.

Identifying and addressing project vulnerabilities is not only the responsibility of a project design and management team, but should be considered a constituent element of the role of the company's risk and security management as well. Where appropriate, external risk management and security vendors might also be used to assess postulated risks and impacts and to offer avoidance or mitigation measures. By bringing the expertise of project and risk management together, the design solution will reflect the most practical and effective business solution to the environment in which the activity will occur. Conversely, this will also reduce the negative impacts on the company's risk management and security division as well as the security vendors, as a solid contingency plan and associated policies and procedures streamlines operations when the project is implemented, resulting in leadership by planning—rather than by crisis management.

PROJECT LIFE CYCLE

Projects are conceived from an idea that triggers the analysis of a business case. Once a defined need and basis of requirement are consolidated, the project undergoes design, development, and testing. This systematic approach establishes the scope and structure of the project to allow it to be implemented and sustained until completion. The products created from the project are then used and evaluated, and further needs are defined, or the project is closed. Product delivery is comprised of getting the work, doing the work, and handing the work over

Exhibit 7.4 Stages of the Project's Life Cycle

Project Management Stage	Remarks
1. Idea	Establish new or unique business need
2. Trigger	Project mandate (authority to initiate an activity)
3. Study	Develop a business case to confirm the validity of the need
4. Design	Design project scope, goals, objectives, and methodology
5. Project Development	Establish a project plan, with associated resources and activities
6. Testing	Confirm project plan and business case prior to start
7. Implementation	Initiate project operations with frequent reviews and controls
8. Handover	Deliver service or product to client or end user
9. Product Use	Utilize service or product, with feedback and adjustments
10. Evaluation	Evaluate product—quality assurance and need justification
11. Further Requirements or Closure	Close the project, either complete or with a management rundown

to the client or end user. It is at the design phase that companies should utilize the resources of in-house or external risk and security advisors, so that the project design is built around risk constraints and considerations from the outset. Risk management can then match pace with the project throughout its life cycle to ensure it is safeguarded from risks until the project is completed. Companies that introduce risk management and security midstream undermine the effectiveness of the project design and impose unnecessary burdens on their risk managers, who are often forced to grapple from scratch with the scope and methodologies of the activity, while project managers are consumed with implementing and sustaining the already defined and underway operational requirements. Risk managers might also need to implement change to resolve unaddressed issues at points in the project process that disrupt or detract from the original design goals, creating management frustration and exposing vulnerabilities that present unnecessary risks to project success. Exhibit 7.4 illustrates how projects should transition through a series of logical steps to achieve a designed end result.

The project life cycle will also involve technical or activity stages, each requiring a separate plan placed within the context of a complete project as well as reflecting generic and unique risks. By breaking the project into stages, the risks are better managed, as each stage may have defined resources and efforts attached to it. If the project starts to underperform in a stage, project management will be able to quickly identify shortfalls and assess whether to continue with the project, accepting that risk thresholds have been breached, or to cease project activities—cutting the company's losses. This is true of both commercial activities and security contracts. Establishing clear and robust program controls is vital to ensure that the project, through effective stage management, remains on track and is not permitted to incur significant accrued risks due to poor oversight of individual components.

If a project is considered a defined path that the business walks toward stated goals, each occurrence at which the business steps from the path should be considered a risk, whether the business returns to the path or must follow a slightly new path to reach the same goal. An exception plan is generated when a change is required from any point within a stage, to the end of that stage boundary. The next stage plan then needs to be managed in terms of any change impacts generated from the exception plan, as illustrated in Exhibit 7.5.

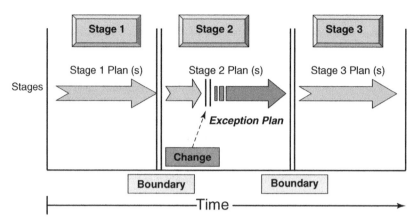

Exhibit 7.5 Exception Plans Resulting from Project Change

In the design phase, project management should seek to identify vulnerabilities that might result in change, and establish contingency plans that will reduce the impact of an exception plan. This contingency planning may include additional resources, funding, or allowances to meet new or unsighted challenges.

PROJECT PLANNING

Project planning determines the product nature and descriptions, resources, activity, cost, and time elements of the activity. Planning rules and templates should be developed, identifying activities and interdependencies through the establishment of flow or Gantt charts, with possible impacts and influences. Scheduling will seek to align concurrent activity with key milestones in order to streamline processes and avoid periods of inactivity or unnecessary excessive work tempos, especially if one stage is reliant on another component to start. Resource surges and troughs should also be identified in order to best manage resources and spare capacity periods, as illustrated in Exhibit 7.6.

Business, operations, and security risk evaluations will be assessed, with agreed tolerance levels, impact assessments, and contingency planning measures. Planning will be layered, encompassing the project as a whole, as well as each stage as an individual element. The value of risk and security managers for planning will be seen both in project design and through the provision of innovations, resource management, and identifying periods where external agencies and capabilities might augment the company's own resources. The project plan serves to enable the project, but also determines whether targets are achievable, what resources are required, and where focuses should lay to achieve success. Associated problems and risk will also be identified during the development of the plan for review and management.

The key principles for project management include:

- **What** the project is intended to achieve.
- **Why** the project is needed.
- **How** the outcome is to be achieved.
- **What** the responsibilities and commitments required to fulfill the need are.

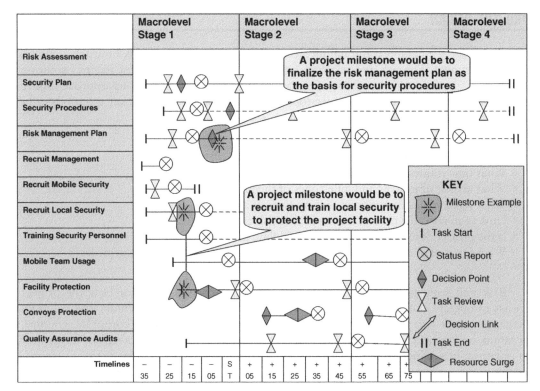

Exhibit 7.6 Simplified Gantt or Project Flow Chart

Risk management may also support project design in developing *effectiveness models*, where convergent services might be provided through different mediums. The use of technologies might provide better security service provision than using guard force personnel, resulting in operating efficiencies and cost savings for the project. Education and training might result in better cross-utilization of personnel or identify shortfalls in the skills required to perform services or operate equipment. Identifying areas of capacity convergence also allows project management to field stronger project teams or seek maximum efficiency from resources. The appointment of a security manager who has secondary skills outside the principal role might result in some project positions becoming redundant, thus presenting a cost saving, or enable the project group to develop new skills sets through in-house training regimes, resulting in increased operational efficiencies. Risk management will also provide program design support through security integration, bringing organic resources, capabilities, and expertise together to provide a unified solution as well as leveraging external group support to augment company resources. Risk and security integration reduces risk exposure to the company, improves compliance to corporate and government regulations, and enables a collaborative approach that best supports business continuity. Resource sharing between multiple projects also reduces costs, strengthens the company's overall performance, and creates more effective risk and security management controls to be implemented.

PROJECT DESIGN

Project design is a complex and unique event, specific to each company, industry, activity, and environment. For risk and security managers, the development of a security solution based around a business activity is often best achieved from a ground-up approach, once some fundamental principles are understood. Managers should ask some key questions prior to tailoring a solution around a project activity, including:

- What is the project trying to achieve?
- What time frames and approach methodologies will be employed?
- What are the objectives and milestones of the project?
- What risk and cost limitations are imposed, or assumed?
- How familiar is the project team with the risk environment?
- Is the project design complete, or is it still fluid and subject to change?
- What internal or external resources can be leveraged to supplement the project?

Risk and security managers will then establish the foundations for how the project wishes to operate and where the priorities lay. In designing a complementary risk solution, managers might also wish to consider layers of project need, including corporate, country, program, and project, rather than focusing purely on the granular-level needs of the project in isolation. In addition, managers should consider whether support areas are static or mobile in nature, when service area changes will occur, and how sequencing will align with project goals, and understand how to differentiate between the provision of consultancy and security services.

Risk managers should design a *concept of operations* around a project, whether it is the development of an agricultural program in Nigeria or the reconstruction of refineries in Kurdistan. Where possible, solution *options* should be provided, enabling the company to select a solution that achieves a balance among risk, cost, and the planned project approach. Risk solutions should also identify project plans that expose the company to risk and proffer recommendations that enable the project to achieve the same results but through more appropriate means. Once the principles of the requirement are understood, it often helps risk managers to visualize the project in terms of space, schedule, and activity. Mapping out remote sites in relation to travel routes, supporting agencies, and volatile areas will place the project into a wider topographical context—color coding risk areas will then define risk profiles in an easily viewable format. Identifying when activities need to occur and comparing these against calendared risk events (e.g., festivals, political events, religious holidays) will enable risk managers to identify conflicts of activity. Creating schematics around facilities with access points, command centers, and perimeter structures will enable managers to quickly identify risk areas as well as manning and equipment requirements. Mapping, Gantt charts, and site schematics can be useful tools to simplify the solution design process as well as indicate to project managers how activities might be best conducted. Exhibit 7.7 presents a very simplistic method by which to quantify manning and operational needs for a simple project task. These graphic representations can be used to design complete facility requirements and allow risk managers to write security policies and procedures to a sketched needs and solution tool.

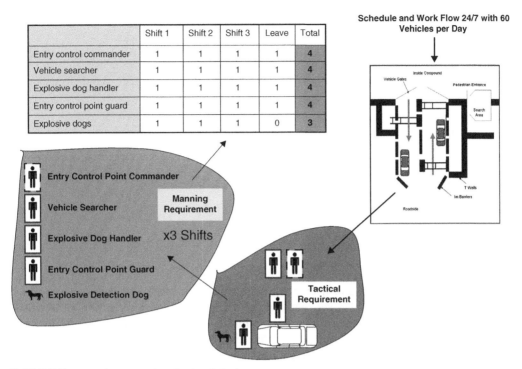

	Shift 1	Shift 2	Shift 3	Leave	Total
Entry control commander	1	1	1	1	4
Vehicle searcher	1	1	1	1	4
Explosive dog handler	1	1	1	1	4
Entry control point guard	1	1	1	1	4
Explosive dogs	1	1	1	0	3

Exhibit 7.7 Visualizing Project Design Solutions

PROJECT START-UP

Starting a project requires an appreciation of what the desired outcome is expected to be as well as the manner in which the project will be initiated, sustained, and completed. The next sections indicate the core elements of starting a project.

Idea

An idea is identifying the need which will drive the establishment of an analyzed business concept. This will lead to a project mandate if the initial assessment deems the activity worthy of pursuing.

Project Mandate

The project mandate is the mechanism required to initiate project deliverables and usually is used as a tool to provide management the scope, structure, nature, goals, and objectives of the activity. The mandate typically triggers the establishment of a project planning team, which defines the start-up of the project. This sequence defines the activities resulting from a project mandate:

- The company appoints the executive or project manager.
- A project design team is established, with involvement from all stakeholders.

- The project activity manager is selected and appointed to manage the activity.
- A project plan is developed, defining the approach, conduct, and risks.
- The project plan is tested or validated and then implemented (*basis for the brief*). The project plan will include:
  - Authorities and permissions
  - Background and objectives
  - Scope and constraints
  - Interfaces and relationships
  - Quality expectations
  - Outline of business case and associated documents
  - Interested parties and stakeholders
  - Risk tolerances and evaluations

Business Case

The business case defines why a project is required and justifies the value it brings to a company. The business case should cover the scope of the benefits, financial (profits or avoided costs), strategic (moving toward strategic aims), and legislative (fulfilling some absolute requirement). The business case should also define the levels of effort required to fulfill the requirement, in order to ensure appropriate focus and resources are understood for evaluation of reward versus cost. The business case should also justify the acceptance of any identified risks, presenting the activity value or gain against the impact loss effects.

Project Approach

During the start-up phase, the project team will determine the approach strategies and policies for the project. This approach will include which elements will be undertaken in-house and which will be subcontracted out as well as whether current products, systems, or elements can be used or modified to support the project. This phase will also be used to define whether products need to be designed from scratch and whether additional expertise needs to be sought for design, development, and production. External risk and security consultancy support may also be required to support project design and implementation. A justification for the rationale behind the approach should also be included, and the project approach should take into account whether risks have been avoided, accepted, transferred, or mitigated against. For projects operating within challenging or remote environments, a risk assessment may be required to place the project expectations and plans within a risk context. These assessments may subsequently influence the approach methodologies used to achieve the desired outcome. Areas of risk that might be of significance to the company as an entity should be addressed by appropriate executive officers before the project is permitted to start.

Project Initiation Plan

The initiation plan includes what is required to start the process as well as the requirements of the actual project plan itself. The initiation plan typically includes:

- Defining and analyzing products
- Identifying activities and dependencies
- Estimating effort, cost, and resources
- Scheduling based on estimates and activity dependencies
- Analyzing risks affecting the project plan
- Completing the plan

A project brief should be provided to clarify with stakeholders and participants the details evaluated and confirmed within the project plan. This offers management an opportunity to raise any final questions and to gain a complete understanding of entire project needs and conduct. Project initiation plans may cover a range of areas and may have specialized subsets outside of the actual project activities, such as security project initiation documents (PiDs) and operations orders. For complex and dynamic projects, identifying confluence points for risk, security, operational, administrative, and logistic requirements will enable project leaders to best manage the process.

Work Packages

The project should be broken into manageable elements that are chained together to form the sequenced components of the entire project. Work packages can be phases or task activities that define a work breakdown structure, forming a stage or an element of the product development or service delivery. Like a faulty cog within an engine, a failure in one work package can have wider repercussions within the system as a whole. An impact assessment of work package failure or delays may indicate entire project delays or costs. Work packages should not only focus on the principal project elements but include supporting activities, such as labor provision, personnel recruitment, materials and asset deliveries, and security provision. Contingency planning and cost versus benefit analysis for additional resourcing of difficult or critical work packages should be conducted to enhance success probabilities of stages and the project.

Project Design

It is important to design a project around the product, gaining a clear understanding of each component of the product as well as what its recipient audience is. The project should be designed around the activity, client requirements, and delivery limitations and capabilities. Project design may have various layers as the project team designs the direct product solution and the risk and security team designs an environment or structure in which the project will operate. Close collaboration is required as independent designs will invariably come into conflict and undermine the process as a whole.

PROJECT INITIATION

Once the project plan is complete, formal initiation is then given to start the management and activity requirements. Project management will need to plan quality assurance measures to quantify client expectations and implications. A configuration management plan will need to be developed to manage the product and its performance throughout and beyond the project life span. A quality assurance plan and associated reports will also need to be developed, using the product descriptions and project plan to provide a checklist of requirements and goals. In terms of security provisions, typically a statement of work defines what elements are needed to support the project activities. This statement should be aligned with the project configuration management plan, as within challenging environments, project operations may be dependent on security provisions. The business case should be updated to reflect new factors or changes, and the risk log should be kept current to reflect typical operational risks as well as external threats. Stage boundaries should be defined and changes managed to keep the project on track. Anomalies and potential shortfalls should be addressed with the client to negotiate delivery issues and modifications, should unique problems arise. Project data storage and management systems should be developed and utilized and, where possible, efficiencies through the use of existing systems, policies, procedures, and templates should be exploited.

Change Management

Effective management of the activity must be through established change policies, authorities, and systems, as within every project, a degree of change will be required. Some will fall within acceptable tolerance levels; others will require exception management approaches and documentation. Change can have a significant impact on cost or productivity and thus must be managed effectively. Risk and security managers should consider the implications that their changes will have on the overall project and attempt to mitigate change impacts by understanding the varied dynamics these changes will have on the core business activities and goals. Project managers must negotiate changes with risk and security managers within challenging environments, as a project change will likely incur a security and risk change. Change effects should be measured in terms of their implications across the whole project team, and change decisions must be measured and unambiguously authorized, rather than occurring as a reflex action following a significant occurrence. Change will have impacts throughout the conduct of a stage and may result in considerable modifications throughout the project life.

Controlling a Stage

Stages should be regarded as individual elements of a project, and managed both as standalone components and as an aspect of the wider requirement. Work packages typically will be released as part of the project plan and accepted and executed by project management, who on completion of the work package will deliver a product for approval and verification. An assessment of the stage progress should be made at agreed-upon intervals, as should a status review in terms of timelines and milestones. Reporting highlights should also be provided for management review, and will drive further directions or future planned amendments to the activity. Project issues and changes will be managed either within tolerance or by exception. Corrections will be made internally, or will be directed by a higher management level within the company. At the end of each stage, or should an *exception plan* be implemented, the project plan should be updated. The business case should be reviewed concurrently, and an end-of-stage report should be provided with impacts and lessons learned. Decision points may be included to determine how future plans will be implemented or whether projects will be dismantled, should requirements not be met. In order to best manage a stage, these reports might be required:

- *Highlight report.* A notification of significant information from the project manager to the project board.
- *Exception report.* A warning from the project manager to the project board that a stage or tolerance is under threat.
- *Checkpoint report.* Points within the project where reports are required to ascertain product deliverable status.
- *Quality management.* The *quality plan* should include the customer's expectations, the provider and client acceptance criteria, and the quality assurance responsibilities. Quality control and auditing should be established to ensure that appropriate checks are conducted prior to the client receiving a product.

Project plans may be initiated by a business unit and then transferred to an implementing division or project team. Within the security sector, a proposal to support a client's business activity may be developed to win work; this proposal amounts to a project plan. If work is won, the proposal may become the basis of the configuration management plan. Project start-ups may be swift and complex, and those who develop plans should seek to create planning documents that not only support business activities but can be modified quickly to assist with administrative and operational mobilizations. In addition, the development of a template PiD that draws from such planning documents will support the swift and effective mobilization and sustainment of a project, within the parameters agreed by the client.

Closing a Project

Project closures are often overlooked in terms of effective project planning. Many security vendors and project staff view the closure of a project as the activity that requires the least attention. This can create long-term problems for the company. Clear and sanctioned authority for project closure must be established and contractually agreed. The decommissioning or closure of a project will require its own stage and an *issue log* to account for any requirements or problems that need to be resolved prior to contract completion. Closure risks must be identified, both as part of the project as a whole, and if unique to the closure process. A *maintenance phase* may be incorporated to move risks or requirements beyond the project closure period, with a smaller management team resolving final matters. The project should be evaluated against the requirements and stipulated product quality standards and deliverables, with an end-of-project report (EPR) being provided internally and, if appropriate, to the client. In terms of risk management, project closures can present a period where complacency occurs, and management and staff expose themselves and the business activities to unnecessary risks.

PROJECT MANAGEMENT STRUCTURES

Each company, industry, and activity will need different layers of management requirement, from the executive elements deciding the overarching needs and strategies, to the project elements managing the actual activities conduct. It is important that a degree of latitude is

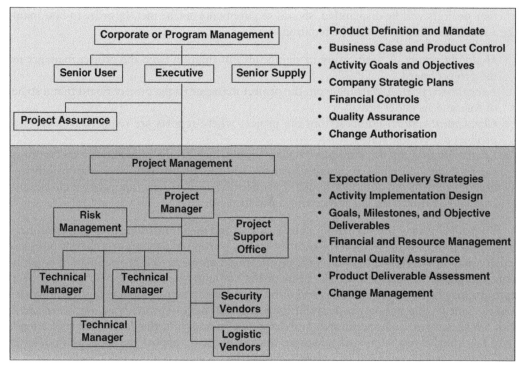

Exhibit 7.8 Project Management Structures

provided for project management to manage by exception, fundamentally being provided parameters and tolerance levels within which they are authorized to make unilateral decisions. This is especially important when projects are operating in remote or dynamic environments where immediate decision-making authorities might be required to avoid crisis situations. For those activities or factors outside of the established decision and management allowances, *exception reports* should be generated to deal with each new or higher need. There are usually five levels of management involved within a project, supported by external consultants and contractors, as illustrated in Exhibit 7.8.

In simplistic terms, the five layers involved in project management typically involve these groups:

1. *Corporate management.* Not part of the project management, this group often defines the needs and strategies for one of more projects, and validates and evaluates project activities.
   - *Executive.* Ultimate accountability for the projects, ensuring the business case is sound and a coherent organizational structure is in place. Responsible for monitoring progress and addressing significant issues.
   - *Senior user.* Accountable for any products supplied by the users, ensuring the product is fit for delivery and meets contractual and client expectations.

- *Senior supplier.* Accountable for the quality of all products delivered by suppliers, representing design, development, facilitating and procuring interests in a timely and effective manner on behalf of the company and their client.
2. *Project direction.* Responsible for the key decision-making activities and directional control of the project as well as assessing and delivering the final product (program manager).
3. *Project management.* Responsible for the day-to-day activities and control of the project (assisting the project manager). This group might include subcontracted vendors and risk managers to support decision making, and may include roles like operations, task order, logistics, security and other task or service area managers.
4. *Technical management.* The management of a component service or product within the project. Technical management may be supported by components of the risk management and security services.
5. *Managing product delivery.* Responsible for individual product production, management, and delivery within a project (team management).

Configuration Management

It is the function of the configuration management (typically within the project office) to identify, track, and protect the product, maintaining clear and accurate records of the project and its stages as well as taking the product from the project process into use once the project activity is complete. For security contracts, configuration management will be led by the security manager and his or her team, overseen typically by a quality assurance group. Each product within a project should be given a unique identifier, and its development and status should be tracked. Changes, delays, or other factors should be clearly recorded and disseminated. A status accountant may be tasked with actually tracking the products within a project as an autonomous internal auditor, verifying management reports and assessments. Configuration management, whether conducted as a stand-alone task by an independent manager within the project team or conducted as part of a wider job specification, is vital to ensure good service delivery. Services or products should be monitored, registered, and documented to ensure that the client has evidenced documentation or materials to represent the stage of the product or the activities conducted within the context of the contract.

Product Assessment

Product assessments may occur throughout their development, with baseline reports recording the status of the product at a specific time. When the product is complete, it should be protected from interference until it can be evaluated by an authorized entity; this action reduces the possibility of release from control without due quality assurance checks. For service-related projects, product assessment may be represented by the frequency a service is provided in relation to contract agreements or perhaps the number of personnel on post. Service delivery tracking and quality assessments, or product protection, amount to the provision of a clearly tested, quantified, and documented product to the client, meeting time, cost, and quality expectations.

Project Estimations

The ability to accurately define the time, effort, and cost of each component of a project is fundamental to effective planning, management, and delivery. At times, mean average estimations will be used to determine the requirement for an element of the project. This averaging approach can be a simple system of determining the most optimistic delivery time along with the most pessimistic, then planning using the medium between the two figures. Often for service-related projects, the requirement may be fluid, and the client may not have finalized the project design. This is common when companies operate within new environments where they have difficulties understanding environmental influences and so estimate schedules and resource needs. Rough order of magnitude (ROM) estimations can be useful to provide a solution to a requirement based on known and estimated factors; ROM estimations permit a degree of maneuverability to both the project team and provider. Basic ordering agreements also provide a shopping list to project teams so that swift and contractually acceptable adjustments or changes can be made when requirement levels shift.

Complex Dependencies

Elements or activities within a project may be reliant on or influenced by external factors or by other stage elements. Resource and efficiency management is therefore essential to avoid loss of time, effort, or resources. Exhibit 7.9 offers a representation of simple and complex project dependencies. Critical path analysis is used to chart complex and significant dependencies that will disrupt project operations. All projects should seek to identify the dependency relationships among different stages, work packages, and requirements in order to best sequence each activity.

Risk Logs

A risk log is retained within the project team to identify and track risks to the project's activities and success. Risks can come in any form, and are defined as those elements that will undermine the business case, impede time goals and milestones, impede quality levels and productivity outputs, or increase financial or commercial threats to the company. Risk management of a project's risks involves the same principles as assessing and countering physical risks; only the risk nature changes. Business and project risk management should be assigned to an accountable manager in order to best mitigate risk levels and to ensure that appropriate risk management resources and focus are applied to offset these threats. Risks should be clearly identified and commercial tolerance levels determined, permitting various layers of management and oversight to monitor how risk is influencing or affecting the project. Risk reporting should be included within the risk log management approach, raising events or activities that might enter into the high end of the company's tolerance levels as well as those exceptions that may exceed stipulated risk levels. Clear parameters of risk acceptance should be defined. Highlight reports should be created when risk tolerances are neared, and exception reports should be created when they are breached, as illustrated in Exhibit 7.10. Events or activities which occur on the outer edge of accepted tolerance levels result in a highlight report, while those which move outside of permissible tolerance levels result in an exception report.

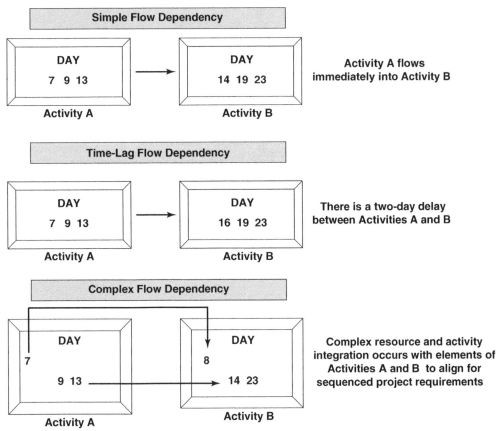

Exhibit 7.9 Project Flow Dependencies

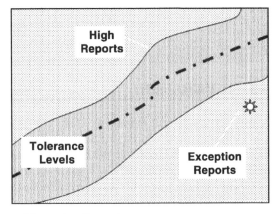

Exhibit 7.10 Highlight and Exception Reporting

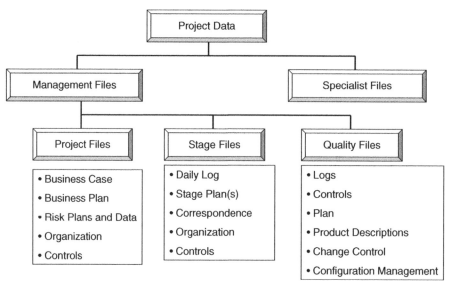

Exhibit 7.11   Project Data Management

Data Management

Sound administration supports effective project management. Frequently project weaknesses and vulnerabilities occur as a result of poor administrative controls and practices. Data management is important to manage significant amounts of information flowing through, or created by the project, both to support decision making, accounting, and quality assurance practices, and also to enable milestone and quality assurance measurements to be assessed. In addition, data management is vital to support internal and external audits, and may be a contracted requirement from the client, especially for government projects. Exhibit 7.11 provides a sample of how project management data should be organized in order to permit effective information management and access.

Custodianship may be shared or centrally stored on an intranet, enabling a range of managers to access core data files. Clear and accurate records and assessments need to be retained, and transparency should be available to appropriate parties. Data mining and referencing should be simplified to make the project management more efficient and to provide a greater degree of transparency to identify and avoid project risks.

RISK AND SECURITY PROJECT MANAGEMENT

Risk consultancy and security service project management should follow the same themes as for any industry project planning methodologies, although some terminologies may be different and the focus and emphasis may be more to identify and prevent physical rather than business or project operating risks. Regardless of the services or products being provided, risk consulting and security service fundamentally strive to achieve the same goals as a textiles or mining project: to produce agreed services or products on time, in budget, and to specification.

While risk consultancy defines and mitigates risks through forward planning and intelligence-driven policies, operational project management within difficult environments is the practical implementation and sustainment of risk policies, delivering the service of safety or protection to project staff, resources, and activities. The integration of product project management with risk and security project management ensures that both elements of an activity are compatibly aligned and work to support each other, rather than creating friction or operating in conflict. Operational planning should also be intelligence led. It is best conducted with the integration of available and appropriate external support, establishing an augmented or mutually supporting project environment rather than allowing the project to operate in isolation or ignorance of the risk climate. At all times a holistic approach should be adopted, with all business and security considerations, groups, and measures being balanced to best support safe and effective project operations.

Security project management should seek to establish project stages and work packages, whether it is a risk assessment stage of an oil installation in Kazakhstan leading to the deployment of security personnel to protect a Caspian Shelf oil facility or the provision of convoy escorts to move medical supplies from San Marcos to Totonicapán in Guatemala. While security project management typically focuses on the delivery of practical services, project planners must still be cognizant of commercial considerations, including:

- Risk and liability tolerances of both the company and the security vendor.
- The safety and welfare of both project staff, as well as the security vendor's personnel.
- Proven and documented risk management and professional diligence for high-risk tasks.
- Cost/benefit analysis of the risk versus business gains.
- Protection of the company and vendor's reputation.
- Performance management and resource utilization measures.

Security project planning can be supported by preestablished policy and procedural templates, which can be modified to meet new or unique project requirements or environmental considerations. These measures typically focus more on granular details within specific service areas, such as risk reviews and audits or mobile and static security. Operational planning is also conducted in alignment with threat evaluations and risk management policies, defined in the risk management plan, as well as a thorough appreciation of the range of threat types, in terms of both softer business issues and harder physical threat impacts. Projects requiring a security component should be supported by a range of systems, tools, mechanisms, and documents, encapsulating every dimension of consideration for the safe, resource-efficient, and productive delivery of services to a product-oriented project.

Intelligence-Driven Project Planning

Intelligence should form the foundation for project management in terms of business risks. It is especially important in hostile regions, where intelligence will form the basis of the risk management and security plans. It should also be an integrated aspect of a company's activity plan, ensuring that its business goals are placed in an intelligence context and that project activities are efficient, safe, and productive. Only by determining the threats in the activity environment can the risk manager develop an effective and rational plan to keep a company's activities both safe and productive. By understanding the nuances and peculiarities of the intelligence process, risk managers are better positioned to provide more pragmatic plans and policies as well as to represent challenges and solutions more clearly to corporate boards and project management elements. Project managers, contracting officers, and project support elements should also understand the principles of risk management and the intelligence process so that their plans more clearly reflect the limitations placed on them by their operating environment. Unreasonable or poorly organized activities can then be planned against as an instinctive and natural activity, and better resource and stage management will result.

Security project leaders must be capable of holding two focus areas in mind whenever planning a stage or work package: (1) to identify and mitigate risks and (2) to meet and support the business objectives of the project itself. At all stages, the project goals, objectives, constraints, and methods of operation should be considered as a fundamental aspect of the intelligence approach and resulting operational plans. It is only by placing intelligence gathered and assessed within the context of the project activity that productive intelligence planning can be conducted. By understanding the project stages and vulnerabilities, the risk manager can identify not only the project risks, but also how external risks may impact or exacerbate the activities' vulnerabilities.

The process for managing intelligence is usually cyclical in nature and is commonly known as the *intelligence cycle*. This process is systematic and consists of five main elements:

1. Direction
2. Collection
3. Processing
4. Dissemination
5. Evaluation

The process should be a continuous cycle as the final evaluation creates new direction, thus triggering the process again. A linear approach will resolve initial risks; however, it will not address subsequent factors that are generated by the process itself. Responsive rather than predictive intelligence processes typically allow companies to track risks and formulate trend analysis; however, they fail to engage in risk estimations and thus to avoid possible conflicts. These key elements comprise the intelligence process:

- *Direction.* Direction is the initial phase of the intelligence cycle and will be dictated by information requirements (IRs) specified by the corporate board, the project management team, the activity itself, or the security vendor. External factors might also trigger IRs: for example, media reporting of hostile group targeting or threat warnings from embassies and military organizations. Fundamentally there are two main types of IRs:
  1. **Priority information requirements (PIRs).** These are critical information needs, those that have a direct or immediate bearing on the overall project activity, such as the assessment of risks for the delivery of high-value equipment on a particularly vulnerable route or a threat assessment for management planning a new project site.
  2. **Standing information requirements (SIRs).** These are more general information needs. Usually they consist of questions or repetitive data gathering designed to help identify the general risk environment for the activity over a longer period, such as general route threat monitoring and local and regional threat awareness or factors influencing a project site.

Establishing how to dedicate intelligence resources provides the foundation for a successful intelligence cycle. The application of direction must be both considered and pragmatic, as poor management of intelligence resources will undermine the project activities' safety and productivity.

■ *Collection.* Collection is the second phase of the intelligence cycle, forming the basis of the information management plan (IMP). The risk manager and the intelligence staff must determine which resources or contacts should be utilized in order to gather the information identified and then how to best exploit the sources and information so that information can be processed into manageable intelligence products to support the business goals. Often limitations are imposed on collecting intelligence, through security restrictions, a lack of reporting, misinformation, or a lack of information management. A lack of detailed reporting significantly impacts the consultant's ability to establish an accurate picture of the operational threat environment for the company.

Intelligence may form a component of a wider IMP or may be a defined subset of policies and procedures which ensure that significant amounts of raw and processed information are managed, used, and distributed most efficiently. Poor planning and management may underutilize valuable materials due to inefficient storage, presentation, and the ineffective delivery of meaningful data. In addition, it is important to ensure that the right people are included in the distribution audience and that inappropriate parties and individuals are removed. The end user audience should be carefully selected in accordance to need for and authority to receive intelligence information.

■ *Processing.* Processing is the system by which information is collated and initially evaluated and analyzed, transforming raw information into a workable and applicable intelligence product. This aspect of the intelligence cycle is the most challenging and requires expertise in analyzing raw data in order to establish an intelligence picture within the context of the company's activity. Processing should combine incident patterns and trend analysis with more lateral assessments that might link multiple information products into a predictive or holistic picture. Processing information requires an understanding of the company, project, and risk environment. In order to be most effective, the risk manager must be able to:

■ Develop a strategic overview of the evolving threat environment across a region.
■ Establish an understanding of the structure, cultural sensitivities, and diversity of the regional and local population.
■ Develop an extensive knowledge of threat groups or individuals, including intent, capability, and methodologies employed.
■ Understand the socioeconomic and political process and its diametric impact on the security situation.
■ Have a detailed regional and local knowledge of tribal and religious affiliations.
■ Understand how all of this information fits into, or impacts on, the company's operations.

The use of multiple sources of information has inherent problems with regard to ascertaining its reliability and accuracy; the probability of rumors or circular reporting also increases. Consequently, information might be evaluated using a simple grading system based on the standard alphanumeric system used by NATO (North Atlantic Treaty Organization) to highlight the reliability of the source as well as the perceived accuracy of the information.

Exhibit 7.12 Grading Intelligence Information

Grading of Sources	
Reliability of Source	**Accuracy of Information**
A Completely reliable	1 Confirmed by other sources
B Usually reliable	2 Probably true
C Fairly reliable	3 Possibly true
D Not usually reliable	4 Doubtfully true
E Unreliable	5 Improbable
F Reliability cannot be judged	6 Cannot be judged

Intelligence products may include formal reports, studies, audits, briefs, statistical tables or graphics, threat mapping, trend analysis, impact assessments, and spot notifications, as well as supporting elements of other security documents. Exhibit 7.12 demonstrates a simple information grading system on which effective project decision making can be based.

- *Dissemination.* Dissemination is the method by which intelligence products are made available to the end user. The end user may include numerous tiers, from the corporate offices to the activity or project management. For that reason, the data provided may differ or be filtered depending on what each user requires or is sanctioned to receive. The proper management and handling of sensitive or classified materials is important, as is the ability to differentiate the critical distinction between classified and unclassified reporting. The specific needs and timelines of the different users are also important factors, as many operations are fast moving and reliant on the swift and accurate reporting of information. The IMP should match requirements to timelines in order to ensure the product is delivered when required rather than after the event.
- *Evaluation.* There is a significant difference between collecting, collating, and processing information compared to the requirement to understand how information impacts at different levels on the company and project. Evaluation can be the most challenging and subjective aspect of the intelligence cycle, and it relies on expertise and experience to be effective. Evaluation also assists in identifying intelligence gaps so that resources can be tasked to address shortfalls. Initial evaluation in terms of the threat types and likelihood can be conducted during the process phase; however, it is usually at the evaluation phase that the full measure of impact on the company and its activities is addressed. Evaluation is a constant ongoing process that ensures maximum efficiency of the process as a whole.

Exhibit 7.13 illustrates the process flow and processes that form the cyclical elements of the information-gathering and evaluation process.

Intelligence Limitations

The intelligence process is subject to numerous challenges, from the practical gathering of information to the subjectivity of evaluation. Assessments are sometimes difficult to quantify

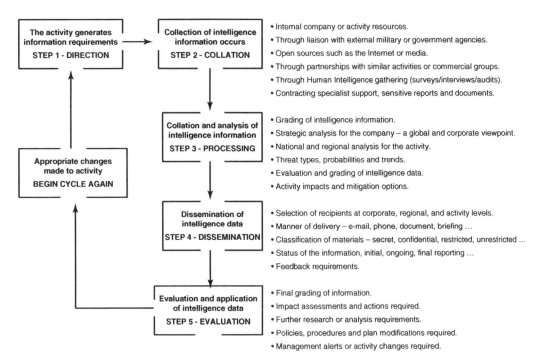

Exhibit 7.13 Intelligence Cycle

or prove until after an event has occurred. Historical reporting and assessment is useful for assessing statistical trends and event probabilities; predicting or forecasting of risks, however, is more difficult to quantify. Project managers responsible for delivering the product often require evidenced information to support change management or exception reports, especially if productivity and milestones are negatively affected. It is by understanding how subjective or problematic evidencing intelligence is that project leaders or corporate officers can better utilize their intelligence resources to the benefit of project design and sustainment. The next list captures some common problems within the intelligence process.

- *Circular reporting.* Information validity can be undermined by rumors and circular reporting, especially from untested human sources and unqualified reviews of technical data. An integrated approach to determine the reliability of both the information and its supporting evidence can mitigate shortfalls to an extent to bring into focus the actual threat versus rumors that confront the activity.
- *Human intelligence (HUMINT).* HUMINT, from internal resources, such as project management and staff, from security personnel, or from visits and meetings, is a useful tool in gathering firsthand information. HUMINT from external agencies, such as security forces, communities, tribal, political leaders, local partners, and employees, yields real-time information for the development of an intelligence picture, although the information is often subjective and prone to perception and bias. The ability to rapidly receive, interpret, and disseminate sensitive and accurate information is vitally important

to maintaining a current threat picture, as this will permit operational staff to develop real-time situational awareness while also permitting project management to conduct strategic and long-term planning.

■ *Analyzing information.* A common error in challenging environments is using available intelligence data for statistical purposes only rather than as a foundation of intelligence assessments. Risk managers and their intelligence staff must thoroughly analyze all available intelligence and formulate clear and concise predictive assessments as to the probability of a particular event occurring in a particular area or time—effectively, they must make sense of partial or complex information and then use the materials as the basis of recommendations or decision making. A retrospective assessment of what has happened in the past is not sufficient. The predictive nature of an assessment must (where possible) be based on historical information, but the assessment must also use trends, risk, event triggers, and other factors to forecast risks on current and future activities. Subjectivity must also be considered, ensuring that the evaluation is least influenced by personal perspective or subconscious preconceived beliefs. In order to better support their planning requirements, companies should request that their intelligence resources provide assessments rather than regurgitations.

MANAGEMENT CATEGORIES

Project management is dependent on the provision of the correct organizational structure to support the activity, populated with the right appointees to undertake the tasks. Labor categories of risk consultancy and security services may be tailored to suit a company's particular requirements or might be reflective of the environment or region in which an activity operates. A degree of innovation is required by both the company and the service vendors to ensure that the right management elements are aligned to the business needs. That said, outside of specific industry, environment, or regional requirements, the project management requirements are relatively uniform in nature. When developing a new contract or reviewing the needs of an existing activity, it is important to establish requirement tiers within each form of service area. Recruiting and funding an expert logistician to manage a pool of six vehicles, for example, is a waste of resources, talent, and budget. Conversely, allowing a manager with little experience to run a multidimensional program with hundreds of staff is under-resourcing a role and will likely result in project difficulties or failure.

It is also important to differentiate *activity* management from *support* management. An activity manager will provide advice and direction directly to manage the company's needs, influencing the manner in which a business activity is planned and conducted at both macro- and micro-levels. Support management typically provides specific control of individual events or systems but generally do not provide advice or control outside of a narrow security or administration field, nor do the decisions of support management normally influence the activity as a whole. For example, an operations manager who plans and supervises secured freight movements will influence how the project is planned, managed, and conducted, while a close protection team manager will determine only how an individual task is planned and conducted in order to support the broader activity. This distinction is, of course, subjective; however, the degree of influence and scope and longevity of impact will separate the two forms of management element within a project team. When structuring the project team within a security organization, it is useful to determine a management tiering system. Such a system might include:

- Senior-level posts dealing directly with the executive board or program manager for complex and significant activities.
- Middle-level posts dealing directly with project managers for individual tasks or activity requirements.
- Low-level posts supporting project teams in management functions, undertaking important tasks, and providing advice and recommendations, but not directing an activity.

Activity Management

The activity management element of a project is responsible for developing strategies, concepts, innovations, and mechanisms to directly advise, support, and improve the company's activity in terms of planning, productivity, and administration. Activity management will be responsible for advising the company in its fields of expertise or managing resources in key areas. Security vendor activity managers should be considered part of, or advisors to, the company's project management team. The level of influence and the scope of an activity manager's role will be determined by the company, contractual agreements, environment, activity, and the caliber of the individual holding the post. A sample of security vendor activity management posts follows.

- *Embedded consultant or manager.* Security risk consultants and security managers are the direct interface between a vendor and the company and provide a full spectrum of security management capabilities on an outsourced basis. This is a cost-efficient method by which an organization can cut its overhead, avoid dedicated resource-specific expertise, and remain fully focused on project goals. Typically embedded consultants are on-site for short periods of time (normally less than 30 days) and conduct security assessments and develop security documents to be implemented by long-term management elements. Embedded consultants and managers may also initiate a complex requirement. Often they draw on the wider resources of their parent company to facilitate contractual agreements. For specific industry or regional requirements, they may provide an initial focal point for establishing strong relationships with military, law enforcement, and governmental agencies in order to allow the company to operate with the greatest degree of safety and efficiency in new or challenging environments. Alternatively, they may provide a conduit for relationship building with local businesses and community leaders based on existing contacts.
- *Program security manager.* Typically a program security manager provides a dual function, providing senior risk consultancy services for complex and dynamic programs as well as managing sizable security personnel, resources, and assets directly with senior-level company project and risk management. The program security manager may also manage strategic operational and contractual planning functions, having both a holistic and a detailed understanding of the operational requirements within contractual and

commercial parameters. Leading the crisis management team, the program security manager will liaise at all levels with multifaceted organizations. This manager will provide detailed, accurate, and well-staffed security documents and exhibits for complex and dynamic projects within the program as well as clear and easily digestible program and project reviews, policy papers, contingency and crisis management plans, training procedures and quality assurance protocols. The manager also will draft contract proposals, scopes of work (SOWs), and ROMs. Directing and accountable for the management of sizable accounting and procurement requirements, the program security manager must have sound commercial awareness and be able to identify commercial opportunities, taking these forward in liaison with appropriate corporate management. Dynamic and proactive, the program security manager will be expected to predict future contractual requirements, placing them into an operational context, while always ensuring that reasonable client expectations are met in full.

- *Regional security manager.* The regional security manager manages multiple complex or simple projects indirectly and remotely for the company, within a clearly defined geographical area, rather than involving him- or herself in their day-to-day management. Supplying advice, guidance, and support to the program security manager, the regional security manager provides regional threat trend analyses, policy papers, documents, and reviews on multiple project requirements, ensuring that policies and procedures are implemented to standard. Strong management skills and focused consultancy provision is required, with liaison with both senior company officers and external agencies. Managing grouped activity accounting, logistical requirements, and control on behalf of the program manager, the regional security manager plays a key role on the crisis management team, providing ground knowledge and local interfaces to support incident resolution.

- *Project security manager.* The project security manager typically manages individual tasks in the program's geographic area or complex and isolated activities on behalf of the program security manager. Dealing directly to the company project manager, the project security manager provides task-specific consultancy and security management functions. These managers should network local relationships, providing the project interface with multifaceted organizations, at senior levels, in order to provide best service provision. Leading the local crisis response team, they should have the latitude to make necessary operational decisions in coordination with senior management. Project security managers should provide the project detailed, accurate, and well-staffed security documents and exhibits for the project as well as administrative and logistical oversight of all activity operations.

- *Operations manager.* The operations manager provides the vendor-to-company interface on a daily basis, at all levels, for practical mobile and static tasks or services. Establishing a clear and intelligence-driven threat assessment for all operational planning requirements, this manager must be able to predict threat trends from available intelligence resources and place the threats into both an operational and a corporate policy context. Delivering operational and threat trend analysis to determine operational requirements as well as associated project impacts, the operations manager must evidence assessments and recommendations with appropriate security documents and exhibits. These managers are part of the crisis response team, providing well-reasoned operational recommendations to the security consultant as well as coordinating and directing tactical resources.

Support Management

The support management element is responsible for providing information, coordination, and the management of functions or specific tasks within the project. These managers advise the activity management elements and may be used to provide expert advice during briefings or policy development, as well as directing and administering their own areas of responsibility. Support management is instrumental in developing the foundations of strategies, concepts, innovations, and mechanisms for the support and improvement of the company's activity in terms of planning, productivity, and administration, although the final product usually is delivered by the activity management element. Support management focuses on systems and processes rather than consultancy and management, and may be more tactical in nature, rather than strategic. For large operations, support managers may have increasing levels of influence and responsibility, leading them to straddle the support and activity service areas. A sample of support management posts follows.

- *Administration and finance.* The administration and finance manager typically manages all vendor-to-company billing issues, document production, tracking, and auditing, and ensures that financial systems and processes reflect logistical accounting and procurement activities. This person also manages all personnel deployments, payment processing, and welfare issues. Liaising directly with the company financial management on invoice and payment matters, procurement, and associated regulatory requirements, he or she advises the program security manager on all matters related to finance and administration.
- *Logistics specialist.* The logistics manager is responsible for the procurement and accounting of contractual equipment, stores, and assets, under the supervision of the finance manager. Maintaining accounts for the receipt and tracking of company and provider-related equipment and materials, including all subaccounts, ensuring that all stores and registers are maintained to the required operational standard, with supportive documentation meeting auditing requirements.
- *Communications manager.* The communications manager is required to establish the communications plan and network interfaces as well as to maintain all security communications and information technology (IT) equipment, supported where appropriate by communications technicians who assist with the maintenance of communications links to remote locations and to security teams. The communications manager also is responsible for the maintenance of the vehicle fleet communications systems as well as first-line repairs and servicing of communications and IT equipment.
- *Intelligence officer.* The intelligence officer establishes close links with civil and military intelligence agencies. This post collects, collates, and analyzes information relating to the threat environment and disseminates the information through reports, briefings, and presentations. This role is critical in providing risk mitigation information for all project operations, thus identifying and avoiding threats. The intelligence manager supports the activities of the program/project security managers and operations managers.
- *Training manager.* The training manager is responsible for the establishment of training and enabling objectives to meet a wide spectrum of professional training requirements, for both expatriates and foreign nationals. Implementing training policies and plans under the supervision of senior management, the training manager retains accurate and

detailed records of training conducted for auditing purposes. The training manager requires strong instructional and administrative abilities.

These sample management positions provide an insight in some of the roles and responsibilities of project management staff as well as the parameters in which they might operate.

Other positions, such as liaison officers, medical staff, camp managers, technical specialists, and tactical command elements, also play a role in complex contractual service requirements.

PROJECT CONTROLS

Typically project offices are established to provide a focal point for project teams as well as a physical location to integrate company and vendor management and external supporting agencies. Often project elements are dispersed geographically within an area of operation. In permissive environments, personnel and resources are usually held in office locations, where other typical functional activities occur. However, within challenging environments, risk- and security-related project management functions may be physically separated from the main project team area due to the restrictions and sensitivities associated with information being processed and the tactical nature of some project decisions. These separated locations might be called a tactical operations center (TOC). They provide a project operations and communications center for the activity, often adjacent to or co-located with the company project management.

The TOC is often the management and communications focal point for regional strategy, planning, management, intelligence activities, and standards liaising at the regional and local levels with appropriate foreign military and ambassadorial staff and other commercial organizations. The TOC ensures that appropriate support is provided to assist the functions of the project and security management. The TOC also provides mission direction and functional management for all mobile, convoy, and static security activities, setting policy and direction and coordinating with military and other agencies. The TOC should also maintain undisrupted oversight and communications with each project location and working party, ensuring that risks and crisis events are best mitigated and managed. The intelligence element of the TOC also provides both strategic and regional intelligence direction, dissemination, and information management. The TOC should maintain a detailed security and intelligence database, with management planning documents such as intelligence reports, situation boards (updated every 24 hours), threat warnings, marked routes, military and government location maps, project site maps, threat overlays, security plans and surveys, risk management systems, standard operating procedures (SOPs) and tactics, techniques and procedures (TTPs), medevac plans, communication networking details, incident and crisis management plans, evacuation plans, and crisis response policies and procedures. These documents allow program and security management to have up-to-date information for most effective project and mission planning.

The TOC might also offer immediate and real-time briefings to appropriate project staff to support dynamic project requirements. It also will act as the administrative center for logistics planning, personnel files and records, training plans, and documents. The TOC should have direct lines of command and communications with the country operations center to integrate management and activities to best support the company's program. It also should be connected to the corporate crisis response center, if one exists.

PROJECT INTEGRATION

It is important that both management and technologies are integrated internally and externally to develop the most efficient project management services, as defined in an effectiveness plan. Effective management structures must be developed to ensure that decisions and information are managed most expeditiously and to ensure that data are streamlined and captured through systems and mechanisms that enable their most effective use and response. The use of semi-automated management systems, alert processes, and templated documents supports the integration of low- and high-end technologies, enabling risk managers and project leaders to focus more on strategic and operational planning. As well as enabling corporate offices to receive a greater flow of detailed and usable information, with least burden upon project teams.

Interfaces with external agencies and governments should also be part of the project integration approach, leveraging support or augmenting capabilities through the development and consolidation of relationships and agreements. Overlapping support and reciprocal agreements can be effective in increasing capabilities exponentially. A company looking only inward at its own resources and capabilities might be failing to exploit or leverage considerable support mechanisms and services from government or other agencies. Risk managers and their security vendors should seek ways of establishing agreements or arrangements with police, military, government, commercial, and other security companies to augment the organic company resources and capabilities.

Ideally technology, communications, and decision making should be managed in such a way as to integrate organic and external resources to produce the most effective risk mitigation and security services, at the most reasonable price. Inefficiencies and a lack of innovation within the security element of project management undermines risk management and incurs unnecessary costs to the company.

Service Delivery

Security project managers should have clearly defined and measurable performance matrixes against which they and their client assess the quality of their performance. The same requirements apply as for any other project: meeting service expectations on time, to scope, and within budget. Chapter 3 captures the main elements of ensuring good service delivery. However, project managers should also be mindful of over- or under-thinking project needs, as often managers overcomplicate a project's solution; conversely, vendors may appoint under-qualified managers who are ignorant of the complexities of the project requirements. Security project management should reach a balance in terms of proposing pragmatic and realistic solutions that meet both holistic and dynamic needs, reflecting both the project and corporate needs.

Effective service delivery should also be based on cross-utilizations and operational efficiencies, where project managers seek ways to best use current resources rather than unnecessarily expand or compound resource requirements. Concurrent taskings are often possible with effective training or educational regimes and sensible scheduling, and vendor project managers should work closely with the company to identify how additional resource mileage can be gained through intelligent development and use of existing resources. Companies should also be aware that some vendors have a tendency to overcompensate in their solution, seeking resources that provide a service which exceeds rather than meets expectations.

At times friction exists between business and project leadership, where the sales team defines expectations that the project team must implement. The balance between an operationally sound but competitive solution can create discord between teams. Where possible, integration of the business and the operational project groups provides an effective method by which to develop and present a realistic and competitive solution that can be implemented with least error or effort. During project sustainment, field project teams and their corporate counterparts may also have differing perspectives and focus areas. Bridging the divide between the two will create an environment for better business results.

Both companies and vendors should also ensure that they address liability requirements when presenting solutions or documents. Often companies include a liability waiver in any formal document so that miscommunications or high-volume reporting efforts do not expose parties to risk.

In summary, effective project management is the coordination and control of resources to deliver a product or service within a defined time and budget, to meet an agreed-upon specification. Projects are dynamic activities with a start point and exit strategy rather than processes that are repetitive with no clear conclusion. Risk management and security services enable the planning of many business activities in remote and challenging environments in a manner likely to achieve the safest and most productive results. Companies can largely limit the probability of project failure through sound planning and the effective mapping of requirements and processes. Process mapping allows project teams to identify diverse group relationships, authorities, and communication channels in order to ascertain where business vulnerabilities lie and how risk impacts might cascade through a project as well as ripple out toward the larger business group.

By understanding what the project is intended to achieve, why it is needed, how it will be conducted, and who is responsible and committed to the task, project teams will have the framework from which to build an effective design solution. For those projects exposed to unusual risks, aligning product and security project management permits the development of a unified plan that meets the company's business goals as well as navigates the project team through a risk environment. Effective risk management brings all capabilities, expertise, and resources together as part of enterprise security, enabling the project to leverage the company's organic resources as well as those of supporting external organizations. Project failure is surprisingly common in commercial and government activities, as most projects exceed time, resource, or budgetary allowances. However, most of the failure can be attributed to poor management and administration. Those project teams that chart out a detailed plan through the project's life cycle—from the inception of the idea and the validation of a business case, to the project plan and implementation involving controlled stages and work packages, to the completion and closure of the project—will invariably identify and avoid common features that lead to failure.

Sound contingency policies that address exception planning and change management requirements will weather crisis events, whereas project teams that have failed to identify and plan against risks will stumble through the business process. For those risk managers designing project solutions, placing the activity in a risk solution framework will present optimal methodologies for companies, allowing them to achieve the desired business results. Establishing effective project management structures and creating configuration management systems to maintain the project on course while tracking deviations and risks will prevent problems from becoming crises. Project teams should also chart out project resources requirements, dependencies, and schedules as part of the project design phase so that risk managers can better align their activities with the business goals and approaches as well as proffer advice and guidance to ensure the approach accurately reflects the operating environment.

As a supporting function to business activities, risk and security managers and their vendors are well placed to work in partnership with business and project leaders to ensure that solutions are tailored from the outside to be both safe and productive. Intelligence lead planning, both in terms of risk consultancy and operational management, should be the foundation for all management approaches. The strengths and weaknesses of the intelligence process should be understood by key stakeholders so that informed decisions can be made to support the overall business goals. Risk and security management can provide a cornerstone to business success, and the sensible structuring of risk and security decision making and supporting groups that complement the project team enable the company both to plan and to sustain the project most effectively throughout its life cycle.

CHAPTER 8

Mobile Security Services

Mobile security services can be broken down into close protection services (people) and convoy protection services (equipment and materials). Companies seeking to operate within unstable or high-risk environments often require mobile security services to enable the conduct of business. Typically the highest-risk element of a program, mobile security presents a challenge at all levels for companies, and the unique factors involved in running mobile security should be fully understood by both risk and program management in order to safeguard the company and personnel as well as seek the maximum level of service delivery from security providers. Mobile security presents a dynamic vulnerability to the company, as personnel and materials are moved, often over protracted periods and distances, within a risk environment.

There are many reasons why mobile security presents the highest levels of risk to a company: Movements and site visits may need to be scheduled and operational information security is easily breached. Visits may be frequent or cyclic in nature, so hostile groups can more easily identify pattern setting, whether from the program staff or associated groups. Routes and access point options are also often limited, and hostile persons may be mobilized when the mobile security element enters a region or site, then lay in wait for the group to depart. Travel also presents a *sustained* period of vulnerability, often removing the group from supporting elements or a safe area as they travel to remote or isolated locations. Also movements may be slow, with large convoys with valuable commodities presenting a slow moving target to criminals or other hostile groups. Thus, companies should consider carefully the manner in which mobile security is planned and conducted, and hold the security provider accountable for the provision of robust and mature intelligence-led security management. Companies should also seek to ensure that auditable management practices are available, not only to enable quality assurance of the services provided, but to also provide an auditable record should an incident occur. Having a robust and documented management process in place demonstrates that the tactical requirements of mobile security are being met by a mature and professional provider, ensuring the company safeguards both employees and the company as an entity.

It is important for the company's risk and program management, as well as the contracting agent, to understand that mobile security services encompass the movement of both personnel and equipment, each coming with separate and unique requirements. The nature of the environment combined with host national laws or external government regulations, industry standards, competitor approaches, company requirements and provider standards will determine the configuration and methodology of service provision. On occasion both services will be provided concurrently, although the operational approach will be different for each, reflecting the unique requirements of each task. Close protective services have been given numerous titles, from personal security details (PSD), armed protection teams (APT), mobile security teams (MST), and security escort teams (SET).[1] The aim of this chapter is not to provide operational or tactical guidelines for the provision of these services to company managers. Rather, this chapter introduces some fundamentals and illustrates some of the core principles for this increasingly required service, to safeguard against physical, liability, and reputational risks as well as maximize the productivity of the program through effective management of security providers, enabling supply change management of both people and resources.

UNDERSTANDING THE NEED

It is often difficult for managers who are remote from the environment in which a program is operating to understand the granular-level requirements of a PSD. Geographic or cultural dislocation can prove challenging even for risk managers who are well versed in tactical requirements, and it is often even more problematic for those managers (program and contract) who do not come from an operational background, but need to procure the services. At all times services within the commercial sector should be operationally sound but price competitive. The problems in gauging the level of resources needed can result in companies accepting unnecessary and unduly costly security services or, conversely, placing their company and personnel at risk by not understanding the practical needs that each unique location may present.

When selecting a security vendor, the company should gauge the past performance and capabilities of the vendor in providing this complex and high-risk service. The level of personnel skill sets and the methodology of approach for PSD operations should not be underestimated. PSD or convoy services are not a simple service, and often the operational approach will morph over time as the environment, both commercial and risk, changes. The *profile* of the PSD required should also be carefully considered by both corporate and field management. A diplomatic client often requires an unobtrusive security approach, whereas a construction engineer working a site in a high-risk environment may require a more robust profile approach. The profile of the PSD will be an important selection aspect; the PSD will represent the company, and any indiscretions by the provider can mar both the company's reputation and its performance on task.

At all times companies should seek close protection personnel who can balance tact and diplomacy with the harder tactical response measures in order to provide the most professional standard of delivery, as often when both a *soft* and a *hard* approach is required. The soft approach is embodied by the stereotypical suited and polite close protection officer who stands in the background unobtrusively. The hard approach is the ability to respond in an appropriately robust manner to threats to the client or principal under their charge. A mature and proven security provider will select personnel who can straddle both areas, employing each where appropriate or needed. There are five fundamental elements a company must consider when engaging a successful PSD:

1. The selection of experienced and qualified personnel or vendor.
2. Appropriate and effective mission and area specific training.
3. The ability to effectively plan and conduct operations.
4. The ability to operate lawfully within a region.
5. The ability to import and sustain specialist equipment and vehicles.

The mission statement that follows captures the consistent theme that defines what a company should seek in a PSD provider. The aim of a PSD is to protect, both by planning around risks and by extracting from risks as quickly and professionally as possible.

> The PSD's mission is to provide an environment in which a client can safely and productively conduct business, and to remove the client from harm's way as quickly and safely as possible in the event of a crisis event.

PSD STRUCTURING

Companies should be aware that there are no industry standards for how a PSD may be configured or indeed operate. Security providers typically draw on past experiences, either within the government sector (Secret Service, military, or police) or commercial experiences (typically a modification of the government approach). Approaches often vary, and will be driven by risk, cost, social factors (the environment, regulations, and culture), and client preference. Risk and program managers should consider how these areas may influence their selection of a PSD configuration as well as how they expect the PSD to operate:

- *Risk*. Risk is usually directly associated with cost, as the higher the risks, the more it will cost to offset the risks. High-risk environments usually result in expensive armored vehicles, equipment, and high-cost expatriate security personnel. Low-risk environments often result in low-cost soft-skinned vehicles and less costly local providers. Risk can be presented in terms of where the company operates, what general threats are present (improvised explosive devices [IEDs], kidnap and ransom, etc.) as well as what activities the company is undertaking and how these activities may increase the level of risk. Vulnerabilities may also come from operating in remote sites, traveling long distances, or traveling through areas of varying hostility. Risk may also be considered in relation to the impact of losing people or resources in terms of company liability, reputation, and productivity.
- *Cost*. PSDs are costly services, involving vehicles, communications equipment, personnel and their equipment, and insurances. Cost will often drive the configuration used, especially in commercially funded operations. The *sticker shock* that often accompanies the realization of how much an armored vehicle or electronic countermeasures equipment costs, as well as the cumulative costs of highly trained personnel, often leads procurers to seek cost savings in terms of what assets are used and the quality of the people employed. Companies should be careful to balance the actual security needs against an effort to be competitive. Where necessary, they should identify where business cannot be done because the costs of security outweigh the commercial gains.
- *Social Factors*. It may be required or desirable to employ local personnel within a PSD, either as a host nation or foreign government initiative to create meaningful employment. This can be either advised or required and will define the size and nationality composition of the team. The value of using local national providers is reflected in regional awareness, language skills, and community interaction. Local employees also often

represent a significant cost saving, in terms of both wage and life support costs. The socioeconomic aspect of a security approach should be carefully considered as it brings both direct and indirect value to the company.

■ *Client preference*. Each company will define the composition of the team according to risk tolerance, employee morale, project cost, and activity requirements. Selection criteria are subjective and may lean toward inappropriate configurations at times, as poor judgment, overzealous cost savings, a lack of understanding, and miscommunication define the approach. Security vendors will also be vying for business and will seek to offer the most competitive bid, which may or may not represent the actual need. The company should seek to establish some clinical criteria for selection, based on specified risk tolerances, technical needs, and cost parameters.

Security Profiles

As a matter of protocol, it is important to determine the security profile required for the company as well as environments where that profile may need to be modified. Where possible, these agreed-upon profiles should be documented, either at the beginning of the contracting process or while operations are being mobilized between the vendor and company. For example, the company may conduct most of its work within high-risk project sites requiring a team with rifles and equipment *on show* (visible), but may also occasionally attend meetings where security personnel must have a much lower profile, with all offensive equipment hidden or absent. As such, establishing the ability to adopt a range of profiles to suit both the changing environment and company needs is important for a professional delivery of service. The same applies to the mode of transport used to move company employees. High-profile vehicle movements generally use armored SUV vehicles, which provide excellent cross-country and urban curb-jumping capabilities. They also offer a higher profile to military forces, which reduces the likelihood of blue on white incidents (accidental firing by the military on civilian personnel). The disadvantage is that SUVs generally indicate Western or government movements to hostile groups. Conversely low-profile vehicle movements generally use armored passenger or saloon-style vehicles, allowing vehicles to travel less conspicuously among the local populace. The disadvantages are increased chances of blue on white, the inability to use cross-country travel options, and an increased likelihood of being caught in urban traffic. In low-risk environments, standard civilian vehicles (nonarmored) may be used, changing to meet the image of the clients and the environmental conditions they are traveling in. It is the responsibility of both risk and program managers to define what profiles they require under different circumstances, and then to ensure the provider understands and meets these expectations.

PSD Tiering

The nature of the business requirements and the risk environment often change during the life span of a project. For that reason, developing a robust PSD tiering system often significantly increases business and operational productivity. While many operations managers state that it is difficult to predict future operational needs, creating a sliding scale of configuration options is a sound practice that enables effective upscaling should the risk

PSD Personnel Key

⊘ Expatriate Team Leader

⊘ Expatriate Team Deputy Team Leader

⊘ Expatriate Team Member

◆ Third Country National Team Leader

◆ Third Country National Deputy Team Leader

◆ Third Country National Team Members

● Local National Team Leader

◐ Local National Deputy Team Leader

● Local National Team Member/Driver

○ Client Passenger

Vehicle Descriptive Key

Counterattack Team

Client Passenger Vehicle

Scout Vehicle

Armored Vehicle

Soft-Skinned Vehicle

PSD Tier 1 : EXAMPLE

Passenger Vehicle

Soft Skinned Vehicle

PSD Tier 3 : EXAMPLE

Scout Vehicle   Passenger Vehicle   Counter Attack Team

Soft Skinned Vehicle   Armored Vehicle   Soft Skinned Vehicle

PSD Tier 6 : EXAMPLE

Scout Vehicle   Passenger Vehicle   Counter Attack Team

Soft Skinned Vehicle   Armored Vehicle   Soft Skinned Vehicle

Exhibit 8.1 PSD Tiering Methodology

environment deteriorate or downscaling should the risks decline and local conditions improve, as shown in Exhibit 8.1. Tiering also creates the foundations for service delivery constancy, ensuring uniformity amongst multiple projects, and an understanding at all levels of the requirement and approach. Tiering should seek to identify the normal range of PSD configurations while not removing the ability to add innovations that are fundamental to security provisions, in challenging environments. Tiering should be based on the considerations of: regional and national threats, specified high-threat areas, route threats, remote or long-range task risks, distances from supporting elements, the ability to secure the venue site, the frequency of visits, whether the passenger or activity is a high-value target, and the ability to respond quickly to increasing risks or tensions.

Tiering should reflect both personnel and vehicles, and if represented visually (as shown in Exhibit 8.1), it can represent the operational approach in a clear fashion. Tiering enables management to affect a staged increase or decrease in PSD profile. Management should be wary of downscaling the configuration without reviewing the need over a measured period, as short periods of threat permissiveness can represent a false image of the risks, and upscaling a PSD requires significant resource management and has considerable additional cost implications (especially for mobilization and procurement). Tiering also lends itself to bolt-ons if a unique activity or circumstance requires an approach currently not accounted for. For example, management may select Tier 3 for a standard task but require the route to be cleared due to recent increases in roadside IEDs and may wish to add an additional soft-skin and two local close protection officers as a surveillance team to clear the route several hours prior to the PSD's task, as illustrated in Exhibit 8.2. This will allow management to borrow

PSD Tier 3 +

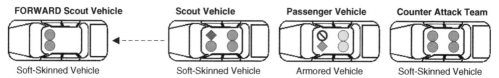

Soft-Skinned Vehicle   Soft-Skinned Vehicle   Armored Vehicle   Soft-Skinned Vehicle

Exhibit 8.2 Bolting on PSD Resources

elements from other PSDs for short durations to achieve dynamic or singular tasks. In addition, risk managers should consider tiering for nonroad movements where PSD personnel can be used. This is especially common in high-risk or remote environments, where air travel may be frequently used and close protection officers may need to travel with clients aboard aircraft, or maritime vessels.

Tiering schedules should also be connected to a configuration table (see Exhibit 8.3); specific projects or activities should be associated with a defined tier.[2] The regularity of travel (frequency) will also be a component of how configurations are selected.

Military versus Civilian Differences

Companies engaging in large-scale government contracts may be offered direct military support, in order to provide security at office and work sites, logistical support, or for the movement of personnel and equipment. Military organizations can be instrumental in achieving productive and safe business activities. Indeed, many military tactics play an important role within PSD operations, especially for high-risk environments where hostile groups may be heavily armed and use complex infantry-style ambush techniques. However, commercial managers should be aware that there is a distinct difference between how soldiers and commercial close protection officers conduct themselves and respond to an incident. Exhibit 8.4 illustrates policy, ethos, and approach methodologies that distinguish how commercial and military close protection is delivered. When operating with mixed commercial and government security provisions, these differences play a fundamental role in determining any risk management considerations and plans.

Exhibit 8.3 Configuration Table

Project	Activity	Risk	Location	Frequency	Tier	Remarks
Balad Prison	Local area movement	Medium	Balad	Medium	R4	Quick Reaction Force (QRF) on standby
	Movement to Tallil Project	High	Route	Low	R6	High risk, long distance
Tallil Hospital	Local area movement	Low	Tallil	High	R2	Military on call
	Movement to Balad	High	Route	Medium	R6	High risk, long distance

Exhibit 8.4 Differences in Focus between Military and Commercial Security Groups

Military Approach	Close Protection Approach
• The mission is to take offensive action against an attacker.	• The mission is to remove the client from the risk area as quickly as possible; aggression is used only to effect an extraction from the area.
• The unit will work as a team but will be responsible for individual protection.	• The unit will work as a team to protect selected (client) personnel.
• Soldiers are trained to conduct operations using infantry skills and are not trained to be accountable for civilians.	• Personnel are trained to protect the client, using infantry and close protection skills.
• Risk tolerances are viewed in terms of achieving the mission.	• Risk tolerances are viewed in terms to injury to people or impact on the company.

It is important for companies to understand the significant approach and skill differences between soldiers and commercial security companies and their staff, so that companies can maximize the value of any military support offered, while not exposing their employees and company to unacceptable risks. The differences cascade from the executive element down to the security personnel—a military commander inherently views risks differently from a business manager, and soldiers will accordingly respond differently from commercially oriented PSDs. Military commanders not familiar with the commercial risk perspective may unintentionally expose civilian personnel to corporately unacceptable risk levels. The company's risk manager and program managers should be mindful of these differences if under the protection of military forces, raising any tolerance inconsistencies with military commanders and seeking to offset these where possible. Risk mitigation when operating under military protection may be in terms of policies or an activity approach, but may also include incorporating commercial elements (e.g., in high-risk environments, commercial PSDs may operate as part of a military escort, responsible for the direct protection of the civilian employees).

PSD Security Elements

PSD planning is a fusion of intelligence and operations. Each task should be treated as an individual and unique requirement, with a detailed risk mitigation process reducing threats to ensure that activities are conducted with the least risk and greatest project productivity achievable. This ensures the safety of personnel as well as the productivity of the project. The configuration of the PSD is often flexible and dynamic, reflecting the fluid threat environment and mission requirements of the activity and area. While the numbers of vehicles and personnel often remains constant due to cost and contractual limitations, their use should be varied in terms of tactical employment: shaped by the size of the team and the risk environment in which they operate. Various elements that may comprise a PSD include:

■ *Surveillance awareness team (SAT)*. This team is usually comprised of local nationals (LNs) who scout routes or venue sites ahead of the client to identify security concerns, redirecting the PSD to alternative routes or to avoid site threats. These teams can, when appropriate, also be used to gather area intelligence for trip planning (limited use only to avoid exposing these personnel to unnecessary risk).

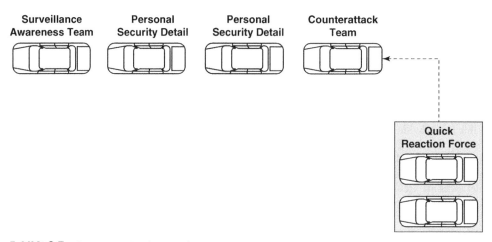

Exhibit 8.5 Augmentation by Quick Reaction Force Resources

- *Personnel security detachment (PSD).* This is the mobile security element that provides intimate protection to a client while moving and when static at the task site.
- *Counterattack team (CAT).* This team may travel in advance or in the rear of the PSD, offering a strong force to assist if extraction of a PSD from a hostile incident site is required. Typically this is a four-person team, but the size varies depending on the specific task requirements and security environment.
- *Quick reaction force (QRF).* A PSD should, where possible, be supported by another PSD as a QRF team. Teams not otherwise tasked with providing other client protection services are best suited for this task, as they are under the direct operational control of the security manager. Even if a PSD is available, a military QRF service should be sought whenever available, as illustrated in Exhibit 8.5. This will require coordination prior to the movement.

The manner in which each team conducts itself will vary depending on established operating procedures, the threat environment, where the team operates, how the program staff need to conduct business, and a range of other dynamic factors. For example, the distance between the SAT ahead of the PSD may change, depending on whether the area is urban or rural, as well as the number of checkpoints on route and the size of a venue to be cleared. The CAT vehicle may also travel slightly outside of the vehicle configuration to better respond to the topographic influences in case of attack. The corporate and field risk managers should seek the balance between establishing agreed operational procedures and policies with a security provider, while also allowing for local tactical decision making that best reflects the dynamic risk environment. The PSD standard operating procedures should be a combination of what must happen and recommendations for how to conduct tactical operations, ensuring best practices are adhered to, without being an unrealistic constraint.

In addition, while the PSD contract may define the configuration of the PSD team, corporate and field risk and program managers should understand and support (where appropriate) the need for a PSD to have the ability to be both flexible and dynamic, reflecting the fluid threat environment and mission requirements of the activity and the location. The selection of suitable PSD security companies who are versed in being both proactive in designing solutions and offering recommendations ahead of requirement, and responsive, meeting company needs quickly and professionally upon request, will support a conflicting corporate need to establish agreed-upon contractual and service expectations, with the ability to also be flexible and responsive. PSD personnel should be able to adapt and combine skills and tactics to suit multiple requirements, including:

- Integration with military forces
- Individual close protection members
- Incorporate counter-attack teams
- Move as mutually supporting PSDs
- High- and low-threat environment tactics
- Mixed nationality teams
- Incorporate surveillance awareness teams
- High- and low-profile approaches
- Venue-clearing and reconnaissance tasks
- VIP and diplomat-level protection
- Convoy configurations
- Personnel air and maritime movements
- Ability to operate within the legal parameters of the host nation

MANAGEMENT PRINCIPLES

In terms of service delivery, PSD operations are typically supported by some form of operations and management element, notably within hostile environments. Within more permissive environments, this operations component may be an office or a manager with a communications team rather than a dedicated control element. For the management of high-risk operations or multiple teams, a strategically focused operational management team might be required, including strategic risk consultancy, security management functions, intelligence collation and analysis, liaison functions, communications and equipment infrastructures, and administrative support, as illustrated in Exhibit 8.6. As with all management organizations, PSD management should seek to provide concurrency of service, meeting both the tactical needs of planning and operating the mobile security teams as well as liaising with external organizations and coordinating resource and activity scheduling, work processes, and outputs to meet the best productivity levels for the company. An effective PSD management team will increase the productivity of a project, offering proactive guidance and recommendations by which to maximize their use, as well as the effectiveness of the project as a whole. Where possible and appropriate, corporate management should seek to integrate a security provider into the project team in order to gain the maximum value from these often-expensive resources. Often this does not happen, and companies undervalue the services they are procuring, to the detriment of their business. When involved in strategic business planning cycles, a risk consultant or security manager often identifies ways to avoid issues or

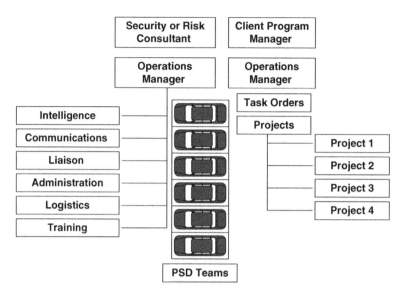

Exhibit 8.6 Complex PSD Management Structures

increase business productivity for long- and medium-term planning, as well as enables sound operational planning that reduces physical risks to traveling personnel.

The corporate risk manager should ensure that the PSD security provider has an extensive array of tactical techniques and procedures (TTPs) and/or standard operating procedures (SOPs) for the contracted PSD services, reflecting the company's requirements as well as host nation and any peacekeeping force stipulations. The PSD management element should demonstrate a flexible and adaptable approach to security and management, showing an understanding that hostile environments create shifting requirements in terms of tactical approaches to security. The provider should proactively advise clients regarding any changes to the risks the company is facing and demonstrate the ability to forecast changing needs, or approaches. The provider should at the very least provide some level of risk consultancy and security management services to manage the actual PSD, whether in the form of an experienced expatriate PSD team leader who concurrently runs the team and draws on the support of their company's larger infrastructure, or a dedicated operations manager or risk consultant who provides higher-level management functions within the contract. Companies should be wary of security providers that have a shallow management structure (direct or indirect) for PSD operations, especially within hostile environments, as this may indicate a lack of knowledge or capacity within the field.

Often complex projects require a dedicated security management team (SMT), which will be designed to ensure the effectiveness, efficiency, and integration of all risk management and security functions provided to the client. The team should act as a fusion center for reviewing, approving, integrating, and promulgating operational concepts, policies, and procedures, ensuring they effectively reflect the intelligence landscape of the project region. The SMT should also provide oversight of operations to ensure policy and procedures are maintained, providing practical and sensible direction to teams as well as to the crisis response component in the event of a serious incident. The SMT often is composed of the tactical operations center staff and might be tasked with developing a pragmatic and established crisis management plan, integrated with external agencies to ensure that resources and information can be quickly processed and delivered in the event of an incident.

Scheduling, Work Process, and Outputs

The procurement of a PSD is aimed at facilitating business. The onus of management and processes should be transferred (where possible) to the security provider to enable the project to focus on business aims. Some oversight, however, is required to ensure that the project operates safely and gets the best value from its PSD resources. Detailed and effective scheduling of these high-cost services will ensure productive utilization, laying the foundation for the most efficient and effective use of the PSD's time to support the project. Scheduling also reduces operational fatigue, an important consideration where the professionalism of PSD personnel will directly impact on personnel safety. Scheduling can also identify high-tempo activity periods where resources will be unable to meet project needs, or show trends that might indicate unnecessary resources, for which resource streamlining could show cost savings.

Scheduling can be through automated scheduling systems (i.e., Primavera or Microsoft Project Manager) or planned manually on whiteboards or spreadsheets. At all times scheduling should encompass operational and managerial experience and knowledge, ensuring that all aspects of the company's requirements are streamlined and integrated, reflecting fluid threat environments and unique project requirements. Scheduling also enables the SMT to conduct intelligence-driven planning rather than be forced into a responsive mode of operation, where tasks are poorly planned (if at all) and expose the company and employees to unnecessary and avoidable risk. Often the lack of scheduling is a reflection of where the security service provider and the client are unable to integrate management approaches and systems. Scheduling is critical for effective, efficient, and safe operations.

It is incumbent on the security provider to support the development of sensible work processes that provide a system that supports effective scheduling, an example of which is illustrated in Exhibit 8.7. By establishing a logical policy for conducting tasks, activities can be made more efficient and safe. While last-notice requirements will always occur, the SMT should reach an agreement with the local risk or program manager to ensure sufficient time is allowed for planning and preparation of any security movement.

The output of a resource should be measured to ensure that it is being fully and appropriately utilized and that all policies and procedures are being implemented in an auditable fashion. During a busy project, it is difficult to dedicate the time and energy to track how resources are being used and whether policies are being adhered to. It is even more difficult to backtrack any historical activities in order to ascertain how and where these resources have been used. To ensure quality assurance at all levels, a simple and measurable output system should be designed and implemented to enable the review of how resources have been used and managed.

To ensure the best management and utilization of the PSD resources, both the procuring company and the contracted security provider should agree to the level of effort and accountability each will contribute to this process.

- *Scheduling.* Who will be responsible for designing and implementing a scheduling system as well as the associated policies that authorize, account for, and manage resource use?

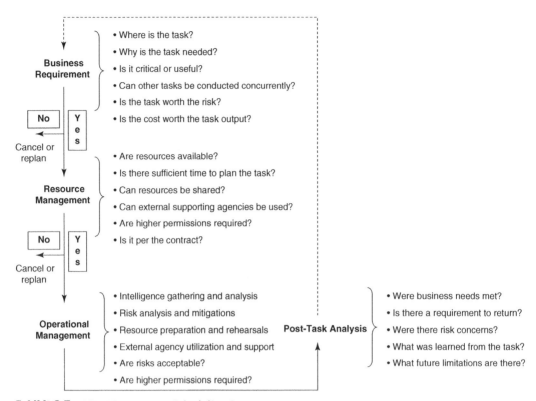

Exhibit 8.7 PSD Management Scheduling Systems

How does scheduling plug into the various departments to ensure resources are available, management is informed, and operational planning is conducted?

■ *Work processes.* Who will be responsible for adapting and enforcing the methodology for both requesting resource use and planning the task? How do the work processes meet changing project needs and environmental risks? Are they connected effectively internally and externally, and are they easily auditable? How does the work process feed into the output element?

■ *Outputs.* Who will be responsible for designing a transparent system by which to record the utilization of resources as well as document that policies and procedures are being adapted where necessary and adhered to at all times? Who is the custodian of all record keeping to allow management at all levels to review how and when resources are being used?

The creation of management SOPs or appropriate project management systems will support all three elements of this management process, ensuring that a system of work is created to support the corporate requirements and to define the needs clearly to those implementing the system. Such policies, or SOPs, should be designed to be clear, simple, and easily used rather than cumbersome, difficult, and confusing. This may sound obvious, but there is a tendency in many companies to overcomplicate policies over time as more elements are added and the original concept is lost in the white noise of corporate jargon.

Risk Sensitization

Managers should be aware that it is natural that project staff who are exposed to risk over a prolonged period can become desensitized to risk or, conversely, oversensitized. Staff members exhibiting a blasé attitude to threats will expose themselves and others to avoidable risk, while others may be less inclined to undertake work as project completion nears. The risk sensitization can also be true of the security provider whose foremost responsibility is to ensure that the company's tolerances are tracked and adhered to. If the security provider's management and operational personnel undertake long duty tours, they may lose a degree of perspective and risk creep may occur, where increasing levels of risk are accepted. PSD operations can be fatiguing and highly stressful for all involved. Strong oversight and sound policies and procedures are required to ensure that consistency of approach and delivery is maintained.

Task Planning Problems

The security provider's goal is to provide the vehicle by which project tasks can be completed. However, the environment in which the project operates often strongly influences how tasks are conducted. The security provider should seek multiple options during the planning process to enable success; the project team must recognize that these options may not always be optimal in terms of how project members wish to conduct business. A sensible middle ground must be reached where risks are identified and acknowledged by the project team, and business goals are sighted and operations geared around by the security component. A good security provider will stand its ground if it believes that the project team members are exposing themselves to an unacceptable degree of risk. The security provider should also be seeking innovations by which to sidestep the risk and allow the project to achieve its goals. A poor security provider will just say no, without seeking alternative methods by which to achieve the business goals, or worse, will accept the project team's lead even if risks are outside of tolerance limits. It is also incumbent on risk and program management elements to realize and accept that there will be instances where timing needs to be changed, longer routes will be used, or tasks will be deferred until a safer period. The task planning process should be collaborative, candid, and cognizant of both business needs and risk issues.

Exhibit 8.8 provides a sample of a program work process and output system at the security provider's operational level.

It is important for all managers to understand that PSD operations require sound planning and that internal company planning time and efforts also reflect the needs of the security provider. Integrated management structures and policies will ensure that both groups work together to achieve a unified product—a safe and productive trip.

PROCESS INTERFACES

When contracting a PSD security company, the corporate risk or security director often seeks a company that has a proven ability to be largely self-reliant—reducing corporate liability exposure, while concurrently ensuring most productive business potential. However, in hostile environments, it is rare that any task is conducted in complete isolation of supporting

Exhibit 8.8 Work Process and Output System Example

Responsible	Work Process	Outputs
Program/project manager generates task	• Security provider security consultant (or designate) prioritizes and deconflicts initial task requirements—*48 hours prior to the task being required.* • Provider's operations manager identifies venue and likely routes to be used. If venue is new, then a surveillance awareness team (SAT) may be used to conduct a reconnaissance and produce an information pack. This will be given to operations manager and intelligence analyst.	• Resources confirmed and booked. • Intelligence and Risk Assessment conducted.
Security provider consultant should confirm which client is authorized to allocate tasks.	• Task is then passed to PSD team leader and deputy team leader, working in conjunction with the operations and intelligence manager who will jointly plan the task in terms of the venue and likely routes. All routes are deconflicted and historical records are consulted to try and ensure the avoidance or setting of patterns and routines—*36 hours prior to the task being required.* • Details of proposed mission will be submitted to sanctioned external agencies 12 hours prior to departure. *This information is critical when requesting security force support in the event of an incident. If this procedure is not adhered to, assistance will not be available. Authorization for the mission to proceed will be obtained at this stage.* • Concurrently the PSD is configured for the task and the SAT controller is briefed on the task. • If for whatever reason the task is delayed, changed, or canceled, consultant is briefed and client program manager is informed. Process may then start again.	• Route and venue reconnaissance conducted where necessary. • Operational plan established—personnel briefed. • External agencies engaged.

elements from government, military, or law enforcement agencies, whether organic or external to the company's resources or capabilities. If available, these external resources should be incorporated into the operational plan where appropriate. The security provider must demonstrate an understanding of the strengths and limitations of external supporting organizations within its policies and approach. This understanding is especially important in terms of intelligence materials and quick reaction forces, where local and organizational interfaces augment both the planning and the executive aspects of PSD operations. Both the corporate and security provider's risk and security management should seek to develop and exploit relationships with multiple external agencies to enhance internal capabilities. Doing so will result in security resource and capability outputs that are significantly higher than the resources (and thus costs) dedicated by the company to the task. Interagency cooperation, integration, and agreements are methods by which to strengthen operational planning and augment internal capacities, usually at no extra cost to the company or security provider. Where possible, a system of internal and external management activities should be developed to ensure that all resources are leveraged in a coordinated and standardized approach, as illustrated in Exhibit 8.9.

Interagency interfaces may also be a stipulated by government bodies. For example, in Iraq in 2007, there was a stated requirement to register movements and tasks with external

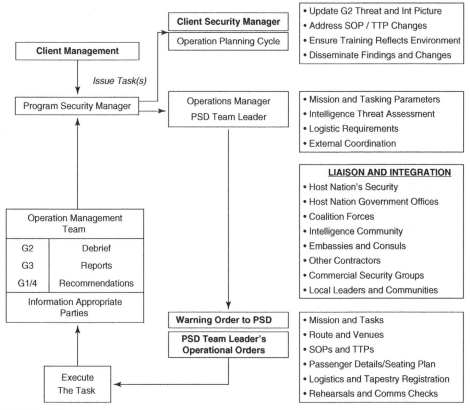

Exhibit 8.9 PSD Process Interfaces

agencies as well as to deconflict activities to avoid possible friction or merge tasks to enhance productivity and safety.

INNOVATIONS

In order to get the most from mobile security services, it is important to understand that this service lends itself to innovation and flexibility at both management and operational levels. Established policies and procedures set the foundation for efficient and well-ordered services; however, leadership and lateral thinking is a key component in meeting ever changing environmental influences. While the contract and costs will require an ordered structure for this service, the correct resource allocation and contract verbiage will enable companies to meet changes quickly and proactively. Both corporate management and the security provider should seek to forecast needs and changes in order to bring innovations and changes to this dynamic service area rather than only being responsive to direct risk or project influences. Reactive changes take place after an incident has occurred rather than addressing problems prior to occurrence, resulting in avoidable risks to personnel or undermining project productivity. Innovations may include:

- Modifying tactics and configurations to meet changing risk factors or project needs.
- Cross-training and skills development of personnel to maximize productivity.
- Intercompany resource sharing to reduce costs and increase productivity.
- Structuring organizations to achieve multiple concurrent tasks—convoy, PSD, crisis response, and so on.
- Creating integrated and redundancy commander structures and management redundancy options.
- Including security provider into management team for project design.
- Establishing management forecasting meetings and reports to identify periods of surge requirement.

PSD TACTICAL PRINCIPLES

Both those procuring and those providing mobile security services should ensure that all PSDs operate through intelligence-driven operational planning, integrating multifaceted agencies and strengths to ensure the task avoids risks or that the PSD is positioned to respond to risks maturely and effectively. This ensures that tasks are conducted with the integration of:

- Training and personnel selection
- Intelligence and risk analysis
- Policies and procedure
- Operational management and integration

to best mitigate risk factors in alignment with the project requirements as well as external party involvement.

Successful integration of these components ensures that proactive management and operational measures are in place to identify and avoid risk during the planning stage, mitigate threats during the task, and ensure that responses to incidents are both effective and lawful. Management elements should ensure that SOPs or TTPs are designed as a central pillar of the management process and that they are implemented so that personnel at all levels, whether within the company or providing support from an external security vendor, are cognizant of how operations should be planned and conducted. Any response to postulated or confirmed threats, whether a suspect vehicle or person, or to an actual attack should be conducted with an awareness that SOPs provide a foundation of approved responses to permit management and security personnel to best respond in an organized, approved, mature, and efficient manner. The development of SOPs also ensures that multiple agencies can more effectively integrate their response activities to bring about the safest resolution to a hostile incident.

While these approved responses will address most of the common threat types and offer support to management and operational personnel by preempting problems and response solutions, it should be acknowledged that responses often do not follow a planned script. A degree of latitude must be incorporated to reflect the peculiarities of each incident, requiring pragmatic, sensible, and measured judgment calls by the PSD team leader. This degree of autonomy requires the PSD and operational management to have the depth and breadth of training, experience, and knowledge to adjust tactical guidelines to suit unique environmental and risk factors, which further emphasizes the need for good selection and training of personnel.

The mobile security service is a fusion of a logical and systematic planning approach, established tactical procedures, and sound operational leadership. The fundamentally operational steps for delivering this service follow.

- The client defines the task requirements.
- The operations manager issues task details to the intelligence manager and PSD team leader.
- The intelligence manager and PSD team leader overlay intelligence with tactical planning.
- The operations manager reviews both intelligence and tactical planning recommendations and determines the viability of the task through a documented task threat assessment (where possible).
- The operations manager determines the configuration and profile of the security group.
- The operations manager decides whether to provide advance clearance security through a situational awareness team.
- The operations manager records the process and raises any concerns to the program security manager or project manager.
- The task is conducted, deferred, or canceled.
- Records are always established and retained for threat assessments conducted.
- All tasks are tracked to ensure patterns are not set using a historical threat matrix.
- Reports and intelligence are generated and recorded for future use.

Information Security

Many companies may not have had projects and personnel exposed to the range of risks that the more challenging environments present. These companies may not recognize the need to withhold administrative information from their management or indeed to mislead them for the sake of security. In the culture of trust that exists in most organizations, it is unnatural, or even repugnant to withhold or mislead management elements, especially senior figures. However, when operating in the most challenging environments, risk and program managers should carefully consider what information should be shared and what information should be guarded. On occasion, misinformation is also a useful tool to maintain operational information security for the safety of personnel and project operations.

The wide spectrum of employee backgrounds and the differences in human dynamics often result in sensitive information being quickly shared outside of the initial planned audience. Many employees will not understand the significance and possible ramifications of sharing such mundane details as when a PSD will be leaving or whom they might be visiting. Limiting information sharing becomes increasingly important in hostile environments, where visits with local leaders, communities, or businesses may provide targeting opportunities for hostile groups. On occasion, therefore, management may need to establish information restrictions or disinformation innovations with agreement and corporate buy- in from executive officers; the probability of employees broadcasting sensitive information publicly should not be underestimated, no matter what instructions they receive.

Standard Operating Procedures and Tactical Techniques and Procedures

A mature and well-established company will have developed comprehensive and pragmatic policies and procedures that govern how it operates. These procedures are especially important for the high-risk service of mobile security. SOPs and TTPs form the basis for how mobile security services will be performed and how incidents will be handled. While many companies incorporate all requirements, SOPs and TTPs, into their policies and procedures because many areas overlap, some break out tactical elements into TTPs. A guideline for those companies wishing to define both areas follows.

- *SOPs* are policies and procedures that govern how management functions are planned and conducted.
- *TTPs* are policies and procedures that define tactical functions and actions.

It is important that these procedures reflect the pragmatic requirements of the task and environment and are kept current to reflect changes in the environment. These procedures should not be unnecessarily restrictive, but should assist management and operators in being more efficient and effective. Management might use these documents to assess the level of detail and competence of a provider prior to an award being made or to confirm the quality of delivery during the contract. The documents might also form the basis of auditable evidence should a liability claim be made against the provider following an injury or death. PSD SOPs might include some of these elements:

- Management responsibilities
- Scheduling and work processes

- Intelligence cycle
- Risk assessment system
- Interagency interfaces
- Communications plan
- Incident management plans
- Serious incident reporting
- PSD recruitment training, and tiering options
- Information security
- PSD briefings
- Internal and external auditing
- Rules of engagement
- Resource management
- Task reporting system
- Special equipment use and issue
- Interagency operations and agreements
- Incident management plans and actions on

SOPs may also include a subcategory called an incident management plan (see Chapter 11), which deals specifically with how incidents themselves are managed.

MOBILE SECURITY CONDUCT

It is important for management elements to understand that there are two fundamental aspects to mobile security: the movement to and the security of the venue site. All planning and operational approaches should focus on these two areas in order to ensure that the best security provision is delivered. Tactical approaches and considerations will be driven by local factors. Each task should be approached as unique, drawing on historical data only for further information and planning support. By determining any patterns set from a historical review of taskings, the risk manager will be better placed to determine whether the company's PSD approach presents an opportunity for hostile groups to more effectively target the project. Some foundational concepts for both aspects of mobile security services follow.

- *Route selection.* The security management team should ensure that route selection reflects not only the risk environment but also road conditions and the location of other friendly groups. Alternative options should the primary route become compromised must be determined, as well as time taken to travel, weather and topographical conditions, and fuel and breakdown considerations. In terms of risk, the operational planners might wish to consider choke points, urban areas, hostile sectors, checkpoints, and other groups' use of routes, which might increase or decrease risk levels (e.g., military convoys drawing fire or clearance operations reducing IED threats). At all times alternative routes, friendly base locations and relationships, trend setting, and known threat areas and levels should be considered during route selection and planning.
- *Venue clearance.* The SMT should be aware that the venue may also pose a significant risk, as personnel are often stationary for extended periods, allowing hostile groups a more measured period of opportunity to engage them. Entry and exit points for vehicles

and pedestrians pose obvious choke points, and the site itself presents an opportunity for attack or detention. If the visit has been planned in advance, information may have also been distributed to inappropriate parties. Therefore, secrecy and disinformation may be required.

By understanding that the task is broken into these two distinct elements, project managers will better understand any constraints placed on them. Often business needs will drive planners to choose the quickest route to a frequent visit site to enable a better use of time; however, this creates trends that significantly increase travel risks. Conversely project management may wish to spend lengthy periods at a venue to get the most from the visit, not realizing that this may allow time for groups to mobilize and prepare for their departure. By understanding the two aspects to mobile security, project staff may better understand the need sometimes to use the longer route and to limit time on-site to offset identified risks.

Planning and Response Considerations

Effectively conducting mobile security services requires a blend of commercial awareness and operational planning. The SMT must establish methods by which the client can safely operate to achieve their goals, taking into account both commercial imperatives and a dynamic risk environment. The PSD's response to postulated or actual threats will be determined by a number of factors:

- Operational and intelligence planning capability
- Nature of the threat
- Environment in which the threat occurs
- Configuration of the PSD
- Application of SOPs and TTPs or operational imperatives to provide a dynamic and lateral approach
- Damages or injuries sustained during the initial period of contact
- Availability of supporting resources

Some examples of considerations a risk manager may wish to consider in order to place mobile security services into a holistic management and operational approach context follow.

Nature of the Threat   A range of possible threats are posed to PSD operations, and the team must assess the nature, scope, and probability of the threat quickly and effectively. If a threat is determined as an insurgent, terrorist, or criminal group, the PSD team leader must identify the different goals and associated threats these diverse groups pose to the PSD. Their intent may range from killing to wounding or detaining personnel. A hostile vehicle may contain a suicide bomber intending to disable, destroy, or channel PSD vehicles into areas for ambush. The initial attack might be only the start of a complex attack involving mines, IEDs, rocket-propelled grenades (RPGs), or other weaponry. Acting under considerable stress, the PSD team leader must quickly determine all of these factors, in order to best coordinate the response utilizing applicable elements of the SOPs, TTPs, incident management plan, as well as training and national laws in order to achieve the safest solution while recognizing the threats posed to the local community.

Environment   Hostile groups will aim to identify a geographic location best suited to achieve their goals. Rugged terrain may disguise a complex ambush site. An ambush within an urban area restricts the PSD response in terms of alternative route selection, either by vehicle or foot extraction, and the application of force due to local laws or moral judgment through risks posed to innocent civilians. Having the PSD engage (with weapons) a vehicle not containing a risk to the team may be aimed (by perpetrators) at sparking local violence or supporting propaganda objectives. The PSD will have identified choke points, high population density areas, route restrictions, safe havens, and likely ambush terrain and hostile group tactical techniques and procedures prior to PSD movement. The SMT's plan will reflect the identification of likely threats in order to enable the PSD to respond quickly, maturely, and professionally to extract passengers and materials from the risk area.

Operational and Intelligence Planning Capability   The aim of operational planning is not to prevent PSD tasks from occurring, but to identify the safest method by which to conduct that task. Operational management integrates strategic planning into operational conduct to safeguard PSD tasks from a range of possible threats. It is only by placing intelligence on local, regional, and national threats into an operational context that PSD planning can be maximized to reduce risk. The use of all intelligence sources allows operational management to determine immediate-, medium-, and long-term threat trends in terms of high-risk areas, time periods, route limitations, support capabilities, and venue factors. Communications are also a key factor, and multiple means of communication are essential, allowing for a real-time awareness of any environmental limitations that might reduce their effectiveness.

PSD Configuration   The configuration of the PSD may change according to task, the profile of passengers, identified threats, and the nature and scope of the movement package. The incorporation of gun trucks" (vehicles with mounted heavy weapons) influences the manner in which a PSD can practically respond to a fast-approaching threat vehicle by allowing better, more obvious visual "gestures" to warn the vehicle to slow down or as a last resort to fire warning shots prior to engaging the vehicle's engine block or tires (to immobilize), thus responding in a graduated and appropriate manner. Counterattack teams may provide additional support capabilities for immobilized vehicles or for extracting injured personnel. The PSD may also embed in a military convoy or have local police escorts. In such cases, the operational plan must incorporate a specific interagency approach as well as appropriate response measures. Cross-training is also required to deconflict multiagency response measures. The formation and operational manner of a PSD also is driven by the environment in which the PSD is operating. Vehicles will space out in open terrain or have closer groupings in restrictive areas in order to provide best mutual support. Foot formations also reflect geographic and threat factors. Speed of vehicle movement must take into account both hostile threats and passive threats, such as road traffic accident risks or driving at night. Tactical approaches must adjust according to the fluid risk environment.

Application of SOPs, TTPs, and Operational Imperatives   Elements of the SOPs and TTPs are firm directives that must be applied under all circumstances. Legal and moral factors peculiar to each environment and circumstance also influence the application of approach and response measures. Tactical responses should be identified and rehearsed to allow security personnel to respond instinctively and effectively to the most probable threats. Security policy documents should also encompass considerable detail regarding threat and risk mitigation measures. However, the actual tactical response reflects operational imperatives specific to each individual incident. The PSD team leader should use the operating policies, training, but above all *tactical judgment* to determine:

- Whether a real threat is posed.
- Whether to issue the order for the graduated use of force, to designate a blocking vehicle to safeguard the passengers.
- Whether alternative road routes can be used to avoid an approaching vehicle threat.
- Whether the team is best suited for a foot or vehicle extraction if under threat.
- Where to relocate to.
- When to cross deck (passengers moving from one vehicle to another) if vehicles immobilized.
- What supporting QRFs as PSDs are required.
- How to most effectively disengage from hostile attention.

Policies and procedures are designed to support, not hinder, tactical leadership. The company should review these policies and procedures to ensure that no conflict exists with their corporate policies or agendas.

Damages or Injuries Sustained   In responding to hostile incidents, the PSD is influenced by damages that vehicles sustain and personnel injuries. Damage to vehicles impedes the speed at which extraction may occur and may require supporting vehicles to support the cross-decking of passengers into functioning vehicles. If vehicles have been rendered immobile or are tactically unusable, personnel might also have to move on foot, requiring specific tactical training and policies to move people to safe areas or waiting vehicles. If passengers do need to change vehicles, vehicles should be placed to provide shielding, with doors interlocking as they cross from one to another. The PSD team leader will need to establish the risks posed by RPGs or heavy-caliber weaponry to armored vehicles, especially those constrained topographically, which may negate the value of using armored vehicles. Injuries to personnel will also influence how the PSD responds; security personnel who are moving casualties must be limited in their tactical responsibilities. First-line treatment of the injured by PSD members also reduces operational capacity.

Support   No PSD operating in high-risk environments should work in complete isolation of military operational oversight, if available. All PSD movements should, where possible, be conducted in conjunction with military planning integration and tracking. In addition, operational and intelligence-driven planning identifies how military or local government operations may influence risk levels for each task. This integration of planning ensures that if a hostile incident occurs, military command centers can effectively mobilize reserves as QRFs, if required and available. The availability and proximity of supporting external agencies as well as any organic resources will influence the manner in which a PSD responds to a hostile incident. The PSD team leader may choose to move to the nearest military base if attacked, may request QRF response to support an immediate or long-range extraction, or request combat air support to permit disengagement from hostile groups. The team leader may also request immediate and comprehensive medical support or may coordinate multiagency support. Multiple factors, notably military footprints within a region, drive the threat environment and associated mitigation and response measures.

Mapping   The use of color-coded routes with spot numbers will provide a level of management control with a degree of security if radios are not encrypted. Spot maps offer a quick and easy method of providing tactical operations center staff with an accurate picture of where the PSD or convoy is at any stage. These codes are difficult for listeners to decipher. Numbers should be randomly selected to avoid establishing a pattern. These maps should be changed frequently to avoid information being compromised, and such mapping should be held in a secure location when not in use. Code words for prominent structures or buildings might also provide a useful tool in informing an operations team of where a PSD or convoy might be as well as when they are leaving or arriving at a venue location. Reference points (obvious point-of-reference structures) can also be provided on grid overlay maps of project sites, to provide further refinement to the grid system which can provide sectoring information, as illustrated in Exhibit 8.10. The SMT should seek to identify any method of clarifying travel and project information through the use of maps, photography, and schematics.

PSD PERSONNEL SELECTION

It is incumbent on the security provider to ensure that each PSD member is carefully recruited, vetted, and trained to ensure all are capable and qualified to undertake these important roles. PSD members often have considerable interaction with the project team and are a direct reflection of the security provider in professionalism and competence. They also often interact with the project team's own clients and thus to an extent represent the company as well. Good security providers require the minimum of several years of military or law enforcement experience with demonstrable tactical skills, proven ability, and inherent judgment as well as specific training to reflect the unique requirements of close protection services. Members' experience should illustrate their ability to counter, deter, detect, and respond to threats as well as an in-depth and practical understanding of threat analysis, personnel security operations, communications, first aid, and the ability to work within a team or in partnership with supporting groups. All PSD members should be vetted to meet these professional standards and should also have a clean criminal background check.

Corporate management must ensure that the security provider requires their personnel to be compliant with host country and coalition military and government standards and requirements, so that their actions reflect and meet legal, moral, and operational requirements. PSD personnel should be trained to respond in a manner that ensures the safety and dignity of local civilians during the response and decision-making process. The safety of civilians should be a core element of any tactical response measure. Poor security providers have loose management policies and procedures in place and may be negligent in terms of adhering to laws or meeting moral obligations. This can reflect as badly on the company as it does on the provider.

Quality assurance must be sustained throughout the life of the contract, not only in the provision of the practical mobile security services, but also the image and approach used by the close protection personnel interacting with the project staff and other external parties.

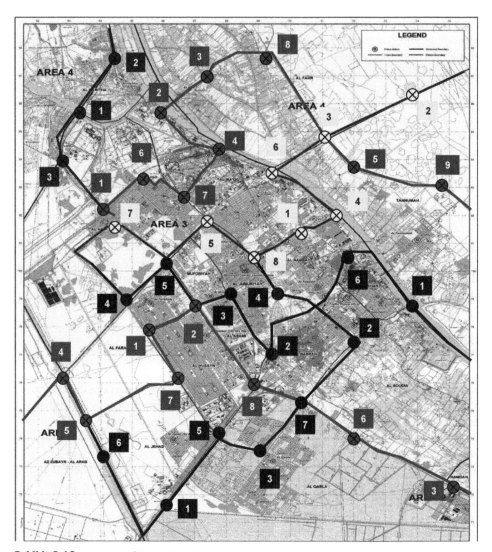

Exhibit 8.10   Route and Spot Mapping

Close protection services must be a balance of quiet professionalism, tact, and diplomacy as well as the ability to respond to extreme threats in challenging environments. Brains, rather than brawn, should be considered as the foundation of personnel selection for close protection services.

Nationalities

Companies may have preferences regarding the use of certain nationalities for PSD and other services. Government bodies may also require or prevent the use of certain nationalities. The use of different nationalities within mobile security operations therefore hinges on a range of factors, including host nation government requirements, community development programs, cost, security, and company preference. Both strengths and weaknesses come with the use of expatriate, third-country national and local national or host nation personnel, and it is important for risk and program management to understand the trade-offs that come from selecting each group. Some of the strengths and weaknesses of each nationality group are discussed next.

Expatriates   Typically expatriates (XPs) have a higher level of professional expertise and security training, which comes from operating in Western military organizations, as well as a better understanding of commercial requirements and operations. These strengths come with a higher cost factor and limitations on local cultural and geographic awareness. Hiring expatriates also might imply to host country leadership that the company is being isolationist and not seeking to engage with the resident community by hiring local professionals and companies.

Third-Country Nationals   Typically third-country nationals (TCNs) from such countries as Nepal, Chile, Fiji, or Africa provide midrange professional expertise and security capabilities. They provide a medium level of professional standard and are often useful for noncritical and supporting functions. TCNs provide lower costs to the project and occasionally have an overlap of cultural interests, which facilities operations. However, often language barriers and cultural differences may undermine their provision of higher-end service delivery.

Local Nationals   Local nationals (LNs) are better integrated with their own environment and communities and can facilitate smoother movement around their own regions and areas. Their native language skills can also be used to navigate problems, and they can provide secondary intelligence support. Often they are also the least costly of nationalities to employ and can be used to develop socioeconomic relationships and programs. That said, local nationals frequently have the lowest level of professional competence and English-language skills, which can significantly increase training and professional development requirements. Ethnic or religious differences might further reduce their effectiveness within different regions, and they are more susceptible to coercion or intimidation.

Training

Companies often overlook the need to permit security providers the time and resources to ensure that pre-deployment and refresher training is conducted. Projects are generally commercially driven, and the common belief is that personnel should arrive on task trained and prepared. While this is an acceptable and logical concept for most situations, within hostile environments a mobilization period is required to refresh or acquaint personnel with their duties, team mates and area of operations. Many companies now accept this need and factor in additional costs and time to enable pre-deployment preparation.

To avoid unnecessary costs and prevent time from being wasted, the security provider should ensure that PSD personnel are selected for their ability to adapt, quickly and professionally, to what is a dynamic and changing role. Personnel should also be selected for their ability to undertake multiple and concurrent functions, thus ensuring that the maximum value is gained from these costly services. Personnel should be able to switch between each role within the PSD, whether as a passenger close protection team member, part of the counterattack team, or as a driver or a rear gunner. In addition, they should be capable of augmenting other security sectors, performing guard services and supporting under extreme conditions the crisis response management team. Each PSD member should be trained to provide the full range of security skills required for protecting high-profile passengers and providing the more robust security function of protecting material convoys in extreme threat locations.

PSD personnel should also be trained and experienced in recognizing the varying threats when encountering terrorist, insurgent, and criminal groups as well as when operating in a wide range of threat environments. They should also be trained to advanced standards for vehicle and foot movement, venue security, and the proper responses to the complex range of threats associated with each. They should all have first aid training skills, as most tasks will be remote from medical support. Personnel should be selected based not only on their ability to conform to comprehensive operational policies and procedures, but also to provide the mental dexterity required for tactical solutions to unique situations. The PSD personnel should also be capable of imparting information to project staff and other external parties— providing detailed PSD or convoy task briefings to appropriate project personnel (delivered at all levels)—as well as relevant procedural training to instill confidence in travelers.

Where possible, PSD personnel should be capable of operating at one level higher than their post in the event of an emergency and to increase operational efficiency for the project. This concept can be implemented in three ways.

1. Personnel are recruited and selected for their ability to adapt to a changing environment quickly and effectively.
2. Their experience is vetted thorough the selection process to ensure that personnel come with a higher-than-required level of specialist and general expertise as well as a depth of subject matter and operational experience.
3. Skill development specifically includes cross-training to ensure that personnel have the skill sets needed to perform additional duties.

Exhibit 8.11 outlines some components that should be considered for a PSD member's skill set.

Training should also be provided to project staff traveling within PSDs in order to rehearse them in response procedures, both in a vehicle and when on foot. Cross-deck training is important to bolster employee confidence and awareness as well as reduce difficulties when

Exhibit 8.11   Close Protection Team Member Skill Set

Close Protection Team Member Skill Sets		
• Hostile environment awareness	• Risk (threat) analysis	• Mission planning
• Route selection and planning	• Close protection training	• Use of intelligence materials
• Venue security procedures	• Operations security	• First-line medical skills
• Convoy command and control	• Communications	• Reporting and reports
• Weapon handling skills	• Team tactics	• Rules of force/engagement
• Tactical live firing	• Tactical driving	• Tactical foot procedures
• Response to small arms fire	• Response to indirect fire attack	• Threat response drills
• Reconnaissance techniques	• Cross-decking procedures	• Evacuation procedures

security personnel are attempting to move passengers from one vehicle into another during a hostile situation.

MEDICAL PROVISION

As PSDs often travel far from medical support, it is the responsibility of both the company and the security provider to ensure that the PSD can provide an emergency response capability as part of each motorcade or meeting, with medically trained personnel integrated as part of each vehicle package. The integration of highly trained emergency responders, capable of providing practical first-line response to injured personnel in terms of airway, breathing, circulation, cardiopulmonary resuscitation, bleeding, immobilization of spinal or bone fractures, and defibrillation significantly enhances the survivability of personnel suffering from post-incident injuries. These personnel will also be better placed to notify receiving medical centers of pre-receivable requirements, where medical staff can be prepared ahead of a patient arriving through notifications or advisory information by PSD personnel. Even in hostile areas, there is a real chance that a passenger will have a heart attack, or suffer some other form of mundane injury or illness. Appropriate equipment should be provided to deal with both mundane and unusual medical problems.

VEHICLE CONSIDERATIONS

The selection of appropriate vehicles has become increasingly important, especially with significant commercial involvement in countries such as Iraq and Afghanistan. Where appropriate, the project may require hardened or armored vehicles. Typically a minimum standard of B6 armoring should be sought for passengers, although levels now range upward of this and the term B6 also has different technical applications across industry standards. To ensure proper installation of the armor plating and to avoid gapping or vulnerabilities in the protection often found around doors and other sealed areas, the company must take care to use reputable dealers. Rhino armor (brand name) can be retrofitted, but this provides less protection than factory fitting and should be avoided where possible. Companies should consider using retro-armored truck cabs for logistical movements as well as personnel movement. While the availability of factory-fitted armored truck cabs is limited, many companies offer up-armoring capabilities that will afford drivers a greater degree of protection.

Although armored vehicles are expensive and procured only if there is a real risk that the protection may be required, it is surprising how often companies fail to assess the quality of the vendor and how often vehicles of the wrong specifications are delivered despite their high costs. When procuring and using armored vehicles, these basic considerations should be considered.

- *Individual protective equipment (IPE).* In hostile environments, both passengers and PSD personnel should wear IPE, as serious secondary injuries can result through road traffic accidents or collisions when a vehicle is engaged in a hostile incident. This IPE includes body armor and, in the case of company staff, helmets.
- *Escape hatches.* Doors tend to jam if the vehicle frame is buckled. When possible, armored vehicles should have emergency escape points in the roof or rear hatch. The PSD should have equipment to pry open doors should passengers become trapped inside.

■ *Cross-deck training.* Passengers should be trained in cross-decking procedures if they are expected to travel in armored vehicles. This ensures they understand how the security personnel will physically move them to an alternate vehicle during a breakdown or hostile incident. This also allows the security personnel to develop a closer rapport with the project staff, gaining their trust and increasing the passengers' own confidence during travel in hostile environments.

CONVOYS

Convoy security is a risk factor that often is partly removed from a company's responsibilities. Often companies contract an external logistical provider to move their equipment and materials from one location to the next and see risk only as a loss or delay in material delivery—possibly resulting in business disruption and insurance costs. As personnel rarely travel within a convoy, the more intimate need for the company to oversee this mobile security service element is removed. That said, some companies do mix personnel and materials for the sake of expediency, or may use their PSD to undertake the secondary duties of escorting freight.

Convoy security is probably the highest-threat activity a company may undertake as it involves large, slowing-moving, and vulnerable targets for criminal or hostile groups. The skills required to protect materials are more robust and aggressive than those required for the close protection of individuals, as the opportunity to extract the material or passengers from the threat area is impeded by ponderous and high-profile vehicles, often driven by civilian personnel. A more robust security posture is required to deter, detect, and respond to threats that convoys face. In addition, following an attack there is a greater chance of losing a vehicle and personnel in large freight movements, as vehicles may be spread over a large area, are difficult to manage and coordinate, and are driven by non-security professionals. Strong management and close attention to accounting for vehicles is required.

Convoy security follows many of the same principles outlined for PSD operations. However, some peculiarities are associated with this different mobile security service:

■ Convoy escort security configurations are calculated based on the number and type of convoy vehicles and the value of the goods being transported as well as detailed threat assessments made for each task. Route clearance and rear protection (capture team for breakdowns or problems) should be interspaced with protective elements throughout the vehicle package.

■ In all cases, a minimum of several B6 armored security vehicles with run-flat tires and comprehensive security equipment should be used in hostile environments.

■ The operations center should track all convoys from departure to return, coordinating the task with the client's logistics manager, project manager, and relevant security infrastructures, where appropriate. Tracking technology is advised.

■ Detailed operational planning must be conducted by the operations manager using detailed intelligence-driven threat assessments, in close conjunction with the client's logistics manager, the client's project manager, the convoy security provider, and appropriate military agencies.

- Reserve vehicles and personnel must be available to quickly replace damaged vehicles so as not to interfere with convoy missions and thus client project requirements—this will affect supply chain assurance.
- Security vehicles in high threat environments must be capable of fighting effectively during an ambush; for example, each should have a pedestal-mounted, medium, belt-fed machine gun enclosed in a 12 mm steel box to protect the gunner so that personnel can fight during movement.
- Clear rules for vehicle and freight destruction must be established.
- Vehicle tracking devices should be considered, either for high value vehicles/commodities, or purely to track sections of the convoy.

Convoy services often see the greatest number of hostile incidents and casualties. In light of that fact, integration with as many supporting agencies as possible and sound planning are essential to mitigate the impact of often-unavoidable risks.

In conclusion, mobile security services are the most dynamic of the direct physical security services a security provider will offer to a company, especially in hostile environments where mobile activities pose the greatest risks to the company's activities and personnel. Mobile security should be considered one of the most important aspects of the project to get right. Thorough planning sound management should be applied to ensure that lethargy does not creep into what can become a daily activity and that complacency does not undervalue the risk mitigation plans, policies, and procedures designed to ensure each task is treated as a unique and separate requirement.

Notes

1. For the purposes of simplicity, mobile security teams will be referred to as PSDs.
2. Measurable values should always be associated with such tables, medium frequency is four to six times per week, and so forth. Subcategories may also be used, such as R for Road and A for Air.

CHAPTER 9

Facility Security Services

Companies seeking to establish or continue business in any environment, whether hostile or benign, typically require some level of facility protection. Thus, static security or guard force services play a significant role in most commercial ventures. Human security services are required to protect facilities, materials, or work sites from terrorist, insurgent, or criminal groups. Effective security management structures are required as well as an imaginative approach if the project's operations are dynamic rather than purely static in nature. The use of supporting technology can also greatly increase the efficiency and cost effectiveness of guard services, providing an integrated risk management and security solution.

The environment in which a company is operating will define the scope and approach of guard services. In the U.S., UK, or Europe, for example, these services will focus mainly on countering criminal threats, with unarmed security personnel reliant on law enforcement agencies to deal with more robust physical risks. In remote or hostile areas, guards may focus more on insurgency or terrorism, requiring significant weaponry and a greater dependence on their organization due to host nation limitations. Passive environment security is also governed largely by government regulations; hostile environment policies and procedures are dictated more by the risk environment.

Guard services can also be broken into two distinct categories—*static* and *mobile*—as sites may have to be protected over the long term, or their activity site may only have a short life span, and personnel and equipment may be applied to a succession of project sites. In this chapter, we consider the requirements of fixed camps or forward operating bases, and mobile site security teams in hostile or remote environments, where security organizations must look to their own resources to meet initial threats and where risk, rather than regulation, governs the approach.

The responsibilities of a guard force should not necessarily be restricted to their primary functions and might include a range of service areas centered around their principal function of physical security, which includes access control, patrolling, perimeter security, and response functions. Their tasks might also include providing basic medical treatment or undertaking duties within a crisis management team. By ensuring that security personnel are well trained for cross-utilization in multiple areas, the provider will have a greater degree of service flexibility, and the project will gain more value for their procurement. A sample of secondary roles a guard force may be required to assist in, outside of its typical guard functions, includes:

- Casualty management
- Mass evacuation management
- Civil disturbance control and response

- Industrial accidents response
- Detainment of unauthorized persons or vehicles

In addition, facility protection is an integral element of supply chain management, as it may be the point from which materials and resources are managed or received. Facility security involves not only protection in terms of authorized intrusion or hostile attention to a site, but also safeguarding the company from authorized materials or information leaving the site. Facility protection can therefore be both outward and inward looking in terms of risks to the company.

FIXED CAMPS AND FORWARD OPERATING BASES

Although differentiating the two forms of permanent facilities is somewhat subjective, a fixed camp might be defined as a permanent structure or facility that the company constructs or utilizes for long-term projects. These locations typically have good infrastructures and life support facilities. A forward operating base is typically a facility constructed to meet a shorter-term activity, or where the company uses other facilities that are not its own. In addition, forward operating base facilities are normally more practical and basic, as staff are not expected to reside there for prolonged periods. The subjectivity in differentiating the two forms involves what time span is considered long and what facility is considered comprehensive.

Planning Approach

Companies should engage external security advisory services early to support project planning stages and to assist with the development of the security requirements of fixed camps. This early engagement between project and risk managers will allow the structural layout of the facility to better reflect the risk environment as well as allow project management to properly budget the required security costs, both human and structural. Typically security providers contracted to support companies establishing operating bases are allowed more time to plan for and develop fixed camps in order to assist the project team plan, budget, and construct such project sites; requirements for mobile sites typically are more dynamic and fast-moving. Companies that hire security advisory support later into the planning process typically must spend additional time and money retro-fixing errors. In addition, security managers should establish security tracking documents and reports to capture facility requirements and shortfalls in order to guide management in evaluating and actioning recommendations or shortfalls.

Facility Security

A fixed camp or forward operating base (FOB) offers projects a well-established and safe environment in which a company can conduct their work and a relatively safe location from which to deploy daily project teams to external work sites. The physical layout and degree of security manning for a FOB is determined by the local and regional threats (both direct and indirect), the profile of the task, the scope and nature of the project and staff involved, and any associated existing site or military support. A FOB may be permanent (for long-term or continued use with a high degree of physical security measures in place) or temporary (where a specific or short-lived project is run). This latter type of FOB might be used for mobile sites, where facilities can be moved from one location to another with relative ease.

External Interfaces

Some project sites have an outer security ring of co-located military forces, such as coalition or United Nations military groups or host nation government or tribal security forces. In some areas, there may be no such forces, or they might not be positioned to support project operations and security. At worst, local security may be unreliable or, in extreme cases, complicit in disrupting the project. Even in the worst cases, however, it is still necessary to consider liaison with local security forces for their inclusion into the outer security ring, so as to avoid unnecessary polarization of the project. The establishment of both fixed camps and mobile site security in the most extreme of environments should incorporate external support such as military organizations and local security into the project security team, ensuring a layered security footprint, with overlapping security arrangements significantly strengthening project operations.

MOBILE FACILITY SECURITY

The provider may need to develop innovative strategies to meet dynamic and unique project requirements, typically where projects have shorter durations and operations may leapfrog between multiple sites. Mobile site security reduces travel time and pattern setting for projects, often the most vulnerable activity in high-risk environments. In addition, by remaining on-site, project teams can better supervise local workforces, increasing subcontractor or partner productivity. Project downtime through movement or travel restrictions is also significantly reduced, while working hours are made more flexible, which is especially relevant during high-tempo or project surge environments. While the concept of mobile site security brings value to the project, it is often costly, requiring significant security personnel and resources compared to day visits. In addition, it may raise the profile of a project site due to a permanent and obvious presence of foreign workers.

Planning Approach

Mobile site security teams require detailed and proactive management in order to be most effective. A close management and operational relationship is required, and the security provider's risk consultant or security manager should liaise closely with the project manager and risk or security staff to determine project requirements, limitations, and goals in order to determine how best to provide security support. This partnership must start at project inception and continue throughout its life, allowing the security vendor's consultant to both understand their company's objectives and quickly and effectively adapt the risk mitigation and security plans to respond to project or risk environment changes.

The security provider should seek to exploit both internal and external intelligence resources on behalf of the company in order to scope the risks and associated problems, producing a detailed intelligence analysis and threat assessment to demonstrate to the project team and executive management the environment and associated influences and risks associated with their project. The company should expect recommendations from the security provider. These recommendations might include the need for a security survey of the proposed project site to determine the overall security requirements. The survey might then be captured in a detailed security plan (see Chapter 12) with associated site-hardening scopes of work[1] defining how security structures, technology, and human resources will secure the site. Thus the security survey identifies the risks and needs, while the security plan defines the practical operational requirements and policies needed to establish a safe working environment for the project.

Although the security provider may offer recommendations for structural changes to the site, an external construction company may be needed to create the security structures. Either the security provider or the project team must supervise and audit such external providers. The selection of movable security structures and materials will allow the team to be more self-sufficient and save the company money. The acquisition of two sets of site resources may also allow the project team to move immediately into the next readied position rather than be delayed by the movement and establishment of security structures at the next project site.

The company should demand that the security vendor provide detailed advice, guidance, and costs that can then be reviewed and rationalized by in-house experts. Once the plans have been agreed and implemented, the company will have established a strengthened work site, determined the level of manpower and resource requirements, and deployed security forces to man the location, as well as created local or external relationships and agreements to support the project's operations. Project staff will then be moved by a personal security detail (PSD) to the site where they can undertake their work at less risk. Once the task is complete, the security provider should establish a demobilization plan to enable project staff to be escorted to a safe area while the process of developing the needs for the next site begins again, as illustrated in Exhibit 9.1.

The mobile site security team should be self-sufficient in terms of security and life support, with physical strengthening of the site through pragmatic security planning and structures. It is preferable that these structures are transferable from one project site to another. To reduce targeting opportunities, logistical replenishment should occur infrequently, preferably only once or twice a month, depending on the size and nature of the project. The team should also have enough armored vehicles for emergency evacuation of all personnel at one time, if the environment warrants such levels of protection. If project teams are dispersed to multiple work sites, security personnel should enhance individual group security bubbles.

Facility Security

The company's program or risk manager should ensure that the security provider's security management team (SMT) managing a mobile site security team establishes a highly flexible and well-organized security organization, capable of quickly adapting to a fluid working and risk environment. As the team may be required to secure a succession of sites, both security provider and project team require an organized but flexible management system to reflect the structural and approach differences of each project as well as changing environmental and risk factors. Supported either internally or by a parent security management structure in terms of intelligence, liaison, and operational management, security on-site should be conducted in close coordination with management structures at all levels. A layered security

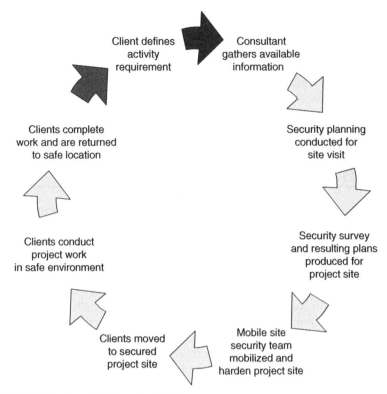

Exhibit 9.1 Mobile Site Security Planning Cycle

approach is often required, with an inner element comprised of the management and close protection personnel (personal security detail). The PSD provides close protection for employees, is the core element of the crisis response team, and also often supervises the static guard force. Key point security then forms the second layer, including towers, access points, and critical facilities. This layer denies and screens access to the work site. A further layer may encompass patrols and in-depth positions to place a final barrier against hostile attention and intrusion.

External Interfaces

Company risk or program managers should articulate to the SMT their liaison activity parameters, defining which organizations and at what level they might engage to support the task, either directly or indirectly. Where possible, the security provider should be permitted to coordinate closely with military and government forces in order to integrate security plans, evacuation measures, and other memorandum of understanding (MOU) agreements. Sensitivity to community relations is paramount, and where possible, support and interaction with local groups will augment security both directly and indirectly. Employment of local employees will also offer a socioeconomic incentive to engender community support, both reducing hostile activities direct from the community and offering intelligence support, should suspicious groups start operating in the local area. The validity of such reporting should be carefully vetted in order to avoid responding to erroneous or misleading information. Poor relations between the project and prominent local figures or communities can adversely affect even the best security plan. Security should therefore be applied in the least obtrusive way possible, while still providing the security necessary to protect the project's personnel and operations. Where possible, language barriers should be addressed through the use of interpreters to ensure that communication and dialog is free-flowing with community and government officials.

FACILITY SECURITY MANAGEMENT

A security location in a remote or hostile area should have a robust security management element to deal with the range of threats that a project might face, from serious incidents such as industrial accidents (fire, toxic chemical leak, injury, and other hazards like H_2S poisoning) to criminal thefts or robberies and armed attacks, as well as dealing with the more mundane contractual and administrative requirements. The management of risk and security should be coordinated from a tactical operations center (TOC), a location that has continuous communications with security locations and personnel within the project as well as with external agencies and corporate offices. The TOC should also be the interface with supporting military of government security organizations. Crisis management and medical support should be coordinated and provided through this management center, assisting in the treatment and stabilization of personnel prior to medical evacuation. A comprehensive array of standard operating procedures, security plans, risk mitigation policies and procedures, evacuation plans, and other management tools should be tailored to suit the unique requirements of each site, and centralized in the TOC.

Tactical Operations Center

The TOC provides a location from which the SMT can coordinate its activities, drawing on technological support to best mobilize resources and access information. The TOC can be considered an agreed-upon and predetermined fusion center from which project team and security provider management can develop strategic policies and plans as well as coordinate relationships and support with external agencies. The TOC acts as a convergence point for both company and vendor managerial and operational elements, and should be the specific focal point for the security management structure as well as the fusion point for external interfaces, as illustrated in Exhibit 9.2.

The TOC should also house the security provider's intelligence element to support the development of strategic and regional intelligence direction, dissemination, and information management. As the management center for the project's security-related activities, the TOC provides mission direction and functional management for all PSD, convoy, and static security activities, supporting the company's management elements by setting policy and direction as well as coordinating activities and plans with military and government agencies. The TOC will maintain undisrupted oversight and communications with each project location and working party, ensuring that risks and crisis events are best mitigated and managed. In the event of an incident, the TOC is an identifiable nucleus for crisis management. All PSD and

Exhibit 9.2   Tactical Operations Center Management Structure and Operational Interfaces

convoy movements should be planned, registered, and tracked by the TOC, which also provides a focal point for static security operations. Centralized coordination will enhance the delivery of service in functional terms, ensuring both the safety and welfare of individuals and the performance of projects. The TOC may also be responsible for quality assurance and contractual compliance, acting as the core management element for the contract. Depending on the scope and nature of the project, the elements that follow may be within the purview of the TOC's scope of work.

Intelligence   The TOC should be a securable facility where intelligence can be collected, collated, analyzed, and distributed to support the project's activities. The TOC should also provide a sorting house for all intelligence data. To provide the project's security management and security personnel with up-to-date information for effective project and mission planning, the TOC should maintain a detailed security and intelligence database, with management planning documents such as:

- Intelligence reports
- Situation boards
- Threat warnings
- Marked routes
- Military and government location maps
- Project site maps, threat overlays
- Security plans and surveys
- Risk management systems
- Standard operating procedures (SOPs)
- Tactics, techniques, and procedures (TTPs)
- Medevac plans
- Communication networking details
- Incident and crisis management plans
- Evacuation plans
- Crisis response policies and procedures

The TOC also offers immediate and real-time briefings to appropriate project staff to support dynamic project requirements. The TOC acts as the administrative center for logistics planning, personnel files and records, and training plans and documents. Secondary TOCs might be required should the main TOC become compromised.

Process Interfaces Managing an effective security location can be a complex, multilevel network of interfaces to ensure that an effective risk mitigation environment is provided in which project activities can be conducted effectively. The integration of multiple internal and external specialist resources, at national, regional, and local levels, will support high-performance work outputs. Managing external interfaces, such as government ministries, host nation military and law enforcement agencies, coalition forces, nongovernment organizations, embassies and consuls, provincial councils, and community leaders at every level, is necessary to access and exploit the necessary expertise and experience to support the project's activities.

Reference Mapping The management of a crisis in a single site is difficult under the best of circumstances but is much more difficult when there are numerous sites involved, and the SMT managing the crisis response (often remotely) is unfamiliar with the area at risk. An effective way to annotate critical locations and routes as well as specific areas of interest quickly and efficiently is to create project site grid overlays. Such overlays allow for the immediate identification of a problem during emergencies, whether they be industrial, criminal, or natural. In order to facilitate process interfaces between the project and the executive security group and any supporting military or law enforcement agencies, the overlay for a specific project should use the same scale, symbols, and numbering systems as those used by external security forces. Exhibit 9.3 is an example of a grid overlay. This integration needs to be done as early as possible in the planning process and should include the locations and routes of external security forces to meet with company security groups, or by which enter the site, as well as to permit external groups to be directed to points of concern of risk with greater ease and accuracy. This form of visual representation is also useful to illustrate existing labor requirements by denoting staffing numbers by post or activity.

Developing Schematics A good security provider's management team will be able to develop detailed and professional project site and building schematic plans and diagrams without the use of graphic artists or complex programs. Such diagrams represent information more clearly to the company's executive and project teams and provide a useful management tool for security management and personnel (see Exhibit 9.4). The diagrams will be especially important if mapping is unavailable or out of date. Schematics and diagrams form an important part of security documentation and should be as simple and clear as possible.

Facility structures should also be captured by the use of floor plans, as illustrated in Exhibit 9.5. This is especially useful if personnel have not visited the site themselves, allowing management to visualize the layout of the local areas and project facilities as well as attribute activities to space in advance of a visit for planning purposes. That said, often floor plans are restricted or not available. The provider's consultant may be required to map out building structures or layouts quickly for reports and plans.

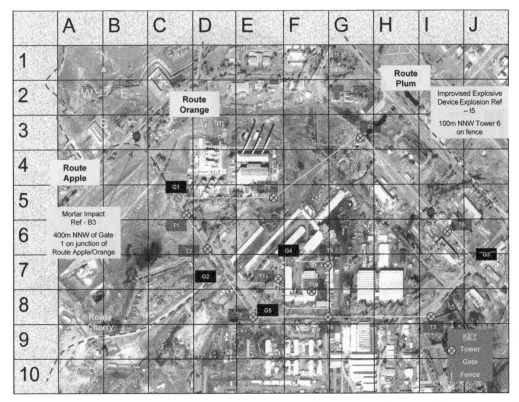

Exhibit 9.3 Reference Mapping and Grid Overlays. Copyright © Iraqi Military Satallite Image, 2004.

Training Local Guards If integrating local communities into the security operations is necessary, training suitable local employees is an effective method of establishing good relations with the local populace or workforces. This training will be especially relevant if the operational area is large or has numerous access control points. A training team should begin training prior to the project start so that adequately trained local security can enhance the security of the outer perimeter and, consequently, the security of the inner working and living areas.

Coalition or International Military Forces Support In countries like Iraq or Afghanistan, where international military forces serve as a key aspect of national security, there may be considerable external assets on which the project or security provider can draw to bolster the project's own resources or provide services the security provider cannot deliver (i.e., air or significant medical support).

Tracking Technology The TOC can manage a range of technologies that enable the satellite tracking of both personnel and equipment. For vehicles, such technologies as MST and Track24 provide vehicle-mounted global positioning system (GPS) tracking, which can also be used as an alternative communications means. These systems are linked to laptop mapping, which can track (real time) the movement of vehicles on maps. Pocket Buddy and other such technologies also permit the tracking of personnel in a similar fashion. Such personnel

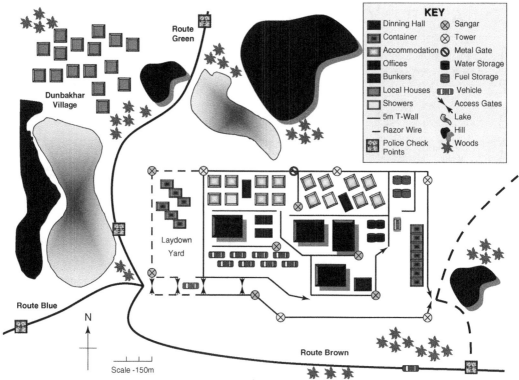

Exhibit 9.4 Developing Simple Facility Schematics

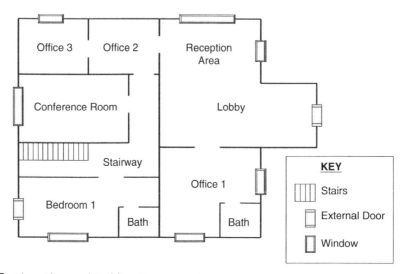

Exhibit 9.5 Floor Plans and Building Representations

and resource oversight has a range of management and security applications, and can reduce the need to have multiple operations centers, as many of the functions can be conducted remotely, and even out of country.

The size and complexity of the TOC and its staff will be largely dependent on the nature and scope of the project task itself. Where possible, companies should seek to make use of central TOCs to oversee and manage multiple projects within a country. In addition, technology may enable a TOC in one country to support operations in another, acting as a redundant crisis and communications center as well as tracking personnel and equipment.

RELIEF IN PLACE

A company seeking to utilize an existing facility or changing its security vendor at an ongoing project site should consider the development of a relief in place (RiP) plan leading up to occupation or change. The occupation of a site or the transition of security from one provider to another is a time that offers the highest level of risk, as the outgoing security provider is focusing on departure, and the incoming security provider might be unfamiliar with the site and will require time to ramp up and understand the operational requirements fully. Program and risk managers should seek confirmation from the security vendor that it has addressed and planned for all key elements of a RiP. A security vendor should consider three aspects of the RiP for large and complex projects, although some vendors may amalgamate all three into a single management plan:

1. *Mobilization plan.* The mobilization plan captures how services will be mobilized, from the identification of a period of a likely service requirement, to the point of transition or activity initiation. The mobilization plan may last for months, weeks, or days leading to transition, and includes all management, administrative, and operational needs and activities. Mobilization plans may be management oriented or operationally orientated, or a combination of both. (See "Operations Order or Mobilization Plans" in Chapter 12)
2. *Transition plan.* The transition plan captures how the transition or occupation of a facility will occur. This plan may be separate from the mobilization plan, or it may be attached at the end of the mobilization plan, when costs start to be expended or resources are mobilized. This element includes specifically the occupation or transition of services.
3. *Project initiation document (PiD).* The project initiation document (PiD) captures what objectives and deliverables are expected from both the procuring company and the security services provider, with milestones, tasks, and trackable achievements. The PiD might contain the mobilization and transition plans as elements or be a separate macro-to micro-level management document that defines both the broader and specific needs for a project start-up. It might also include management policies, procedures, procurement, logistical and administrative tasks, and any other component required to successfully start a project.

Exhibit 9.6 provides an example of a simple management transition plan for a site. It will be supported with further documents or standard policies and procedures that specify tasks and activities which meet the overall objectives stated within the plan.

Exhibit 9.6 Management Transition Plan Example

Phase 1: RiP − 20	Phase 2: RiP − 10	Phase 3: RiP − 1	Phase 4: RiP + 10
• **Select Key Personnel.** Ensure management personnel meet task specifications and experience requirements. Source *all* personnel to best fit requirements.	• **Risk and Security Managers.** The security provider's management and operational team liaises with the project team ensuring all operational requirements and expectations are understood to effect a seamless and safe transition plan.	• **Liaison.** Program Management liaises closely with the project staff and other external organizations to ensure all handover requirements are fulfilled.	• **Contractual Confirmation.** Confirm contractual obligations and expectations are met in full, identifying shortfalls or deficiencies.
• **Establish Operational Transition Requirements.** Ensure that correct resources and management elements are prepared.	• **Program Management Mobilized.** Key personnel will assume responsibilities for the Transition Plan, personnel will be deployed and trained.	• **Operational Transition.** Shadow operational management is conducted for a pre-agreed time leading to the transition, ensuring that a seamless transition occurs. Ensures that the security provider's policies, procedures and plans are in alignment with the established approach.	• **Operational Confirmation.** Management elements confirm all operational activities are in accordance with the project requirements.
• **Identify Start-Up Resources.** Ensure that surge staff are pre-identified and prepared to support the mobilization, especially during high tempo work activities.	• **Information Transition.** Request access to information on the incumbent regarding personnel, policies and procedures, ensuring the transition is smooth and well coordinated, maintaining consistency of service during the transition period.	• **Operational Tasks.** Formally assume tactical management of the security functions during a formal hand-off, mitigating potential risks. Patrolling and other operational tasks start.	• **Management Confirmation.** Management integration is consolidated with clear policies and procedures to link the project team to the security providers.

- **Draft Project Initiation Document (PiD)**. Draft a PiD and work plan laying out the requirements and plans.

- **Policies and Procedures**. The security provider will identify special requirements or regulations associated with this contract to support the effective transition.
- **Contract Compliance**. Provider Contracting and Legal Directors will ensure that all contractual and legal requirements are fully understood in order to meet all company requirements.
- **External Liaison**. Relationships developed with supporting organizations.

- **Management Transition**. Program Management will shadow operations to ensure a seamless transition of responsibilities and operational services and information.

- **Contractual Management**. Contracts liaises closely with the project team to ensure that all contractual requirements and processes are compliant.
- **Equipment Auditing**. All project security equipment is audited and accounted for in preparation of the transition. Logistics managers identify any deficiencies.

- **Security Risk Assessment**. Security Provider conducts a formal Risk Assessment and presents the Security Plan for the location to ensure that an independent audit is conducted and modification requirements are raised with the project management team.
- **Equipment Hand-Over**. All equipment is sited and signed over to the new security provider. Shortfalls are registered.
- **External Consolidation**. Agreements and management integration with external organizations is finalized, plans and support agreements are consolidated.

- **Quality Assurance**. An agreed quality assurance program or process is consolidated to measure the performance of the provider.

- **Reporting**. Periodic reporting of service delivery and important facts is established and maintained throughout the lifespan of the contract.
- **Meetings**. A meeting schedule is finalized between internal and external management and operational planning teams.

- **Audits**. Internal and external audits are conducted to maintain service delivery quality.

SECURITY CONSIDERATIONS

Each project site will have different security requirements, governed by the company's activity, environmental risks, local and governmental permissions and authorities and cost parameters. Due to the stand-alone nature of many project sites, as well as the inherent risk posed to the high-value sites or activities by hostile groups, it is often necessary to create and implement a full set of tactical procedures to ensure security of the site, key terrain, and site approach routes. Where possible, previous security plans should be used as the basis of new plans, to utilize existing concepts and materials as well as to ensure a degree of consistency. The next sections provide samples of tactical concept considerations that the security vendor should focus on when offering recommendations for facility security requirements to the company.

Boundaries   Boundaries are necessary tools for indicating publicly accessible areas from secured areas as well as allocated responsibilities for different parts of the project site. Where possible, the boundaries should be on a clearly identifiable line, such as a road, path, fence line, power line, or building. All areas should be assigned to a security team or personnel to minimize the threat of blue-on-blue incidents, to ensure that all terrain is covered, and to identify firing sectors and impact areas/beaten zones to prevent bystander casualties or industrial accidents. Boundaries also provide an identifiable demarcation zone for local personnel to prevent unintended intrusion into a secured area. This is especially important if the local populace is nomadic or consists of farming or transient communities that might migrate periodically or seasonally through the project area. Accommodations should be made to assist such local groups in their usual activities to avoid unnecessary friction.

Communications   Companies should establish a detailed communications plan within the SMT components, within the company as a whole, and to external organizations. Often the basic factor that undermines a company's ability to respond effectively to a crisis event is the inability to convey information and instructions efficiently to multiple organizations. Companies should establish nodal points where nominated individuals are responsible for cascading or sharing information with other individuals or groups. Companies should also consider developing decision matrixes for significant issues: for example, who can order an evacuation, who should speak to the press in the event of interest, and who can call on military support if required.

Trigger Points   Companies should establish defined events or factors that require a predetermined action or activity. Trigger points are connected to the decision matrix and will be the catalyst for decisions; for example, increased local tensions may result in a scaled response from the project leading to only critical external work being conducted, to the measured evacuation of the site itself. Trigger points may be aimed at the executive management; for example, the injury of a project employee by hostile action may require the board to review whether it wishes to remain on task, or increase security measures. Thus trigger points and decision matrixes may be engineered at three levels: corporate, country, and program. However, all levels should overlap as a corporate decision or trigger will have repercussions on country and program activities and policies. (See "Crisis Management" in Chapter 4)

Friend or Foe Recognition   In order to reduce the likelihood of fratricide, all security person-nel must be easily identifiable to one another day and night and identifiable by outside military or host nation security forces. Identification will revolve around the wearing of uni-form, weapons system identification, and the use of infrared illumination on personnel and static positions. The use of range cards, limits-of-engagement measures (firing arc restric-tions), and sound appreciation of the site layout is important both for the site security team and external supporting arms. Well-planned and coordinated interagency agreements and procedures are required to ensure support is positively managed rather than posing an addi-tional risk to the facility and personnel.

Control Key Terrain   Key terrain must be identified and assigned to specific security elements. Where possible, this ground should be occupied as part of the defensive plan with relevant surveillance and weapon systems installed. During the initial assessment, terrain that is not observable must be identified and alternate means of observation employed. Such security coverage can be achieved by establishing additional observation points, frequent patrolling, or use of electronic technologies.

Security Positions   Sufficient security positions are necessary to allow for complete observa-tion of the site, control key terrain, afford sufficient protection to allow security personnel to return fire accurately and effectively, provide mutually supporting or interlocking security with adjacent defensive positions, and cover all access/egress routes. On large sites, these positions may need to be placed depth (i.e., positions are layered so that the forward posi-tions have rear locations protecting them). Where multiple groups occupy one site, careful liaison and coordinated security plans are required to ensure that boundaries of responsibil-ity do not present areas of confusion or weakened security or, worse, areas devoid of ad-equate security.

Positions in Depth   Depth positions generally support forward security positions, but should also provide a secondary line of defense for the key areas within the facility and be manned with more robust weaponry. Depth positions often are responsible for protecting access con-trol points, main routes to vulnerable or important infrastructures, or exposed flanks to the facility.

Fire Sectors   In environments in which guard forces are issued weapons (individual weap-ons or crew-served weapons, such as light and medium machine guns), it is important to site weapons individually with sector limits clearly set for both day and night engagements. Weapon coverage areas (or arcs) need to be interlocked with the fire sectors of adjacent posi-tions, and impact areas must be identified and accounted for so that rounds do not leave the perimeter of the security zone and pose a threat to the surrounding local populous or create secondary hazards from industrial accidents.

Patrolling   Areas for patrols need to be identified, and a full patrolling plan needs to be docu-mented and deconflicted. Patrolling is both a physical and psychological security measure; it also offers security structures checks: fence breaks, open buildings, and so forth.

Mobile Reserve Force   A mobile reserve is a key component to the security plan. It must be a dedicated force at a constant level of readiness commensurate with the threat and operational activities of the forces it is supporting. This groups may be additional security personnel or off-watch guards. The mobile reserve force must be fully briefed, equipped, and inspected; have completed tactical rehearsals, communications, and weapons checks; and be familiar with the project and surrounding area.

Illumination Matrix   An effective illumination matrix (or lighting plan) is required using all forms of illumination, including lighting plans, illumination equipment, and response measures in order to ensure that the site has sufficient methods to permit good visibility for security staff. The illumination matrix also ensures that the site has lighting that augments security, in terms of deterring unwanted attention while concurrently providing good observation for security personnel on boundaries and key areas. Lighting should also work in the favor of the facility security group, facing outward to blind and illuminate intruders, without skylining security posts or personnel. (See Exhibit 9.7.)

Rules of Engagement   A significant risk faced by companies is liability, whether they are directly accountable or have associated responsibilities as procuring agents. It is the responsibility of both the company and the security vendor to ensure there are clear and documented rules of engagement (ROE) and that personnel are trained and adhere to these policies at all times. In principle, ROE that are set by outside forces or by executive leadership should not be altered by field management; this ensures consistency of rule but conversely often makes the ROE less stringent, as they are generalized rather than specific to the area. The company may wish to empower local security managers with the ability to make the ROE more restrictive if the local situation requires it. However, executive management and indeed the security provider should always be involved in such changes. All security personnel must be trained to a very high level of ROE proficiency under stressful scenarios to ensure that they can react properly to incidents within the limits of the ROE. Additionally, all personnel need situational awareness training, which enables staff and management to identify and avoid

Exhibit 9.7   Illumination of Project Operations. Copyright © K. Smith, 2005.

dangerous situations early and deal with any resulting incident in a manner that may be less dangerous or threatening to the company, project, and local population.

Liaison Officers   Companies should give serious consideration to the value of active liaison with outside military or security forces as well as with host nation agencies and the local community. Often some level of external interaction is essential to ensure that the maximum supporting capabilities are included in the security plan through a seamless integration of all layers of defense. Liaison will also significantly reduce the threat of blue-on-white incidents. Liaison officers may hold a defined post for complex and dynamic projects with multiple participants, or may be carried out as a secondary role for a security manager.

Close Protection   Companies should consider the close protection of project staff on-site, as it should not be assumed that (perimeter) static security measures alone will prevent threats from intruders or indirect fire attacks. Often security vendors provide PSD personnel to ensure the close protection of key or vulnerable project staff. Where large work areas need to be secured, additional static guards may man overwatch posts or conduct roving patrols to provide satellite security. Thus layers of security may be required to ensure the safety of project personnel within some facilities rather than relying only on perimeter security measures.

Surveillance and Target Acquisition Plan   Located in the security plan, the surveillance and target acquisition plan (STAP) should document and allocate what human or mechanical means are to be employed for risk management and security provision, as well as who is responsible for emplacing, inspecting, and responding to alarms. This plan might include technological devices as well as human resources to maintain surveillance intelligence for the site and surrounding area. The STAP can also be visually represented, to illustrate which areas are managed by different groups and where gaps or greater areas of weakness might occur.

Observation Posts   Companies should consider the value of observation posts (OPs) when planning risk mitigation measures for their facility. OPs often have the capacity to dominate significant amounts of real estate, without significant resource or cost issues. Where appropriate, a combination of overt and covert OPs may be used to identify any hostile activity and to cover terrain not otherwise observable from other defensive positions, or where areas are large and would otherwise require considerable infrastructure or manpower to secure it. The OP must always have secure routes of egress and reliable communications, and be within range of defensive fires. Communications must be checked constantly. Because OPs might be outside of the main secured areas, if communications are lost with an OP for more than a predetermined time, a quick response force (QRF) should be dispatched to investigate.

SOPs and TTPs   The SMT should ensure that all security personnel have access to and understand relevant SOPs and TTPs. SOPs and TTPs may be detailed and cover a wide spectrum of company and project needs. Nevertheless, security personnel should, at the very least, be familiar with sections related to emergency response actions, reporting, site diagrams, evacuation routes, guard orders, mobile operations procedures, ROE, personnel requirements, supply and equipment accountability procedures, weapons security and storage, maintenance, communications, and other administrative issues associated with their duties. Frequently SOPs and TTPs are only paid lip service to. Some form of accountability should be imposed to ensure they are read and understood, such as having personnel sign to acknowledge review at the start of each deployment or simple periodic tests of key areas.

Access Control   All personnel must be positively identified and searched before entering the site. Access control presents one of the highest-risk areas as it often involves significant amounts of pedestrian and vehicular movement through one geographic point. A full access control plan should be developed and sustained by the security vendor to ensure best management of this critical security service. All processes and procedures should be captured within the facility security plan. Vehicles and equipment are to be searched to prevent unauthorized movement of materials, explosives, or weapons into or from the site.

Improvised Explosive Device/Unexploded Ordinance Sweeps   Explosive devices pose a significant risk to facilities, especially if the devices are strategically placed, such as within an area of high staff use or on a vulnerable aspect of the facility's structure. All personnel should be educated to be constantly vigilant against the threat of IEDs. Sweeps by roving security personnel, with dogs if available, is a critical component of security in areas prone to improvised explosive device (IED) use. IED sweeps should occur prior to project staff entering new areas or after an intrusion or break of security has occurred. IED/unexploded ordnance (UXO) sweeps should also occur following an indirect fire attack to locate any unexploded ordinance.

Individual Protective Equipment   Project staff and security personnel should wear individual protective equipment (IPE) whenever the threat dictates. IPE is often uncomfortable, especially in hot climates, and a pragmatic balance should be struck between security and health and safety.

Special Security Equipment   The incorporation of technology into a security plan or STAP can both enhance risk mitigation and provide cost-saving advantages. Equipment may include volumetric devices, infrared, closed camera televisions, ground sensors, and other specialized equipment. Technology often requires direct support, both for management and response to technology measures. Nevertheless, technology often can significantly reduce the labor pool required to secure large sites.

Explosive Detection Dogs   The use of explosive detection dogs provides an excellent deterrent and a highly efficient method by which to search vehicles, materials, and personnel. Trained handlers and significant logistical and administrative support is required to care for these security resources, often with the requirement for explosive training materials, food, housing, and cooling equipment as well as veterinary clinics. Attack or patrol dogs are also very useful as deterrents and to reduce risks to security personnel when used to locate or secure intruders into a facility.

Medical Plan   Companies should ensure that there exist appropriate levels of organic (in-house) medical support for emergency requirements for projects operating in remote and hostile locations as well as ensure that some form of medical evacuation measure is in place to relocate staff to adequate clinics or hospital facilities. A comprehensive medical plan, including treatment plans, casualty evacuation, and repatriation policies and procedures, should be developed to support companies in managing injuries or fatalities effectively, as shortfalls in response effectiveness have significant moral and liability repercussions. These plans may be integrated with military and government agencies to augment the effectiveness of a response. In addition, companies may wish to engage medics or emergency medical technicians (EMTs) to provide appropriate day-to-day health and welfare support services for all project and support staff as well as first-line stabilization of more serious casualties. The EMT should have adequate facilities, which can act as a dispensary, health care location, and triage center for serious incidents of multiple casualties. The integration of a highly trained emergency responder, capable of providing practical first-line response to injured personnel, in terms of airway, breathing, circulation, CPR, bleeding, immobilization of spinal or bone fractures, and defibrillation (using automatic external defibrillators [AEDs]) will significantly enhance the survivability of project staff suffering from post-incident injuries. EMT personnel will also be better placed to notify receiving medical centers of pre-receival requirements (information or notifications provided by security staff to receiving medical centers). As a secondary function, EMT staff may also train PSD and static security personnel to ensure that all security personnel have an appropriate level of first-responder skill.

Personnel   Typically, different nationalities will be used for different security functions, depending on the economic and social nature of the project area as well as the level of training and reliability of the different national groups. There are no hard and fast rules regarding the use and integration of different nationalities, as each project, location, and ethnic and social group is unique. A flexible and pragmatic approach should be adopted when determining how different groups will be employed, being sensitive to but not constrained by moral or equal opportunity policies and regulations when it comes to security and safety.

Companies should seek a combination of the most pragmatic solutions for their facility prior to expending capital on manpower or resources. The construction of a costly 20-mile fence line to secure a sizable work area may not be as operationally and cost effective as spaced towers, technology-based virtual fence lines (intruder detection systems [IDSs]), and response teams. Sensible planning and security versus cost options should be balanced prior to commitment. Often there is a point of diminishing returns where additional costs do not result in equivalent security gains. This point should be established so that funds can be better spent on securing the site and its personnel.

LAYERING SECURITY

Security is best served if the project operates within a layered security environment, in which threats must pass through several sets of barriers before the project staff or their activity is at risk. Security management should consider at least three conceptual layers (see Exhibit 9.8):

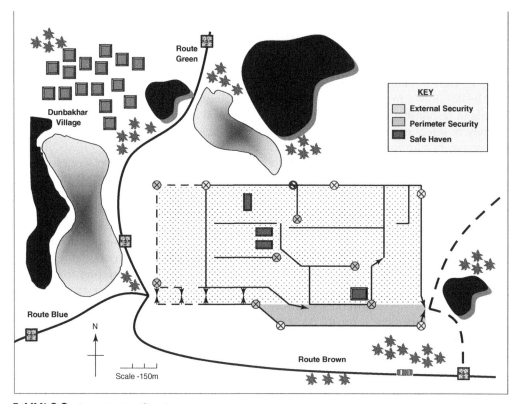

Exhibit 9.8 Layering Facility Security

1. The area surrounding the site but outside the remit of the organic security elements
2. The boundary to the site manned by project security
3. Safe locations within the site

Layers may be physical, psychological, or technological in nature, and may include incorporating external agencies into the overall site security plan in order to augment project resourced security measures. Companies should ensure that their security provider considers the value of layering within the security plan and draws on any external organization that might create additional buffer zones to support the facility's organic security measures.

Outer Perimeter Security Layer

The outer perimeter represents the ground beyond the site perimeter itself, outside the domain of the project or security provider is responsible for securing. A demarcation between the external area and the secured area is usually denoted in physical terms, using security structures such as razor wire, a fence, or a wall, or a psychological barrier, such as signs that sanitize an area between the static site perimeter and the adjoining local area. This demarcation prevents the local populace from unintentionally approaching or entering the site, and thus reduces the risks of mistaking an innocent person for an intruder. In addition, this layer also acts as a deterrent and physical barrier for hostile persons approaching the static site, giving security personnel more time to identify and react to an intrusion. If multiple commercial activities are occurring in an area, an effective perimeter may lead to hostile groups seeking softer targets. This outer layer should be secured by host nation or coalition forces where possible; in such cases, liaison and integration between the site security management and these groups is required for integrated planning and agreement responsibilities.

Site Perimeter Layer

The site perimeter layer acts as the first true barrier between the surrounding environment and site security. It should be both a physical and a psychological barrier and should be secured and patrolled by project-owned security personnel operating from interlocked defendable security positions and/or towers that can oversee the perimeter and provide clear fields of fire. Secondary site perimeters may be established for individual work sites in a large project catchment area, or for special, high value or critical areas within a project site.

Safe Haven(s)

Safe havens are hardened locations where project staff can gather in the event of a threat. They often provide safety from explosive hazards, and should be defendable. Security provider security personnel often provide the final layer of security at safe havens, directly managing project security management and being augmented by other security personnel (guards and external forces).

PHYSICAL SECURITY STRUCTURES

Physical security structures provide a means of deterring, delaying, and detecting unauthorized or hostile persons. The nature of physical measures used will be determined by the project's budget, profile, and task's activity requirements as well as the risk and topographical influences. Local community factors may also be relevant to the structuring and placement of physical security measures, and these local factors should be considered by companies during the planning phase. The next sections capture a sample of some physical security options that might be associated with both fixed and mobile security sites.

T-Walls

T-walls (see Exhibit 9.9) are a costly but effective and movable asset, providing an effective means of countering physical and intrusion threats. T-walls are constructed of prefabricated T-shaped reinforced concrete panels designed to deflect and withstand the detonation of an IED or indirect fire. It may be necessary to subdivide large compounds with further T-walls to limit the effects of indirect fire if the compound is shelled, individually protecting such structures as accommodation and office spaces; various sizes of T-walls can be used to best achieve compartmentalization. Car parking areas should also have blast walls to mitigate the threat of a vehicle-borne improvised explosive device (VBIED). Fuel storage areas should be compartmentalized to reduce secondary explosive hazards. T-walls offer long-term

Exhibit 9.9   T-Wall Example. Iraqi Military Base. Copyright © M. Blyth, 2006.

protection, providing excellent protection against direct fire and fragmentation from indirect fire. T-walls also provide a good physical barrier against intruders, prevent VBIED intrusion, allow for good arcs of fire for tower guards, provide a strong physiological barrier against potential insurgents and criminals, and prevent hostile ground-level observation of the compound site. However, T-walls take time to construct or deliver, requiring external supply of materials, and are costly and raise the profile of a site.

Hesco-Bastion Barriers

Hesco-Bastion barriers are large wired baskets filled with soil and/rock, typically topped with at least two-high razor wire on external facing walls. These structures provide medium- to long-term protection, are excellent protection against direct fire and fragmentation from indirect fire, and are a good physical barrier against pedestrian and vehicle intrusion. They also allow for good arcs of fire for tower guards, provide a strong physiological barrier against potential insurgents and criminals, and prevent hostile ground-level observation of the compound site. They are less costly than concrete barriers, are faster to install, and require far less material support. That said, Hesco-Bastion barriers have a tendency to degrade after extended periods of use (especially in wet conditions) and are more easily damaged from direct and indirect fire than concrete or earthen barriers.

Earth Berms

Earth berms are simple security structures to create, as they are piled-earth defenses. These structures are usually topped with three-high razor wire and a ditch on the outward-facing area. Earth berms provide long-term protection, good protection against direct fire and fragmentation from indirect fire, a limited physical barrier against pedestrian intruders, and prevent VBIED intrusion. They allow for good arcs of fire for tower guards, provide an adequate physiological barrier against potential insurgents and criminals, prevent hostile ground-level observation of the compound site, and require no external supply of materials.

They can also be constructed higher than typical concrete or Hesco-Bastion barriers. However, earth berms are more susceptible to heavy rains, their slopes are easier to climb, and usually their establishment requires a much wider perimeter area, and the availability of soil for construction.

Chain-Link Fences

Chain-link fences are cost-effective security structures, usually comprised of a minimum of a six-foot-high heavy-gauge chain-link fence topped with razor wire. These fences provide long-term protection, delay intruders' entry, act as a psychological barrier, provide good arcs of fire for tower guards, and are relatively quick to install. However, they do not mitigate direct or indirect fire threats and do not prevent VBIED intrusion. In addition, they only delay unauthorized access and permit hostile observation of the compound area (unless fabric sheeting is used to prevent surveillance).

Razor-Wire Fence

Razor wire is a simple and expedient method of creating a security perimeter quickly and cost effectively. Usually razor-wire structures are comprised of a three-high coiled razor-wire fence, supported by additional wire for the top of each razor-wire strand, linked to 12-foot posts spaced every 10 feet. Such fences provide a long-term security protective measure, delay authorized access, act as a psychological barrier, provide unrestricted arcs of fire for tower guards, and are very easy to install, repair, replace, and move. However, razor wire does not mitigate direct or indirect fire threats, and does not prevent VBIED intrusion; it only delays insurgent or criminal entry and permits hostile observation of the site.

Entry Control Points

Entry or access control points (ECPs) are potentially the weakest point in any security perimeter, being subject to vehicle-borne explosives as well as providing clear physical access to a site. They also form a choke point for pedestrian and vehicle traffic, and can be crowded and busy security service areas. ECPs should be structurally layered to limit exposure to risk, including screening, visitor control, inspection, overwatch, and staging areas for cargo delivery. The structural layout of an ECP should permit the early identification of possible threats and protect security personnel from external site threats as well as potential threats posed from those attempting to gain access or departing a site. The physical security structures should be sufficiently robust to prevent unauthorized access by both pedestrians and vehicles, and may be structured as illustrated in Exhibit 9.10.

A comprehensive set of SOPs and TTPs should be developed to ensure effective search policies and techniques for visiting personnel and vehicles as well as to prevent hostile intrusion. Access must be limited to authorized personnel and visitors, with a stated need to gain entry. The procedures must be clear and consistently enforced to avoid frustrating those engaged with routine access and to prevent humiliating important visitors with inappropriate or unreasonable searches or lengthy delays. The procedures at access control points must include physical barriers preventing forced entry, methods for positively identifying

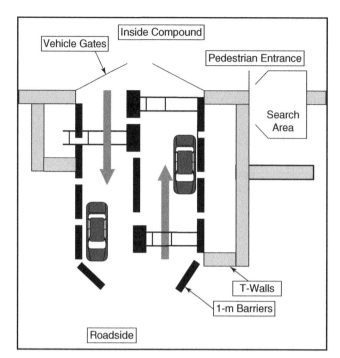

Exhibit 9.10   Entry Control Point Structural Layouts

personnel, issuance of visitor badges, escorts, areas segregation and detention, and armed oversight from secure positions of security personnel conducting access procedures, with communications to operations centers.

Should workforce or management personnel require movement into the site project, management should identify both long-term contractors and frequent short-term visitors in order to expedite their entry. The right to search personnel and their belongings and the procedures to be followed should be sensitive to local religious or social customs and clearly explained to security staff, with agreement from the project or risk manager. The project site may also require compartmentalization in order to restrict the access of certain types of employees from certain areas. If this is needed, additional internal fencing or blast walls will need to be constructed, with inner access or entry control points.

Security Gates

A physical barrier should be erected at road or pedestrian entrances to control the movement of vehicles and personnel entering and leaving the site. Gate hinges should be designed to prevent the gate from being removed from the outside. Gates should also work on the double or air-locked system so that personnel enter via a secure area protected from direct fire, where they are searched and identified and then allowed to pass through the second barrier. All gates should be designed to protect the guard force from external and internal threats. A metal screen gate allows the access point to be secured at night and locked down in the event of increased hostilities. Strategically placed sandbagged positions should be constructed to afford security personnel protection from attack. Unmanned gates should be kept locked and inspected regularly, with keys for emergency exit gates securely held but readily available. Manned gates are to be supervised from a position that enables the guard to communicate directly and effectively with the security control room (i.e., tactical operations center or TOC).

Door Strengthening

Doors to key areas should be especially strengthened in order to prevent access by unauthorized or hostile persons. Hinges should be placed on the side of greatest security. The use of observation ports or spy holes will allow security staff to view those requesting access. The door should be capable of withstanding forced entry, small arms fire, and the blast effects from limited explosives. This access control measure will permit areas to be sealed in order to compartmentalize areas to support daily security procedures as well as support the security response to hostile incidents or persons. Door strengthening should be considered for all safe havens.

Blast-Resistant Windows

While the threat of an indirect fire attack achieving a direct strike on a project building is relatively minor in most environments, the threat of direct fire should not be discounted. To mitigate this threat, it is recommended that for high-profile sites (typically diplomatic residences or significant Western projects), windows facing toward main streets should all be fitted with B6-level equivalent blast/bullet-resistant windows.

Blast Film

Improvised explosive devices are a common choice of weapon by insurgent groups in challenging environments. The effects include the blast, heat, and shrapnel injuries, plus secondary injuries resulting from the blast wave, which often cause structures such as glass windows and lightweight doors to fragment, thus creating secondary hazards. The use of inexpensive blast film on windows will reduce the threat of secondary injuries to the project staff should an explosive detonation occur nearby.

Safe Havens

The mission of an effective security plan is to provide an environment in which a project can operate safely and most productively. However, even the best risk mitigation plans and security measures may be breached. Therefore, contingency planning should include methods beyond the provision of a close protection and crisis management team in order to secure the project staff while a crisis event is being managed. Typically the staff will be removed from the risk area. In the case of hostile environments, the staff will be secured in a safe location while the incident is being addressed.

A safe haven is a location that allows personnel to be placed in an area of greatest protection while security management deals with a crisis event. This location should be a defendable room or area that has overhead protection and preferably two hardened entry and exit points that can be secured against intrusion. In addition, the area should be capable of housing all key staff for an extended period in relative comfort. Firefighting and survival items, water, food, and other critical equipment should be prepositioned in the safe haven. Strict management of safe havens should be implemented to ensure that they can be used effectively as required. There should be a safe haven on all building floors as well as a preferred safe haven for the residence/office location as a whole. Should a hostile incident require personnel to evacuate the project site, alternative or external safe havens may be required. These may be foreign government or military locations or existing secured areas. It is critical that SOPs and evacuation plans reflect any agreement with external agencies offering their secured location for an alternative external safe haven.

Overhead Protection

Projects operating within hostile environments with the threat of direct or indirect fire will require buildings and shelters hardened by concrete, berms, Hesco barriers, or sandbags to provide lateral protection from blasts and projectiles. The shelters must also provide adequate protection against penetration through the roofs into occupied areas. Access and exit points should have additional barriers to protect against ground-level hazards, such as the direct effect of rocket or mortar shrapnel, spalling of secondary hazards, or falling ground debris resulting from the blast effect. There are a number of ways to provide this type of protection (see Exhibit 9.11):

- *Buried shelters.* These shelters are fully or partially buried with the excavated earth placed over the top to provide the necessary blast protection to safe guard personnel.
- *Concrete.* Concrete may be used to provide protection either alone (U-bends) or as a rigid base for earth and/or sandbag augmentation. This augmentation may be necessary for existing concrete-roofed buildings that were not designed to withstand indirect fires.
- *Sandbags.* Sandbags are an effective means of mitigating overhead blast threats. If the supporting roof structure—concrete, wood, steel, or other materials—is insufficient to hold the weight, occupants may be in greater danger from a collapsing roof than from the effects of the overhead blast.

Exhibit 9.11 Hesco-Bastion Barriers Example. Iraqi Military Base. Copyright © M. Blyth, 2005.

Since shelters typically are used in emergencies, there is no time to provision them after an alarm has been sounded. Therefore, shelters need a dedicated on-site supply of food, water, seating, cots, heating and cooling if applicable, lighting, communications equipment, batteries, radio, medical supplies, and even books and other items to occupy time if the attack is of a sustained nature. Toilet facilities that provide the same level of protection should be nearby as well. A personnel accountancy rosters should be located at the command shelter, with the warden communicating with external support agencies.

SECURITY SURVEILLANCE AND LIGHTING

Companies should give serious consideration to the use of technology to augment security provision for facilities. Technology is often a means by which to enhance protection of a site while also reducing costs. The ability to proactively prevent a serious incident from occurring is preferable to relying on reactive security measures. The establishment of a surveillance security plan or a STAP is therefore fundamental to protect a site and staff. The extensive use of security lighting, guard towers, security staff patrols, and surveillance technology will increase security provision, integrating human resources and technology to significantly enhance the effectiveness of security measures. Close liaison with adjacent and patrolling military forces must also be established within the security plan to augment the project's security resources as well as avoid unnecessary friction or confusion. The next sections provide a brief insight into elements that might comprise a surveillance plan.

Intruder Detection Systems

An intruder detection system (IDS) offers a less labor-intensive option to monitor the security of a project site, and is an especially useful option for areas that cover sizable real estate or that have difficult or undulating terrain to survey. Technological security devices can also exceed human resources in terms of providing thermal, motion, ground sensor, and infrared security and can remove personnel from high-risk areas while still maintaining an overwatch capability. Many systems can provide enhanced security at a lower cost than guard forces. Cameras, passive infrared sensors, volumetric measuring devices, and ground motion sensors can be used, often programmed to include an automatic alarm system to alert management personnel immediately to the presence of an intruder, allowing the monitoring station to supervise multiple sensors indirectly. Transmissions may also be wireless to remove threats to physical disruption, and digital, increasing the view ability of a system as well as providing real-time feeds to corporate crisis response teams. Video devices also record events, permitting an effective post-incident review or confirmation of any alarm-triggering events. An integrated site security plan with technological detection systems integrates guard services with technological support, ensuring the most effective detection, deterrence, and response to unauthorized intrusion. Some of the uses of technology to support risk mitigation and active security provision for a project's operations are described next.

Detection The IDS should be capable of detecting an intruder penetrating vulnerable areas of the perimeter. It should also be able to detect an individual moving in areas out to a specified distance (e.g., 1500 feet) from the perimeter. When an event occurs, the system should automatically alert the TOC and activate the cameras or devices for immediate tracking and recording of an intrusion and incident. The operator should then be able to visually identify the nature and extent of the threat using the detection system from the management center, informing security personnel as to the nature of the threat, directing them towards the breached area, as well as advising project management where necessary to enable better decision making.

Radar   Radar detection can enhance the automated capability of the system, reduce operator fatigue, and add an additional layer of alert to security provision. Radar and digital infrared detection allows the system to gain an accurate fix on intruders, permitting the operator to acquire further information by manual use of a camera system. Detection ranges up to 5000 feet for pedestrian intruders (terrain dependent), with vehicle detection often exceeding 7000 feet. Digital infrared sensors are available on some systems and decrease the false alarm rate, as compared with analog infrared sensors. The system should be configured to establish virtual fence lines, determining the delineation between the external area and the perimeter demarcation line.

Cameras   A high-resolution camera is recommended for identification of the threat type and extent over a large operational area. Thermal imaging capabilities will allow the identification of intruders at night and in inclement weather conditions, and camera systems may have rotation and tilt capabilities as well as automatic motion identification and tracking capability. They must be able to withstand a wide range of weather conditions while requiring limited technical maintenance. Typically, infrared and thermal cameras perform within a range of 150 to 1200 feet. Cameras can be set automatically to pan areas and lock onto movement, tracking possible intrusion while sounding an alarm. They can be set in remote or difficult terrain with a wireless feed, allowing security personnel to survey ground outside of the project area with no physical risk. Systems can also be concealed to prevent identification, although power source requirements can pose limitations.

Command Station   The radar and camera system should connect to a command center through physical or wireless communication mediums. The command center should have monitors and relevant systems to accurately display the location of possible intruders; some systems may do this on a computer-generated map overlay. The operator must be able to adjust and control cameras and other sensors from the command center. On some systems, an audible alarm accompanies intruder acquisition. Many systems also include data storage facilities in order to track intrusions for post-incident review. Command systems should be designed to monitor a range of devices, ensuring a complete technological integration solution as well as real-time information provision to management and security personnel. These centers can also keep real time data and images to corporate offices in other countries.

External Lighting

External lighting provides an effective deterrence and should be positioned to expose the intruder, but conceal the occupants inside the project site. In high-risk areas, lighting should be angled away from the office areas and security positions in such a way as to illuminate the entire perimeter. Lights should shine into the eyes of any intruders and cover dark areas that would otherwise give cover to an intruder approaching the site. Dark areas should be illuminated by waist-high subdued lighting. Areas around all external doors giving access to offices or accommodation blocks should also be well illuminated in order to aid the identification of callers. If possible, external lights should be connected to an alarm system so that they are switched on automatically whenever an alarm is triggered.

Security Patrols

The use of security patrols provides a firsthand method of monitoring perimeter security to identify physical security deficiencies or unauthorized access and acts as a good deterrent measure, if conducted properly. Patrols should avoid pattern setting and should be tactically planned and conducted, with routes, times, and cleared areas being varied to establish a degree of unpredictability. The use of both vehicular and foot patrols allows large areas to be secured and a more measured or considered security posture to be adopted. Patrols rely on effective communication systems and well-defined procedures to allow effective coordination and response measures. The SMT should also divide the site into sectors, ensure that patrols are familiar with the area, and prevent areas from being missed. Patrols should be coordinated with other security groups (towers and external agencies) to prevent accidental alarms or response measures being taken.

Towers

High-profile projects in hostile areas may require security towers in order to detect and deter unauthorized access or to dominate areas surrounding a project site in order to deter unwanted attention, detect potentially threatening activities and to respond to hostile activities before a breach of the site may occur. Such observation points provide a position from which to detect hostile persons, sound the alarm, and delay threats from a range of threats, including terrorists, insurgents, and criminals. It is important to establish a sound security plan that stipulates response measures and specifies where other security locations are sited through the use of schematics, sketches, and clear static guard instructions. To be most effective, guard towers should, where possible, provide mutual support and interlocking arcs of observation and fire.

CONVENTIONAL SECURITY POLICIES

It is tempting for security management to focus on mitigating physical threats in high-risk environments rather than consider the normal challenges that occur in passive environments. A complete security review of a project's requirements should include those measures normally associated with conventional environments, such as theft, commercial espionage, and power loss. The next sections provide a sample of conventional security considerations risk managers should address when operating in more challenging environments, where typically the focus is drawn away from conventional threats.

Lock-and-Key Security

Lock-and-key security forms a vital element in the protection of buildings within the site, protecting companies from theft, espionage, and vandalism. Locks may be attacked by picking or force, or breached using lost or stolen keys. Key security is designed to reduce the exposure to such an attack. No unauthorized person should have access to keys, and the number of keys for each lock should be kept to a minimum, with spare keys strictly controlled and secured by the security manager. If a key is lost, the lock should be changed immediately; replacement keys should not be obtained.

Sensitive Data

Information security is often poor in most companies, even (or especially) within the security division. This problem can be exacerbated in temporary or makeshift work areas where office lock-and-key policies are difficult to enforce and work hours are long. As a result, information may be left accessible to unauthorized attention. Restrictions should be applied to areas that contain sensitive data—in both commercial and security terms. Where possible, office spaces should be locked and patrolled at night to prevent theft or criminal damage. Materials considered restricted in nature and content should be placed in safes or locked cabinets. Where necessary, cameras, thumb-drives, and other recording devices should be restricted to prevent unauthorized removal of data. Information technology security policies and procedures should be implemented to prevent data loss or system infection.

Power Sources

Most remote or hostile region project sites have no reliable power sources, and power is intermittent at best. Thus, sites may rely on project-resourced generators to provide energy. Ideally generators should not be co-located in case of damage, and they should be shielded to the same degree as work and living areas. Redundant power sources should be established, should generators break or need repairs. Fuel supplies should cover anticipated logistical replenishment periods, with a surplus to meet delays in reprovisioning. Additional fuel should be stored separately from power sources or other important structures.

Parking

Parking should be by permit only and restricted to specific areas. While vehicles should be thoroughly inspected for unauthorized or harmful materials prior to entry, in some areas they should still be considered a potential risk for VBIEDs, and a final layer of protection between vehicle parks and office/residences is a sensible precaution. Vehicle inspections and protection also prevent the unauthorized removal of sensitive or high-value items from the site. Vehicle parks may be bordered by T-walls, Hesco-Bastion barriers, or earth berms to protect against unidentified explosives contained within vehicles or from damage sustained by indirect fire or explosively created shrapnel. The potential trajectory angles of explosive materials should be considered when determining the height of perimeter defenses for vehicle parks, to protect both vehicles and surrounding buildings, as illustrated in Exhibit 9.12, as often second. Story levels may not be protected due to trajectory angles.

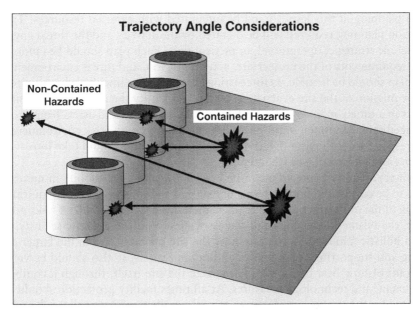

Exhibit 9.12   Trajectory Considerations for Protecting Facilities, Personnel, and Assets

Warden System

Companies should establish, or request from their security provider, a warden system that can be used during emergency situations to direct the movement of personnel to designated secure locations and then account for their safety and determine medical or other needs. Accountability and reporting must be done in accordance with SOPs. If project staff are mobile, they will need to phone or radio their location and status to the SMT or TOC. Since project staff sometimes ignore alarms and other security protocols (especially late at night), the site should be swept to ensure that all personnel have gathered as required. Primary and alternate medical points, if necessary, should be established as gathering points for injured persons. Entry control point guards should routinely list who enters and leaves the central life support area to facilitate accountability during emergencies and drills. The site accountability register should be the security manager's primary tool for maintaining accountability for all personnel physically located at the primary or subsites; often the main weakness of the response plan consists of the accounting for personnel during a crisis event.

EVACUATION PLANNING

Companies should consider evacuation planning an essential part of risk mitigation and security services. Evacuation planning should reflect local, regional, and national level needs. While local or regional evacuation should be within the resource capability of the security subprovider, rarely can the project's own resources manage a national-level evacuation.

Evacuation planning at this level should be integrated with external resources. The level of the evacuation planning required will be dictated by the activity and the threat environment, and may include strategic, operational, or tactical tiers. Each plan should be tailored to meet the unique requirements of the project site, activity, region, and threat environment. In addition, each plan should be flexible, as forecasting risk events is difficult and subject to constant change. The mission of the site evacuation plan is to identify the need to demobilize personnel or assets in a timely manner and to safely extract personnel and assets from project areas to prearranged safe location(s) in the event of deterioration in the risk environment. Evacuations may respond to both natural and man-made threats, and should take into account different factors and influences (see Chapter 10).

In summary, facility protection can be both static and semi-mobile in nature, and requires risks to be considered both in terms of external and internal threats, requiring a sound appreciation of the most practical and realistic methods by which to offset risks posed to the project site, the business activities, and the associated workforce. Static security should be viewed in a holistic manner, considering how the site operates within the larger context of surrounding and supporting communities and organizations. It also should be viewed from the standpoint of how best to secure and manage the site itself, through a combination of physical, human, and technology measures. At all times facility protection should be guided and supported by comprehensive, but user-friendly, policies and procedures by which management identifies the risks and applies the solutions.

Note

1. Building physical security structures to strengthen the site's existing security.

CHAPTER 10

Evacuation Planning

Companies should consider evacuation planning as an essential part of risk mitigation and security services, especially when operating within remote or unstable environments. Evacuations are singular events in that they directly often involve entire project teams, and indirectly corporate offices, under stressful and difficult conditions. Evacuation plans should be reflective of local, regional, and national influences, and should be applied to both static and mobile activities. Evacuation planning should also be considered in terms of management levels. Typically it will have different requirements on executive, country, and project leadership.

While a local or regional evacuation should be within the capability of the project or security provider's resources, rarely can the project's own resources manage a national level evacuation. Thus, evacuation planning at this level should be integrated with external resources and managed strategically by at the corporate level. The level of evacuation planning required by a project will be dictated by both the activity and the threat environment, and may include strategic, operational, or tactical tiers. Each plan should be tailored to meet the unique requirements of the project, activity, region, and threat environment and also should have a degree of in-built flexibility, as it may be difficult to forecast risk events, which might be subject to constant change.

The mission of the evacuation plan is to identify the need to demobilize personnel or assets in a timely manner and to safely extract them from operational areas to prearranged safe location(s) in the event of deterioration in the risk environment. Evacuations may respond to both natural or man-made threats, and should take into account the different factors and influences associated with each.

Decision making within the evacuation plan should be clearly defined at each level, as the plan will have a significant impact on the business activity as well as the safety of personnel. Typically as risks increase due to political or social instabilities, or pending natural influences, a project's activity may start to draw down and become more limited in nature to reflect the uncertainties of the environment in which staff or resources are operating. This is not necessarily the case for companies with higher threat tolerances or those that have significant infrastructures or resources in the area. In addition, those companies that have entered the area aware of the challenges and instabilities the environment may pose will be less likely to withdraw; they will be more likely to attempt to weather the storm and achieve productive results in the face of shifting threat levels, maintaining an effective level of business continuity through well-established contingency plans. Typically these types of companies include reconstruction, engineering, and aid agencies operating in areas that have recently undergone tumultuous political changes, are emerging from periods of conflict, are experiencing tenuous political transformations, or any situation in which the sovereignty and leadership of the country is in question. These companies may also be those who are experienced with operating within regions where severe weather or techtonic conditions may present frequent natural hazards.

Besides considering extreme political volatility and social unrest, it is necessary to understand the rapidly changing commercial needs of the company that may impact the requirements and directives within the evacuation plan, such as decreasing risk tolerances. The plan must therefore be able to adapt to a dynamic commercial environment and to a changing political and security situation, or changing natural influences. In order to be most effective, evacuation planning must be seen as a process embedded in the management planning structure. Evacuation planning at all levels should become part of the normal business practice. The evacuation plan should form a component of the project or program's risk management plan.

EVACUATION PRINCIPLES

Evacuation planning is not the responsibility of purely the security management team (SMT), but will involve every element of a company's structure. All participants must therefore be identified and take ownership of the plan and their responsibilities in the event of implementation. A clearly defined management structure with lines of authority and responsibility should be established within corporate, country, and program structures. Where each layer overlaps, or where key managers are responsible for organizing supporting elements, nodal point personnel should be identified.

In the unlikely event that a project team is required to withdraw from a specific area, region, or country, the evacuation management team (EMT) should coordinate details with executive management as well as government and military organizations and local agencies to ensure that assembly areas, safe locations, interagency plans and support, transit routes, exit points, and asset and information planning are conducted in accordance with predetermined management requirements.

To support management decision making and activities an information management plan (or communications plan) should be prepared in order to ensure that the correct people are informed or enlisted within a crisis response. Nodal points, those posts designated to funnel information, should be identified and briefed to ensure that information cascades throughout the company through predetermined managers to make the response most effective.

The alert state plan should identify predetermined trigger points, which in turn drive decision making. Triggers can include a rise in civil disturbances, political unrest, incident increases, changes to weather patterns or initial indicators of forthcoming earthquakes. The acquisition and passage of accurate information is critical for good decision making and co-ordination. Networking and closed and open reporting is useful to quickly establish a threat picture that might trigger phases of an evacuation response. Multiple forms of communication should be in place to deal with the likely failure of normal communications mediums, typically resulting if communication infrastructures are damaged or otherwise adversely affected or overload during and following a crisis event.

Sound administration typically provides the foundation for success or failure for an evacuation. Companies should ensure that both the security elements and the supporting logistical and administrative structures are in place to support evacuations, as personnel and materials will require transportation, life support, and other administrative support.

It is important for project management also to understand that initiating evacuation procedures may not actually result in a withdrawal from the project site; it might only prepare management teams and resources for a possible evacuation. A series of measured steps should be taken prior to initiating the significant requirements of moving personnel and key equipment from a facility. It is important to maintain business continuity as long as safely possible in order to avoid undermining the productivity of the project's operations. Evacuation planning should include these principal elements:

- *Ownership.* Clearly defined ownership and delegated responsibilities, at all levels.
- *Decision making.* Based on alert states, triggers, and the use of external advice.
- *Information.* Timely and accurate situation assessments to help the EMT form balanced decisions.
- *Communications.* Reliable communications systems (with alternate means) supported with clear reporting procedures that are checked regularly, guided by the information management plan.
- *Administration.* Planned administrative details and readily available resources. Regularly updated records of locations and contact details of all potential evacuees.
- *Business continuity.* Maintaining the security of operations and personnel in an atmosphere of speculation and rumors.
- *Business recover.* Establishing plans by which to most effectively return to an evacuated location and resume operations.

EVACUATION PLAN ELEMENTS

Not every evacuation plan will look the same, and each should be tailored to meet individual company and project needs. That said, consistency of structure and content should be sought so that the company's management is assured that pertinent points are addressed within multiple evacuation plans. The overarching goal for evacuation planning is to effect a timely and safe evacuation of personnel leading up to, as well as during, a crisis event. To that end, sound contingency planning measures are necessary to avoid confusion and issues during the plan's implementation. The sections that follow discuss elements that should be factored into evacuation plans.

Resourced

Evacuation planning must be regarded as an essential task at all levels of management, from strategic through to tactical and from corporate down to project. Too often, contingency planning is neglected across all business functions, and the consequences of poor evacuation planning in both passive and hostile environments can have significant impacts upon the company overall, as well as the activities the actual event impairs. Companies should seek to ensure that evacuation plans are resourced in terms of development, sustainment, and actual implementation.

Understood

Companies and their security providers should ensure that all staff (including local nationals and subcontractors for whom they have responsibility) fully understand what is required of them should the evacuation plan be executed. Part of this will be ensuring that movement and location logs are always kept up to date and that communications details and mediums are kept up to date and operable. Briefing managers and making elements of the evacuation plan accessible is also a useful method of sharing information and ensuring group understanding.

Scalable

The evacuation plan should be scalable, able to be applied to a single location where a highly localized threat triggers withdrawal or to wider areas as the situation dictates. Having common procedures regardless of the area to be evacuated lessens the burden on the coordinating staff and the evacuees at a time when stress levels are likely to be high and rising. Staged evacuation measures might also enable a degree of business activity to continue during the early stages of evacuation implementation.

Flexible

Although the overall plan must be fully understood by all, it must also be capable of being quickly revised to reflect a wide spectrum of influences, whether risk or corporate need related. A robust means of communicating any changes to all coordinating staff is required to support a flexible approach to plan revisions. Management should review the original planning assumptions against changes in the risk environment and alter the plan parameters and requirements accordingly. Where appropriate, executive leadership should sanction significant changes.

Rehearsed

Evacuation plans at all levels, from corporate to project, should be rehearsed on a regular basis to ensure that they are effective and realistic in the event of a withdrawal. It will not, of course, be practical to withdraw personnel and resources from the site, as this will undermine business activities and may present greater risks to personnel. However, management tabletop exercises and initial evacuation response measures can be conducted periodically to ensure that plans can be implemented effectively.

Coordinated

It is unlikely that an evacuation plan will be triggered in isolation. Rather it is likely that other agencies and companies will also be triggering their own evacuation plans. It is also highly likely therefore that routes, safe havens, major assembly points, and the like, will be common to some or all evacuation plans. In evacuation planning, it is essential to ensure that neighboring organizations are consulted to explore how plans can complement each other/deconflict with one another. The use of supporting external organizations will also augment organic capabilities and resources in order to reduce risks to project staff and materials.

EVACUATION MANAGEMENT

Companies should understand that typically there are three tiers of management involvement in evacuation plans: (1) corporate or executive leadership within the headquarters element, (2) country-level management overseeing national activities, and (3) the project itself, an individual task site that may need to withdraw. Each will have unique but overlapping areas of interest, and each should have defined sections within an integrated evacuation plan that span not only the internal management levels but also how these plug into external support organizations, whether they are specialist commercial bodies contracted to support an evacuation (air transportation, medical, logistical, counseling) or government agencies (embassies, military, police). Risk managers should consider how nonsecurity-related professionals might be required for an effective evacuation, as an evacuation is not simply the practical movement of people and equipment from a risk environment, but will also require executive-level management awareness, authority, and input.

The typical crisis response teams will be augmented with logistics and administrative staff during an evacuation, as large numbers of personnel and equipment may need to be moved within a country or to adjoining or other nations. The tactical operations center (TOC) may also act as the evacuation coordination center, coordinating internal and external resources, expertise, information, communications, administration, logistics, and authorization levels. An evacuation authorization chart and associated decision matrix should be agreed on within the company, as well as with the security provider, to determine which management levels are authorized to make decisions under different circumstances. Consider this example:

> Project evacuation management are authorized to evacuate personnel and resources from the project site if a direct and imminent threat is posed to the activity, location or personnel, withdrawing to the program management center or another appropriate and predetermined safe location. If no immediate threat is apparent, but threats are increasingly likely to occur in the near future, permission must be sought and arrangements made through the program evacuation manager.

Different levels of authorization should be pre-formulated by the company to prevent immediate threats from posing an unnecessary or increasing level of risk to the project if senior management personnel are required to grant permission to evacuate. Key positions within the evacuation management structure include:

- *Corporate executive evacuation manager (CEEM).* Higher-level authority and management should rest with the corporate board in terms of macro-level considerations, strategies, decision making, and interagency liaison. The corporate team will also be responsible for media handling, family liaison, legal affairs, liability issues, diplomatic discussions, and other supporting functions as well as overseeing and managing company-level considerations—in addition to strategic and complex decision making. The corporate element can also provide the funding and resource allocation to support new requirements more effectively.
- *Country evacuation manager (CEM).* The CEM should have overall decision-making authority for the programs in the country. The CEM will determine the alert phases and

decide with corporate management if and when to execute an evacuation. The CEM should maintain close links with military and security organizations as well as appropriate embassies and diplomatic missions.

■ *Local evacuation team (LET).* The LET (typically the program or project) plans, organizes, and supports an evacuation of personnel and vital equipment for a specific commercial site, activity or region. The team will maintain close liaison with the diplomatic missions, nongovernment organizations, (security) authorities, and military headquarters within its area to facilitate an evacuation.

■ *Site evacuation managers (SEMs).* The CEM will designate site (or project) evacuation managers (SEMs). They could be the project manager, a contracted security manager, or other qualified staff member responsible for the risk management and security of a particular project or facility, for evacuating a project back to a program location or other defined site.

■ *Reception team.* Reception teams should include a senior company representative to provide employee briefings and enhance moral support as well as a range of support and administrative staff. The reception team function is to manage the reception of evacuees at a regional or national safe haven or one located outside of the activity country. Information management, accountability, liaison functions, travel, accommodation, and life support provision and medical support will be included within their responsibilities.

Supporting these management elements will be legal, human resources, finance, administration, travel, public relations, logistics and procurement, and other back-office elements. In addition, liaison with external organizations such as embassies, military organizations, or indeed other companies should be conducted to augment the project's own capabilities through mutually beneficial and pre-agreed planning.

Information Management Plan

Companies should seek to establish an information management plan (IMP) to ensure that all security operations, including evacuations, are well structured and effective. The management of information is critical to ensuring not only balanced and timely decision making for the evacuation itself but also that a consistent and trusted source of information provides a focal point for evacuees, friends, and family, rather than the snippets and rumors that might otherwise create confusion or unnecessary concern. Management of information will also contribute to the public relations effort that is so often necessary in hostile media environments. There is thus a need for both a robust communications infrastructure, both in management and technology terms, with built-in redundancy to ensure the passage of information is technically and organizationally achievable and an IMP that sets out who receives information and who it is passed to. Clear and recognized channels of information flow that are rigorously maintained are an essential part of an effective evacuation plan.

A detailed and predetermined IMP can also focus on agreed decision-making and information-sharing protocols, as companies may elect to have different individuals or groups be part of the information management process during the different stages of an evacuation. For example, during the initial stages, the broader company group might be included to ensure that all personnel are aware of heighten security awareness requirements. During the actual physical evacuation, only a smaller management group may be included and receive detailed instructions so as to avoid confusion, panic, and poor management and operational activities. Conversely, in situations where project sites frequently ramp up to initial evacuation preparation points, senior-level corporate leadership may elect not to be informed until an evacuation is likely to be required; planned actions may be the purview of executive managers.

Strategic Mapping

Companies should seek to identify the location of project- and country-level management or work sites, as well as other facilities or groups of use or interest in order to ensure an understanding of where company and influential sites lay in relation to each other. Mapping should also include multiple extraction routes or points, such as roads, rivers, and air transportation points, as illustrated in Exhibit 10.1. The locations of military bases, safe havens, and areas of risk should be identified in relation to company operations. Mapping provides an excellent visual medium to place the projects into a physical context and prompts managers to call on supporting organizations for assistance. Mapping extraction route options also reduces the need to communicate complex information should projects need to withdraw from a site, and maps using color codes and spot marking, as well as code names will allow managers to pinpoint locations or routes with greater ease and accuracy.

Exhibit 10.1 The Evacuation Principles

Destruction Plan

Evacuations that are staged and conducted over a measured period usually allow for the withdrawal of vital information and high value or sensitive materials from the site. However, where extraction resources are limited or when the speed of evacuation is swift, valuable materials and information may be left behind. The company should consider the need to establish a destruction plan, which might involve cleansing hard drives, burning paper files, or even destroying or making inoperable certain equipment. During the stress and confusion of an evacuation, destruction requirements can be easily overlooked, leading to the loss of valuable business and operational information as well as sensitive or harmful materials. Persons should be designated to have authority to sanction and carry out destruction. To avoid unnecessary loss of valuable information, it is useful to have data grab bags where information can be downloaded onto external hard drives or important paperwork can be boxed for withdrawal. Important equipment might also be packaged in prepositioned containers or carried by designated personnel from the site.

PROCESS PLANNING

The evacuation management process is a logically driven system that should contain sufficient detail to enable a crisis management team to understand why, when, and how to evacuate personnel and assets. A solidly developed evacuation plan should include the components of preparation, decision making, the evacuation implementation process, tactical evacuation procedures, the consolidation and processing of evacuees, the movement to an airhead or port, and evacuation to a regional safe area, and the reception in a regional safe area, followed by movement back to a final destination.

Preparation

Companies should seek to ensure that adequate time and resources have been provided for the preparation phase and that it meets both short- and long-term objectives. The short-term objective is to ensure that if an evacuation crisis happened tomorrow, the planning groups at all levels would have the means to effect an evacuation. The long-term objective is to put in place an integrated evacuation planning process, with sufficient controls, relationships, and management systems to provide the most effective evacuation measures. This preparation for evacuation planning may include:

- *Strategy*. Confirm with all stakeholders, executives, and program management the overarching strategy and concepts of the evacuation plan, establishing group agreement, understanding, and participation. Determine initial and long term focus most vunerable sites first.
- *Resourcing*. Provide the evacuation management group with the resources and expertise required to establish an effective evacuation plan as well as identify tactical resource, relationship and budget requirements.
- *Plan*. Establish an integrated evacuation plan drawing on internal company resources and knowledge and exploiting external agency support and expertise, where possible. Liaise closely with external supporting agencies to gain plan support and buy-in. Maximize security vendor support, both in terms of contract and regional resources.

- *Policies.* Ensure that security and risk policies support the evacuation plan and are fully integrated into the requirements, especially site and mobile security, logistics, administration, communications, and liaison responsibilities and functions.
- *Management.* Confirm the different tiers and management structures within the evacuation plan, consolidating plan responsibilities and functions as well as liaising with external groups to gain agreement and understanding. Establish management centers and structures.
- *Assessment.* Continually assess the threat environment and inform the management structure(s) of significant changes or predictions. Reviewing the evacuation plans to ensure it reflects the current environment.

Evacuation Decision   At all levels, within management teams of both the company and the subcontracted security providers, the decision to evacuate must be both balanced and unambiguous, as well as decisive and based on a clinical evaluation of the threats facing the project directly as well as peripheral risks that might affect it. The EMT, led initially by the company program manager, or risk or security manager, should define the threats in alignment with contingency planning policies (see the section titled "Alert States"). Different levels of evacuation may be required, from nonessential personnel, local employees, to the final critical staff departing the project area or country. Also, different areas within a geographic space may need to be evacuated, as a particular threat types may focus on certain areas. Evacuations may also occur in stages, with each stage requiring a decision from authorized management elements. Each step toward an evacuation, whether local, regional, or national, requires further engagement with internal and external organizations and groups as well as additional resources, management, and administrative support. Corporate crisis management teams should be in-step with each stage of an evacuation, to ensure it is both authorized and supported.

Tactical Evacuation   During the tactical withdrawal of personnel and assets, it is important to reassess the threats that each activity faces, as these threats may dictate a change in the evacuation planning and implementation measures. Personnel should be advised of the threats and the evacuation plan as well as what they must do to support or participate in the withdrawal. Elements outside of the project should be fully engaged in supporting a full or staged evacuation, from the project site to an adjoining area or to another country. In addition, national and local crisis management teams should assess the most effective means of effecting a withdrawal, whether via road, air, or sea, working in close coordination with diplomatic and military organizations. Assembly areas, routes, and predetermined safe locations (havens) should be confirmed and appropriate external resources mobilized to effect the plan.

Tactical evacuation may require the use of military or government facilities as an interim staging point prior to departure from country. Bridgeheads from airports, borders, or ports may also need to be established to administratively to cater to large numbers of personnel awaiting final transportation from the risk area. Communication networks should be in place to ensure that all stakeholders and decision makers are kept abreast of developments and strategies and that interfaces with military or consular offices are maintained. Security may also be needed for staging points and media handling and liaison with families and subcontractor management offices should also be initiated. All necessary administrative, logistical, life support, security, financial, and resource procurement measures should be addressed to support the evacuation.

Strategic lift planning should be considered, integrating the project's requirements with other groups, so that resources can best support the movement of personnel and materials from affected sites or regions. Larger movements might attract greater support from military authorities. Combining activities from different security companies might significantly enhance overact project security. It is important to secure or destroy high-value or sensitive items that may be left behind at the project site. Parties that might not be subject to the same risks as the project staff might be hired to stay behind as part of the contingency planning measures to secure facilities and resources until a return to the site is possible.

Consolidation The evacuation process, however well planned and organized, will inherently result in a degree of confusion. Sound contingency planning well in advance of an event, as illustrated in Exhibit 10.2, is important to reduce confusion and enhance management systems and processes.

Managers should be aware that evacuation management involves not only those physically involved in extracting personnel and materials from a location but requires logistics, public relations, human resources, administrative, and other back-office support functions. The tactical extraction of people and materials from a specific site is but one element of a more complex and dynamic operation. Strategic reviews and assessments should be ongoing during the evacuation to assess the speed of requirements needed to support current withdrawal as the threat picture changes as well as macro-level impacts, considerations, and requirements which might affect longer term and more strategic needs. Thus the EMT will need to draw on in-country operational resources as well as supporting groups to be most

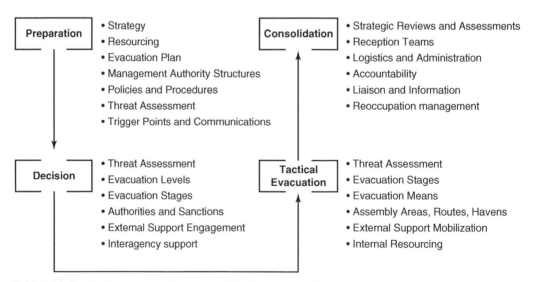

Exhibit 10.2 The Evacuation Planning and Implementation Process

effective. Reception teams will receive the evacuated personnel at predetermined safe locations, processing them in terms of rosters, life support, and further transportation requirements. In high-threat environments, stress trauma advisors might be required to care for the project staff. While the local crisis response teams should be responsible for personnel and equipment accountability and tracking, secondary management checks should be conducted at reception sites. The information cycle between the SEM, LET, CEM, CEEM, and reception teams should be closed to confirm that all personnel and high-value items are accounted for, with onward responsibility allocations so that tactical management elements can pass responsibilities onwards as people and materials are safety extracted from their areas of responsibility. The IMP should also include the documentation and dissemination of important information within the company, to diplomatic and military missions, and to family members and communities so that information gaps do not appear and responsibilities are clearly defined. This is especially important if subcontractor companies rely on the contracting company to coordinate and manage all evacuation requirements, as the project may be inclined to focus more on its own personnel or concerns.

EVACUATION TRIGGERS

Implementing an evacuation can have far-reaching consequences for a company. For that reason, the decision to withdraw should be carefully planned, where possible. While the speed of deterioration may vary, having established plans and trigger recognitions will ensure more effective management of an evacuation process. Triggers may include political or social unrest, increased threat incidents, direct targeting, climatic or volcanic risks, or a change in the company's tolerance levels. The influence or factors that determine and evacuation of project staff or assets can be an accumulation of incidents over a prolonged period leading to a staged and measured withdrawal, or may be a high-impact event or situation that requires an immediate decision. Two forms of situations might necessitate an evacuation: progressive deterioration and rapid deterioration.

Progressive Deterioration

Progressive deterioration occurs when a gradual risk level increases, or a series of events enables sufficient information to be gathered by managers to identify and track a gradual deterioration of the overall risk environment. This allows a set of predetermined responses to be taken by the company at a measured pace to facilitate a timely evacuation of personnel or assets. The decision to implement an evacuation based on a progressive deterioration usually is made by the corporate offices.

Rapid Deterioration

Rapid deterioration is when there exists little or no warning of impending hostilities, adverse reactions, or natural threats. The decision to implement an evacuation based on a rapid deterioration usually is made by the project or country management and requires immediate implementation—typically along pre-agreed-upon decision lines and authorities.

ALERT STATES

Preparing an evacuation plan requires detailed preplanning measures that determine agreed-upon alert states at both corporate and field levels. Alert states are agreed-upon points within a threat environment where a risk or event triggers management activities or warning notifications. Threat levels are often the key indicators of alert states; however, threat levels are extremely volatile and do not necessarily reflect actual risks to personnel or equipment and can also be subjectively assessed. Assessing alert states in terms of the threat to and vulnerability of a project will provide a more tailored and realistic local alert state system. The process should be a continuous one of assessing the risk environment in which the project is operating at local, regional, and national levels; it should not be associated solely with evacuation requirements.

Sound judgment forms the basis of a decision but the development of agreed-upon alert states provides a common vocabulary, context, and structure for assessing and reacting to the threats that confront the project. In essence, these alert states provide a simple and effective way of conveying the severity of a situation to local, national, and corporate management in order to facilitate their decision-making process. Alert states can also be used to trigger internal risk and security reviews and measures, increasing awareness, initiating contingency measures, and mobilizing resources to be positioned to respond to a need.

Alert states can be influenced by internal assessments and/or guided by government, military, or civil assessments. Differences may exist between what a government considers just reason to evacuate and what commercial organizations see as the final trigger for a withdrawal. Typically businesses will bear the brunt of financial or project losses in the event of an evacuation; whereas diplomatic warnings are more advisory and perhaps not audience specific.

Different Alert States

Alert state risk assessments can also be tied directly to actions required and policies implemented. The development and refinement of alert states will assist in a semiautomated process following the risk assessment. Alert states vary from low, medium, high, to extreme. In each instance, to avoid personal perspective or ambiguity, an explanation of what drives the classification should be provided as well as what actions are required to reflect a risk change. Alert state tables may be complex or simplistic, depending on the complexity of the project requirement.

Alert states should be connected to a response table (see Exhibit 10.3), which defines what occurs at each alert state. This table may be managed at three distinct levels—corporate, country, and project—where each alert state drives a certain response or requirement. The response table itself should be associated closely with a decision matrix, defining who is authorized to implement decisions.

The simplified response table in Exhibit 10.4 indicates some considerations that might be applied in different alert state levels. Each bullet point should be supported by more detailed incident management plans or by associated company policies.

EVACUATION PLAN COMPONENTS

An evacuation plan should be clear and detailed, offering very specific guidance on how an evacuation is both planned and coordinated. Preparation significantly reduces problems associated in dealing with a crisis rather than purely crisis managing the event. A sample of

Exhibit 10.3 Simple Alert State Table

State	Description	Response
Low	Political stability and low levels of criminal or civil activity	Business activities continue uninterrupted, with limited out-of-bounds areas.
Medium	Peaceful demonstrations and changes in political environment and structures through peaceful means	Limitations placed on some activities to avoid peaceful demonstrations. Security awareness and vigilance enhanced, site security augmented, and evacuation requirements reviewed.
High	Demonstration frequency increasing in number and size, with violent clashes between protestors and security forces. Political leaders resign in protest or under duress.	Only vital external activity tasks conducted, any political or demonstration areas avoided. Site security hardened and mobile security augmented. Advice sought from diplomatic and military missions. Evacuation readiness implemented. Nonessential personnel removed from country. Crisis response team mobilized at national and corporate levels.
Extreme	Violent demonstrations frequent with the closure of political offices. Security forces unable to contain clashes. Looting occurs with no clear governance and political control.	All external activities cease. Close liaison with diplomatic missions and military forces. Personnel and assets readied for evacuation. Site access control points closed and local employees return home. Crisis response team active, and full evacuation implemented if required.

considerations that might be included in an evacuation plan follows. The use of marked mapping, photography, check sheets, and pre-developed management systems (of which some have been discussed) greatly enhance the management of this form of crisis situation.

- *Assembly areas.* The locations to which employees move upon notification of an evacuation, typically within a work or project site.
- *Embarkation points.* The locations at which project staff board aircraft, ships, or vehicles for evacuation from the local or regional areas (airports, ports, parking lots). This may be within a project site or at a regional extraction point.
- *Safe havens.* The locations, within and outside of the project region (residence, work site, hotel, diplomatic mission, military facility), to which project staff are relocated to ensure greater protection until the situation stabilizes or until they are transported to their ultimate destination.

Exhibit 10.4 Simplified Response Table

State	Corporate Level Decision	Country Level Decisions	Project Level Decisions
1	• Conduct a business risk review • Reduce investments to the task • Reduce project expansions • Require security review of tasks	• Review project activities • Limit nonessential tasks • Practice evacuation plan • Request information from military or embassies	• Advise staff members • Review and update evacuation plan • Review overall security measures • Discuss with local military commanders
2	• Discuss with embassy officials • Conduct executive review of business case • Seek legal and insurance liability review • Limit country-level activities, review risks	• Restrict movement in affected areas • Seek information from local military and embassies • Increase security measures at all appropriate sites • Prepare next-stage resource requirements	• Advise staff members and subcontractors • Only essential movement conducted • Increase guards at access control points • Confirm and exercise next level requirements
3			
4	*Escalation of Decision and Response measures as the risk situation deteriorates*		
5	• Stand-up crisis response team • Mobilize internal extraction resources • Advise family and subcontracting companies • Request embassy and military support	• Liaise with military commands for support • Mobilize bridge head for national extraction • Prepare to review project staff and materials • Standby armed response teams to support	• All personnel evacuated to safe havens • All sensitive materials removed or destroyed • Area locked down and secured • Military forces informed of actions

- *Evacuation coordination center (ECC).* The EEC may be an already existing management location (for example a TOC), or one created to deal with a specific evacuation event. Where possible preparations must be in place to ascertain availability of communications between management groups, as well as other administration and support resources. Hastily prepared ECC's often will struggle to deal with an evacuation event.
- *Movement.* Without the proper intelligence, protection, and training, travel in certain countries can be lethal, especially during higher risk periods or events. As a result, movement is intensive in terms of assets, resources, and manpower, and difficult due to possible hostile activities and ongoing military operations. While travel by air might be possible, helicopters are extremely vulnerable, and hull insurance on commercial fixed wings is often prohibitive. Road convoys are often exposed to both opportunistic and deliberate ambushes, and if large numbers of personnel or assets require withdrawal, frequent movements of personnel or resources might set patterns along common routes increasing risks substantially. The safe movement of personnel therefore is a significant challenge. Movement of personnel and assets needs to be carefully coordinated and controlled through an integrated journey management system using report lines and other

tracking and monitoring tools. Movement should take into account terrain restrictions, urban areas of concern, high threat areas, bridges and tunnels, weather limitations on travel, and local factions. The SMT must assess the benefits of air, maritime, and land evacuation options, with close liaison and integration with military and government agencies.

- *Communications.* As many hostile and difficult environments begin recuperating from violent conflicts or as events build to an assuredly volatile situation, effective media management is critical for company reputational concerns. Related to this, and as equally important, is effective internal communications for employees and subcontractors. An effective communications strategy, both internal and external, is an essential part of any successful evacuation. In addition, the practical requirements of coordinating activities and needs between the crisis team in the threat area and external supporting teams is essential.

- *Threats.* It is vital that the immediate threats against the activity which is driving the evacuation requirement are adjusted and aligned with any subsequent threats generated by the evacuation activity itself. An assessment of both forms of threat will determine how the evacuation should be conducted or modified, or indeed whether it is safer to remain at the project site. These types of threat might be reviewed:

- Civil disturbance
- Flood
- Volcanic eruption
- Landslide
- Mine threats
- Unexploded orndance (UXO) risks
- Disease and injury
- Crime
- Social infrastructures
- Road traffic accidents
- Heat or cold injuries
- Insurgency
- Terrorism
- Political instability
- Indirect fire
- Direct fire
- Improvised explosive devices (IDs)
- Kidnap and ransom
- Ambush

- *Agreements.* Memoranda of understanding between different companies or with military organizations should be sought, either formally or informally to augment organic resources for evacuations.

Accountability

It is critical that personnel and high-value assets are properly accounted for, tracked, and administered. During the evacuation of a complex and large-scale operation, enormous potential exists to leave personnel (especially security) or equipment behind. All personnel should move through multiple checkpoints and roster confirmations prior to departure from the project site to ensure that every individual and each piece of valued equipment is accounted prior to the evacuation being complete. Clear management, administrative, and operational responsibilities should be established to prevent misunderstandings or assumptions. This should also include clear transport load plans, as travel is the most vulnerable aspect of the evacuation, and the loss or damage to vehicles in transit will require immediate passenger or equipment identification and coordination.

RECOVERY MANAGEMENT

Evacuation of a site or country may be only temporary, leading to the staged return of people and materials to the project site, a situation that enables business to recovery and continue after a delay. Companies should consider recovery or reoccupation plans that will enable business activities to start again in a planned and safe manner. The evacuation may have resulted from man-made problems or a natural disaster. The implications of the cause of the evacuation should be carefully considered in each instance. Reoccupation of project sites and a restart of operations should be considered almost as a limited version of the mobilization plan, plus some additional factors are to be considered in terms of security measures as well as the likely implications of damage and looting that might have resulted following the withdrawal. Heightened local tensions and government responses may have also changed the threat picture, and floods or other natural disasters may have undermined the rule of law and created additional security instabilities or health hazards that compound the effects of the initial problem. The circumstances that led to the evacuation may have made the region temporarily more volatile or, conversely, safer due to the increased presence of security forces. A simple planning process is illustrated in Exhibit 10.5.

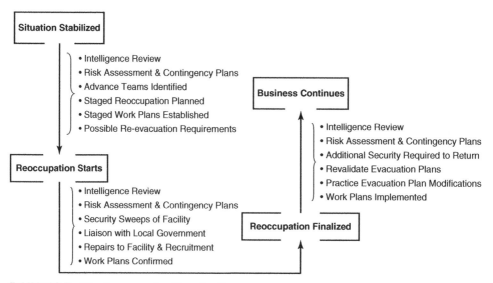

Exhibit 10.5   The Reoccupation Planning Process

When the risk environment has stabilized following the evacuation of a remote site or a region as a whole, a detailed intelligence and risk assessment should be conducted to determine the known and possible new threats facing a reoccupation. These threat considerations should focus not only on physical threats, hostile groups, and criminal elements, but should also consider disease, logistics resupply, and other more mundane factors. Contingency plans should be reviewed and modified to reflect the changes to the operating environment as part of a return planning process. The company should have already identified an advance team whose responsibilities are to liaise with local leaders or embassy officials in order to gauge the viability of return and to deploy with appropriate security support to review the needs associated for reoccupation, including reviewing the project site itself. The advance team should draft, or consolidate, an existing reoccupation schedule and plan as well as project work plans so that a measured return with appropriate lead groups is achieved. This should be a collaborative effort between risk and business or project managers. The reoccupation goals are for a safe and productive return of project staff, and it is important that productive business activities can start as soon as personnel and resources arrive on-site. Resources sitting idle at the project site cause the company to incur unnecessary costs and expose personnel to unnecessary risks. Personnel should deploy only when they can do so safely and when they can operate. During the entire planning process, reevacuation considerations should be at the forefront of planning.

When reoccupation begins, a continued process of intelligence and risk reviews should be conducted. The facility should be swept for any harmful materials that may have been planted by hostile groups, or audited for natural hazards. A registry of damages and materials thefts should also be established to ascertain information or material loss that might affect the business goals or the security or safety of the site and activity. Ideally a destruction plan will have been implemented, meaning that little valuable information or equipment was left behind. Liaison with external groups should be conducted as part of the overall reoccupation process. Needed repairs to the facility and material requirements should be identified and the supply chain system mobilized. Recruitment of local labor forces, including security personnel, may be problematic following an evacuation, as locals may have been involved or affected by the cause of the withdrawal. Time may have to be spent reestablishing communications and reenlisting local labor forces. Project work plans should also be considered to determine which project staff should return and in what order to avoid unnecessary exposure to risk and to ensure productive business activities.

The staged return of project personnel is likely to require additional security resources, both in terms of movement and possibly heightened security at the facility while reoccupation occurs. All plans should be revalidated to ensure they are consistent with any changes to the risk environment following the evacuation, and continued liaison and threat reviews should be conducted. The security posture should be more robust immediately following a return, as tensions or problems in the area will likely remain or be exacerbated. In many cases the reoccupation presents more challenges and risks than the initial occupation of the site.

In conclusion, evacuation planning is a significant element of any security plan and should be applied at all levels, from the methods by which a PSD extracts from a compromised route or venue site, to how to extract significant numbers of personnel and materials from a project facility. An evacuation is the most significant event a company may face, as it involves large numbers of people and often is conducted quickly and without time for management planning or preparation. Evacuations are confusing and beset with unforeseen problems under the best of conditions, but especially within challenging or remote environments. A sound evacuation plan will leverage internal as well as external resources and capabilities and should be engineered to provide simple and effective methods by which managers can extract personnel and materials from project sites based on standard operating procedures. Companies operating without a clear understanding of who makes decisions, what processes and protocols are required, and how to practically undertake an evacuation, before it occurs, will likely expose themselves and their staff to avoidable risk. Business recovery and project reoccupation is also the means by which the company can initiate business activities again safely and productively. Management should give careful consideration to establishing mechanisms and plans by which the impacts of business activity cessation can be mitigated by sound and practical forward planning.

CHAPTER 11

Disaster Response Management

Disasters come in many forms, from wars, political coups, and civil unrest, to floods, famines, and earthquakes. Whether they are natural or man-made, both forms of disaster present unique sets of challenges, exacerbated by regional, economic, environmental, political, and ethnic differences as well as by the actual impact of the disaster event itself on the community involved. Natural disasters present their own challenges. Floods are characterized by extensive damage to property and agriculture, with some loss of life in the acute stage, and long-term health risks due to damages to the affected regions infrastructure. Earthquakes present many similar problems, but there is generally more death and injury in the acute stage and fewer medium- and longer-term health risks than floods. Natural disasters also present endemic problems in the area (e.g., malaria, measles, cholera, dysentery, typhus, dengue fever). Crime and social instability can also present challenges to project teams operating within a natural disaster–struck region, as well as logistical, communication, and infrastructural problems, outside of the risks and challenges presented by the disaster event itself.

Man-made disasters such as war, intrastate conflicts, political instability, civil disturbances, insurgency, industrial accidents and terrorist acts can present the same problems seen with a natural disaster, plus additional threats: physical threats due to unexploded ordnance and mines, social and political instability, and possibly a residual or continued threat from crime and hostile groups. Man-made threats may also shift from area to area, constantly changing the dynamics of the risk environment, and requiring flexible and real-time responses.

Companies supporting government or humanitarian operations within disaster-struck regions will need to determine and address risk issues for projects before entering an unstable or challenging environment. Projects will face the typical risks associated with a region; however, these may be compounded by weakened infrastructures, instabilities in governance and security, and heightened risks of disease and injury. Risk natures and levels in disaster-struck regions can also quickly change, and risk managers will need to understand both the typical and the unique environmental changes that projects may face. Companies with operations already in a disaster-struck region will also need to understand the nature and impacts of disaster management, in order to effectively crisis manage the event in order to enable business recovery and continuity.

Risk management and security companies are often well attuned to the unique needs of operating within such dynamic and challenged environments and might be ideally placed to support global disaster relief programs throughout the life span of a project, from program conceptual development to project implementation and sustainment. Disaster relief typically involves the use of aid resources and reconstruction expertise within the sectors of water and waste, transportation, energy and power, telecommunications, and facilities and structures.

Often there is a conflict between a company's desire to respond to emergencies immediately and delaying the response to allow time for a proper risk and needs assessment. Companies should consider engaging a risk consultant to enhance the business and operational planning and implementation requirements of disaster response requirements within the context of safety and security from the outset, allowing companies to understand and plan for the problems they may face. Security companies can also be used to great effect in supporting not only company planning, but also implementation and sustainment of project operations, whether the vendors are engaged at the start of an event, or midstream through a crisis.

To place risk mitigation and security services within the correct context, it is important that the company understands the nature of disaster environments and the associated processes and impacts as well as the unique challenges project activities will have to manage within the field, and corporations will have to contend with strategically. The next sections provide insight into some fundamental principles of disaster response requirements.

HUMANITARIAN OPERATING ENVIRONMENT

In disaster-struck regions, different aid organizations or commercial companies may be required to work together even though they may not share the same values and objectives. The company or vendors may be required to facilitate the integration of different groups, goals, and approach methodologies through significant levels of diplomacy and management. Managers should be aware of the values and principles of development organizations in order to better understand how to operate with or alongside organizations whose methodologies and objectives might be significantly different from commercial infrastructure or development companies. Some of these values are expressed documentally, such as in the Code of Conduct of the Red Cross Movement and International Non Government Organizations.

WORKING WITH GOVERNMENTS

The company often needs to work closely with the host nation government, leveraging its support and acceptance in order to operate effectively. Some governments can be problematic under normal circumstances, a situation which can be exacerbated significantly after or during a disaster situation. Relationship building through an understanding of the strengths, weaknesses, capabilities, and limitations of national, regional, and local governance is important.

Working with Local Communities

It is important for companies to interact with the local program stakeholders (i.e., those who will benefit from the services they provide), recognizing the need to proactively manage broad-based relationships with multiple authorities and local communities. Companies and their vendors should seek a community approach strategy that best reflects the unique cultural and social factors of the environment. This can be achieved through a combination of acceptance and local capacity building.

A management approach based on the principles of acceptance, deterrence, and prevention can reduce or mitigate some of the challenges a company may face from local and national opposition. By establishing company interfaces with multiple local authorities and communities in terms of program impacts, conduct, values, and problems, greater levels of acceptance can be leveraged to facilitate the activity goals and reduce the risk environment.

The effectiveness of local security increases significantly when local national personnel are trained and provided with energetic and intelligent leadership. Training increases the throughput of personnel, as trained employees find employment elsewhere, assisting in the socioeconomic development of a community. As a result, training increases the capability of both project management and local employment and business, allowing local security personnel to perform central functions within the security organization.

MANAGEMENT PREPARATION

For those companies in regions subject to natural or man-made disasters, comprehensive risk management and security plans should be developed to identify possible risk events and develop solutions and responses that can enable the most effective management of a disaster. Companies should determine when to stay and when to withdraw and whether preemptive or staged evacuations are required. A comprehensive risk management plan will address these issues and ensure all levels of management are best prepared and equipped to deal with disaster situations.

Management structures and organizations as a whole operate more effectively and safely if management and project personnel are trained and adequately prepared to deal with the unique challenges they might face in new and unstable environments. Training can include crisis management programs, delivered through seminars focusing on kidnap/hostage situations and emergency evacuation procedures, utilizing tabletop exercises and a number of scenarios to bring the subject to life. Some useful management training programs that might support project staff preparing to deploy or currently undertaking operations include:

- Crisis management team: what is its role and what are its responsibilities?
- Key considerations for development of a Crisis Management Plan.
- Communication with next of kin and employees.
- Cooperation with government and law enforcement authorities.
- The handling of families, media, and other stakeholders.
- Key elements of an evacuation plan and how to implement one effectively.
- How to monitor an escalating threat situation.
- Development of a series of evacuation triggers.

Hostile environment training (HET) is designed to benefit those who intend to travel to, or work in, challenging environments. HET focuses on personal security, situational awareness, land mine awareness, and first aid. The training provides deploying personnel with the necessary knowledge and skills to deal with conflict situations, emergencies, and traumatic events with specific focus on understanding and mitigating the risks they will face. Training can be conducted domestically, in a transition country (final point prior to project country entry), or if necessary within the project country itself.

PRINCIPLES OF DISASTER RESPONSE

Companies should understand that typically a disaster response by governments or aid agencies involves two main assessment phases. This approach can also be modified to reflect considerations a company might take into account during a disaster event. By defining two stages of disaster response the company can develop an understanding of the project resource and support needs, as well as management planning stages.

1. Initial (Rapid) Assessment Phase
   - Identify urgent needs of the affected population or project, with short-term planning activities and resource needs.
   - Identify areas of risk and support focus for in-depth assessment(s).
   - Identify immediate risk factors and mitigation measures.
2. In-Depth Assessment Phase(s)
   - Identify, in detail, specific (sectional) needs of the population or project, taking into account local response capacities, with medium-term planning requirements for local managers and supporting response groups.
   - Identify the risk mitigation needs for project establishment and sustainment throughout the life of the activity, including capacity building of local employment, business engagement, and skill development.

Planning

The amount of time a company spends collecting information before designing and implementing a program to support disaster affected regions will be determined by the magnitude, dynamics, and likely evolution of the disaster crisis as well as the current and potential public health impact on the affected population. If the situation is one of rapid deterioration, an immediate or urgent response may be required. Programs or activities that can be implemented immediately are unlikely to be delayed by a requirement to complete detailed and more measured assessments. Sound management and planning systems and the ability to reach out to multiple vendors will enable an effective response to immediate operational or business needs. Security vendors well versed in the disaster response field and in the task region will enable the rapid deployment of project staff to an affected location, although this movement will present a combination of established and unpredicted risks to the company and the vendor. Where companies are already present in a disaster region, a crisis management or extraction policy might be implemented (if already designed) or companies might require an immediate assessment and associated plans to deal with the risks that have not already been planned or resourced against.

In situations where there has been a slower evolution of humanitarian needs (relatively more gradual deterioration in the health status or infrastructure requirements of a population as a consequence of a prolonged conflict or the collapse of the state), more time may be available to the project assessment team. For more measured situations, detailed assessments on the associated risks and mitigations can be conducted, allowing a more refined and staged approach for project planning teams.

During assessments, risks should be identified through the utilization of intelligence gathering and analysis from multiple and complementary sources, in terms of both risk and security analysis, as well as crisis management expertise associated with specific types of disasters. Local or regionally experienced consultants offering a grassroots perspective on the project area, and who are better placed to draw on local and other agency resources can also offer a more comprehensive and realistic approach. Approaching the requirements in this holistic manner enables companies and their vendors best to define the risks in terms of dangers to both project staff and materials as well as to the project goals and corporate interests. The aim is to mitigate or avoid risks while allowing the project to proceed or withdraw in the most efficient manner.

STAGES OF DISASTERS

It is important that companies understand the nature and sequencing of typical disaster scenarios in order to conduct sound planning before committing to an engagement or course of action. Conversely, companies that have existing operations within an affected region will need to understand the consequences a disaster will have on existing operations and personnel in order to determine how they will conduct crisis response: Do they remain or do they withdraw? Vendors must also understand the processes associated with disasters in order to provide sound advice and services to support company operations. Exhibit 11.1 illustrates the typical cycle of a disaster process.

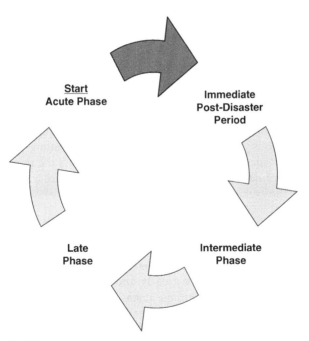

Exhibit 11.1 Stages of a Disaster

Acute Phase

The acute phase consists of the disaster itself and the phase when most casualties occur. In natural disasters this phase may be short—minutes (earthquakes) to hours or a few days (floods, hurricanes)—or long and drawn out (famine, epidemic). A war is effectively a continuing disaster, but since fighting often shifts around an area, parts of the country may be in the immediate post-disaster phase while others are still in the acute phase. The acute phase will present the most dynamic risks to a company and will be the period when most confusion occurs. Success in navigating this phase will rest heavily upon local leadership, training and well establish policies and plans.

Immediate Post-Disaster Period

During the immediate post-disaster phase, the high and immediate casualty rate usually is replaced by a steady but declining toll of injury and death. The main medical problems are generally the treatment of injuries. In earthquakes or hurricanes, most of those who are going to survive are found in the 12 hours after the disaster. Most of those injured will have been treated in the first 24 to 36 hours. This phase presents a chance for projects to consolidate actions undertaken within the acute phase, and to start to draw more upon company resources and management structures. Well-established plans would have resulted in response actions being implemented during the acute phase, with resources and support now arriving at the affected location.

Intermediate Phase

In natural disasters (or individual events in a man-made disaster, such as a massacre), the intermediate phase typically begins after 3 to 5 days and tends to peak at 10 days. It is the period during which the diseases brought about by acute exposure (to heat or cold), lack of clean water supplies, and poor sanitation appear, as people are often crowded together in temporary shelters. It is characterized by a rise in acute respiratory infection (ARI) and diarrheal illness. Toward the end of this period, diseases such as dysentery, cholera, typhoid, and hepatitis become more common. Measles may also occur, and the lack of food and the ability to cook it may begin seriously to affect the more vulnerable, leading to higher malnutrition rates and decreased resistance to infection. This phase presents the opportunity for companies to start recovery of project operations, suspend activities until a defined point of stabilization, or to complete the evacuation and closure of a project.

Late Phase

The late phase is usually the one in which actual reconstruction begins. The timing of the start of this phase and its duration vary greatly and depend on many factors, such as the health care infrastructure and what damage it has suffered; availability of shelter, clean water, food, and the like; and the diseases endemic to the area. Typically companies will have started new operations to support related disaster response requirements, or will have conducted business recovery to enable operations to resume in some capacity.

The company supporting a government- or aid-funded response may need to deploy from the acute phase onward. An immediate assessment of all forms of risk in the context of the environment and activity is required, with appropriate and realistic mitigation measures to enable the activity to begin and continue throughout the different stages of the disaster. The decision to withdraw existing operations hinges on how well prepared the crisis response plans and resources are and whether the risk assessments indicate that personnel will be safer remaining on-site as opposed to attempting an extraction from the region, which poses its own risks.

DISASTER MANAGEMENT

Effective disaster management requires a blend of crisis response, risk consulting and security services, project management, information and research analysis, and evacuation planning and delivery capability. An appreciation of the activity area, culture, and industry field(s) is also essential to provide the correct advice, guidance, and support to the company. The establishment of communication centers and networks in remote and difficult regions either as part of an existing pre-disaster project infrastructure, or in advance of new teams entering an affected area, will support strong management, and control of operations. Developing relationships with multiple agencies prior to a disaster, as well as during the recovery stages will support project staff in operating safely and productively, laying the foundations for the success of the initial activity period.

Management structures and communication networks will need to be established both within the project area as well as with the corporate board and supporting agencies outside of the project country. In addition, liaison with representatives from the Office of Disaster Assistance (OFDA) Disaster Response Teams (DART), local government and law enforcement agencies, and foreign military, diplomacy, and aid groups will enhance the project team's initial and medium-term success.

Exhibit 11.2 provides an example of the layers of nationality management and staff used within management teams within disaster-struck regions.

Exhibit 11.2 Management Layers Example

Expatriate Staff		
Consultant	Project Manager	Operations Manager
Comms Manager	Comms Technician	Administration Manager
Logistics Manager	Training Manager	Liaison Officer
Security Advisors	Close Protection	Medic

Third-Country Nationals				
Drivers	Close Protection	Administration	Trainers	Guards

Local Nationals			
Drivers	Liaison Officers	Guides	Logistics
Close Protection	Static Guards	Procurement	Administration

Based on the number and nature of the locations where company personnel will perform work, gaps and needs for interconnectivity can be determined. Various levels and forms of risk management and security provision may be required, involving multinational blends of personnel.

PREPAREDNESS PLANS

In order for a project team to be capable of deploying effectively and quickly to a new, challenging, and potentially threatening environment, a preparedness plan (or mobilization plan) should be developed to enable effective and immediate assessments and deployment during the acute phase. This plan will allow project planning and implementation to be conducted most efficiently in terms of risk assessment, safety, security, cost, and actual project deployment. The next sections discuss aspects that should be included or considered within a preparedness plan.

Risk Analysis Network

An integrated intelligence and project management capacity, both in terms of qualified managers and reports, should be developed by either the company or a contracted vendor. This service monitors the risk status of every possible area of interest, permitting an immediate risk and needs assessment to be conducted. This capacity enables company executive and program management to receive detailed and accurate advice, guidance and reports on specific areas of interest on a daily basis, allowing project management to retain a global appreciation of the risks associated with immediate deployment requirements. A global disaster monitoring capability allows the company to identify, ahead of government notifications, a likely deployment task. This form of forward planning and awareness provides advance planning and preparation time, maximizing a company's response effectiveness.

Contingency Planning

The company should establish planning and policy requirements prior to initiating an activity. Doing so will permit the company to focus on achieving an objective rather than discussing issues that could be resolved at a more measured pace. The development of pragmatic and tactical solutions to a range of situations, which should be run through realistic simulations to test response plans, will enable better preparation for disaster response. Contingency planning can include:

- The establishment of a communications plan, with information nodal points and cascade systems for the swift and centralized information distribution to enhance response times and project planning efficiency.
- The integration of a security consultant in the corporate project planning team to ensure that project requirements are placed in the context of associated risks for best planning protocols, from the outset of a task response.

- Planning documents to ensure that all deploying project staff members receive pre-prepared and quickly modified travel briefs and deployment packages, allowing them to focus on project requirements rather than personal administration—for swift and effective mobilization.
- A deployment plan, with prepositioned specialist equipment for immediate deployment, allowing project planning logistical support to be in place and ready for immediate use.

    Establishing fundamental deployment equipment requirements and procurement/sourcing protocols allows the project team to operate within natural or man-made disaster areas in an expedient and effective manner.

The establishment of deployment notification information will ensure that project staff can conduct critical predeployment administration without unnecessarily hindering actual project requirements, allowing managers to deal efficiently with what would be otherwise complex laborious communication and administrative burdens, including mundane but necessary medical, logistical, and administrative requirements. The following rapid deployment list indicates points that should be considered when deploying to a disaster-struck region:

- Inoculation requirements
- Training requirements
- Project area and risk predeployment briefs
- Travel security requirements
- Medical advice
- Transit country information
- Accommodation information

Equipment and Assets

For companies with purchase planning policies and identified project resource needs, managers might opt to have pre-positioned deployment stores which allow initial requirements to be met with organic supplies, or via procurement through domestic or local project area suppliers. Specialist vendors can assist companies to understand what items might be required within a staged or sequenced process, ensuring that critical resources are procured and costly or longer lead-time items are bought only at the time of need. Managing resource needs, expectations, and provisions contributes to ensuring that security risks are minimized, communications are established, and critical project assets are in place for immediate use. Pre-positioned deployment equipment should be available for immediate deployment with advance management teams to ensure that all critical functions are in place and tested prior to project teams arrival in the affected area.

Crisis Response Team

The establishment of a *virtual* crisis response team avoids unnecessary costs to the company while still permitting management to quickly mobilize (at no residual cost) both corporate and project planning teams. Crisis response or program management teams must be structured to respond to the unique requirements of each disaster response, including:

- Coordinating multiple activities in the most effective and efficient manner.
- Identifying the project requirements and associated security and safety risks.
- Identifying threats to project staff and operational conduct, and how such threats will impede project performance.
- Identifying personnel and equipment to best mitigate security and safety impediments.
- Authorization to commit resources and finance to support the activity.
- Authorization to initiate engagement in the task, activity or courses of action.
- Ability to mobilize appropriate personnel while initial planning is under way, to ensure that projects are streamlined and most efficient.
- Ability to mobilize extraction teams which will secure personnel or facilities, as well as manage their safe extraction from a risk area to a reception point (see Chapter 10).
- Ability to mobilize advance management teams (if appropriate) to:
  - Establish base camps in terms of life support for project staff.
  - Source equipment and transport.
  - Liaise with local government and agencies in advance of the project team arrival.
  - Receive the project team to ensure immediate work can commence.
  - Establish all crisis and evacuation planning requirements.
  - Source and recruit local labor forces.

MOBILIZATION

Effective mobilization of project personnel and resources relies on a timely appreciation of the project area and associated risks as well as the ability quickly to provide detailed analysis on specific areas of interest or impact. Mobilization may occur in a sequence of events, from gathering data to establishing a secure environment ahead of company staff arrival, or may be the movement of the entire project team at once. Mobilization is followed by sustainment, once the project foundations are established and the initial challenges and uncertainties are overcome.

Security and Risk Plan Development

A risk/security consultant should be embedded in the company planning team, assisting with the establishment of task requirements, management, and conduct. External resources, such as embassies, military missions, and other companies, should be leveraged to gather all available information as normal public information and communication infrastructures and mediums will usually be undermined during a disaster situation. The consultant will develop a detailed security or risk plan, based on the unique project requirements of each task as well as environmental factors, so that the activity planning team's effectiveness is assured throughout performance of a specific activity or task. For companies extracting from an environment, this support can augment their capabilities and knowledge in order to safely and effectively implement response measures to mitigate risks during the withdrawal of personnel from the affected area. Each security plan is tailored to suit the unique requirements of each task, and places the activity goals into the context of some of these risks:

- Civil disturbances
- Natural risks (floods, earthquakes, tornados, tidal waves . . .)
- Mine threats and unexploded ordnance
- Insurgency and terrorism
- Heat and cold weather injuries
- Disease and traumatic injuries
- Crime and looting
- Famine and draught
- Medical provisions and support
- Government coordination
- Social infrastructures
- Road traffic accidents
- Political instability
- Stress and psychological trauma

Even well-established projects can face rapid deteriorations of conditions, as illustrated in Exhibit 11.3. The vendor's consultant should provide the company support at both corporate and project level in such areas as:

- Briefing the activity planning team on the immediately known facts of the task location.
- Gathering specific information on the country, region, or location for detailed project planning.

Exhibit 11.3 Sandstorms Affecting Project Locations. Iraqi Military Base. Copyright ©
Peter Jones, 2004.

- Establishing any specific or peripheral risks that might affect planning or conduct.
- Offering recommendations to support planning while safeguarding personnel and assets.
- Recommending or drawing on supporting elements to:
  - Develop intelligence-driven planning.
  - Provide project team with training or project specific training (i.e., HET).
  - Provide corporate planning support throughout the life of the activity.
  - Provide transit country information to ensure the safety of project staff while moving to the project location.
  - Facilitate basic project requirements in advance of the team's arrival (accommodation/ transport/liaison/entry/reception, etc.).
  - Provide project team in-country support for functional security and management support (advanced management teams).
  - Cover any areas of specialist requirement (medic/linguist/guides/communications/ administration/logistics/liaison officers, etc.).
  - Provide the security management element of a crisis response team.
- Identify project critical equipment, facilitating local procurements as necessary through advance party management.
- Brief project staff on the status of the project area, answering specific questions and gathering stated information to support planning—liaising with both core and project area consultants.

Project-Limiting Factors

Physical risks may limit the project activity; however, after disasters, a range of more practical and psychological limitations may be prevalent. Projects, whether providing specialist expertise or more physical products, rely on administration and logistics to operate effectively. In hostile and disaster-struck regions, these infrastructures may be absent or damaged, hampering the project activity as well as undermining the confidence and morale of project staff. An assessment of available support mechanisms and structures, as well as those the company must resource itself, is required, including:

- Transport
- Life support
- Food and water
- Medical support
- Liaison and networking
- Critical equipment
- Communications
- Confidence and morale
- Equipment and resources

Advance Management Teams

While project planning is being conducted within the company's corporate offices, advance management teams can be used to establish the operational and administrative foundations for the project staff to implement project plans, without being burdened by initial logistical or administrative requirements and delays. Advance management teams will serve to enhance the efficiency of the project team, ensure that the project team operates from the start in a safe environment, and act as a cost-saving measure for the funding agency by avoiding costly project delays or false starts.

Advance management teams can also ensure that the project team enters a secure project site, offering a completed security plan and incident management plan as well as detailed advice and guidance to the project planning team prior to or during deployment. Advance management teams can also facilitate local arrangements and serve as a liaison on behalf of the project team to establish a network of contacts within the multiple agencies involved within a disaster area. Advance management teams can source, identify and arrange some of these requirements:

- Accommodation
- Food and water
- Medical support
- Prepositioning locations
- Local points of contact
- Meeting coordination
- Conduct site/route reviews
- Liaison with local authorities
- Support the arrival of the project team
- Provide project team training
- Recruitment of local nationals
- Training local nationals
- Transport and movement
- Power sources
- Specialist stores
- Safe havens
- Evacuation centers
- Evacuation routes/exits
- Country, region and area entry and exit points

An advance management team might be required to demobilize when the project team arrives, or elements might remain to integrate within the project team, continuing to support the project during its life span. Needs will be determined on a case-by-case basis, based on requirements and cost. Advance management teams should also be supported by a depth of expertise within the region and from central or core management and information centers outside of the country, allowing security and project staff to call in for real-time answers to specific regional or project-oriented questions, which enhances the efficiency of planning and operations. This ability will be especially relevant during any crisis situation.

Advance management teams might come from existing projects already in-country, or within adjacent countries, moving into specific areas ahead of a mobilizing team, or to meet and support withdrawing projects from an affected region.

Resource Capacity

The company will require immediate human resources, in both specialist expatriate fields and possibly from local providers. The nature and impact of disasters vary, with geographical, social, and political factors further complicating the situation and resulting resource needs. Dynamic, flexible, and capacity-positioned vendors are required to support risk mitigation and security provision. Resource requirements may also be driven by changing external influences and factors, and the company will need security subcontractors to be responsive and adaptable. Companies can identify likely resource needs ahead of an event and ensure that they have agreements in place, whether through retainer arrangements or basic ordering agreements—in order to ensure they can source support quickly, as well as avoid administrative delays in contracting services.

Predeployment Requirements

Before deployment, the project team should meet at a central location for briefings and any necessary training and final planning requirements. By gathering deploying staff together at a physical location it supports the provision requisite knowledge and equipment before entering an unstable or high risk environment. Risk managers or subcontracted security vendors should fully brief team members on real-time information regarding the project location and requirements as well as the political and risk situation (using question-and-answer sessions between project teams and advance management teams). Risk managers should also offer practical advice and recommendations concerning such factors as:

- Endemic diseases
- Available medical services
- Medical needs
- Cultural awareness
- Security and safety
- Local support and logistics
- External relationships
- Prominent figures
- Emergency procedures
- Communications and points of contact
- Management structures and decision makers
- Diplomatic and military presence

An administrative manager should also ensure that practical requirements are met by:

- Checking that visas, passports, money, tickets are in order, contracts are signed, and so on.
- Ensuring that vaccinations are up to date.
- Ensuring that relevant malaria prophylaxis is obtained.
- Discussing the trip with the public relations department.
- Providing relevant telephone numbers, including all emergency and satellite phone numbers.
- Ensuring that individual records (next of kin, etc.) at corporate offices are up to date.

SUSTAINMENT AND DEMOBILIZATION

Activity sustainment is delivered through the risk management and security policies and procedures already outlined, culminating in the demobilization or withdrawal of project staff once the activity is complete or should risks or other external factors require early departure from the area or country. Normal program management activities should apply once the activity has started, reflecting any unique requirements associated with the region and threat elements facing the company activity and personnel.

In summary, companies with existing infrastructure or personnel operating in a disaster-struck region should draw on existing crisis response plans to guide their decision to remain on location or to effect a withdrawal to a safe location or adjoining country. Effective contingency planning enables a company to quickly mitigate risks, whether due to political instabilities, insurgents, or increases in criminal threats. Or resulting from floods, earthquakes, or other natural disasters. By understanding the nature and sequence of disaster situations, companies can make solid judgments on how to best respond to them.

For those companies deploying to disaster-struck regions to support reconstruction of humanitarian efforts, an understanding of the different groups operating in the region and of the need to integrate with host nation and foreign governments in order to be most effective is essential. Preparedness planning, understanding the need for rapid and in-depth assessments, and aligning the likely stages of a disaster with an entry or sustainment plan will determine the project's success and personnel's safety. Disaster management requires established plans and resources as well as sequenced deployments, which include advance teams to ensure projects arrive ready to operate, with risks mitigated prior to arrival. An organized and rehearsed crisis response team will manage entry, business recovery as well as effect project withdrawal if required. Operating within a disaster struck country relies on sound operational and administrative management, reflective of the risks facing the company's operations.

CHAPTER 12

Security Documents and Exhibits

Companies operating in any business environment, but especially those that present phys-ical challenges, should ensure that their risk and security management information, deci-sions, and plans are captured on paper to ensure that professional standards are achieved and maintained, as well as to best illustrate and share information. This supports a best practice approach. Both consultancy services and security management require the delivery of formal security documents to support the project's activities. These documents consist of white pa-pers, reports, or exhibits to support information-gathering, decision-making, and manage-ment activities or items that may be exhibited to evidence or display information. Security documents may be viewed by field project staff, engineers, administrators, contract manage-ment, security personnel, and program managers. The documents may also be viewed by various groups in the corporate offices and may be used as the basis of contractual agree-ments, historical reviews, audits, or liability suits. Thus security documents serve not only the immediate purpose of presenting information or procedures as logically and digestibly as possible but also have longer-term implications and wide repercussions for both the com-pany and vendor.

Despite the value and significance of security documents, the lack of consistency and de-tail of security documents can be surprising, both within risk and security consultancy as a whole as well as within specific companies themselves, with only a few companies having a well-defined and mature approach. Many companies will provide little to no guidelines to their personnel, and consistency is lacking, with individual consultant approaches and meth-odologies more commonly used. This lack of uniformity is hardly surprising given a lack of industry standards as well as the unique and personal requirements brought by each project activity, risk environment, provider preference, and project peculiarities. That said, it is very useful to establish a degree of consistency in a company's approach to creating security docu-ments and to ensure that security providers adopt some degree of standardization in terms of principles and formats. Such consistency saves time and effort and improves overall manage-ment confidence. While standardization is important, the designated task manager or consul-tant should always tailor reports to suit a dynamic environment and the particular project being serviced. Documents must meet professional standards as well as the project's expectations.

Security documents may be engineered to meet the needs of a varied audience or tailored to meet a particular requirement or client group. Typically executive-level documents have detailed executive summaries, with most details and facts contained within appendices and attachments, as senior-level leadership may wish to review only the supralevel elements or specific factors. Reports written for program or project management may also be more gritty, providing local factors and details that would not interest board members. Under-standing the final target audience is therefore an important element of structuring security documents, as well as being cognizant that a secondary audience may result from comments or recommendations made within the report.

Consultants should seek to exploit existing security documents that may contain reusable data or concepts as well as over time to establish their own library so that each report is based on established work, with innovations and additional research providing the basis of the unique report requirements. There is often significant overlap of information within different documents, with each subsequent document drawing on previous efforts. An appreciation of how best to write and structure each report in terms of secondary uses will also allow consultants to be more productive. That said, there can be a tendency to shortcut the process too much and insert erroneous information to pad out the report. Only relevant and accurate information should be used from other documents, and all information should be tailored to reflect each unique requirement.

Consultants may also wish to gather other reports or information examples to supplement their own work, while being mindful of any moral or legal restrictions that might apply. A wide range of security documents may be required when delivering consultancy services. The company or project may define the requirement, having particular methods, approaches, formats, or standards, or the environment and project may dictate the scope, content, and structure of a report. Consultants should use any existing templates or examples as a starting point and efficiency tool rather than being constrained or limited by them, applying ingenuity and logic to avoid stale and meaningless document production and delivery. Frameworking is also a useful process if previous templates are lacking in areas or do not apply to new tasks.

Where possible, data should also be imparted using visual representations (maps, photography, schematics) or tables and charts. Visual representations are a useful way of imparting large amounts of complex data succinctly. The aim of this chapter is not to define the scope, nature, content, or style of a particular security document or exhibit, but to suggest some generic security document types as well as a sample of content materials that might be included if appropriate. This chapter should be used only to broaden both the company's and any internal or contracted consultant's sense of what forms of document are used and what content materials are commonly included.

It is useful to differentiate security forms from security documents and exhibits, although this is a subjective division. Security forms might include weekly security reports, standardized intelligence reports, or individual but frequent task risk assessments. Security forms could therefore be classified as any document that are part of a standardized and scheduled process or management system rather than as a unique and significant business or project supporting report.

CONSULTANCY PROCESS

There is no defined industry standard for the consultancy process, as the company or project provides its requirements to any service provider and the scope of requirement is broad and often specialized. In an ideal world where budgeting does not constrain the services provided, a logical system can be used to develop a measured understanding of the environment in which a new activity hopes to operate. Ideally this process is included at the outset of the business cycle, although more commonly the consultancy process starts midstream and has to contend with established constraints and preconceived concepts and allocated budgets and resources. The sections that follow capture a logical consultancy process in terms of establishing a project activity in a challenging environment.

Stage 1: Direction

The business and project team defines the nature, goals, and requirements of the business activity, issuing tasks or seeking advice from a risk management company. The service needs are defined and the contractual requirements of the initial tasks established.

Stage 2: Intelligence Review

An intelligence assessment is made of the activity country, region, and local area. Factors and influences that may impact conduct of activities are collected, collated, and analyzed. This process paints the scene in which the client will operate and begins to provide an understanding of the restrictions and threats the client may face.

Stage 3: Threat Assessment

The threat assessment provides a granular review of the macro- and micro-level threats the activity will face, providing mitigation recommendations to offset risks in order to enable the client to operate successfully within the risk environment. Threats will cover a spectrum of areas, or may be restricted by the client's needs.

Stage 4: Security Survey

A physical review of a site or activity itself is conducted to establish the actual requirements needed to undertake the venture. Drawing on and expanding the intelligence review and threat assessment, this report provides a granular and local perspective, focusing on policies, procedures, resources, and funding required to mitigate the threat environment.

Stage 5: Operations Orders (Mobilization Plan)

Operations orders or mobilization plans are developed to establish the management policies required to implement an activity. The planning documents typically are the dynamic start-up or close-down aspects of the task. They merge the tactical risk mitigation requirements with other logistical and management needs. They might also be called a mobilization plan and may be a core component of the PiD.

Stage 6: Security Plan

The security plan may be developed in advance of an activity starting (unlikely but preferable) or once services have commenced. The security plan provides the basis of how risk management and security services will occur, both internally and with the integration of external resources. The plan is a practical document coordinating policies, procedures, and relationships. The risk management plan itself might include the security plan as an component, but will address both strategic and granular level company needs.

Stage 7: Proposal

The security survey and security plan define the activity needs in terms of risk mitigation and security provision. These needs may be captured in greater detail in a proposal for services, a legally binding document that defines services against value, initiating the delivery of resources or services stated within the security survey and security plan. The issue of a work order is authority for services to be delivered and payments to be made. The proposal should come before any monies are expended by security providers, but may be changed at various times throughout the business activity. Proposals may be required for each stage.

Stage 8: Security Services

Security service delivery occurs throughout the consultancy process in order to provide the management tools to understand how the project must be supported to achieve success. However, the final dimension of service usually accounts for the bulk of services, the investment for project security support. Further surveys and assessments may be made throughout the life span of an activity to ensure that services and policies reflect a changing risk environment. Security services should be supported by policy documents such as incident management plans, standard operating procedures, and tactical techniques and procedures. Services typically occur once all initial planning is complete and a proposal has been accepted.

Stage 9: Security Audits

Audits may be conducted internally or may be provided by impartial and external consultancy services. Audits confirm that service delivery contractual requirements, quality assurance, and realistic provisions are being provided. They may confirm the validity of existing policies and procedures, or may require modifications to risk management and security provisions. Audits ensure that risk and security approaches are kept current and ensure management accountability and quality assurance.

In summary, the process from defining a potential need to the delivery of services varies depending on the nature of the company, project, and circumstance. For large contracts, especially for government clients, the process will be well defined and systematic, ensuring that every aspect is taken into consideration prior to a contractual award being made, as illustrated in Exhibit 12.1. For commercial ventures, the process may be significantly shortened or simplified. Exhibit 12.1 lustrates one potential process, from requirement inception to service delivery.[1]

INTELLIGENCE REVIEWS

The content, style, and structuring of an intelligence review or assessment is largely driven by the project requirements, regional influences, information availability, and nature of the project itself. Project or executive management will define the nature of the information required (the direction). The consultant must then make best use of internal and external resources to collect information for processing and initial evaluation (the report). The intelligence review is a consultancy service that provides evaluated information for dissemination to the company for its own business evaluation, either at a strategic or local level

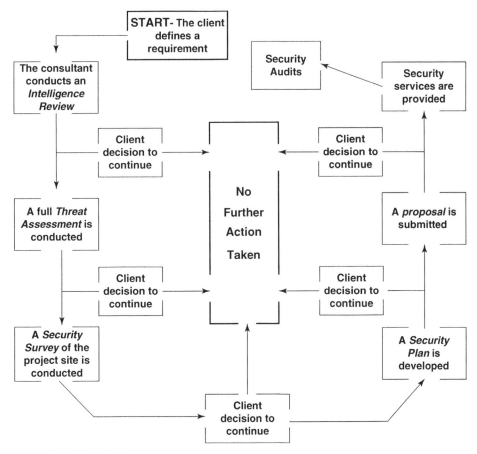

Exhibit 12.1 Consulting Process

focus. Where necessary, intelligence reviews can be conducted independent of physically visiting the project site. Indeed, the intelligence review is usually used to assess the viability of conducting physical site assessments. There is a significant difference between regurgitating facts and figures without drawing observations or recommendations and actually analyzing the data and providing pragmatic advice and guidance. The intelligence review should avoid stating only facts and figures, but should also seek to provide the company with assessments, evaluations, and predictions where possible. There is no strict format for the provision of an intelligence review; however, the next sections offer a sample of areas that might be covered.

Part 1: Executive Summary

The company's corporate management typically relies on the executive summary to establish an initial picture on the situation their activity will be facing. Often most management do not read past the executive summary and selected portions of the report, so it is important to crystallize the key elements of the report up front as well as any major recommendations.

Demonstrating an understanding of the business activity will place the report in the proper context. Clearly stating the principal threats and their impacts on the company, as well as grading the information's reliability, defines the premise of observations and recommendations.

1. Introduction
   a. Aim of the Intelligence Report
   b. Business Mission and Objectives
   c. Evaluation of Intelligence Picture
   d. Evaluation of Threat Factors
   e. Grading of Intelligence Sources
   f. Recommendations

Part 2: Intelligence Background

The intelligence background sets the scene in terms of national and local influences and factors, both historically and currently. It might be worth briefly defining the general geographical factors also to place any risks into a physical context. These factors should only be overarching observations, as a more detailed review of the physical aspects of a project site usually is conducted during the security survey. The background should also cover political groups, leaders, and events, as these have a significant impact at macro- and micro-levels, as well as the socioeconomic status of the country and particular areas, which often provide foundations for unrest or particular forms of risk. Ethnic and religious tensions are also a key component to understanding the social drivers for instability as well as methods by which to foster community relationships to support the company's activity.

1. Historical Factors
   a. Political and Tribal[2]
   b. Social and Cultural
   c. Religious Fractions
   d. Table of Key Historical Events
   e. Key Annual Calendar Dates
   f. Evaluation of the Business Impacts
2. Topographical Factors
   a. Description of Physical Environment and Climatic Influences
   b. Map of Region and Project Area
   c. Evaluation of Business Impact
3. Political Factors
   a. Supra Regional Political Situation (surrounding countries)
   b. National Political Situation
   c. Political Groups, Agendas, and Influences
   d. Political Figures and Agendas
   e. Map of Political Regions or Areas
   f. Evaluation of Business Impact

4. Regional and Local Factors
   a. Governorate and Provincial Leaders
   b. Community Groups and Leaders
   c. Community Relations and Projects
   d. Evaluation of Company Interaction or Impacts
5. Socioeconomic Situation
   a. National and Local Industry and Business
   b. Poverty Levels and Employment Levels
   c. Map of any economic bandings or social areas
   d. Social Infrastructures
       i. Hospitals
       ii. Schools
       iii. Transportation Services
       iv. Power, Water, and Energy
       v. Evaluation of Business Impact
6. Ethnic and Religious Regions
   a. Ethnic Groups and Influences
   b. Religious Groups and Influences
       i. Map of Ethnic and Religious Divides
   c. Evaluation of Business Impact
   d. Map of ethnic and religious divides or hot spot areas

Note: Duplication of details can be avoided by creating simple tables to demonstrate how different factors impact the business goals. If impacts are spread throughout the document, a summation table might be useful to capture the key points in one place.

Part 3: Threat Factors

The intelligence review should seek to capture the relevant details on terrorist, insurgent, and criminal groups, focusing on their motivations, methods of operation, and prominent figures. These threat factors will often define their choice of both targets and approach in terms of threats to the company. Any group associations or historical data or trends should also be discussed to establish a better understanding of how these organizations or groups operate and think, and how they might seek to harm or disrupt the company's business activity. The threat types should also be defined in terms of how hostile groups target business activities and the associated impacts in terms of damages or risks to both company and personnel. The consultant should also look outside of the national borders of the country in which hostile groups might be working, as external subversive groups or governments may play a significant role in threatening a client's commercial interests abroad. A threat matrix may depict the risks a client may be facing in terms of probability and impact.

1. Threat Groups
   a. Terrorist: Groups and Leadership
   b. Insurgent: Groups and Leadership
   c. Organized Crime: Groups and Leadership

    d. Other Criminal Influences
    e. Historical or Statistical Data
    f. Evaluation of Client Impact
  2. Threat Categories (Brief Insight[3])
    a. Threat Types and Associated Groups
    b. Targeted Groups and Individuals
    c. Trend Analysis and Threat Predictions
    d. Projected Threat Influences
    e. Evaluation of Business Impact
  3. Hostile Foreign Influences
    a. Political and Diplomatic
    b. Military and Law Enforcement
    c. Intelligence Organizations
    d. Others
    e. Evaluation of Business Impact

Part 4: Government and Foreign Organizations

The consultant should provide the company an understanding of how the host nation operates on both a political and security level and how the relevant agencies and offices conduct their business. Such an assessment is especially important regarding the ministries of defense and internal security. An understanding of the various governmental security apparatuses which influence or directly affect the company and business activity is useful, as this might determine how much of the company's own resources are required to mitigate risk, and where external group resources may be leveraged to mitigate threats. Non-government security groups, such as tribal elements or secular or regional paramilitary organizations, should also be addressed. The consultant should illustrate how foreign governments and security organizations operate in a region, so as to define how much support (or obstruction) a company might expect during the course of normal operations as well as during crisis events. Other organizations undertaking similar activities might be of interest or use to the company, as well as groups whose allegiances or activities are as yet undetermined.

  1. Host Nation Government and Security Agencies
    a. Host Nation Government
    b. Host Nation Military Forces
    c. Host Nation Law Enforcement
    d. Tribal Paramilitary Groups
    e. Other Paramilitary Organisations
    f. Evaluation of Influences on the Company
  2. Friendly Foreign Influences
    a. Political and Diplomatic
    b. Military and Law Enforcement
    c. Other Security Organizations
    d. Aid Agencies and Reconstruction
    e. Evaluation of Influences on the Company

3. Neutral Parties
   a. Political and Diplomatic
   b. Military and Law Enforcement
   c. Intelligence Organizations
   d. Others
   e. Evaluation of Influences on the Company

Part 5: Conclusion and Recommendations

The intelligence review should submit final observations and recommendations based on the information gathered and evaluated during the study of a particular subject or area. The need for further assessments, either through indirect or physical means, should be stated. Any unambiguous risks to the company should be raised prior to a full threat assessment being conducted. The intelligence review should provide the company with a clear picture of the threat environment and different groups that might affect or influence the company's commercial activity.

THREAT ASSESSMENTS

The threat assessment specifically defines the scope, nature, and impacts of risk the company may face during the life span of the operation. It should be written in the context of both the risk environment and the company's risk tolerances, as these will define what risks are considered noteworthy and which fall within acceptable ranges for a project. The consultant should not assume that the threat assessment will be read in conjunction with the intelligence review. Therefore, the key elements from the intelligence review should be included (if available) to clarify the environment in which the business activity will operate. The threat assessment can be conducted in isolation of a site visit, although specific risks associated with a project will be difficult to ascertain without firsthand knowledge through an actual visit. A secondary threat assessment may be done concurrently with, or as part of; a security survey to provide the final specifics for the project itself, as opposed to the more overarching initial assessment.

Part 1: Executive Summary

Executive management may read only the executive summary and selected portions of the document, so it is important to capture succinctly the key elements at the front of the report. The consultant must also demonstrate an understanding of the company's operations in order to assess how component parts may be subject to risk, aligning the threats to specific project activities or policies. The company's tolerances and perceptions should also be captured in order to set agreed-upon parameters of threat and define what threats mean to the company. A brief intelligence picture will set the scene for the subsequent observations and recommendations. The consultant should represent calculated key risks as well a macro-impact assessment.

1. Introduction
   a. Aim of the Threat Assessment
   b. Company Overview and Threat Tolerances

    c. Intelligence Picture
    d. Risk Calculations
    e. Threat Impact Assessment

Part 2: Risk Picture

Based largely on the intelligence review, the risk picture places political considerations, socio-economic factors, ethnic issues, religious factors, terrorism risks, insurgency problems, and criminal factors into a threat picture. Each group, area, or element should be reviewed in terms of how it may pose a threat to the company's national, regional, or local operations. Doing this provides a macro-level look at who or what may pose a risk to the company and how this risk can be viewed in the short, medium, and long terms. A historical perspective can also provide a good foundation of understanding if long-standing feuds or instabilities exist and might reflect or be associated with current threats, allowing trends to be established through evidenced information. The company risk manager or contracted consultant should consider such elements as commercial espionage or data theft within the risk picture rather than focusing purely on physical threats. Mapping threat group operating areas, poverty zones, or ethnic and religious divides can help the company understand some of the local and regional areas of concern.

    1. Threat Groups
        a. Historical Factors
        b. Political Instabilities
        c. Socioeconomic Issues
        d. Ethnic and Religious Issues
        e. Terrorist Groups and Targeting
        f. Insurgent Groups and Targeting
        g. Organized and Opportunistic Criminal Issues
        h. Commercial Problems and Limitations
        i. Trending Observations
        j. Evaluation of Likely Impacts on the Company

Part 3: Risk Probability

It is important to specify whether a threat assessment has been established based on hard, empirical, or statistical data or through more intangible methods, such as professional judgment or experience-based assessments and predications. Presenting evidence to the company to substantiate an assessment often gains more traction, although providing hard empirical data may be difficult to accomplish. Visually presenting risk probabilities against impacts is also an effective way to capture a company's attention regarding important risk factors.

    1. Threat Nature
        a. Objective or Supported Risk Assessments
        b. Subjective or Predicted Risk Assessments
        c. Overall Risk Probability and Impact Assessment

Part 4: Threat Types

A detailed focus on threat types provides a granular review of exactly how a hostile person or group will subject the company to risk. Threat types cover a wide spectrum of risk areas, in terms of both tangible and intangible risks. Covering each risk type in detail by describing what it is, how it is conducted, and what impacts may result allows the company to assess how such risk might impact the project at different levels.

1. Physical Threats
   a. Armed or Complex Attack
   b. Indirect Fire Attack
   c. Small Arms Fire and Direct Fire Attack
   d. Kidnap and Ransom
   e. Improvised Explosive Devices
   f. Civil Disturbances
   g. Complex Ambushes or Attacks
   h. Travel and Static Threats
   i. Industrial Threats (explosive and toxic risks)
   j. Climatic and Geographic Threats (flood, fire, earthquake)
   k. Summary of Impacts on the Company
2. Nonphysical Threats
   a. Coercion or Intimidation
   b. Reputational or Brand Threats
   c. Financial Threats
   d. Information Technology
   e. Intellectual Property
   f. Morale and Welfare
   g. Productivity Impairments
   h. Summary of Impacts on the Company

Part 5: Risk Mitigations

The company should seek recommendations on how to avoid or manage the threats presented within the threat probability and type sections of the report. Risks may be mitigated (or exacerbated) by a range of external activities occurring independently of the company's operations. The consultant should seek to understand how the activities and influences of external groups, from host nation elements to foreign influences and commercial activities, may influence risk levels within a region or area or to the company or project specifically. It is also important to understand at this stage how external groups might be resourced to assist in directly reducing or managing risks to the company through the establishment of relationships or agreements. The reliability of such groups should be addressed as well as whether evidence might suggest that elements may be coerced or in collusion with subversive parties. The consultant can also offer recommendations on how risks may be mitigated or reduced through company policies, procedures, resources, and expertise as well as agreements with external agencies. These factors will be explained in greater detail in the security plan.

1. External Agencies
   a. Host Nation Government
      i. Military and Law Enforcement
      ii. Civil Administration
      iii. Diplomatic Groups
   b. Foreign Governments
      i. Military and Intelligence
      ii. Diplomatic Missions
   c. Others
      i. Commercial Groups
      ii. Nongovernment Groups
      iii. Security Organizations
2. Internal Mitigation Measures
   a. Policies and Strategies
   b. Procedures and Plans
   c. Relationships and Agreements
   d. Equipment, Expertise, and Resources

Part 6: Impact Assessment

The impact of the threats should be defined in terms of project performance and reputational risks as well as whether the threats might have tangible impacts, such as the loss of life or equipment. Intangible impacts adversely affecting morale or the company's credibility should also be discussed. The threat type should be defined, as to whether the threat impact remains constant throughout the project's lifespan, or whether the impact of a specific threat will change over time. The influence of external factors should also be assessed: For example, if the military leaves, a certain threat level will increase, or if humanitarian aid is provided, threat levels may be reduced. Threat impacts should be calculated or reviewed in terms of the current situation and should also be predictive in nature, specifying what might happen if an event occurs or a decision is made. Threats should also be viewed in terms specific to the company—such as if site A is attacked, this will happen. Generic threats that might not be aimed specifically at the company but that might nevertheless affect it also should be detailed.

1. Threat Impacts
   a. Tangible
   b. Intangible
2. Threat Types
   a. Dynamic
   b. Static
3. Threat Probability
   a. Short, Medium, and Long Term
   b. Locations or Defined Sites
   c. Matrix or Graphics
4. Specific Threats
   a. Personnel and Facilities
   b. Equipment and Assets

      c. Performance and operations
      d. Reputation and liability
      e. Other
   5. Generic Threats
      a. Personnel and Facilities
      b. Equipment and Assets
      c. Performance and Operations
      d. Reputation
      e. Other

Part 7: Conclusion and Recommendations

The threat assessment should deliver both a macro- and a micro-level review of the threats facing the company and its operations, at both a strategic and granular level. A spectrum of risks should be considered, evaluated, and calculated in terms of probability and impact. Recommendations should be provided to offset risk to the company, and should exploit or capitalize on internal and external resources. Polices, procedures, and resources should be addressed in order to assist the company in planning the activity within a threat context. The company executive leadership and risk and program managers should gain from the threat assessment a clear picture of the threat environment and an understanding of what will be required to permit the company to operate in a particular environment most productively. A proposal for services may follow a detailed threat assessment if the company uses the document for budgetary and project planning purposes, although typically a threat assessment does not define resource-oriented solutions, and a full security survey and subsequent security plan, as discussed next, are better suited to provide a detailed appraisal of the complete security requirements for a new project.

SECURITY SURVEYS

Ideally the security survey draws on the information contained in the intelligence report and observations and recommendations made in the threat assessment to establish the foundations of the threat environment in which a project will be operating. The security survey pays particular attention to the project site or activity itself as well as the risk and security management procedures and policies. The consultant should place information gathered from the site or activity into the context of the specific area intelligence picture and threat factors, providing a review of the policy, procedural, and physical security measures associated with a site, along with observations and recommendations. The security survey is the foundation for the security plan, the document that specifies actual policies and procedures required to protect a project site or activity. The security survey may also be used as the basis of contractual requirements, defining the resource and approach needs. The consultant should base the security survey on the company's own tolerance levels rather than attempting to impose his or her tolerance levels or judgments onto the activity. In other words, the security survey should be built around the company's approach and activity rather than a consultant's or a vendor company's personal views.

Part 1: Executive Summary

The executive summary should capture the critical components of the intelligence picture and threat assessment to set the foundations of the review of a site or activity. Again, the report should be written with the assumption that earlier reports may not be reviewed by the recipient audience. It is important to demonstrate an understanding of the company and its activities, as this will determine the approach and methodology of the survey. The observations of the security survey should indicate the nature of the environment and the associated risks in the context of what the company is attempting to accomplish. An overview of the overarching resource and budgetary requirements may also be included if the company is trying to decide whether to proceed with an activity or will use a negative report to disengage from the business opportunity. The executive summary should clearly state whether the consultant advises the company to undertake an activity, and if so, what would be required to enable it to succeed. In the survey, it is important not just to repeat what the client already knows but to offer professional insights and recommendations to assist in corporate and programmatic decision making.

1. Introduction
   a. Executive Summary
   b. Company Overview and Threat Tolerances
   c. Intelligence Picture
   d. Risk Calculation and Threat Impact Assessment
   e. Nature of Project Activity
   f. Policy, Procedure, and Resource Needs (Recommendations)

Part 2: Activity Requirements

Only by having a comprehensive and detailed appreciation of the company and its activity requirements can the consultant develop a professional security survey. The survey should be built around an understanding of what the company is attempting to achieve: project plans, milestones, and stages (see Chapter 7). The consultant must also understand how the company envisages the project will be conducted as well as any policies and procedures the company has in place that may influence the survey and any resulting security plans. Understanding how the project may fit in with other groups is also important, as the company may be funded by a government agency that can leverage assistance, or may have diplomatic connections with a host nation, engendering support. Community projects in surrounding regions may also be exploited to strengthen the company in a new project. The company may also have teamed or subcontracted with other companies whose relationships, experience, and activities may assist or undermine the project. While it may be assumed that some of the client audience will consider this section as stating the obvious, in large, amorphous organizations containing different groups and departments often have no visibility over the activities or capabilities of other departments, and this section may bring together disparate concepts and information into a unified summary—assisting organizational convergence.

1. Goals and Objectives
2. Project Timelines, Phases, and Milestones
3. Company Operational Approach and Methodologies
4. Company Policies and Procedures
5. Company Relationships and Interaction with External Groups
6. Company Partner or Subcontractor Arrangements
7. Relationships or Capabilities which Might be Leveraged

Part 3: Site Description

For security surveys focusing on facilities or work sites the consultant should describe and illustrate the nature of the site itself as well as surrounding terrain and key features, communities and structures. After reading this section, the company should have a clear understanding of the facility, surrounding area, and current security measures and structures in place. The use of diagrams, photography, and mapping develops a greater appreciation of where the activity will be conducted as well as any areas of concern. The consultant should also discuss the existing management and security personnel in place, as these may form part of a decision to proceed with a venture, and may be integrated into any future security organization or management plan. In addition, the consultant should explain how the site currently operates on a day-to-day basis, the number of workers, schedules, deliveries, and other factors that might require modification or may influence the final security plan approach and resources. Local communities and groups may be included in this section as they may directly influence how the site operates.

1. Topographical Considerations
2. Climatic Factors
3. Travel Options
4. Nature of the Site
5. Site Security Structures
6. Local Site Management and Security Personnel
7. Site Work Practices and Routines
8. Urban Areas and Local Communities

Part 4: Supporting Agencies

The consultant should seek to draw on any available resources within the international community as well as host nation support, if available. By understanding the organizations and key office holders at the local, regional, and national level, the consultant may be able to leverage additional support for the company's activity. In addition, while some forces may conceptually support the company's endeavours, they may have limitations or weaknesses that will undermine their use in terms of actual support capability. Friction between competing national groups may also present a risk or instability that should be noted and addressed. Where possible, the consultant should seek to engage external agencies (with the company's agreement) and seek formal understandings in terms of medical support, evacuation, response capability, and other augmentation measures. The consultant should not merely state the types of groups available in the report, but should geographically situate them in the context of the company's project sites and logistical routes as well as recommend seeking formal relationships where appropriate.

1. Host Nation Agencies
   a. Military and Police
   b. Specialist
   c. Tribal and Religious
   d. Other
   e. Locations of Bases, Facilities, or Urban Areas
2. Foreign Agencies
   a. Government
   b. Diplomatic
   c. Military and Security Agencies
   d. Locations of Bases and Facilities

Part 5: Threat and Mitigation Analysis

This section can be taken largely from the intelligence report and threat summary, with particular attention to the site itself and how operations should be conducted. A granular level of focus and attention should be paid to how the site itself may be subject to threats and risks presented to routes to and from the project area. The consultant should seek to leverage a national and regional understanding of the threat types, levels, and trends, and bring this down to a local level. Mitigation measures should be associated with the threats; these measures will feed into the security recommendation portion of the survey. Referencing to external supporting agencies and groups may be used to indicate how the threat picture is affected by other parties and how mitigation measures can be integrated with these elements.

1. National and Regional Threats
2. Hostile Groups, Organizations, and Individuals
3. Threat Types, Categories, and Impacts
4. Trend Analysis and Predictive Risks
5. Specific Travel Threat Analysis
6. Specific Site Threat Analysis

Part 6: Recommendations

The recommendations section brings together an understanding of the company's project, how it intends to conduct itself, and under what policies and methodology it does, or should, operate, aligning the policies and approach with the threat environment and site itself. The recommendations should engage and exploit available resources within the site as well as external agencies, and augment or resource risk management and security areas as appropriate. If resourcing or policy is based on a concept or premise, it should be defined in order to allow the client to understand that certain approaches may be subject to external influences or decisions and may require further levels of effort to engage or confirm. The use of schematics, maps, and tables succinctly captures key requirements. Recommendations will be tailored to each unique project requirement, and environmental factors:

1. Security Strategy and Concepts
2. Security Policies and Planning
3. Security Procedures and Documents
4. Resources Identification and Allocation
5. Physical Security Structures
6. Secured Personnel Movement
7. Material or Freight Movement
8. Static and Guard Force Services
9. Technological Security Devices
10. Liaison and Agreements
11. Communications Plan
12. Medical Services
13. Crisis Management and Evacuation
14. Security Budgets and Financing

Part 7: Administration and Logistics

If the security survey's role is to provide recommendations that will form the basis of a proposal for services, a section covering manpower and equipment resources should be included. All associated requirements—mobilizations, physical structures, life support, and facilities, administrative, and logistical support—should be included, as these may form the basis of a pricing section of a proposal and will provide the company with insight into the scope and nature of the resources required for the project.

1. Personnel, Mobilization, Schedules, and Procurements
2. Vehicles and Equipment
3. Physical Security Structures
4. Life Support and Facilities
5. Communications and Information Technology
6. Subcontracting Arrangements
7. Resource Matrix
   a. Personnel
   b. Equipment
   c. Assets
   d. Subcontracts

Part 8: Conclusion

The conclusion may provide a brief summary of key points. However, most aspects should have already been addressed in the different parts of the survey, with the recommendations and resource sections covering the core observations and recommendations of the report. The consultant may wish to include several appendices to supplement areas of the report—such as intelligence and threat assessment reports from which observations or recommendations might have been drawn. Other useful information, such as maps, tables, reports, and graphics, may be included as subsections.

Part 9: Appendices

    a. Intelligence Report
    b. Threat Assessment
    c. Mapping and Schematics
    d. Statistics and Graphs
    e. Interview Notes and Supplemental Documents

Note: The security survey normally precedes the development of a scope of work by the company, which defines the services desired from subcontracted security providers who might be engaged to support the project. The security plan is typically used only once resources have been confirmed; the plan establishes the manner by which risk and security will be managed and conducted for a project. For large contracts, however, the company may use the security plan as the basis of a request for proposal rather than the security survey. Either may include a rough order of magnitude in order to estimate the costs associated with the measures recommended in the security survey or defined in granular detail in the security plan. The approach is typically dictated by the company, depending on style, operating methodologies and requirement.

OPERATIONS ORDER OR MOBILIZATION PLANS

The mobilization of personnel or resources should occur once a security plan is in place. However, this is not always the case. A mobilization plan or operations order is a document that defines the immediate security needs of the site to protect arriving personnel as well as the manner by which personnel and resources will be moved safely and effectively to the facility. It may also form the basis for the project initiation document (PiD) and is similar to the military management system employed to initiate operations, although with a commercial bent. At a tactical level, this document is practical in nature, and should be used as a method of coordinating resources and personnel as well as mitigating immediate site occupation and travel risks. Drawing on the intelligence report and threat assessment, this document has a short life span and is redundant once a project site is established. A separate demobilization plan should be drawn up when personnel and equipment depart the project site at the end of the task. Typically operation orders are written specifically for security management and personnel rather than for the project management, although aspects of the document have obvious applications for the business activity (timings, logistical requirements, procurements, agreements with facility owners, briefings, etc.). The document should also be considered sensitive, as it will define routes and other information that could pose a threat if made available to unauthorized personnel. Simplicity is essential for this document to be user friendly.

Part 1: Executive Summary

The executive summary should quickly outline the groups involved in the task, the nature of the requirement, and the threat and risk overview. The order of march, or configuration, as well as management positioning should also be established to set the framework of how the project management and security team will conduct the operation. This is very similar to a military-style operational approach and should be succinct and pragmatic.

1. Introduction
   a. Executive Summary
   b. Company Overview
   c. Intelligence Picture
   d. Risk Calculation and Threat Impact Assessment
   e. Groupings and Configurations
   f. Management Structures and Communications
   g. Timings and Schedules
   h. Information Restrictions

Part 2: Ground

The ground section should provide information regarding the nature of the threat picture as well as the topographical aspects of the region and site itself. This section explains what the security personnel and project staff can expect while traveling to and arriving on site. Routes should be covered in detail, as these often are the most vulnerable parts of the project's activity. Maps, photographs, and/or schematics should be used to illustrate this section where possible.

1. Project Region
2. Project Site
3. Routes

Part 3: Situation

The situation section indicates the intelligence and threat picture plus relevant external security or government agencies that might play a part in the movement or occupation of the project site. Threats should be clearly articulated in terms of their nature and the methodology of the plan's employment. This section can be succinct extracts from previous reports, focusing on the specific needs of a particular mobilization plan.

1. Intelligence Picture
2. Threat Assessment
3. Friendly Forces
4. Hostile Groups
5. Civilians

Part 4: Mission

The consultant should clearly articulate the requirements of the task and, if necessary, further break down the functions and responsibilities of subgroups within a team. Defining the mission and tasks will be especially relevant if multiple teams are used to clear routes, secure the venue, and move the project staff into a facility.

1. Mission
2. Group Taskings
3. Configurations and Roles
4. External Groups and Agencies

Part 5: Mobilization Execution

The concept of operations is effectively a mini–executive summary that talks the security group and company management through how the task will be accomplished, from administrative and logistical requirements, to occupying the facility. Effectively the concept of operations provides a full walk-through of the task in general detail: *Here is how we will do it!* The operation phases provide more granular detail, with questions if necessary. The consultant should break the task into manageable sections to enable management and support personnel to follow the different aspects of the task more easily. At each stage, response or crisis management actions should be stated if they relate to a specific section; if they do not, the response measures should be stated at the end of this section.

1. Concept of Operations
2. Operation Phases and Conduct
3. Crisis Management
4. Configurations

Part 6: Coordinating Instructions

The coordinating instructions will include the timetable of events, the integration of external agencies, and any other integration of information requirements.

1. Timings
2. External Agency Integration

Part 7: Administration and Logistics

The mobilization of significant numbers of project staff and resources require vehicle support, equipment allocation, life support and a host of other administrative and logistical support requirements. This section should identify those needs and specify responsible parties with time frames for delivery captured within the coordinating instructions timetable. In hostile or remote environments, it is especially important that all equipment is serviceable and accounted for prior to departing a safe area or base camp.

Part 8: Command and Communications

It is important to define the management chain to both security personnel and associated project management personnel in order to ensure that tactical decision making and crisis response measures are quickly and effectively coordinated. This unambiguous definition or roles and responsibilities is also important if the consultant has security management responsibilities that supersede those of project staff during the vulnerable movement and occupation stages of a project. In addition, a clear communications plan with frequencies, codes, and numbers should be provided, along with any overarching crisis management responses in case of emergency. It is not common to include the security survey in full as an appendix, although appropriate sections may be copied, along with the threat assessment and any relevant mapping or photography of schematics.

1. Management Structure
2. Communications Plan
3. Crisis Response Plan

Part 9: Demobilization

The demobilization aspect of the plan captures all of the same elements as the mobilization aspect, but it also closes the project in terms of how the extraction will affect the site after departure and the accountability for resources used during the task. The demobilization may also account for the destruction, write-off, or transfer of materials or information to other parties, typically those inheriting the project facility. Any residual tasks, such as project confirmation visits or close-down procedures, should be identified, as should logistical and administrative support requirements for the returning project staff. Often this information is best captured on a table of requirements.

1. Information Management
2. Resource Accountability
3. Resource Destruction and Transfers
4. Project Extraction Impacts
5. Residual or Follow-Up Tasks
6. Reception and Staging Requirements
7. Replenishment and Support
8. Documental Requirements and Closure Report
9. Relief in Place Requirements

SECURITY PLAN

The security plan is a practical policy and procedure document that covers how every dimension of risk will be mitigated and security provided. It might form a key component of an overall risk management plan; however, it is tactical in nature and is designed to last the duration of the project activity, rather than act as a snapshot review or task specific concept, to which the intelligence reviews, threat assessments, and mobilization plans are more aligned. The security plan's focus is on the security needs and delivery of services for a site on a macro- and micro-level, looking inwards as well as externally. It should contain appendices to encompass supporting policies and plans (standard operating procedures [SOPs]; tactics, techniques, and procedures [TTPs]; evacuation; incident management) and should contain appropriate references to internal and external agreements and understandings as well as graphic representations to simplify data delivery. Much of the information contained in the security plan will have been determined by the intelligence review, threat assessment, and security survey. However, the security plan provides granular and tactical measures used to support a particular activity or site. Each security plan must be tailored to meet the unique requirements of each company, activity, and environment. The sections that follow provide a sample of elements that might be included in the document.

Part 1: Executive Summary

As with all security documents, it must be assumed that this report will be read in isolation. Thus it should contain all critical information to allow the reader to understand the context in which the report is written. The company, its mission, goals, and objectives, as well as the nature and conduct of the activity itself, should be briefly introduced. Discussion of company constraints and threat tolerance levels will allow the reader to understand why certain measures are being implemented and why others are not. A list of reference or supporting documents should also be provided for further reading or clarification. A summary of the intelligence and threat picture will also lay the foundations of what risks are being countered as well as the impacts and repercussions that might follow successful targeting of the activity, although intelligence reviews and threat assessments will have a shelf life, which the security plan might outlive.

1. Company Background
   a. Mission, Goals, and Objectives
   b. Policies and Procedures
   c. Activity Details
   d. Operations and Methods
   e. Constraints and Tolerances
   f. Document References

Part 2: Intelligence and Threat Review

The intelligence picture should be clearly articulated and updated in the security plan, along with the threat assessment with scheduled or event-driven reviews—this element of the plan will drive change and enable the plan to evolve to match changing threat conditions. Security plans typically are updated only rarely, or after an incident, although managers should identify where environmental or project changes require a revision to the plan. The consultant must determine how time-specific the intelligence element of the plan will be; the aim is to avoid negating the value of the document by making it too date-specific and thus too cumbersome and costly to manage. Risk types should be reviewed in terms of threats to the activity or site itself as well as to logistical and personnel movement requirements. A threat probability and impact assessment should be included to focus corporate and project management on why the security plan is of significance and why appropriate resources should be provided to mitigate identified or postulated risks.

1. Intelligence Picture
   a. Intelligence Overview
   b. Intelligence Assessment
2. Threat Assessment
   a. Threat Assessment
   b. Risk Types
   c. Risk Probability and Impact Matrix

Part 3: External Factors

The consultant might wish to explain the layout of the region and local area in terms of geography, landscape features and influences, local urban and rural communities, and any important climatic factors (river levels, road conditions, mountain pass accesses) that might be relevant to the security plan. External agencies that might influence, threaten, or support the company's activity should also be referenced, citing their location, area of influence, and any part they may place within the risk picture or mitigation measures.

1. Ground and Area
   a. Local Area Topography
   b. Site Topography (Boundaries)
   c. Ground Restrictions and Threats
   d. Local Urban and Rural Settlements
   e. Climatic Factors
   f. Mobility Corridors
2. External Agencies
   a. Military
   b. Law Enforcement
   c. Government
   d. Tribal
   e. Diplomatic
   f. Community
   g. Commercial Businesses
   h. Commercial Security
   i. Nongovernment and Aid Agencies

Part 4: Integration Plan

A clear understanding of how external agencies and groups are integrated within the security plan should be covered, including discussion of whether there exist any formal and documented agreements or informal arrangements. Any relationship development and sustainment plans and methods should be addressed to ensure that internal company management changes do not omit knowledge or awareness on useful outreach programs.

1. Integration of Security Procedures
   a. Memoranda of Understanding
   b. Alert States and Response Procedures
   c. Communications (Communications Plan or Information Management Plan)
   d. Intelligence and Threat Warnings
   e. Recognition Measures
2. Community Relationships
   a. Liaison
   b. Community Leaders and Groups
   c. Meetings and Events
   d. Goals and Agendas
   e. Projects and Support

Part 5: Management

The management of the security plan should be clearly defined in order to streamline decision making and attribute responsibilities and accountability for the range of risk management and security delivery requirements. Organizational structures, responsibilities, authorities, and agreements should be addressed. Management plans covering communications, mobilizations, and quality assurance should also be included. Management integration, within the company and the security provider's organization, should be clarified, as should their integration and relationships with external agencies. Overarching security management policies may also be included, in order to integrate physical and technological measures within the complete security plan approach.

1. Management Plan
   a. Organizational Structure
   b. Responsibilities and Duties
      i. Decision Matrix
      ii. Trigger Points
   c. Policies and Documents
   d. Orders and Instructions
   e. Crisis Management and Incident Management Plans
   f. Communications Plan
   g. Memoranda of Understanding
   h. Interagency Cooperation Plans
   i. Mobilization (and Demobilization) Plan
   j. Orders and Instructions
   k. Journey Management
   l. Quality Assurance Plan
   m. Medical Plan
   n. Registers and Reports
2. Surveillance and Target Acquisition Plan (STAP)
   a. External Support
   b. Technology Measures
   c. Lighting (illumination matrix)

    d. Towers and Observation Points
    e. Patrols

Part 6: Instructions

The instructions issued to both security personnel and appropriate corporate and project management should be covered in an instructions section. This section may largely refer to supporting documents (SOPs, TTPs, evacuation and incident management plans, etc.) but should localize generic instructions to reflect any unique requirements of a project site. Security orders, personnel administrative matters, and detailed supporting plans might also be included or referenced.

  1. Security Force Instructions
    a. Incident Response
    b. Personal Security Details and Convoys
    c. Guard Force Patrols
    d. Guard Force Towers
    e. Access Control Points (Access Control Plan)
    f. Buildings and Escorts
    g. Quick Reaction Forces
    h. Medical and Health
    i. Rules of Engagement and Use of Force
    j. Disciple and Training
    k. Incident Management Plan
      i. Armed Attack
      ii. Indirect Fire Attacks
      iii. Kidnap and Ransom
      iv. Industrial Hazards
      v. Suspect packages and the Like[4]
    l. Improvised Explosive Device/Unexploded Ordnance Clearance Sweeps
    m. Evacuation Plans and Safe Havens
      i. Project Site Routes
      ii. Bunkers
      iii. Internal Safe Havens
      vi. Evacuation Routes
      v. Alternative or External Safe Havens
    n. Complaints and Liasions
    o. Media Management

Part 7: Quality Assurance Plan

It is useful to define self-regulating measures to ensure that the security plan reflects a changing risk environment and to ensure that professional standards are sustained and delivered. These policies or procedures may be contained in a separate quality assurance plan or may be briefly covered in the security plan itself. Training, development, and how weaknesses will be addressed might also be included. External audits should be defined, detailing the frequency and responsible parties.

1. Professional Standards
2. Quality Measurement
3. Audits and Gap Analysis
4. Training and Development
5. Shortfall Rectifications
6. Reporting and Authorities

Part 8: Conclusion

Although no conclusion may be necessary, in some instances a short summary of key points at the end of the security plan is a useful tool to refocus the company on key issues after reading through rafts of details.

Part 9: Appendices

In order to avoid duplication as well as make the security plan more manageable, a series of attachments or appendices may cover elements of the requirements in greater detail. Having appendices will also allow the consultant to utilize existing materials that might be appropriate for the plan. These appendices might be included:

1. Intelligence Report
2. Threat Assessment
3. Incident Management Plan
4. Memoranda of Understanding (s)
5. Evacuation Plans
6. Mapping and Schematics
7. Quality Assurance Plan
8. SOPs and TTPs

SECURITY AUDIT

The scope and nature of a security audit is driven by a company's requirements (see "Auditing Consultancy" in Chapter 6) and may include areas such as the auditing of a company or vendor's policies and procedures, management approaches, or an assessment of a site or the practical services being delivered by vendors. A post-incident review audit may also be required following a crisis event to ensure that management responses were correct and that shortfalls are identified and resolved. The company may require documental and record checks or that the auditor determine the level of professional ability and experience of staff or a subcontractor. Security audits are sensitive issues; often recipients are concerned that their professionalism is being called into question, or that their jobs or contracts are threatened. The consultant may be viewed with varying degrees of skepticism, hostility, or suspicion.

The structure, scope, and content of an audit is therefore a fluid and complex issue that must be defined based on what the company requires of the consultant. An audit may cover some of the next areas.

Part 1: Executive Summary

The executive summary should demonstrate an understanding of the company and project's activity and define what the company requires from the audit in terms of mission, focus, and scope. The audit aims should be in alignment with the goals and methodology of the company's activity and reflect the manner in which the company wishes the audit to be conducted. It is important that the company defines what parameters and authorities the consultant has for the audit; for example, is the consultant permitted to interact with the program manager, or should the consultant liaise directly through the security director? In addition, it is important to detail what levels and types of information sources the consultant is permitted to have access to: documents, reports, databases, sites, and personnel. The consultant must work within these parameters so as not to frustrate the company engaging his or her services while being sensitive to the local management who are the subject of the audit. The executive summary should also define what information restrictions have been imposed by the company or recommended by the consultant. Finally, the executive summary should offer overarching findings and recommendations to indicate the major strengths and weaknesses of the audited party or activity as well as offer recommendations to address gaps and shortfalls. Finally, as audits are often sensitive documents, a list of those authorized to receive a copy should be indicated to ensure that only appropriate management have oversight of this document.

1. Company Corporate and Project Overview
2. Aim of the Audit and Focuses
3. Audit Approach, Parameters, and Authorities
4. Information Restrictions and Allowances
5. Findings and Recommendations
6. Audit Report Distribution List

Part 2: Background

The background section should succinctly capture the nature, scope, and methodology of the company's activity, as this section forms the foundation of what services or activities are being audited. A summary of the intelligence and threat picture (where appropriate) sets the scene for the audit, illustrating why services are being provided and providing the company with a degree of spatial and situational awareness. An explanation of what specific services or activities are being audited focuses the report on the stipulated goals of the audit, so that consultant and reader are not sidetracked into areas that are not part of the requirement. It might be useful to explain the management structures, key personnel, and company and external agency interfaces as well, as these may influence how activities or services are being performed. A description of the site (if relevant) also allows the reader to envisage the project and thus place the information into context.

1. Company's Activity Summary
2. Intelligence Picture and Threat Assessment

3. Threat and Incident History
4. Reason for the Audit and the Services Being Audited
5. Management Structure and Key Personnel
6. Interfaces and External Agencies
7. Groupings and Configurations
8. Site or Facility Description

Part 3: The Audit

The scope and nature of the audit is defined by the company's requirements. The consultant should attempt to define a systematic and logical approach to different areas of requirement, especially if the activity is large, complex, and involves multiple agencies. The consultant should remember that the report audience may not be fully informed of how the activity is structured, managed, and integrated with subcontractors, partners, and external organizations. The audience may have never visited the activity or may have no experience in the work practices of the project and thus might find it difficult to place the report into any easily understandable context. The company that hires the consultant for this service should state how much detail is required as well as how granular the explanation in each section should be. Some audits succinctly state the subject area with strengths, weaknesses, and recommendations. In others, some explanation of the subject area may be required to place this information into an understandable context. The organization of each section is usually shaped by the audit focus. A sample of areas a consultant may be required to audit follows.

1. Management Structures
   a. Company and Subcontractor Organizational Structures
   b. Internal and External Networks and Communication Lines
   c. Decision Making and Authorities
   d. Group Capabilities and Capacities
   e. Internal and External Resources
   f. Contractual Agreements and Requirements
   g. Incident Control Teams (Site)
   h. Crisis Management Teams (Corporate)
   i. Security Organizational Structure
2. Policies
   a. Project Management Activity Policies
   b. Local Community Integration, Agreements, and Relationships
   c. Military and Diplomatic Office Integration, Agreements, and Relationships
   d. Subcontractor Policies and Quality Assurance
   e. Risk, Security, and Crisis Response Policies
   f. Discipline, Warnings, and Dismissals
   g. Complaints and Redresses
   h. Media Handling
   i. Information Security
3. Procedures
   a. Risk Mitigation

    b. Mobile Security

    c. Static Security

    d. Crisis Response

    e. Repatriation

    f. Reporting

    g. Document Control

    h. Quality Assurance

4. Security Document Audit

    a. Site Security Plan

    b. Incident Management Plan

    c. Evacuation Plan

    d. Medical Response Plan

    e. Communications or Information Management Plan

    f. Standard Operating Procedures

    g. Tactical Techniques and Procedures

    h. External Force Agreements

    i. Surveillance Target Acquisition Plan

    j. Training Plans, Reports, Returns, and Records

5. Personnel Audit

    a. Management Team

    b. Recruitment and Vetting

    c. Contractual Requirements and Standards

    d. Quality Measurement Systems

    e. Contractual Performance and Delivery Standards

    f. Training and Records

    g. Tested Responses and Service Delivery

    h. Reliability and Experience

6. Administration and Logistics

    a. Vehicles, Watercraft, and Air Assets

    b. Mobilization and Travel

    c. Procurement and Accounting

    d. Invoicing and Billing

    e. Weapons and Ammunition

    f. Personal Protective Equipment

    g. Towers, Gates, and Perimeters

    h. Lighting, Closed-Circuit Televisions, Intruder Detection Systems

    i. Communications and Information Technology

    j. Life Support and Facilities

    k. Specialist Items

    l. Registers and Accountability

    m. Equipment Damages, Losses, and Write-Off Documents

Part 4: Strengths

While the audit section comments on the granular level of the strengths of the services being provided, a short description or table of the most pertinent strengths of the audited party might be useful. Companies and consultants should be mindful not to focus purely on negative aspects of an audit, but also point out what is being done well.

Part 5: Weaknesses

Although the audit section should address shortfalls or gaps at a granular level, it can be even more important to highlight the major deficiencies within a separate section—in order to focus the company on what key areas need to be resolved. These weaknesses should be represented in a balanced and clinical manner rather than be presented purely as negative elements.

Part 6: Recommendations

Recommendations may be included within Parts 4 and 5 or may be formally stated in a separate section that defines what remedial measures are suggested in order to address weaknesses and gaps. The recommendations section may provide a checklist of items that need to be actioned and can form the basis of a follow-up audit to see how far corrective action has progressed. The final recommendation might be that an independent and impartial auditor confirm at a later (defined) time that agreed improvements or actions have taken place.

Part 7: Conclusion

The audit conclusion might address the possible impacts if certain remedies are not met and provide an overall assessment of the activity as a whole. This section is likely to be similar to the executive summary and provides only a general statement of the audit findings as a whole. Appendices may also be included where appliable.

INCIDENT MANAGEMENT PLANS

The incident management plan consists of the actual response protocols to any crisis event, enabling more effective business recovery. It is a management tool used to predetermine likely threats and consolidate and document predetermined and systematic response measures. The incident management plan does not define policy (the risk management plan does that); it is more a checklist and user tactical guide used when a crisis is occurring to assist and enable management to deal with an event more effectively. The protocols should not be considered restrictive but guidelines of useful tips and checks. The sections that follow might be included in an incident management plan.

Part 1: Incident Management Organizations

These organizations should be considered as elements of the incident management group:

- Executive Management Team
- Incident Control Team

- Special Response Team
- Technical Management Teams
- Local Management Team
- External Agency Participation Teams

Part 2: Responsibilities and Functions

The company should define the responsibilities, parameters, authorities, and roles of each level of the project group, including:

- Executive Management
- Project Management
- Program Management
- Site Management

Part 3: Serious Incident Reporting

The incident management plan should address the methods by which serious incident information is captured and processed from the point of occurrence to the executive board, including:

- Serious Incident Verification
- Report Templates and Details
- Documentation Requirements
- Reporting Claims
- External Notifications
- Data Storage

Part 4: Incident Management

Incident management should also address the postulated requirements or threats likely to face the company's management elements. By forecasting likely incident events, pragmatic management protocols can be developed to support incident management requirements, to best enable business continuity and recovery. Typical examples of incident events or requirements include:

- Lost Communications
- Missing Persons
- Medical Emergency
- Emergency Medical Evacuation
- Personnel or Site Evacuation
- Kidnap and Ransom
- Equipment and Resource Evacuation
- Explosion or Sabotage
- Armed or Violent Attack
- Facility Intruder or Breach

- Intimidation and Coercion
- Family Liaison Following Fatality or Kidnap
- Media Management
- Local Government Coordination
- Vehicle-Borne Improvised Explosive Device Threat
- Improvised Explosive Device and Suspect Packages
- Unexploded Ordnance Clearances
- Post-Incident Reviews
- Information Security
- Repatriations
- Road Traffic Accidents
- Communications Plan
- Injuries and Casualties
- Espionage
- Investigations
- Civil Unrest
- Loss of Weapons
- Detention by Local Authorities
- Loss of Sensitive Information
- Information Technology Security Breach
- Detaining Persons
- Hostage Response
- Industrial Accidents
- Personnel Discipline
- Theft or Fraud
- Military Force Coordination
- Possession of Illegal Substances
- Complaint Management
- Indirect Fire Attack

Part 5: Supporting Materials

Incident management should also be supported by tools that depict the event location as well as by rules, policies, and reports that crisis management teams, often remote from the event, can use to understand the local environment and situation, allowing them to make better informed decisions. Supporting material may include:

- Maps
- Orders
- Schematics
- Photography
- Reports
- External Communication Plans

In conclusion, security documents and exhibits are usually developed according to individual company requirements. Some companies have detailed and well-established templates and protocols; others have limited structures in place or reinvent the process repeatedly. The unique nature of each task also demands a fresh review of the structure and content of each document to ensure that it matches the current need. On occasion circumstances may require different types of document to be merged into an amalgamation of several elements, especially if time is short and concurrent details are required. Lateral thinking and common sense will define how reports are blended and merged to meet concurrent or new requirements. By establishing a stable of detailed and well-structured reports companies will be better placed to enter new markets or activities, sustain productive operations, and recover from business interruption with greater ease.

Notes

1. Security documents typically should be delivered to the audience or client in PDF format to prevent unauthorized modifications. In addition, for sensitive documents, password protections might be used to limit public access to the information. It is also advisable to include a liability waiver so that the consultant or their company are not held accountable for recommendations or observations made within a report.
2. Notable elements include political instabilities, terrorism, and insurgency.
3. Greater detail is normally contained in the threat assessment report.
4. See this chapter's section "Incident Management Plans."

CHAPTER 13

Government versus Commercial Contracting

It is important for companies to understand the differences between government and commercial contracting, whether their immediate client is commercial but financed by a government body or whether they work directly for the government as a prime contractor. The implications flow down to all management elements, and companies' risk and program managers should understand the rules under which they, and their security vendors, operate. By understanding the regulations associated with government contracts, all parties can align their processes and policies to ensure, from the outset, that they conduct themselves in a manner that will withstand an audit. Failure to understand the rules of government contracting can place both the company and its vendors at significant business risk. It is incumbent on all parties to operate with a full understanding of the applicable regulations.

For those companies operating under a purely commercial contract, the differences can be marked. Management should understand both the obvious differences and the nuances between government and commercial contracting. This chapter is designed to introduce managers to the differences between government (specifically the U.S. government) and commercial contracting, with an emphasis on government contracting, as this provides an established regulatory process whereas commercial contracting policies are based largely on company-specific requirements.

DIFFERENCES BETWEEN U.S. GOVERNMENT AND COMMERCIAL CONTRACTS

Commercial and U.S. government contracts differ in some significant areas. Commercial contracts have fewer (external) legal requirements binding them and are usually driven by factors such as those that bring the greatest benefit to the commercial company, either through profit and performance, or value gained by developing intra-company relationships (see Exhibit 13.1). Personal relationships, company histories, and branding may play a greater part in the commercial company selecting a provider than with a U.S. government contracting authority. U.S. government contracting has strict and well-established guidelines and parameters that, in theory, level the playing field in accordance with who can provide the best service, regardless of relationships, branding, or other factors. In theory, exploiting federal opportunities is simpler and more evenhanded than exploiting the commercial market, as the rules are known and the selection criteria are clearly provided.

Exhibit 13.1 Differences between Government and Commercial Contracting

U.S. Government	Commercial
Governed by strict and clear regulations	Contract by negotiation
Forced open competition	Alliances play a part in selection
Socioeconomic factors included	Performance and cost driven only
Very slow process (6 to 12 months)	Usually a fast process
Can terminate for convenience (quit)	Closure through "breach of contract"
Competition contracts are publically available	Contracts protected through confidentiality

GOVERNMENT CONTRACTING

The U.S. government implemented a standardized system for procurement (or acquisition) of commercial items and services after the Revolutionary War, as considerable defrauding of the U.S. government occurred during this period. The Federal Acquisition Regulation (FAR) has been developed and simplified over successive generations and is now captured in a series of guidelines designed to clarify the rules and regulations that relate to U.S. government procurement activities.

While the FAR is intended to be a clear and simple guide, as with any complex and sizable legally binding process, it can be difficult to understand the regulations at first; both explanation and subsequent use ease the process. This introduction provides a basic understanding and offers some useful reference points to allow navigation of the FAR itself. This introduction should not be considered a definitive guide, just a useful introductory briefing tool.

MARKET SIZE AND SCOPE

Commercial organizations whose funding comes directly or indirectly from the U.S government need to understand the FAR, as the U.S. federal government is the largest global buyer of services and equipment. In 2003, the U.S. government, through over 1,500 federal acquisition offices, spent over $290 billion. Contract modifications made up 50% of procurements; new awards, 14%; task and work orders, 33%; and small purchases, 3%. The Department of Defense (DoD) makes up the largest buyer ($21 billion in 2003), including the U.S. Army, Air Force, Navy, and Defense Logistics Agency (DLA). The Department of Homeland Security is the second largest buyer. NASA (the National Aeronautics and Space Administration) procured $11.8 billion, and the General Services Administration (GSA), $15 billion. Services make up 64% of sales, with equipment and supplies accounting for 36%. Research accounts for approximately 12%.

By understanding the federal procurement system and its basic rules, companies can better understand how to win business. Some online sources of information include:

Federal acquisition Web site: www.arnet.gov

Federal procurement data system: www.fpds.gov

FAR Web site (newest FAR): www.acqnet.gov/FAR/

GAO Red Book—the Principles of Federal Appropriations Law: www.gao.gov/legal.htm

U.S. GOVERNMENT STRUCTURE FOR ACQUISITION

Acquisition falls under numerous branches of the U.S. government, from the beginning of the process of identifying a possible need and the funding required for such an activity, to awarding money through a series of agencies until a final contractor provides an actual service. The sections that follow briefly capture the roles of the core government agencies, to enable a better understanding of the stages of monetary award for an acquisition activity.

Executive Branch

This branch develops the plans, programs, and budget activities for consideration by Congress, then executes the budgets, with plans and programs authorized by Congress. The Executive Branch also develops and maintains the FAR, via the Office of Federal Procurement Policy (OFPP).

Legislative Branch

Congress passes laws and appropriates money for obligation to service or supply acquisition. Congress controls the budget process, authorizing the release of money for procurement, appropriating money to specific agencies, and providing apportionments of that budget to specific procurements within a wider purchase. The GAO works for the Legislative Branch (see the GAO Red Book) investigates matters related to receipt, disbursement, and the application of funds. It also evaluates the performance of U.S. government programs, has broad authority to audit contractors (sellers), provides guidance over issues and protests, and is the deciding authority for pre-award disputes and protests.

The GAO does not have the power to enforce recommendations or observations on a U.S. government procuring agency; however, it can report the matter to Congress, which may intercede. The GAO can, however, during periods of political uncertainty pass a continuing resolution, to provide a stopgap measure to enable continued funding to certain activities at the same amounts and under the same conditions as for the preceding budgetary year.

Judicial Branch

The Judicial Branch interprets the laws passed by the Legislative Branch or the policies and regulations originating in the Executive Branch. It also renders decisions to the terms and conditions of a specific contract and ensures the constitutionality of laws. It also provides:

- Sources of federal law which come from the U.S. Constitution, the U.S. government having implied inherent powers to use contracts to carry out its duties. Statutes are laws enacted by the Legislative Branch and signed or vetoed by the president. Administrative law is a body of rules and regulations, while common law are decisions handed down by judges in courts of law, establishing precedents.
- Federal statutes and regulations are covered through many laws, including the U.S. Codes (USC), Code of Federal Regulations (CFR), and the Federal Register (FR). There is no single procurement law, and different agencies may use different laws to conduct their procurements.

ACQUISITIONS

For those seeking to pursue business opportunities or for managers holding a contract and sourcing and contracting vendors to support their business activities, it is useful to understand the acquisition goals of the U.S government. The U.S. government is seeking *quality, timeliness,* and *price,* while minimizing *business* and *technical risks,* accomplishing *socioeconomic objectives* while *maximizing competition,* through an integrity-based approach. The acquisition plan seeks to maximize competition, acquire commercial items where possible, and integrate the efforts of all stakeholders to ensure that needs are met most effectively. According to FAR 7.104, these areas form the basis of an acquisition plan:

- *Statement of need.* Sources of possible provision.
- *Applicable conditions or rules.* Contractor competition through clauses and requirements.
- *Cost factors and budgeting.* Estimation of budget requirements.
- *Performance characteristics.* Product description and standards.
- *Delivery requirements.* Timeframes and delivery standards.
- *Trade-offs.* Balanced value versus cost.
- *Risks.* Contract types to be used.
- *Acquisition streamlining.* Milestones and planning.

Legal Framework for Acquisitions

An acquisition is the acquiring by contract, with appropriated funds, of supplies and services by and for the use of the federal government through purchase or lease, whether supplies or services already in existence or must be created, developed, demonstrated, and evaluated. A contract is a binding legal relationship obligating the seller to furnish supplies or services under certain conditions and agreements to the buyer (U.S. government). The acquisition requirements can flow from the contract holder to subcontractors, each having to demonstrate the quality of the service, with appropriate documentation and processes.

Federal Source Selection

Unless a restricted procurement is involved, the U.S. government will seek competition through various means, known as full and open competition. The government will use a group called the Agencies Market Research to promote full and open competition to identify commercial products and services that are to the benefit of the procurement activity. The procuring agency can seek contractors through GSA scheduling of providers, acquisition histories, catalogs and periodicals, Web sites and publications, advertisement for services through FedBizOps and notice boards, trade and professional associations, and known providers. Pre-qualifications may be applied (i.e., security clearance, business size, proven experience, and capabilities). By understanding where federal agencies market or advertise acquisition requirements, commercial companies can best position themselves to identify opportunities and respond most effectively.

Fundamentals of the Acquisition Process

The amount of money allocated to a procurement decreases significantly as it moves through the standard procurement chain. It is important to understand the procurement process (see FAR 7.105), as it defines how much money a contracting agency will place against procurements rather than expectations that might be associated with company's expecting to see a contract award amount. The U.S. government is seeking services or materials provided or performed when and where contracted, performing to an acceptable level in alignment with the contract terms, and compliant with the terms and conditions of the contract, FAR, and other regulations. Typically the process follows a sequence, such as this one:

1. *The initial budget is anticipated.* The figure set at $200 million as an anticipated cost.
2. *The Office of Management and Budget (OMB) apportions the money.* Management fees from the OMB are removed and the remaining balance (now $80 million) is apportioned, unless the award is specifically appropriated, then no fees can be removed.
3. *The budgeted agency (i.e., DoD) receives money for procurements.* An agency is given funding and also removes management and overhead fees, normally 25%; the amount now is $60 million.
4. *The receiving agency allots money to procurements.* In this case, the Navy receives $20 million, the Army $20 million, and the Air Force $20 million.
5. *Procurement agencies allot monies for individual procurements.* The receiving agency may remove its own costs before it allocates monies to a provider for specific procurement activities—final amounts are now at $5 million per activity.

Determination of Need

The contracting authority often plans years in advance in order to ensure that future needs are accounted for and budgeted against. The process typically follows the process outlined in Exhibit 13.2.

The process can be further defined by the next five steps, which lead to the provision of a solicitation or request for proposal (RFP):

Step 1. *Determination of need.* Program managers often plan up to five years ahead to prepare program plans, schedules, and budgets for consideration of Congress.

Exhibit 13.2 Contracting Process

Pre-Award	Solicitation and Award	Post-Award
Determination of need	Solicitation	Initiation of work
Analysis of requirement (SOW)	Bid evaluation	Quality assurance
Extent of competition	Proposal evaluation and negotiation	Payment and accounting
Source selection and planning	Contract award	Modifications and closeout

The contracting officer develops a mission strategy through understanding of the customer's mission and helps draft a realistic acquisition plan, schedule, and budgets.

The commercial sector might assist by drafting realistic plans, schedules, and budgets, with recommendations for long-term strategies.

The U.S. government prefers to procure from commercial sources, as this reduces development and infrastructure costs and is a more expedient method of acquiring services/materials.

Step 2. *Description of need.* The statement of work (SOW) and the contract clauses and requirements define the nature of the procurement and how it should be delivered.

Step 3. *Estimate of costs.* The contracting office will estimate the cost of the procurement and seek funding apportionment—an act of Congress—to permit an agency to obligate monies from the U.S. Treasury for specified purposes. The Office of Management (Executive Branch) will then be requested to apportion budget amounts for specific activities, projects, or objects.

Step 4. *Contract budgeting and financing.* There are three types of money:

1. *Committed funds.* This internal process within the Comptroller's Office sets aside money for an activity. If the funds are not used in a timely manner, they can be transferred to another procurement activity.

2. *Obligated funds.* Is the legal binding of money to a contract award by the government contracting officer to a company contractor, with legal liabilities associated with a contract action. Obligated money can, however, be "descoped" to use on another (similar) task order or through a termination of convenience if the U.S. government wishes to discontinue an activity.

3. *Expended.* Funds are expended when they have been invoiced and committed to a service provider.

Step 5. *Authorization to acquire.* These funds are gained through purchase requests (PRs); internal processes that put the acquisition plan into action and provide the contracting officer with the information and approvals necessary to initiate the procurement.

The PR moves money from the Comptroller's Office into obligated funds and includes certification of available funds, quantity, and description of procurement activity, required delivery dates, special requirements, provisions and clauses, with evaluation factors for the award, recommended sources, and justifications and approvals required for other than full and open competition.

Note: Money has a "life" and must be obligated within that life span. The money does not have to be spent within its life span; it has an additional obligated life of five years, after which the budget is canceled and returned to the U.S. Treasury.

Basic Elements of the Acquisition

A brief insight into the core elements of the acquisition process conducted by the U.S. government follows. This is also a system which might apply between the prime contractor to the government and their subcontractors:

- *Solicitations.* An advertisement for a supply or service (can be through a draft or final RFP).
- *Offer.* A proposal or binding offer for services and supplies, which should be written in a form to accept the commitment to provide goods to a buyer. The proposal might be subject to negotiations or counteroffers if the buyer wishes to modify the offer.
- *Consideration.* The flow of value between parties (money or other), effectively between the seller in terms of services and goods and the buyer in terms of payments or other valued items.
- *Execution.* Execution must be by competent parties (sane, sober, and of legal age). Only an "agent" who can legally bind the seller to the buyer has authority to bind the company to the U.S. government. For the U.S. government, this agent is only the contracting officer (CO).
- *Legality of purpose.* Only a legal pursuit is binding.
- *Clear terms and conditions.* An unambiguous set of agreements between the seller and buyer to bind both to provide consideration for both parties, ensuring that contractual objectives and compensations are met.

FEDERAL ACQUISITION REGULATION SYSTEM

It is important for commercial companies to remember that the FAR is not designed to be equal but is intended to be fair. The FAR is structured to conduct business with integrity, fairness, and openness where possible, fulfilling public policy objectives while minimizing administrative operating costs and satisfying the customer. The FAR applies only to contracting (procurement) for appropriated funds and is not applicable to grants, cooperative agreements, and nonappropriated fund activities.

The FAR applies to the prime contractor (the company holding the government contract) and typically does not flow down to the subcontractors working for a prime contractor, who are obliged to follow their customer's contractual requirements. That said, the prime contractor typically ensures that FAR requirements are included in subcontracts to ensure that compliance is met at all levels, as these requirements will affect the prime contractor's ability to meet government audit requirements as well as invoice effectively. While flow-down may not happen usually, subcontractors should be mindful that the government has the right to audit and review their activities and might take action if serious breaches of the FAR are found. Both primes and subcontractors should therefore seek to be as FAR compliant as possible, in terms of meeting both their contractual obligations to their direct customer as well as the ultimate customer's requirements. Doing this ensures that service delivery and invoicing will be more expeditiously managed to the benefit of both the prime contractor and subcontractor. The guiding principles of the FAR 1.102-2(c)(3) are to:

- Satisfy the customer (funding agency of the U.S. government).
- Minimize the administrative operating costs.
- Conduct business with integrity, fairness, and openness.
- Fulfill public policy objectives.

These organizations maintain the FAR:

- Defense Acquisition Regulatory Council (manages Defense Federal Acquisition Regulations [DFARs]). Provides revisions through Federal Acquisition Circulars (FACs), published in the Federal Register, with advance notice of proposed changes, using proposed or interim rules and a final rule.
- Civilian Agency Acquisition Council (CAAC).
- FAR Council with representation from all agencies.
- FAR Secretariat. Manages the FAR.

Organization of the FAR

Contracts are bound to the FAR clauses (see Exhibit 13.3) and regulations at the time of contract. New clauses and regulations do not apply to old contracts. Management should therefore retain a copy of the FAR at the time of contract award or seek the archive version through the Internet for reference.

Agency Supplements

The FAR is broken into agency supplements: 48 CFR Chapter 2-59, DoD Chapter 2, HHS Chapter 3, GAS Chapter 5, and NASA Chapter 18.

Each U.S. Government Agency has its own FAR supplement which provides additional, specific regulations that pertain to its contracts. For the DoD it is the DFAR (www.acq.osd.mil/dpap/dars/dfars/index.htm). For the U.S. Agency for International Development (USAID) it is the AID Acquisition Regulations (AIDAR). In addition to a U.S. government agency's FAR supplement, each has innumerable policy guidelines, administrative procedures, and rules that govern contract design, implementation, and management. USAID, for example, has a number of such regulations, which can be found at www.usaid.gov/business/regulations/

Awards are issued by the U.S. Government Prime Contracting Office (PCO), which was subsumed into the Corps of Engineers (USACE) in 2006. USACE usually states the nature of the program and project tasks to several bidders, then requests a proposal from potential prime contractors. The winner of the award will then use the U.S. government SOW to determine which work they will do themselves and which aspects will be subcontracted.

Exhibit 13.3   FAR Parts

Parts 1–4	**Subchapter A.** General
Parts 5–12	**Subchapter B.** Competition and Acquisition Planning
Parts 13–18	**Subchapter C.** Contracting Methods and Contract Types
Parts 19–26	**Subchapter D.** Socioeconomic Programs
Parts 27–33	**Subchapter E.** General Contracting Requirements
Parts 34–41	**Subchapter F.** Special Categories of Contracting
Parts 42–51	**Subchapter G.** Contract Management
Parts 52–53	**Subchapter H.** Clauses and Forms

Security and life support are common subcontracted tasks; most clients do not have the in-house security capability to do either. Typically layers of subcontractors exist. Tier 1 are those who are directly subcontracting for the prime contractor (client); lower-level tiers are subcontracted by the subcontractors.

Rules Outside of the FAR

If a policy, procedure, particular strategy, or practice is in the best interest of the government, and is not specifically addressed in the FAR, nor prohibited in law (statute or case law), Executive Order, or another regulation, the Acquisition Team will not consider it prohibited—the absence of direction should be interpreted as permitting innovation and sound judgment, consistent with the principles of the FAR and other policies and guidelines.

The FAR applies only to procurement contracting with appropriated funds, not to grants or non-appropriated fund (NAF) activities. Deviations from the FAR are not permitted without clear authorization, normally from the head of an agency, but may be contained within the guiding principles of the FAR 1.4 and other regulations and statutes. Some rules are automatically "read" into a contract (known as the Christian doctrine), such as termination for convenience and rules applying to disputes. Selected core FAR clauses cannot be excluded, even if the contracting officer permits exclusions.

CONTRACTING AUTHORITIES

The agency head is the ultimate source of contracting authority and establishes agency policies. The head of the contracting activity works with the senior procurement executive to establish the major procurement policies. The chief of the contracting office makes local policy and designates authority to procure through warrants to contracting officers. Contracting officers rarely have time to oversee the management of contracts, and designate contract management to contracting officer's representatives. The contracting structure typically includes:

- Head of the agency
- Senior procurement executive
- Head of contracting activity
- Contracting officer (CO)
- Contracting officer technical representative (COTR) or contracting specialists

For the majority of contractors, the only person who is authorized to bind the U.S. government to a contractor is the contracting officer, who holds a warrant for that procurement activity. The warrant is held against a post, not a person, and defines the limits and parameters of the contracting authority. Any obligations made by noncontracting officers are considered unauthorized commitments and bind the individual to the obligation, not the U.S. government. Should this occur, the contractor might need to sue to gain consideration for any services performed or materials provided.

The contracting officer serves as a business manager and advisor to the customer (contracting authority), performing the functions of a procurement contracting officer (PCOs), administrative contracting officer (ACO), and termination contracting officer (TCO). The contracting officer has a positive responsibility to ensure that the contractor is compliant with the contract requirements.

Types of Contracting Officer

The PCO plans acquisitions, solicits and evaluates offers, negotiates terms and prices, and awards contracts. ACOs and TCOs have authorities delegated by the PCO and may be resident with the contractor and administer the contract management on behalf of the PCO. TCOs also settle termination claims and negotiate termination settlements. These elements may be present to represent the contracting and program offices:

Contracting Officer (CO)	Program Office
COs and specialists	Program managers
Business advisors	CO technical representative
Contract negotiators	End users
Contract administrators	Engineers
Price and cost analysts	Legal counsel
Contract termination specialists	Legal counsel

Most agencies have a centralized acquisition policy office that issues FAR supplements and provides procurement management reviews and contract clearances. Executive agencies also might have separate boards or offices for contract appeals, small and disadvantaged business utilization, and legal counsel.

Contract Management

Some government agencies "borrow" contracting officers from other agencies; these COs advertise and manage the contract award process under the agency title. Monies are internally transferred and "considerations of value" moved between agencies, typically due to a shortage of resources. It is important for contractors to search such advertisement tools as FedBizOps by the nature of the contract activity rather than the agency name for solicitations and contract award information; otherwise contractors may miss opportunities.

PROCUREMENT METHOD

As discussed, the contracting authority establishes the foundations of a need first, in order to decide how best to market and structure the award. Core aspects of the procurement method are listed next.

- The contracting authority determines whether an item exists or must be developed: Can the item be bought off the shelf, or does it need to be designed and manufactured? Where possible, the U.S. government seeks to procure services or materials from the commercial sector, as this is the most cost-effective solution.

- The contracting authority plans for an anticipated cost for procurement or design and development: How much should be budgeted for the award?
- The complexity of the work to be performed must also be established, to determine the scope and nature of an award.
- Who might provide such services or materials? Are there identified providers, how much marketing of the award might be necessary, what type of competition factors might be included (small business, 8(a), etc.)?
- The urgency of requirement must be established. Can a measured bidding process be used, or does the contracting authority need to speed up the process by limiting competition or making a sole-source award?
- How much discussion is required between the government and offerer? Is it in the interest of the government to enter into detailed discussions in order to best define the requirement, and thus get a better return for the investment, or is the requirement clearly understood by the contracting authority?

Types of Procurement Method

There are a number of procurement vehicles designed to meet differing government requirements. The negotiation procurement option is becoming increasingly used as contracting authorities realize that commercial companies can offer innovations that reduce cost and increase performance. The most common types of acquisition processes are listed next.

- *Sealed bidding.* Typically the government establishes performance criteria, and then chooses the lowest bidder meeting those standards.
- *Simplified acquisition procedures.* These are used for defined award amounts under which a sole-source award might be made—for example, counterterrorist services under $250,000, commercial item procurement under $5 million. This permits organizations to procure services or items quickly from known and trusted providers, without going through the RFP and award process.

  Normally more than one offerer is required; however, awards can then be made under blanket work orders if a sole source aware is selected, or where IQC awards are made.
- *Two-step sealed bidding.* The government first reviews technical compliance, then requests costings to determine the lowest bidder.
- *Negotiation.* A series of evaluation criteria are provided, weighing performance against cost, and the offerer and government might negotiate to achieve best performance for cost.
- *Special procedures.* Special services are required, such as research and development.

Procurement Planning

Once the type and nature of the award is determined, procurement planning can start. This planning might include establishing the documents and records required for procurement planning, identifying tasks necessary for an award, and establishing key decision points and those responsible for undertaking certain functions, with milestones and defined authorities and responsibilities. Procurement milestones often include:

- Provide a solicitation to multiple offerers.
- Proposals received from offerers.
- Complete a technical and price evaluation.
- Rank the offerers against established technical and price criteria.
- Hold discussions if not a sealed bidding process.
- Offerers submit modified proposals and best and final cost offers.
- Reevaluate the ranking of offerers.
- Execute the contract award.

Solicitations

Solicitations may come in several stages, leading to an RFP. Depending on the complexity and requirement, the contracting officer will provide between 30 to 60 days to respond to an RFP. A prime contractor may provide less time. According to FAR 6.303, some notices that may be released from a contracting authority include:

- *Invitation for bid (IFB)*. Normally for a fixed price contract.
- *Broad agency announcement (BAA)*. Proposals for requirements, without defined timelines.
- *Research announcement (RA)*. Normally for grants.
- *Request for information (RFI)*. Soliciting for information or interest, with no contractual obligations. There is no requirement to notify the contracting agency of interest; however, the government may use this method to gather information to develop the RFP.
- *Request for proposal*. A soliciting document stating the requirement and terms necessitating a proposal. A draft RFP might be released to allow offerers the chance to better understand the requirement, as the contracting authority develops and refines a final RFP. This will be the vehicle used to gather offerer's proposals for assessment and award.

Pricing Arrangements

The pricing of an award may differ, based on the nature of the requirement and the manner in which the government wishes to ensure best performance from the provider. The government will seek to minimize the risks to itself in terms of cost and performance while being mindful (to an extent) of the needs of the provider. Costs are based on being *reasonable*, *allowable*, and *allocatable*. According to FAR 15.3 and 15.4, trade-offs between a technical solution and price is permitted for nonsealed bids, if a higher cost is outweighed by superior performance and delivery.

There are two main categories for pricing: fixed price and cost reimbursements.

1. Fixed Price
   - Fixed sums paid as services provided, in alignment with performance objectives set.
   - Least cost risk to the government.

▪ Most cost risk to the provider.
▪ Payment tied to performance.
2. Cost Reimbursements
▪ Provider reimbursed for allowable costs, after they have occurred.
▪ Subject to review and audit.
▪ Most cost risk to the government.
▪ Least cost risk to the provider.
▪ Not tied to performance.

A limitation of funds might be included within the RFP. This can reflect the need for further funding authorization to be approved from Congress or the fact that the contracting officer is still defining the final budget amount. In order to make pricing and ordering efficient for frequently used services, a basic ordering agreement (BOA) may be established, representing a pricing schedule (e.g., a price shopping list associated each a series of labor categories, services, or materials).

Base Years and Options

Contracts usually have an initial base period, with a series of option periods. For example, a contract may be for a base year with four one-year options. This means the U.S. government has the right to hold the offerer to the terms and conditions for a total of five years, with the flexibility to use only a portion of that period. The contractor cannot refuse to service an option period, although economic adjustments can be requested to reflect changes over long time periods.

RFP AND THE UNIFORM CONTRACT FORMAT

U.S. government agencies can use any format they desire in terms of an RFP and how they require an offerer to respond in terms of structuring their proposal. The uniform contract format (UCF), however, provides a template for government agencies in terms of the structure and content of an RFP. The requirements of a solicitation may be changed during the proposal/bidding phase, with amendments reflecting questions posed to the contracting authority by bidders, or new and additional factors being identified and thus included by the contracting officer. The solicitation can also be delayed or canceled at will by the contracting authority, with no redress options by bidders. The contracting agency may also permit a site visit or inspection to be conducted prior to the RFP being released; during the RFP process it may allow questions and offer a bidding conference to clarify complex or ambiguous issues.

According to FAR 14.210, the UCF is structured to cover these general aspects:

Part	Elements covered
Part 1 – Schedule	
A	Solicitation and Contract Form
B	Supplies, Services and Prices (CLINs—Cost Line Item Numbers)
C	Description/Specifications/Work Statement (SOW)

(continued)

Part	Elements covered
D	Packaging and Marketing
E	Inspection and Acceptance
F	Deliveries and Performance
G	Contract Administration Data
H	Special Contract Requirements

Part 2 - Contract Clauses

I	Contract Clauses

Part 3 - List of Attachments

J	List of Documents, Exhibits, or Other Attachments

Part 4 - Representations and Instructions

K	Representations, Certifications, and Other Statements from Offerer
L	Instructions, Conditions, and Notices to Offerers
M	Evaluation Factors for the Award

Government Negotiation Strategy

The RFP or solicitation will be defined by what the contracting officer is seeking from the offerer. This RFP will include identifying the best- and worst-case performance outcomes for each requirement, the objective and priorities for each requirement, strategies for accomplishing the award needs, preparing a pre-negotiation plan, with briefings to the evaluation team to ensure the requirements and objectives of the procurement activity are met. According to FAR 15, the contracting officer will seek to provide clear guidance to the evaluation team in terms of strategies and tactics, concessions and trade-offs, target objectives, issues and concerns, and the structure of the team and individual and group taskings, as well as a time or sequence schedule for the activity. Negotiations with the offerer can cover bargaining and discussions on how best to perform services in relation to cost.

Key Parts of the RFP

RFPs vary in complexity, structure, and format. Some are well written and provide a solid and logical framework in which to respond with a proposal. Others provide limited information that can be contradictory in nature, making a responsive (winning) proposal difficult to write. The art of providing a responsive and innovative proposal comes with the ability to understand what the contracting officer is asking for as well as identifying ways to respond to what he or she may have missed in what is a technically acceptable and price-competitive manner (see Chapter 2).

The most pertinent parts of the RFP for a security consultant or manager to be cognizant of are Part 1B, 1C, and 4M, discussed next. A proposal capture manager and finance staff will focus on certifications, packaging, pricing, and all other documents and inclusions stated within an RFP. Those unfamiliar with an RFP should review several versions to better understand the content and differences within these documents.

Part 1B, Supplies, Services, and Prices   Price will be an aspect of the evaluation section (Part 4M); however, it is be captured at the front of the RFP under Part 1B. Typically the RFP offers a cost line item number (CLIN) sheet that provides a list of labor categories or services to be delivered. These may seem restrictive in that they do not reflect the detailed costs or labor categories required, in which case bundling of costs is required (i.e., where a group of services is included under one item).

If the RFP asks for a level 1 manager monthly rate, mobilization, life support, insurance, and equipment costs might need to be included in a wrap rate (i.e., every cost element required for that individual to perform the requirement—unless the CLIN offers separate sections to address these costs). Typically the cost analysis includes:

- Direct materials
- Direct labor
- Other direct cots
- Indirect costs
- Subcontractor costs
- Profit or fees

It is important to understand that a single line item cost may not be calculated simply in terms of obvious cost factors—labor wage and profit fee—but can also include rotational costs, mobilization costs, Defense Base Act (DBA) insurance, equipment, uniforms, management fees, incentive bonuses, danger and hardship pay, morale and welfare costs, recruitment fees, attribution factors, infrastructure overheads, life support, training and qualification costs, administration fees, and numerous other factors that might change a single cost category into a complex wrap rate of all costs pertaining to a simple function bundled together. The accuracy of costing is made difficult when an RFP asks for several labor categories and all their individual costs to be captured in a single CLIN.

Part 1C, Statement of Work The SOW defines the procurement activity required. The SOW should be a clear, unambiguous, and detailed explanation of the services or materials required, but rarely is this the case. Most security-related contracts are service contracts, whether these are procuring individuals or are performance-related service activities (construction, security, consultancy).There are three types of SOW:

1. *Functional.* Describes the service in terms of end objectives, not how the service must be performed. It may specify the essential characteristics to satisfy the intended use.
2. *Performance.* Describes the technical requirements of the operational characteristics and indicates what the service must accomplish rather than how it must be conducted.
3. *Design.* Describes precise measurements, tolerances, processes, and deliverables.

The solicitation SOW may define what specific performance requirements are necessary for group or individual services (performance work statements [PWSs]), against which the proposal will be evaluated.

Part 4M, Evaluation Factors for the Award The contracting authority should provide guidance on how the proposals will be evaluated. This guidance explains to bidders what factors the contractor finds most desirable, whether it is cost or performance, or a balance of both. This information can be presented in percentage terms: The management component is valued at 20%, the technical solution at 50%, and the cost aspect at 30%, for example.

Alternatively the evaluation balance terms might be more vague, with the contracting authority stating that the technical solution will weigh more heavily than price. Three mandatory factors are required to evaluate a bid:

1. Cost
2. Technical competence
3. Past performance

Other factors may also be included, depending on the nature of the contract and the objectives of the contracting authority (socioeconomic, innovations, small business set-asides, etc.). The evaluation factors are designed to minimize business and technical risks to the U.S. government while providing an opportunity for the best competitor to deliver the highest-quality service, on time, in budget, and at the expected cost. The offerer must not assume that the evaluation team knows or understands the company's history or performance and must recognize that each proposal is written as an individual and isolated offer. The first requirement is to answer the questions or requirements posed in the RFP; the second is to consider where innovations (or discriminators) might improve performance and reduce cost.

The contracting officer should establish a clear and unambiguous evaluation matrix to be used by the source selection evaluation board (SSEB) to score the proposal against the SOW and any PWS and assessment criteria included in the RFP. Some key considerations are discussed in the next sections.

Late Bids

Late bids will not be considered. Contracting officers are usually very specific on this issue (to the second), and multimillion-dollar proposals submitted five seconds late have not been accepted. The contracting authority's clock, not the offerer's, must be used to avoid confusion over timing. In addition, if an electronic submission is provided, the contracting authority will accept a late submission only if the bidder can prove that an e-mail version was sent at 1700 hours the day before the submission was due. E-mail delays, losses, or other failures will not be considered under any other circumstance. Postal problems, weather, and other delay factors also are rarely accepted. A request for additional time (extension) can be made to the contracting officer, but this must occur well in advance of the submission date and time.

Nonresponsive Bids

Bids might be deemed nonresponsive if they do not answer the questions posed in the RFP, are structured incorrectly according to the instructions provided, do not have the correct information included (certificates, supporting documents), or are considered technically or financially incorrect (unrealistic solutions and costs). The contracting officer has the right to increase costs submitted by a bidder (without discussion) to reflect what he or she believes is a more realistic cost for a technical solution, even if this then makes the offerer the most expensive bidder—little recourse is open to the company or bidder to respond or address these contracting authority adjustments and associated impacts.

Sealed Bids

Sealed bids are evaluated based on meeting established technical requirements and at the lowest cost to the government. According to FAR Part 14, often bids are provided in a ballot box format, with an expedient award period based on responsive and cost elements.

Responsible Bidders

Offerers will be considered responsible if they have adequate financial resources and the ability to obtain project funding. Also, they must be able to comply with the required or proposed delivery and performance schedule. They must also have a satisfactory performance record and proven integrity and business ethics. Offerers must have the necessary organization, experience, accounting, operational controls, and technical skills to perform the work, with access or ownership of the necessary facilities. They must also be eligible to receive the award under U.S. and host nation laws and regulations.

EVALUATION

Evaluating Team Structure

The size and complexity of the evaluation team will be determined, to an extent, by the size and complexity of the award, as illustrated in Exhibit 13.4. The source selection authority (SSA) makes the final determination for the award of a contract, advised directly by their SSA council. The source selection evaluation board (SSEB) chairperson oversees the board members—each of whom might view sections of numerous proposals (e.g., one board member may view all of the pricing elements, another all of the management sections).

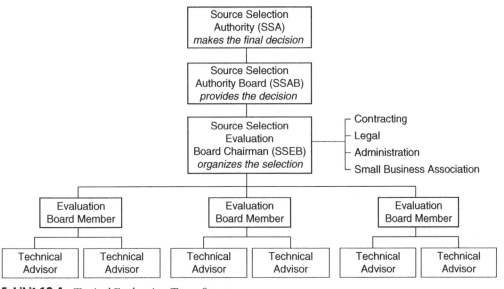

Exhibit 13.4 Typical Evaluation Team Structure

Alternatively each may review the complete proposals from each bidder. The goal is to achieve a consensus from the evaluation team, which enables the chairperson to advise the SSA council of a decision.

According to FAR 15.3, the technical evaluation seeks to rank proposals based on the evaluation team's understanding of the requirement, the best solutions to the requirements stated, the most efficient use of labor and materials, and innovations that might enhance performance while reducing cost to the government.

The evaluation process typically consists of these steps:

Step 1. *Proposal delivered.* It is received in accordance with time and packaging requirements.

Step 2. *Initial proposal evaluations.* Weaknesses and deficiencies are identified. Offerers who are noncompetitive or noncompliant are removed from the bidding process. A debrief can be asked for at this stage; however, this will be limited, and a second debrief is not permitted.

Step 3. *Committee discussions.* The short-listed proposals are reviewed and clarification points are identified.

Step 4. *Clarifications.* Questions may be posed to the bidders on areas of uncertainty within their proposals.

Step 5. *Communications.* If a proposal is borderline, specific questions may be asked to allow the evaluation board to determine whether the proposal is competitive or should be removed from consideration.

Step 6. *Competitive range.* Those final proposals that are technically responsive and price competitive are reviewed for final ranking.

Step 7. *Final evaluation.* The final decision is made on which proposal provides the best solution, at the best cost.

Step 8. *Award (roll-ups).* The contract is awarded.

Step 9. *SSA briefing.* According to FAR 15, the "losers" can ask for a formal debrief on why their proposal was not successful. The debrief does not indicate the specifics of the other proposals, only the deficiencies of the individual proposal. Debriefs must be requested within three days and are normally provided within five days of the request.

Past Performance

According to FAR Part 15, past performance will play an import role in evaluation, in order to determine the offerer's ability to perform the service. Past performance will be considered in terms of:

- Currency and relevance of experience (usually no older than five years).
- Sources of information (references and confirmation).
- Context of the experience (Does it relate to the requirement, either directly or indirectly?).
- Trends of performance (Is there evidence of performance consistency?).

Note: If an offerer has no past performance in an area, a neutral score is awarded, unless past performance is a criterion for the award, and then the offerer will be noncompliant.

Competition Factors

For certain contracts, the U.S. government offers preference for other U.S. government agencies to provide services (interagency support) or from state institutions, such as prisons and other government providers. In addition, the U.S. government might award preference to support socioeconomic goals, such as small business set-asides and 8(a) set-asides, as discussed in FAR Part 19. Some contracting authorities have a Small Business Administration (SBA) that is tasked with identifying awards that might offer smaller companies an opportunity for growth. Small businesses must register and are permitted to remain in the 8(a) category only for eight years. To be considered a small business, the business must have an approximate annual revenue of $50 million or less and approximately 600 employees or fewer.

The contracting officer might also set aside provisions for veterans (based on FAR subpart 22.13) or companies owned by those with disabilities. A consortium of companies might be required for certain awards to ensure that these requirements are met. According to FAR Part 25, the U.S. government can also add an additional 25% of cost onto foreign company proposals in order to offset U.S. commercial interests under the Buy American Act.

CONTRACT AWARD AND ADMINISTRATION

The award contract must be signed by the contracting officer, who has ensured that funds are available to initiate the delivery of services. The offerer may (through a bilateral agreement), or may not (through a unilateral agreement) be asked to sign a contract. The contracting officer has the right to use the offerer's proposal as the basis for a single-signature contract. The offerer can withdraw the proposal prior to signature, although this can create problems in terms of company reputation. The award notification may be made by telephone, letter, or e-mail, or at a meeting.

Normally sizable contracts are awarded after 1700 hours on a Friday to avoid disrupting the stock market. FedBizOps will advertise the contracting authority's synopsis for the award within one to two days of the award being made.

Contract Award

The award brings a considerable amount of contractual and delivery issues. Some key factors are discussed next.

Debriefs Unsuccessful offerers must requested debriefings within three days of the award being made, and they usually are provided within five days of the request being made. Debriefs are useful to help offerers determine how to improve future proposals. A debrief typically lasts no more than one hour and does not include any details on the content of the other proposals. Subcontractors to a prime contractor are not entitled to be provided a debrief, and only one debrief is permitted.

Protests An unsuccessful offerer may issue a protest within 10 calendar days of the award being made, if it considers the award unjust. This protest can result in a stay of contract award during the consideration period, although the contracting authority has the right to waive the stay of award if it deems the delivery of service necessary. A protest can be made directly to the contracting officer, moving then to the Government Appeals Office (GAO) if the appeal is declined by the contracting officer. The GAO should provide a recommendation within 100 days of the appeal being made. The GAO does not have the authority to overrule the contracting officer, although the office can report the matter to Congress. (This is likely to occur only if the contract is significant.) According to FAR 52.233, the protester can also choose to appeal to the Court of Federal Affairs, a costly, time-consuming, and uncommon remedy.

Award   It is important for the contracted party to arrange a kick-off meeting with the contracting officer shortly after the award is made, in order to discuss areas of concern, ambiguity, or importance so that both parties have a clear and mutual understanding of all contract requirements. This meeting also allows for modifications to be discussed if the RFP lacked clarity in areas that were not addressed by the proposal (such factors which might incur costs are often left out by companies until the negotiation period in order to first win the award). Funding may also be incremental; if so, a clear understanding of how invoicing and payments will be processed is required. Contractor and contracting authority milestones and objectives can also be clearly established as well as the identity of the contracting officer's technical representatives (COTRs) and other key management personnel.

Contract Administration   Administering a contract correctly from the outset is critical to avoid performance and invoicing problems. According to FAR Parts 42 to 51, some key factors include administration, and negotiations and errors.

During the life span of the contract, the contracting officer typically has little involvement after the award with the daily running of the contract delivery. Often these officers defer to their COTRs to ensure that contract deliverables are overseen in terms of security requirements, technical delivery, administration, and that logistical needs are met and modifications are reviewed and presented to the contracting officer. Other administrative staff will ensure that invoicing and billing are proper. The COTR cannot bind the provider and U.S. government to new acquisitions, only oversee existing ones.

The U.S. government has the right to hold an offerer to proposed services and costs, even if circumstances change or unintentional errors or unknown factors have been included. However, government contracting authorities tend to view errors or changes evenhandedly in order to ensure that continued business opportunities exist between the government and providers. If the contracting officer notes an error, he or she may ask an offerer to verify the bid. If the offerer notes an error, it must ask permission to adjust or withdraw the bid. The reason for the mistake must be evidenced and clear for the contracting officer to review and sanction changes or allowances. Mistakes made after the award may be corrected with modification to the contract, or the contract may be rescinded or terminated.

Task Orders and Work Orders

Funding may be broken into specific deliverables to provide the contracting authority with the flexibility to adjust requirements to suit fluid or unknown requirements. Typically an indefinite delivery contract (IDC) asks for costings against an estimated requirement and then awards task orders (a collection of work orders) or work orders against an established price schedule. For example, Task Order 1 is the establishment of military bases in Afghanistan, Work Order 1 is a base in Kabul, and Work Order 2 is a base in Kandahar. The task or work orders will detail amounts, times, and services required. The contractor must notify the contracting authority when 70% of the funds has been spent on each order and must stop work when all funds are expended, until further funds have been awarded for continued work.

Modifications

Contract modifications may be requested by the contractor to reflect changes to the environment or task/order requirement. The contracting officer may also make unilateral changes, without necessarily getting permission from or involving the contractor. According to FAR Part 43, the contractor is legally bound to undertake those changes, even during a dispute period, or it will be considered in breach of contract.

Invoicing

Typically the U.S. government is required to make payment to each invoice within 30 days of submission. The correct data must be included on each invoice, including the name and address of the contractor, the invoice date and number, the contract number, and the description of the service, unit, and quantity. Failure to submit correct and full information will result in the invoice being returned for correction. The Cost Accounting Standards (CAS) regulate and audit the financial activities of contractors. The GAO Red Book provides useful information regarding financial and procurement matters (refer to the U.S government Prompt Payment Act).

Failure to Perform

There are numerous reasons why a service may not be delivered on time or to standard. The fault may lie with either the contractor or the contracting authority. An inexcusable delay is where the fault lies with the contractor; an excusable delay is where the fault lies with the U.S. government. A mutual delay is where the fault is shared by both parties. On occasion a delay in delivery or service outside of performance failures from either party may result in a failure to perform (act of God, war, etc.). If a failure occurs through reasonable cause, a request for equitable adjustment can be made to the contracting authority, to compensate the contractor for additional costs or unforeseen lower performance levels. Typical performance problems include:

- *Schedule.* Failure to deliver or make progress on time.
- *Cost.* Exceeding estimates or budgets.
- *Quantity.* Supplies or services do not meet the requirements.
- *Compliance.* The delivery does not meet the terms and conditions of the contract.

The contracting officer typically seeks to resolve contract problems rather than terminate a contract. Termination comes with significant problems and costs. The contracting officer normally provides the contractor a full brief on the problem(s) as well as the status of the issues. The process normally includes:

- Providing documental evidence of the problem.
- Determining the impacts and whether the problem is excusable (who is to blame).
- Whether a formal or informal resolution is required.
- Whether a contractual remedy is required, or a modification is necessary.
- Whether a stop-work order should be issued or the contract terminated for default.

Stop-Work Orders

A stop-work order occurs either when a contractor is not performing within the contract scope of requirement or when the contracting authority might be required to change the nature of a contract or terminate it for convenience. The stop-work order might apply to a section of the service or for the whole contract. The order can occur only for 90 days prior to a final decision being made. In theory, an assumption that work is permitted to continue will allow the prime contractor to recommence work unless told otherwise at this point. The contracting officer will take this recourse only after serious consideration, as it has significant impacts on both the contracting authority and the contractor. The COTR can issue a temporary stop-work order in the event of an emergency; however, only the contracting officer can issue a long-term order. The prime contractor can choose to continue requesting deliverables from their own subcontractors during this period, as their contract is removed from the U.S. government. According to FAR 52.242, a detailed explanation must be provided to the prime contractor by the contracting officer as to the rationale of this order.

Notices

The contracting authority might choose to provide a show-cause notice to give a contractor time to resolve any contractual difficulties, providing an evidence plan to resolve shortfalls in delivery. A cure notice is the next step and permits the contractor only 10 days to resolve the problem; otherwise, a termination for cause might be issued. Cure notices and terminations for cause are problematic and generally are instigated only for serious failures.

Descoping

Descoping is removing tasks due to financial shortage or change. If too many tasks are dropped the contract might be considered *partially terminated*, at which point the contractor can claim costs (e.g., if 25% of tasks are descoped). The contracting authority may choose to allow the contract to run until natural completion, as a *termination for convenience* (i.e., not a fault of the contractor) can often incur more costs than a natural completion.

U.S. Government–Furnished Property

According to FAR 45, the contracting authority might provide equipment, services, or life support to support the contractor delivery a service. These will be outlined in the RFP and included with a subsequent contract. Equipment loaned for the use of a contract must only be used on that specific activity, and must not be used (without written permission of the CO or COTR) on any other government, or commercial project. Property provided by the government to the contractor is accepted on Form DD250 (FAR 46.5) and title transfers are covered under FAR 46.505/46.601. Equipment must be returned at the end of the contract or correct destruction documentation (authorized by the COTR) provided in place of equipment (Standard Form 1424). Materials and resources may be restricted to components of a wider contract. These rules apply to any vendors using the contract's resources.

Contract Closure

The prime contractor must confirm that the contract is physically complete and satisfies the contract requirements, providing the necessary reports and closure documents. Settlement of outstanding issues is also required, identifying any outstanding issues and claims. Final payments must be made and monies not used deobligated. (Note: Closure documentation is required prior to close-out being complete and no further invoicing being permitted.) According to FAR 4.804-1 through 4.804-5, a contract completion statement will be issued, with directions for the disposal of files. A contract closure period can last up to six years after the final services are delivered. It is therefore important that vendors provide all necessary documentation and materials as part of the overall contract closure process because subcontractors may have vital information that the company may require some time after the project is closed.

Subcontractors

The company working for the U.S. government, known as the prime contractor, may hire subcontractors to perform services under the contract. Rules may apply to the subcontractors, as defined within the RFP and resulting contract. However, generally rules and obligations do not flow down from the U.S. government to the subcontractors; rather a separate contract (commercial) is provided between the prime contractor and subcontractors, as described in FAR Part 44. Managing subcontractors' conduct is as important as running the company's own operations, as any subcontractor failures can be held against the company and its officers.

Transportation and Travel

Failure to adhere to FAR guidelines in Part 47 regarding travel regulations often results in considerable costs to the contractor. A clear understanding of what can and cannot be charged, and the documentation required to permit invoicing, is essential.

Audits

The U.S. government has wide-ranging authority to investigate/audit both the prime contractor and its subcontractors. The government typically audits accounting procedures and practices according to cost U.S accounting standards policies and procedures—reviewing books, records, and financial documents and other evidence based on cost, pricing, and delivery data. Typically the Defense Contract Audit Agency (DCAA) undertakes this function.

Property registries, policies, and procedures ensure that materials are correctly accounted for, managed, and, where necessary, disposed of. The forms in FAR Part 53 provide guidance on this issue.

TYPES OF CONTRACT

It is important for managers to understand the nature of the contract as this will define how they conduct their operations. The U.S. government has established a number of contract types to meet different award requirements. The award of the contract can be through sealed bidding (lowest price, technically acceptable offer) or through negotiation to weigh best performance to cost. Most contracts are now conducted through negotiation, as discussed in FAR Part 16, as the U.S government recognizes that the cost to additional value benefits provided by companies are sometimes offset by higher service performances which make small funding increments a sound investment. The main contract types are shown in Exhibit 13.5.

Note: Fixed price contracts tend to result in contractors budgeting higher than the expected costs in order to reduce their own risk as well as increase profit margins.

Other contract pricing types include:

- *Fixed-price-incentive (FPI)*. This contract is for a fixed price with an incentive fee, which can be up to 25% of the award fee (normally it is between 6 to 10%).
- *Cost plus fixed fee (CPFF)*. This contract is for the cost of the project, plus a determined fee amount.
- *Cost plus incentive fee (CPIF)*. Here the contract covers the cost of a project plus a series of fees (normally 3% base fee, 8% target fee, and 15% if above expected performance levels). This contract is designed to provide incentives to the provider.
- *Cost plus award fee (CPAF)*. This unpopular price vehicle can result in no profit to the provider.
- *Cost or cost sharing (C/CS)*. This type of contract is usually used for university or research development projects where the government derives some benefit and ownership from a product and the awardee receives grant funding to assist funding requirements.
- *Time and materials (T&M)*. This contract buys labor hours, materials, and equipment, loaded with fee costs and overheads.
- *Labor hour*. In the labor-hour contract, loaded costs are accrued for time rather than performance or products.
- *Letter*. This type of contract is undefined. Often it is used for immediate requirements while a formal contract is established. A letter contract should have a short life span, as it is a temporary measure.

Unsolicited Proposals

Should a company identify a need or requirement that might not have been identified by the U.S. government, an unsolicited proposal might be offered. This proposal allows the offering company an opportunity to recommend innovative or unique services that the U.S. government might buy, either directly as a sole source from the offerer (FAR 6.302) or through

Exhibit 13.5 Different Forms of Government Contracting

Contract Type	Explanation
Firm Fixed Price (FFP) *Definitive price for a definitive product*	The requirements are defined and the costs are estimated to remove risk to the government. The risk is to the contractor, especially if the marketplace is unstable (notably hostile locations). A contractor incentive can be applied whereby every dollar saved is reflected as an additional dollar added to the contractor's fee. The firm fixed price is for every line item, or groupings of line items, procured—the level of effort and schedule is fixed.
Fixed Price with Economic Price Adjustment (FP/EPA) *Definitive price, with allowances for economic influences*	The requirements are defined; however, certain costs are known to fluctuate—*local labor rates and cost change*. This poses risk to the contractor that is accepted by the government, who makes certain adjustments possible. A fixed ceiling will be applied, with the dollar for dollar cost saving to profit approach being applied. The levels of effort and performance are determined, however, inflation rates permit variations to the contract and line item cost values.
Indefinite Delivery (ID) *Requirement is known, however, delivery is not confirmed*	The scope and size of the requirement has not been defined and may not exceed the minimal value offered (e.g., *"we will need security services for Iraq military bases for the next three years, award valued at $3 million to $475 million"*). The costs are per units, or a period of performance. Normally a maximum and minimum budget is established. The same saving to profit, dollar for dollar, incentive approach may be used. The level of effort reflects the procurement of the unit or performance time. These are usually long-term contracts for supplies and services.
Definite Quantity (DQ) *Requirement is defined*	The size of the requirement has been defined; however, this does not mean the timeframe for delivery has been decided—this can occur through successive Task or Work Orders (e.g., *"we will need 500 type A battle tanks over the next ten years"*).

(continued)

Exhibit 13.5 (continued)

Contract Type	Explanation
Indefinite Quantity (IQ)	The need has been established, but the size still requires definition (e.g., *"we will need type A tanks over the next ten years"*).
Requirements (R)	The general concept of a draft need has been established, but the size, time, and actual details are not known (e.g., *"we will need second generation fighter aircraft in the future"*).
Indefinite Delivery/Indefinite Quantity (IDIQ)	The need is known, however, the size and timeframes are yet to be defined (e.g., *"we require disaster response support for global engineering services for the next five years, Task Orders reflective of future global disaster"*).

open bidding. (In the latter case, the offerer still has the advantage of knowing more about the requirement than the competitors, having established the need.) The government recognizes that certain circumstances might prevent full and open competition (FAOC) and instead require a sole source award. These cases include:

- Only one responsible source
- Unusual and compelling urgency
- Industrial mobilization or research and development capability
- International agreements
- Authorized or required by statute
- National security
- Public interest

Contract Factors

If a proposal has not identified a requirement, and the gap is considered fair and acceptable, the contractor might ask for a ratification to be paid for this additional requirement (although this payment is not assured). If an additional requirement is identified by the contracting officer, outside of the original proposal and subsequent contract, these services would be defined as out of scope and a modification to the contract will be required, according to FAR 1.602-3. No services or materials should be provided unless covered under a contract or authorized modification. Should circumstances that could not have been foreseen occur (say drastic change in the security environment, major economic change), an extraordinary contractual relief clause might be invoked (see FAR Part 50).

Clauses

Some clauses will be included in a contract. However, some clauses that are not included or written into a contract can be legally considered read in automatically under the FAR. It is important that the provider understands that these automatic clauses cannot be ruled out under U.S. law, even if the contracting authority has agreed (illegally) to remove such clauses. (For details, see the clause index in FAR Part 52.)

Standards of Conduct

The U.S. government will seek to avoid illegal acts through the establishment of standards of conduct (FAR 3.101–9.5). Failure to adhere to these standards might result in criminal proceedings or the government preventing companies or individuals from seeking work with any contracting authority. The key guidelines to government contracting officers and representatives include:

- Avoid a conflict of interest or a perceived conflict of interest.
- Conduct your activities in the spirit of full public disclosure.
- Avoid accepting items which might be construed as bribes/gifts ($20 meals or coffee) or gratuities.
- Do not represent contractors.
- Avoid making or recommending official decisions in which you or your family have an interest.
- Do not conspire to defraud the U.S. government.
- Do not disclosure source selection or proprietary information.
- Do not engage in, or accept offers of employment.
- Do not participate in collusive pricing.
- Do not engage in antitrust violations.
- Do not discuss or agree on contingent fees: *if we win we will provide.*
- Do not accept subcontractor kickbacks.
- Do not impart improper disclosure of information on pending or ongoing procurements (draft RFPs).
- Do not slant specifications to favor specific vendors without good cause.
- Do not suppress bids by limiting of complementary bidding.
- Do not engage in bid rotation or market division.
- Do not provide false invoices, mischarging, or intentional failure to update cost or pricing data.
- Do not falsify government furnished property records.

If a subcontractor is in a technical support role, clinically it is permitted to provide data that might be used to establish such documents as a SOW, as the contracting officer will use the data as he or she deems fit in a larger document. This, however, implies a conflict of interest. Providing a complete contractual document, however, would be considered a clear conflict of interest and would prevent the subcontractor from bidding on that work. It is essential that subcontractors protect themselves from clear or perceived conflict of interests, if they intend to pursue a solicitation on which they are providing information.

In summary, management at all levels should understand the contractual parameters under which they and their company operate. Often significant errors can be made through a poor appreciation of the regulations that define the project operations and how security vendors might also place the company at risk. The U.S. government procurement and contracting system is designed to protect not only the government's needs but also contractors and their subcontractors. Understanding the broader rules and regulations can support more productive business activities and avoid liability and performance risks. Not only the prime contractor, but also security subcontractors, must understand how they should conduct business, what records they should keep, and the scope of quality assurance mechanisms and permissions that should be established to avoid contractual risks and enable productive business.

Printed and bound by CPI Group (UK) Ltd, Croydon, CR0 4YY

23/04/2025

14660930-0002